CONJURING
SPIRITS

THE MAGIC IN HISTORY SERIES

FORBIDDEN RITES
A Necromancer's Manual of the Fifteenth Century
Richard Kieckhefer

CONJURING SPIRITS
Texts and Traditions of Medieval Ritual Magic
Edited by Claire Fanger

RITUAL MAGIC
Elizabeth M. Butler

THE FORTUNES OF FAUST
Elizabeth M. Butler

The MAGIC IN HISTORY series explores the role magic and the occult have played in European culture, religion, science and politics. Titles in the series will bring the resources of cultural, literary and social history to bear on the history of the magic arts, and will contribute towards an understanding of why the theory and practice of magic have elicited fascination at every level of European society. Volumes will include both editions of important texts and significant new research in the field.

CONJURING SPIRITS

TEXTS AND TRADITIONS OF MEDIEVAL RITUAL MAGIC

EDITED BY
CLAIRE FANGER

THE PENNSYLVANIA STATE UNIVERSITY PRESS
UNIVERSITY PARK, PENNSYLVANIA

Copyright © 1998 M. Camille, C. Fanger, J.B. Friedman, R. Kieckhefer, F. Klaassen, J. Lidaka, R. Mathiesen, E.I. Wade, N. Watson.

Published in 1998 in the United States of America and Canada by The Pennsylvania State University Press, University Park, PA 16802

First published in 1998 in the United Kingdom by Sutton Publishing Limited.

ISBN 0-271-01862-3 (cloth)
ISBN 0-271-01863-1 (paper)

Library of Congress Cataloging in Publication Data
A CIP catalog record for the book is available from the Library of Congress.

Printed in Great Britain

It is the policy of The Pennsylvania State University Press to use acid-free paper for the first printing of all clothbound books. Publications on uncoated stock satisfy minimum requirements of American National Standard for Information Sciences—Permanence of Paper for Printed Library Materials, ANSI Z39.48—1992.

CONTENTS

MEDIEVAL RITUAL MAGIC: WHAT IT IS AND WHY WE NEED TO KNOW MORE ABOUT IT

W hat is ritual magic? While magic itself has been the subject of much argument (over what it is, whether it is necessarily or only accidentally a pejorative term, and even whether it can be defined in a way that makes it useful at all),[1] the sense of the composite term 'ritual magic' (or 'ceremonial magic') is easily circumscribed by pointing out that it labels a certain readily identifiable genre of text. I intend to sidestep, for the moment, the theoretical questions surrounding magic in general. This is not because I believe they are unimportant, but rather because, in the area of medieval intellectual magic, there is a strong risk of prejudicing the issues raised by the texts under discussion, many of which are themselves concerned with the question of what magic is, and whether it is a category to which they can appropriately be said to belong.

As a genre of text, then, ritual magic has certain characteristics: it describes what are normally fairly long and complex rituals for obtaining a variety of different kinds of benefits to the operator through the conjuring of spirits (whether demonic or the reverse). These texts emerge from a literate environment, and the ritual elements as well as the entities conjured or petitioned derive from a Christian framework (with some admixture from Arabic neo-Platonic and Jewish sources).[2] Ritual magic may thus be distinguished – again on the basis of genre – from medieval spells, charms and folk magic, which generally involve much shorter rituals, need not have been composed or performed by literate people, and in the early period might sometimes invoke recognizable local pagan entities in addition to Christian ones (as in the case of a few of the Anglo-Saxon charms). The type of magic we are concerned with in this volume is largely a late medieval phenomenon, and no text under discussion here is witnessed in manuscripts much earlier than the thirteenth century.

There are two basic forms of ritual magic (that is, for our purposes, two subgenres of text) which I will refer to as 'demonic' and 'angelic'. The typical apparatus of the demonic variety is familiar to most people from ancient and modern literature and folk tales as well as modern horror films – magic circles, animal sacrifices, written or uttered words or characters (often cryptic or foreign), suffumigations and the like. Demonic magic has also been referred to since the time of the composition of these texts as 'necromancy' (literally 'divination by the dead') or in corrupted form 'nigromancy' ('black magic', more or less) though the meaning of the term 'necromancy' (like that of 'magic' itself) varies with context and does not always or invariably designate the conjuring of demons in medieval or later usage.

If the terminology is imprecise, demonic magic as a textual genre nonetheless has certain discernible common features. The magical effects sought for are often (if not invariably) of a rather spiteful and petty-minded sort – causing disease, harm, or deformity in another person; manipulating the emotions of others to induce love or hatred between two people, or to get a person of the opposite sex to submit to the operator's desires. Demonic magic normally involves a ritual process whereby demons are forced to obey the request of the operator after being summoned and bound, not strictly by the operator's own powers, but by calling upon superior spiritual entities (angels, Christ or God) – so that while demonic magic may invoke benign spiritual powers it does so in a different way and for different purposes from the type of magic I am referring to as 'angelic'.

The operations of angelic magic are generally less familiar to the public from literature and folk tale,[3] though they are conceivably of yet greater interest to the historian due to their intermingling of magical, devotional and mystical elements.[4] Texts of this type discussed in the present volume include the *Sworn Book of Honorius*, the Ars Notoria,[5] and the *Liber visionum Marie* (in fact an Ars Notoria revision and variant). In all three texts the primary magical effects sought for by the operator involve obtaining visions and being infused with heavenly knowledge. The Ars Notoria and variants add to these the infusion of worldly knowledge (in the form of the seven liberal arts) and the improvement of the intellectual faculties (memory, eloquence, understanding).[6] While angelic magic was condemned by theologians with no less frequency than demonic magic (and sometimes on the basis that it, too, must have relied upon demons for its effects, whatever it declared to the contrary), the texts themselves claim to be most holy, to do the practitioner nothing but good, to involve no demons, and to operate only through benign entities and at the will of God.

Rather than the magic circles, sacrifices, conjurations and bindings that we find in demonic texts, the angelic operations involve lengthy prayers to God, Christ, the Holy Spirit, the orders of angels and other benign entities, which are petitioned at length and with elaborate biblical metaphors to grant the operator's request for knowledge and/or visions. All prayers involve ritual preparation in the form of fasting, confession, and periods of silence and meditation. From this description, the designation of these texts as magical or sorcerous may at first appear somewhat mystifying. However, since the reasons for considering these individual texts to be magical (or not) are discussed at length elsewhere in this volume, I will not rehearse them here. I will say, however, that if it is possible for scholarship to argue two sides to the issue of their magicality now (which it is), this is the case only because there were two sides to the issue of their magicality then. Thus, neither the view that these works are 'magical', nor the view that they are Christian works more or less legitimately (if eccentrically) 'devotional' can be taken as a modern projection onto a distant or alien cultural context; rather it is a question, in the end, of whether the scholar chooses to side with the theologian who condemns the work or the operator who upholds it. (In the case of the *Sworn Book*, of course, the claim that the work is magical is maintained by the composer simultaneously with the claim that the work is Christian and most holy, showing how many different threads may be woven into the same garment.)

Like all such categories, demonic and angelic magic have permeable boundaries. As will be seen, some portions of the text of the *Sworn Book* straddle the line between demonic and angelic magic, as do other texts both earlier and later. The incorporation of astrological magic (magic that might be classified as 'natural' under other conditions) into ritual magic texts is rather the norm than the exception. Yet the categories I have described here are nonetheless useful in a rough and ready way, if only as a departure point from which the texts themselves may be examined with greater nuancing.

THE AIMS OF THE PRESENT VOLUME

Over the past four decades there has been a rapid growth of interest in the intellectual magic of the early modern period, instigated most notably by the work of the late Dame Frances Yates. Until comparatively recently, however, the area of medieval intellectual magic has received much less scholarly attention, and as a consequence there is considerably less information available about the kinds of texts under discussion in this volume. It may be noted that this dearth of secondary information is not the consequence of a lack of manuscript material. Despite a tendency on the part of medieval authorities to confiscate and burn them, magic texts of various kinds seem to be relatively abundant in manuscript (no doubt at least in part due to a prudent impulse on the part of medieval compilers and collectors to keep them hidden).[7] Though there is no systematic catalogue of the magic texts extant in Europe and North America,[8] it is clear from the survival rate even of those texts we know about that the practices attested in them were fairly widespread in medieval Europe and transmitted over a considerable period of time. For this reason, if no other, these texts seem deserving of more serious attention from historians than they have received. And yet to date Lynn Thorndike's monumental *History of Magic and Experimental Science*, completed in 1958, remains not merely a base reference for scholars interested in texts of this kind, but in some cases the only available source of information about them outside the manuscripts themselves.

As all such rich and ambitious works must be, Thorndike's *History* is riddled with errors, false leads, gaps in, and misconstructions of, the evidence. This should be seen as no serious discredit to Thorndike, as anyone who has had the humbling experience of extracting evidence even from much smaller quantities of manuscript material will know. It is likely that Thorndike's *History* will remain useful for many years to come. Yet it should also be plain that brief or fragmentary synopses of texts written by a scholar whose primary interest was in tracing the early roots of experimental science are insufficient as a basis upon which to construct an accurate or balanced history of ritual practice. Additionally, the imbalance witnessed here affects not only our knowledge of the occult practices themselves, but also the larger context of theology and intellectual history, of the medieval religious and devotional practices against and through which the occult and magical practices must be read.

Magic may be a marginal pursuit; certainly it has been known to represent itself this way. Yet what precisely does it mean for a practice to be 'marginal' if it is widespread, if it is transmitted over several centuries, if textual evidence for it is relatively abundant? What new shades and colours of rhetoric can we see in the condemnations of occult arts by medieval authorities when we consider how attractive the occult arts themselves appeared to be to monks, doctors, clerics and other literate people with some cause to be grounded in the theological issues at stake? Indeed how seriously should we take the claims of magic itself to being oppressed, threatened and on the verge of extinction, when texts proclaiming such things can survive in multiple manuscripts?[9] Both sides surely had their justifications; my point is that the notion of the marginality of magic is in serious need of re-examination, and more so – rather than less – because it is a claim upheld by both sides. The fact that condemned texts survive at all becomes much more interesting when one considers simultaneously the injunctions to secrecy and privacy contained in them, and the recurring claims on both sides of the issue that the practices involved ought to be, or are in the process of being, extinguished.

There are other broad issues of considerable interest. It has been argued, most significantly by Edward Peters and Norman Cohn,[10] that the rise in witchcraft accusations in the early modern period is not unconnected to the problematic status of medieval ritual magic and the unsavory mythical aroma which surrounds the medieval necromancer in literary sources. This in turn suggests a variety of reasons why the intellectual magicians of the early modern period might have been unwilling to profess an open debt to their medieval antecedents – an unwillingness which has in turn certainly played some part in justifying the comparative scholarly neglect of the medieval materials until lately. Though much work remains to be done on the medieval materials, it is still possible to speculate that the real or apparent rise in the popularity of intellectual magic in the early modern period may be traced directly to the ways ritual magic was constructed as a problem in the later Middle Ages – a problem that the early modern writers were engaged in an attempt, more or less deliberate, to resolve.

But how in fact was the medieval problem constructed? We return once again to our informational hiatus: before any of these broader questions can be satisfactorily elaborated there is a primary requirement simply for more information about the medieval texts, a need for more editions and more codicological studies to assess the frequency and patterns of occurrence of the texts in question and to bring the manuscript materials into a more accessible form.

It is this information gap which the present volume is designed to address. Clearly it cannot fill it. Editions, in particular of lengthier texts, are labour-intensive and time-consuming to produce. Some of the essays in this volume deal with manuscripts still unedited; in other cases editions of the subject texts are in progress but incomplete. I have asked the contributors to share the understanding they have of the texts they are working on even where uncertainties still exist about readings, manuscript origins and textual histories; the information presented here will necessarily be subject to change and revision as the texts are edited, new manuscripts are discovered, and new questions are put to them. The essays presented here are meant first and foremost to open up an area of thought and action too little discussed, too little related to other and better understood areas of historical study.

This is particularly important with respect to the texts I have described as containing angelic magic. It may be noted that more than half the essays included here are concerned in one way or another with texts of angelic magic, in particular with the Ars Notoria and variants thereof. There are strong reasons for this, since this is the group of texts which have in the past suffered the most extreme neglect, about which least is presently known, and whose broad dispersal and relative popularity in the Middle Ages ought to make them of particular interest to cultural, intellectual and religious historians. As I hope will become clear in the essays that follow, it is chiefly by comparison of the contexts and concerns of purportedly divinely derived texts (like the Ars Notoria and the *Sworn Book of Honorius*) with those of the slightly better known necromantic texts that the peculiar problematic issues of medieval magic can begin to become visible in all their complexity.

THE ESSAYS OF PART ONE

The essays of the first part look at a diverse array of texts, all of which provide valuable insights into the varied contexts of the idea of magic in the later medieval period and the sources upon which it drew. Frank Klaassen's work on English magic manuscripts from 1300 to 1500 offers an overview of the codicological context for several genres of magic text in this period and provenance, including image magic, necromancy and the Ars Notoria. While Klaassen surveys only a small sample of existing magic manuscripts, his essay nonetheless covers the broadest territory of any piece in this volume, and is helpful in giving insight both into how the various genres of magical text relate to each other, and how they were thought of by the people who collected, compiled and used them. As Klaassen observes, the texts in question fall into noticeably different codicological categories: image magic texts were collected most frequently by those whose other interests lay in the area of natural philosophy, astrology and magical theory, while necromantic texts occur most often by themselves, or with other texts of the same genre. The codicological context of Ars Notoria texts can be compared to that of the relatively more innocent and less problematic texts of image magic; versions of the Ars Notoria, where they do not travel solo, may be found in conjunction with works on natural philosophy and astrology, as well, in some cases, as devotional works of a more traditional and less questionable nature. Many of the suggestions Klaassen makes here about the nature and context of broad groups of texts are filled out by more detailed discussions of single texts later in the volume.

With *The Book of Angels, Rings, Characters and Images of the Planets,* Juris Lidaka provides the only edition of a complete text contained in this anthology. Despite the title, *The Book of Angels* proves to be a work chiefly demonic in its orientation, though with a strong admixture of astrological magic.[11] Its invocations of angels are primarily of the brief demon-binding sort rather than the extended *orationes* petitioning divine entities on their own account which are to be found in the angelic texts. *The Book of Angels* involves rituals with typical necromantic ingredients such as blood and the skin of sacrificed animals, and the goals of the experiments, too, are consistent with magic of the necromantic genre: effects sought for include creating apparitions of various kinds, causing diseases or deformities, bringing good luck (usually to one's self) and bad luck (to someone else), or inducing love or ill will between two people. Almost all the experiments in the first half of the text include some inscription of astrological signs and characters as part of their working, and the second half is devoted to instructions for making planetary magic squares. These latter experiments do not involve any demonic names or invocations; however, the magical effects sought for through these mathematical talismans are often the same as those of the demonic rituals found in the first part. The brief introit, attributing the text to one 'Messayac' (whose name appears to derive from the Hebrew word 'Messiah') encourages the reader to think of the work as being in the tradition of sacred texts despite the demonic content and base designs visible in many of the experiments.

The next two essays deal with material that does not itself constitute ritual magic, but which helps to provide a broader context in which the practices of ritual magic may be located. John Friedman presents us with a text of a rather different kind from *The Book of Angels*, which nonetheless seems to inhabit a similar intellectual atmosphere. As Friedman notes, manuscripts of the *Secrets of the Philosophers* are found in books which also contain alchemical tracts and secrets literature as well as medical writings. Yet the *Secrets of the Philosophers* is not in fact a work of ritual magic, nor are the secrets it contains of the sort that might seem to be implied by such a title. Friedman describes this late thirteenth-century work as 'faux-theurgic'.[12] It promises, in a manner reminiscent of genuinely hermetic works, to disclose certain secret processes reputed by the common crowd to be impossible; but instead of delivering rituals of demonic conjuring, angelic invocation, or anything else which one might be compelled to understand as genuine magic, the text discloses such practical things as methods of secret writing, codes, riddles, tricks with mirrors and other means of deceiving the five senses, as well as instructions for more straightforward chemical, mathematical and engineering projects. Some of the procedures were intended to be used as party tricks or entertainment among groups of friends, and (like the tricks of stage magic through the ages) offer to replicate through chemistry or sleight of hand the kinds of disclosures that works of genuine ritual magic promised *in re vera*. Friedman's essay serves as a useful reminder that the contexts of the idea of magic in the Middle Ages were as varied and ambiguous as they are now: the line between magic and charlatanism has always been as visible in principle as it is smudged in practice.

Elizabeth Wade's discussion of the fifteenth-century divination device in Wolfenbüttel, Herzog August Bibliothek, Cod. Guelf. 75.10 Aug. 2°, relates to the broader context of occult philosophy in yet more unexpected and suggestive ways. The device she is concerned with is a simple fortune-telling wheel: a paper circle embedded in the wooden cover of the codex, which is surrounded by letters of the alphabet coordinated, in a separate key, with brief statements predicting the good or bad fortune of the querent. Classified by Johannes Bolte as a type of party game, this device is the first item to confront the reader in a book whose orientation is otherwise literary, comprising a set of popular narratives all reflecting on the theme of Fortune's wheel.

At first glance the device, and the codex in which it is embedded, would seem to have little to do with the more forbidding and risky intellectual atmosphere of the magic texts whose primary concern is the invocation of spirits. However, Wade's exploration of the historical analogues for this type of divination, particularly in Arabic and Jewish sources, lead her to intriguing speculations which relate both the device and its key to Kabbalistically inspired Lullian circular diagrams. It becomes clear after reading Wade's discussion that even such an innocuous entertainment as the alphabet wheel device must be considered in the larger intellectual context which equally fostered the practices of genuine ritual magic.

Michael Camille's work brings the perspective of art history to the magical images or *notae* which are an integral part of the Ars Notoria ritual practice. These *notae* are not in fact found in all manuscripts containing Ars Notoria texts – something which may be accounted for by the fact that they were complex and difficult to execute, so that the cheaper manuscripts are less likely to contain them. The images treated by Camille, particularly in the thirteenth-century Turin manuscript (Biblioteca Nazionale MS E.V. 13), are deluxe productions on their own account, and seem to be fairly independent of text, as though the long version of the ritual text and the images may have circulated separately. Camille discusses the background of the design elements in these manuscripts, and the ways in which the *notae* both reflect and distinguish themselves from other kinds of medieval pictorial and diagrammatic contexts. While Camille shows the images incorporated into the *notae* of the Ars Notoria to be different in many striking ways from more conventional depictions of the seven liberal arts, nevertheless, as he points out, the visual elements of these images 'are not only intimately connected with, but built out of the very structures of orthodox discourse against which they are so often opposed'.[13]

THE ESSAYS OF PART TWO

The second half of this volume comprises essays discussing the texts of the *Sworn Book of Honorius* and two versions of the Ars Notoria. It is appropriate to group these texts together since all involve rituals aiming to procure visions and divine knowledge, and all may be considered to involve angelic magic in the sense defined above.

Robert Mathiesen discusses the *Sworn Book of Honorius*, a late medieval text which is of considerable interest not only for its ties to Jewish mysticism which are discussed by Richard Kieckhefer later in this volume, but also on its own account, because it takes a far more explicit and even aggressive pro-magical stance than is usually found in medieval sources. In his lengthy prohemium, the composer of the *Sworn Book* issues a challenge to the earthly hierarchy of the Christian church with regard to its condemnation of magic – a condemnation which he calls not merely foolish but demonically inspired. God, the writer claims, is on the side of the magicians and not the pope. Following this prohemium are instructions for the performance of an extended ritual which involves prayers and fasting over a lengthy period to obtain a divine vision and 'to know God . . . as Adam and the Prophets knew him'.[14] Mathiesen argues that the extravagance of the introductory claims may have seemed well justified from the perspective of the practitioner, who, if he did not see God, very likely would have seen *something* by the end of the elaborate twenty-eight day rite – an effect which would have been quite unlikely to alleviate the qualms of the theologians about the claims of the text's prohemium and the theurgic dimension of its invocations. Mathiesen's discussion of the *Sworn Book* brings out the fact that the argument between magic and established Christian religiosity need not be a projection either of Christian theologians onto magical practices otherwise unconcerned with it, nor of modern views onto a more innocent past, but a genuine issue in the medieval conception of magic which could be articulated from both sides.

In the next two essays Nicholas Watson and I discuss the newly discovered text *The Book of Visions of the Blessed and Undefiled Virgin Mary*: a work which attempts to recuperate the frequently condemned Notory Art of Solomon into the domain of legitimate religious practice. *The Book of Visions* was composed, as it is claimed, with the approval and assistance of the Blessed Virgin, by one Brother John, a monk of Morigny. The McMaster text of the *Liber visionum* (an anonymous reworking which revealed nothing about its composer) was discovered only four years ago and quite by accident; the Munich version (which provided us with the name of the author as well as some of the circumstances of the text's composition) was unearthed a year or so later, though somewhat more purposefully.[15] Just one week before this volume was originally scheduled to be sent to the press, we received a microfilm of a manuscript discovered earlier in the summer (Graz, University Library 680) which contains a third redaction of the text, with rather more new information about John of Morigny than we have yet had time to absorb. We have done our best to incorporate as much of this new information into our essays as possible and practicable under the circumstances. Three other manuscripts, which appear to be of the Graz version of the text, have also been located; we have not yet been able to look at these.[16] It is quickly becoming apparent, however, that the *Liber visionum* will turn out to be a very important work, both in the sense that it was clearly relatively widely dispersed by the fifteenth century, and also in the sense that it gives us a good deal of unexpected information about the magical and mystical traditions to which it relates.

Watson's essay discusses the relation between the Munich and McMaster redactions of this text, situating John's work in relation to the mystical and devotional traditions of composition on which it also draws. My own essay examines Brother John's relation to the Solomonic Ars Notoria, the text on which *The Book of Visions* is loosely modelled. Both of our essays represent prelimary work done to an edition which we hope to accomplish collaboratively in the next few years. Much remains to be discovered and clarified about John's text, but it seemed important to present what we had learned of the text to this point despite the many remaining uncertainties.

Richard Kieckhefer's essay also discusses the *Liber visionum* in conjunction with the *Sworn Book of Honorius* as well as a third text, a brief collection of spells from a manuscript now in the Bodleian. Kieckhefer's essay opens up the question of Jewish influence on medieval Christian magic – an important issue as it touches not only on the under-examined topic of the prehistory of Christian Kabbalah, but also because, as Kieckhefer points out, the fundamental continuity between mysticism and magic which is manifest in Jewish writings both earlier and later appears foreign to Christian culture. Kieckhefer argues that the overlapping of theurgy and mysticism evident particularly in texts of the angelic magic genre most likely owe something of their conception to direct or indirect Jewish influence. The issue of the medieval Christian distinction between magic and mysticism is important in another way as well, for certainly it is true that modern academic disciplines have traditionally tended to separate magic and mysticism as objects of study – a hiatus which I hope Kieckhefer's essay, along with the others in this book, will do something to bridge.

CURIOSITY AND BEYOND

While curiosity is a vice traditionally associated with magic (a vice which may be said to afflict the scholar as much as the practitioner), I hope it is possible, even from these brief synopses, to see the ways in which these texts, curious as they are, open avenues for investigation into much larger areas. Beyond the variety of ways they show magic being argued, condemned, justified, exalted and revised, they also possess a richness from which, despite their arcane content, more subtle details emerge of the way the people who used and collected these texts lived and thought and felt. Even where the practices they describe seem distant, their desires, their frustrations, their fears, are deeply familiar. The challenge to the church hierarchy issued by the composer of the *Sworn Book*; the desire and frustration evident in the aims and ends of the demonic summonings in the *Book of Angels*; the desire both to be wise witnessed in the Ars Notoria, and to appear so witnessed in the *Secrets of the Philosophers* – all these speak to us of human things we know. The composers of these rituals were clearly not saints or philosophers; the texts themselves do not contain, even where the writing is more subtle, the spiritual blessings which seem to be on offer from the writings of the more famous mystics. The composers and operators of these rituals are rather people like you and me – people who, with the best will in the world, still sometimes kicked their dogs, grew irritated with the vaunting or pedantry of the monk in the next cell, or cursed the neighbor who uprooted their favorite tree without asking. They were jealous. They wanted to be smarter than they were. They went to parties; they played games; they were overlooked in inheritances; they made mistakes. And like us too, perhaps, they were sorry for their mistakes afterwards; they wanted life not to be such a jumble. Magic, if I may be permitted a few words of polemic, is not, or not wholly, about the next world or spiritual perfection; it is more often about real life, which includes both spiritual imperfection and the desire for something better, more perfect, whole and true, to be manifest here and now, not later, not after death or at the Last Judgment. It is about those attempts to control the intractible forces (whether they are in truth angelic or demonic, or whether they merely appear so) which frustrate our desires to see ourselves as good and wise and knowledgeable and just.

    Sometimes, we may be sure, these attempts to attract and compel the upper and lower worlds were successful. Sometimes they were not. Sometimes the stolen objects were found, the angels and demons appeared, the accursed did fall sick, the practitioners did grow wiser. Sometimes they did not. But the stories buried here are familiar ones. Whether we ourselves indulge in petitions to the angels or demonic summonings is not the point. We know these people. We may or may not be fond of them, but they are our neighbors, our kin, ourselves. I hope that this book will bring to its readers an enriched sense of anticipation about the things yet to be learned in the history of medieval life, thought and ritual practice. The essays included here are meant to constitute small openings into a larger realm which is no less real and no less curious than our own lives – a realm about which in due course we must and shall learn more.

Notes

1 The anthropological context of the argument is briefly and lucidly summarized by Michael D. Swarz in *Scholastic Magic* (Princeton: Princeton University Press, 1996), pp. 18–22.

2 The precise nature and extent of this admixture has not yet been explored, though see the final essay in this volume by Richard Kieckhefer.

3 As Frank Klaassen points out with regard to the Ars Notoria in his essay in this volume; see Klaassen p. 15.

4 For further analysis see Kieckhefer's essay in this volume.

5 Ars Notoria (or Notory Art) is capitalized throughout this book because the term can refer both to a specific work (the Notory Art of Solomon) and to a class of magical texts intended to procure knowledge, also often called 'Notory Arts' although they are not closely related to the Solomonic text. For more information see Klaassen, pp. 14–19 and Fanger, pp. 218–22.

6 The recent study by Michael Swartz (*Scholastic Magic*, cited above, n. 1) discusses the Hebrew Sar-Torah literature – a type of ritual magic emerging from the context of Jewish mysticism which is similarly intended to infuse heavenly knowledge and memory into the operator by angelic means. I do not see in the texts analyzed by Swartz any obvious or clear-cut similarity to the Ars Notoria variants I am familiar with, though the question of a direct Jewish influence on the Ars Notoria is by no means closed and surely requires further study.

7 See Robert Mathiesen's comments on this topic in this volume, pp. 143–5.

8 There is in fact no systematic catalogue of any kind of ritual magic texts specifically, though in respect to other forms of intellectual magic Great Britain is well served by Dorothea Waley Singer's *Catalogue of Latin and Vernacular Alchemical Manuscripts in Great Britain and Ireland*, 3 vols (Brussels: M. Lamertin, 1928–31). This catalogue cites a number of magical texts not strictly of an alchemical character.

9 I refer to claims made in the prohemium to the *Sworn Book of Honorius*; see Mathiesen, pp. 147–50 and Kieckhefer, pp. 253 in this volume.

10 Peters, *The Magician, the Witch and the Law* (Philadelphia: University of Pennsylvania Press, 1978) and Cohn, *Europe's Inner Demons* (New York: Basic Books, 1975).

11 This combination of demonic and astrological magic is not unusual. Richard Kieckhefer describes some similar combinations of astral and demonic magic in some of the experiments

detailed in his *Forbidden Rites* (Stroud: Sutton Publishing, 1997), pp. 176–80. There does seem to be a higher percentage of astrological references in *The Book of Angels* than in the text analyzed by Kieckhefer, however.

12 Friedman, p. 77.

13 Camille, p. 135.

14 Mathiesen, p. 151.

15 Nicholas Watson had been commissioned to deliver a five-minute talk on the manuscript (whose modern binding labelled it simply a 'prayer book') for an educational videotape put out by McMaster University about its small manuscript collection. Expecting the book to contain essentially what the binding promised, he was surprised, as he read on, to discover that the text included what he described as a 'technology' for procuring visions of the Virgin Mary, followed by a set of extended prayers for the taking of the seven liberal arts, and, at the end, instructions for the making and consecration of a magic ring. Watson's background in medieval spirituality did not cover rituals of this type, and he quickly telephoned Richard Kieckhefer, Frank Klaassen and me, to find out whether it might be something known to us. It was not. However, some connection with the Ars Notoria tradition was immediately obvious, and Richard Kieckhefer further suggested that it might be a text similar to the one condemned in the *Grandes Chroniques* entry for 1323. (That it was, in fact, the same text, did not become clear until later, after I found another text of the McMaster manuscript prayers in Munich, Bayerische Staatsbibliothek Clm 276, and Watson and I had had a chance to transcribe its contents.) If it had not been for the educational videotape, however, there would have been no reason for anyone ever to look closely at the text at all – a testimony, perhaps, to the value of making educational videotapes.

16 See Watson, p. 165 and pp. 182–3, nn. 7–12.

LIST OF ILLUSTRATIONS

ACKNOWLEDGMENTS

For their comments and corrections to my essay on John of Morigny and the introduction to this volume, I would like to thank John Friedman, Wouter Hanegraaff, Frank Klaassen, Nicholas Watson, and David and Virginia Fanger. I am particularly grateful to Richard Brzustowicz, who has not only been a useful reader but has also promptly and gracefully supplied me with information from the OCLC and other library catalogues on various urgent occasions during the course of putting together this book. I am also grateful to Richard Kieckhefer for his input on various aspects of the volume's content, and to Jennifer Stevenson for her help with data entry. Finally, members of the list MEDTEXTL have been most helpful with my occasional queries. Errors which remain are, of course, my own.

Part One

CONTEXTS, GENRES, IMAGES

English Manuscripts of Magic, 1300–1500: A Preliminary Survey[1]

Frank Klaassen

nterest in literate magic[2] in the late medieval period whether practical, academic, or prurient took many forms. The manuscripts which attest to this interest give us access to the world view of their authors, scribes and collectors, and frequently betray a great deal more about these individuals, their professions, names, education, status, or relative wealth. Integral palaeography[3] can provide a perspective unavailable through the more commonly used sources such as trial records, literature, art and philosophy, all of which represent magic in ways that may or may not reflect the realities of individuals and their interest in magic. Medieval literary or philosophical discussions of magic and trial records tend to witness peculiar kinds of ritual magic, in particular, the flagrantly unorthodox or seditious varieties. While study of these sources may provide valuable insights into the preconceptions which were brought to bear upon such trials, the history of witch trials, or upon the trappings of magical practice, such sources are less valuable for a general study of those who were interested in or practicing learned magic. For such an enquiry, the manuscript evidence provides a more reliable starting point as a witness to a wide range of people interested in magic who would never have found their way into court or into the literary or mythological representations. To be sure, the study of manuscripts is subject to its own set of problems (selective survival, questions of authorial intent, forgery, etc.). However, by surveying a large number of the surviving manuscripts and catalogues many of these problems can be overcome.

This paper is thus a tentative exploration of the interests of the owners, collectors and scribes of magical manuscripts, of the kinds of works they collected, and of the attitude towards magic suggested by the way in which they treated magical texts in their books. This discussion is based upon a survey of manuscripts of British origin or significant British provenance from 1250 to 1500, which include works on magic, and of medieval library catalogue/inventory entries containing magical works.[4] To use an individual manuscript as evidence for the understanding and practice of ritual magic we must take into account both the content of the work and whatever its context within a codex can tell us about the interests or approach of the scribe or collector.

BOOKS OF IMAGES

The story goes that the thirteenth-century astrologer Guido Bonatti took pity upon a poor apothecary with whom he used to play chess. 'Guido gave him a wax image of a ship, telling him that if he kept it hidden in a box in a secret place he would grow rich, but that if he removed it he would grow poor again.' In time the apothecary did grow rich but began to worry about the condition of his soul and confessed to a priest who counselled him to destroy the image. The hapless apothecary did as he was told and, predictably, was soon reduced to poverty once again. Evidently having reconsidered the matter, he returned to Bonatti to ask for a replacement. Bonatti chastised him saying that the effects of the image were not magical but natural, and were derived from astrological conditions which would not recur for fifty years.[5]

This wry reversal of the familiar moral tales about magic illustrates a significant division in the late medieval understanding of image magic. The apothecary's concern was an understandable one because, philosophical arguments aside, the trappings of image magic could very easily leave one in doubt about the nature of the effect and its ultimate source. To put it another way, the apothecary was concerned that the image had derived its power from or through an inappropriate rite. Had he been familiar with the literature on magical images he might have been less concerned, since most of the texts would appear to have been regarded by their collectors as natural magic. On the other hand, a portion of the texts of image magic would have justified the apothecary's concern since they could feasibly be identified as necromantic magic, and it is true that images made of wax are frequently associated with necromancy in literature and court records. In the end, he would have had to take what solace he could from the fact that most collectors of the texts of image magic appear to have collected this material from an interest in natural philosophy or the natural world and not from illicit religious interests.

Of the works expressly devoted to magical images[6] most are comparatively innocent; i.e., very few are explicitly necromantic in orientation, and only a portion of them make extensive use of the techniques usually associated with necromantic magic such as incantation, suffumigation, the summoning of demons and other rituals. The most obvious general feature of collections including works on images is that the overwhelming majority (all but one) are made up of some combination of astrological or astronomical works, alchemical works, books of secrets, natural wonders or recipes, or medical works. In other words, these texts of images were almost always collected with books about the natural world. From this we can reasonably infer that their scribes and/or collectors regarded them as at least potentially connected with the natural world rather than demonic forces.

Just over half of the collections including works on image magic have explicit astronomical and astrological interests. Because works on images often occupy a very small portion of the text, not least because many of these texts run to only a few folios, it is prudent to ask whether the work on images found its way into the collection purely by chance, or by 'piggy-backing' in with other non-magical texts.[7] For example, Selden Supra 76, a late thirteenth-century codex, appears to be a collection of booklets produced by a single British scriptorium. The gatherings are of irregular number of bifolia, making it possible for the texts to end somewhere near the end of the gathering. In principle, then, a short text could easily be tagged on at the end as a bonus to the reader, in order to provide the right amount of text for a gathering which would otherwise end in a folio and a half of unused parchment. Yet in practice this is not the case with Selden Supra 76, and I cannot find any instance where this may have happened. There is an analagous problem with a magical text like Thebit ben Corat's *de Imaginibus*, which, as only one of a number of works by this author in circulation, might be thought to have travelled with his non-magical works simply by virtue of having been written by the same author. Once again this does not appear to happen. Although his works frequently travel three or four abreast, the *de Imaginibus* generally does not travel with other works of Thebit ben Corat. As a rule, magical texts are transmitted with other magical texts rather than with astrological or other material by the same author.

Works of images are thus not accidental parts of the collections in which they are found. The content of these texts are integral to the world view suggested by the other works in the collections which contain them.[8] To return to the example of Selden Supra 76, this codex includes a section of al-Kindi's work on astrological/magical theory, usually referred to as the *De radiis stellarum*. This makes it clear that the compiler was very much interested in magical images, if only in a theoretical sense.[9] The *De radiis* provides a strong theoretical foundation for image magic by making explicit the later neo-Platonic theory which underlies the practice. Al-Kindi argues that all sublunary motion derives from the stars and that this motion is transmitted through stellar rays. These 'rays' vary in form depending upon the disposition of the heavens and the variations are reflected in sublunary effects. These celestial forms have connected mundane forms in sounds, images, gestures and suffumigations which can produce produce their own rays and, hence, change, due to their connection with their original celestial form. Manipulation of these rays through something with the appropriate form, like an image, allows 'magical' operation. Much of this kind of theory was incorporated into Scholastic treatments of magic (such as Albertus Magnus' *Speculum astronomiae*),[10] which lent a certain legitimacy to image magic in the later Middle Ages that was not available to necromantic and other ritual material. So long as there was some clear connection to the stars and no connected ritual such as incantation, suffumigation, or ritual gestures, the magical operation was less at risk of being identified as demonic. Charles Burnett has discussed how the science of images was sometimes represented as a branch of legitimate study under the rubric of 'necromancy' as the seventh liberal art.[11] His analysis of Adelard of Bath's translation of Thebit Ibn-Qurra's work on magical images reveals a similar attitude toward images, probably that of Adelard himself.[12] It is not likely coincidental that a section of the *Speculum astronomiae* coincides in the fifteenth-century codex Digby 228 with a work of image magic, the *Liber lune*. As part of a discussion and evaluation of astronomical and astrological texts, the *Speculum* seeks to divide good and bad magic on astrological grounds, in particular good and bad images. There are also Continental examples of this configuration of texts combining theory and images.[13] So it is clear that some of the scribes and collectors were making explicit use of the theoretical works on the subject, and it seems unlikely that the remainder did not understand the connections, especially given their obvious interest in the natural world.

It would be hazardous to suggest that all of these works represent compilers or scribes with active and practical magical interests. However, the evidence suggests that the number of such people might have been relatively high. Of the twelve codices in my survey which betray astrological and magical interests, all but one have more than one work on magical images, which suggests that a person likely to collect or copy one work on magic would likely be serious enough to copy others. Sloane 312 contains two collections of the fifteenth century, both of which betray very practical and involved interests. Largely devoted to judicial astrology, the second collection also includes a work by Sahl Ibn Bishr on magical images that is followed by a short section of further images added by the scribe. In the first we find a typically practical collection including a text of judicial astrology, a text discussing the natures and properties of the planets, a text of image magic (Thetel on images) and an astrological method for discovering thieves and stolen goods. The collection is more crudely written than many of the image magic texts, and was likely for personal use. In both cases we have evidence that the interest in the material was quite practical, if only insofar as both involve judicial astrology and practical activities such as discovering thieves. In addition, both collections betray an active interest in the material. The first text appears to be a personal notebook and the second includes notes and personal additions to the magical material.

Medical doctors as a group are historically associated with astrological images, or at least suspensions, ligatures and rings. Medieval medicine was inextricable from astrology, but in addition to this, ligatures, suspensions and images appear frequently in medical literature. This historical association is also strongly reflected in my sample. Six of the twenty-two collections show an interest in medical material, and two of the collectors can be independently identified as medical practitioners. *Society of Antiquaries 39* contains part of a collection by John Argentine, who was provost of King's College, Cambridge, in the late fifteenth- and early sixteenth-century and doctor to Edward V and his brother Richard,

Duke of York.[14] The collection includes Thebit ben Corat's book of images and a work on images attributed to Ptolemy. Interestingly, it contains *no medical material*, so that in the absence of the 'Quod Argentyn' we would have no idea it was written by a physician at all. Interestingly, Argentine makes the only fifteenth-century reference to the *Picatrix*, the infamous work of Arabic magic, so it is clear that Argentine was actively interested in magical texts.[15] The texts in Argentine's collection appear in the same order in Ashmole 346, the collection of another physician, Thomas Scalon, who was a junior Fellow at King's at the time Argentine was there.[16] We are fortunate to have all 164 folios of this collection, which is made up largely of astrological and medical works, but also includes secrets and recipes. In addition to the material of John Argentine, Scalon has collected two works of magic giving directions for finding thieves or stolen goods.[17]

Although medical practitioners frequently collected magical texts, the largest identifiable group of collectors were clerics, usually monks. Motivated by the same intellectual forces which drove medical doctors, this composite group could also draw upon a long-standing tradition of using wonders of the world to direct attention to the divine. The well-known Dominican encyclopedic writer, Thomas of Cantimpré, performed a valuable service for the preservation of texts of magic when he included in his *De natura rerum* the entire text of Thetel's work on the images used by the sons of Israel while in the desert.[18] He concludes this work with a short piece which describes the blessing of a stone to return it to its pre-lapsarian (and thereby more efficacious) state. Thomas did not see the text as altogether trustworthy, nor did he regard all sculpted gems as effective. Although the form of the stones is to be honoured for its virtue, 'yet hope is not to be put in them but, according to what is written, in God alone from whom the virtue of stones is derived'.[19] Thomas's rationale for writing *De natura rerum* was that should people not be moved by sermons of the usual kind, they might be moved to religious devotion by stories of the wonders of the natural world.[20] So the purpose of recording this information was certainly not to encourage the reader to sculpt gems, but rather to give a credible report of their behaviour.

A similar project may have been involved in the assembly of Oxford, Corpus Christi 221, which includes extracts from an encyclopedia of the same name by the Carmelite John Folsham, in addition to another copy of Thetel and a treatise on sculpted gems by Marbod.[21] The remainder of this codex is taken up with recipes, medical recipes and medical notes. So far we have nothing out of the ordinary; one thinks of a collector interested in recipes, medicine, and aspects of the natural world with a particular interest in sculpted gems. What is very interesting about this fourteenth-century collection is that it is bound together with a twelfth-century collection which includes the Dialogues of Gregory the Great and two saints' lives in a late medieval binding. As David Pingree has noted,[22] this volume was part of the collection of Michael Northgate, monk at St Augustine's, Canterbury, the author of the *Ayenbit of Inwyt*[23] (a translation of a

French work, *La somme des vices et des vertues* written by Laurentius Gallus in 1279
for Philip II of France). Three of the twenty works recorded under his name in
that library contain works on magic – a high enough ratio to demonstrate an
interest in magic on his part. The catalogue of the Abbey's library records the
codex with the the *Dialogues* of Gregory the Great, and the age of the binding
could easily date its assembly to the lifetime of Northgate.[24] It would be
presumptuous to assume that this is in itself firm evidence that the binding
together of these two codices indicates that the new composite codex was used
with Thomas of Cantimpré's project in mind or, for that matter, that Northgate
was responsible for its assembly. However, the circumstantial evidence suggests
that the combination was not coincidental. Northgate was interested enough in
magic and the natural world to collect quite a number of works on both topics
and interested enough in devotional literature to write a vernacular work on the
subject. His collection of books is composed of approximately even numbers of
devotional works and works concerned with medicine, alchemy, secrets, astrology,
magic and natural philosophy. If Northgate did not regard his devotional and
'scientific' interests as coherent in the manner of Thomas of Cantimpré, we can
certainly say that both of these interests are represented in Oxford, Corpus
Christi 221.

The collections of those interested in or practicing alchemy are often much
more focused in their interests. They will occasionally include a work of image
magic and there are three of this kind in my sample.[25] The magical texts are
usually short and buried in a host of small alchemical texts. In all of these
collections, at least some of the texts of image magic involve the use of engraved
stones. Selden Supra 76 and Ashmole 1416, contain a magical text concerned
with images engraved on gems. In the case of Corpus Christi 125, we find two
works on images in addition to the tract on fifteen stars, fifteen herbs, fifteen
stones and fifteen images frequently associated with alchemical texts.[26] So while
magical and alchemical interests do cross over, the attraction of texts on image
magic for those interested in alchemy might have something to do with a more
diffuse interest in literature on stones. The alchemists' interest in symbols and
symbolic language might also have attracted them to engraved images.

The overwhelming numbers of astrological, medical and alchemical texts
found with texts of image magic might serve to demonstrate this body of writings'
primary association with the natural world. However, there is a significant
additional literature present in these collections which needs to be examined.
Lapidaries are to be found in four of the manuscripts[27] and recipes,[28] herbal
lore,[29] weather prediction[30] and books of secrets[31] also recur. As I have
mentioned, the connection of lapidaries to works on images is a logical one as
several of the texts on images concern images engraved on stones. Although most
of the collections are still best characterized as alchemical, medical or
astrological, Sloane 1784 is exclusively concerned with stones of magical and

non-magical varieties. Corpus Christi 125, while containing alchemical and astrological material, also contains a high percentage of material on properties of animals, recipes, chemical experiments, secrets and even a book on tree planting. Although these examples suggest a distinct set of interests, even these texts could have been regarded as falling under the rubric of natural philosophy and astrology insofar as it was thought that occult properties, whether derived from an image, stone, plant or animal, all derive ultimately from the stars. This, as the title suggests, is the rationale for the hermetic text on fifteen stars, fifteen stones, fifteen herbs and fifteen images.

The patterns of collection evident from descriptions in medieval manuscript catalogues are substantially the same as those of surviving manuscripts I have examined. Of the ten volumes containing works on image magic recorded in medieval British catalogues which I have identified to this point, all but two may be classified as astrological/astronomical or alchemical.[32] The works of images generally included are also the same: Thebit ben Corat, *De imaginibus*; *De lapidibus filiorum israel*; *Liber lune*; the *De sculpturis gemmarum* attributed to Marbodius; *Liber hermetis de xv. stellis* . . . and the *De imaginibus* attributed to Ptolemy. Of the collectors of works on images identifiable from medieval catalogues and inventories, all are monks – a predictable fact given the relatively large number of surviving monastic catalogues. However, two notices do not initially appear to fall into the standard pattern and deserve independent treatment.

The collection of Thomas Erghome became a substantial part of the library of the Austin Friars at York sometime in the late fourteenth century.[33] Among the approximately three hundred books which the library catalogue lists as having belonged to him, seven notices include works on magic. None of these have been identified with any surviving manuscripts.[34] All but the books listed in the catalogue as items 362 and 364 follow the pattern we have discussed so far. The first contains a collection of magical works unparalleled in its size and in the variety of its contents.[35] To my knowledge, no existing codex contains so complete a collection of the magical works available in the fourteenth century. What is significant for our present purposes is that this codex contains not only the standard configuration of works on image magic with astrology/astronomy and magical theory (again represented by al-Kindi's *De radiis*), but also includes a substantial number of explicitly necromantic or ceremonial magic texts as well. These include the *Liber sacer* or the *Sworn Book of Honorius*, *Vinculum solomonis*, *Tractatus de penthagono salomonis*, *Ars notoria*, *Ars notoria nova completa*, *Liber rubeus qui aliter dicitur sapiencia nigromancie* and *Tractatus de nominibus angelorum et effectibus eorum*. The second book (364) includes the *Liber lune*, al-Kindi's *De radiis stellarum*, another work on images, a work on magic tricks and a *Liber sacratus petri abellardi*.

Erghome would have been one of very few with the resources to compile such a collection of magical works from such disparate traditions, and if he did not collect each piece individually, he may have combined several volumes in a single codex. As we shall see, the grouping of the texts by subject suggests that these were originally separate volumes, and also gives us some idea where the divisions might have occurred. One way or another the chances are high that Erghome was at least in part responsible for the collection of these texts.

Both of these codices are collected under the heading 'Prophecie et Supersticiosa', which likely means that on average these codices were not regarded as legitimate natural philosophy, astrology or astronomy. In the case of item 362, the list provided (see note 35) should be ample explanation for this classification. The case of 364 is somewhat different. Why is it that a work including images and magic theory would be classified as superstitious, when the *Liber lune* and at least four other works on magical images occur in another of Erghome's books (375) in the company of works on astrology, classified as astrological and astronomical? Al-Kindi's *De radiis* appears twice more in Erghome's collection (385 and 452), also among the astrological and astronomical works. Although the works on images tend to be relatively short and thus might not have played a part in a decision about how to classify a codex, the *De radiis* would likely have occupied several quires and have taken up a substantial part of a codex. A workable explanation for the classification of 364 as superstitious is that the last work is not a work by Peter Abelard (certainly no work of his exists by such a name) but the *Liber sacer* or *Sacratus* also known as the *Sworn Book of Honorius*, a relatively large work, and one of the most significant works of ritual magic during this period in England.

As no works of this kind of ritual magic appear elsewhere in his collection under other headings, it could be assumed that a volume with any such lengthy work of ritual magic ought simply to be classified among the volumes of superstitious works. It might also be that the problematic contents of the *Liber lune* may have moved Erghome to classify the whole codex in this way. But we cannot answer this question conclusively. Given the breadth of material commonly found in individual codices, a cataloguer who had to classify an entire codex under a single subject heading would have had to make a decision based on the average content of a book, the relative importance of the included texts, or perhaps the first text in the codex. As a result, not a great deal of weight can be placed upon the choice of one classification over another without a very careful analysis. As it stands, we can regard the classification of this codex only as an indication of what he thought (or wished others to assume he thought) about magic in general. But this cannot be taken as evidence for a synthetic approach to all magical texts, or an indication that Erghome assumed no internal divisions existed among the constituent texts. In other words, Erghome could well have regarded Thebit and al-Kindi as belonging to quite a distinct category from the *Liber sacer*, as the rest of our scribes did, and as the scribes of most of Erghome's other volumes including magical works would appear to have done also.

In the event that they were acquired as a piece, these two volumes of

Erghome's would provide two exceptions to the standard configuration of subjects in being codices which combine image magic with more ritually oriented texts like the *Vinculum Salomonis* and the *Sworn Book of Honorius*. Yet even in that case, the manner in which 362 is organized would not appear to be at all random. That the texts on images and theory all appear together in this codex (a-i, n-r and ah-ao), and in blocks separate from works of necromancy or other more explicitly ritual magic, further confirms the standard divisions among the surviving manuscripts and other catalogue notices. In addition, al-Kindi's *De radiis* appears in both volumes (362g, 364c and possibly 362b, as suggested by Humphreys) side by side with works of image magic as does what could only be Thomas Aquinas' *De occultis operibus naturae* (362e) which further demonstrates the association of image magic with theoretical interests. It is a strong possibility that these texts were either grouped in this fashion by Erghome, or were assembled in this way as discrete collections prior to assembly by him. Assuming, for the sake of argument, that Erghome saw no differences between the texts he compiled, these volumes would have to be regarded as in some measure exceptions to the rule. Nonetheless, it would remain that the standard groupings of texts are reflected here despite what Erghome may have thought, and that the overwhelming majority of these standard texts on images do not usually travel with works of more explicit ritual magic.

The apparently ambiguous case of these two volumes from Erghome's collection ultimately adds to the evidence for a classificatory division being upheld between ritual and image magic. The existence of texts of image magic which contain a significant quantity of ritual operation suggests that the division is not altogether hard and fast; nevertheless, codices containing such works reveal that the scribes' interests lay in the direction of natural philosophy rather than illicit ritual practices. They also furnish further evidence of the necessity of examining such works in their manuscript context.

Digby 228 is a late fourteenth-century codex written on parchment by three scribes and running to seventy-nine folios. The magical text is an incomplete version of the *Liber lune*, an Arabic work of image magic which runs to one-and-a-half folios. Contemporary quire marks suggest that the codex is complete to quire 'h', the end of the extant codex, although it is possible they indicate reassembly. The major hand of the codex, mid-fourteenth century, begins at quire five (f. 15), and the texts it records run over the quire divisions until the end of quire seven, where it stops. It emerges again through quires eight and nine. At the end of quire seven there was enough room for the second scribe to include part of the *Liber lune*. The *Liber lune* is incomplete, but the scribe did not use up all the available space, so there is no indication that there is a missing quire, although that is possible. In a similar way, scribe two filled in a significant section of the *Speculum astronomiae* of Albertus Magnus at the end of quire nine. The scribe of the *Liber lune* (scribe two) dates all but ff. 8–15 as a late fourteenth-century compilation as he fills quires one through three and the last leaves of quires seven and nine. Another fourteenth-century hand fills quire four. What this boils down to is that we can treat the material written by scribe two as a collection, and the original material to which he added (the material written by scribe one) as a supplementary indication of his interests.

The *Liber lune* is a work of Arabic image magic attributed to Hermes. The magical effects sought for are often of bad intent, ranging from binding someone's tongue, to twisting a man's limbs, to destroying an entire region. The instructions concern the engraving of images as the moon moves through its houses, and the magical processes involve the reciting of angel names and suffumigations. To distinguish this text from the works of necromancy on the basis of content would be difficult. We have a complex array of ethereal beings, we have images and we have incantations. The ritual features of the process receive a considerable amount of attention. However, the codicology of this version of the *Liber lune* is very much like that of other works on images and, as we shall see, unlike that of most necromantic texts.

Digby 228 also includes the standard array of astrological and theoretical works we have demonstrated to be the usual company of image magic. In the first three quires a scribe has copied a few short astrological and astronomical texts, including a short commentary on the *Sphere of sacrobosco*, and a text which explains the astrological significance of being born on a particular day. In addition, this scribe copied a section of the *Speculum astronomiae* concerned with distinguishing good and bad images, which indicates that scribe two was very much interested in magic, although it is not clear whether this interest was practical or theoretical (or, in fact, whether the material might have been collected as part of an anti-magical project). One way or another, however, the scribe has chosen to approach the material through a work of magical theory and in conjunction with astrology.

In the manuscripts containing works on magic that I have surveyed, the two major medieval works of magical theory make frequent appearances: the *Speculum astronomiae* appears once[36] and the *De radiis stellarum* of al-Kindi appears eight times. In every case, the text of magical theory appears together with works on images; and in every case except Erghome's *codices superstitiosae*, it does not appear in a codex with ritual magic texts. As we shall see, among works of magic involving the conjuring and binding of spirits, there is very little evidence of an interest in theory. (This is despite the fact that al-Kindi is, in the first instance, interested in developing an astrological basis for the function of incantation, and takes on images as a supplementary issue.)

Astrology is as fundamental to most works on images as hierarchies of demons and angel names are important to works on conjuring, so it is logical that these theoretical works appear in company with image magic. Moreover, the *De radiis* is Arabic, and the *Speculum astronomiae* refers to the tradition of images which is largely Arabic as well. These works also tend to be associated with speculations that there are certain forms of magic which are allowable on the grounds of being 'natural' (this is an explicit argument in the case of the *Speculum* and implicit in the *De radiis*). The theoretical grounds for the 'natural' functions of an image are fundamentally connected to the theories about occult properties (which might explain the presence of a version of the *Secretum secretorum* in Digby 228 although it was written by the first scribe, not the scribe of the *Liber lune*). Works on images and secrets appear together elsewhere in my survey.[37]

The question remains whether the *Liber lune* in general and this version of the text in particular ought to be included under the umbrella of ritual magic. It clearly belongs there if content has anything to do with it; on the other hand, as a text in Digby 228 and in the context of the tradition of Arabic astrological image magic, it belongs to a group of texts with a markedly more innocent agenda. Its collector understood the work to be connected to the theoretical context of image magic, and may have had no practical interest in the subject at all. It is quite possible that the collector may have decided, upon reflection, that the *Liber lune was* bad magic, and not attributable to astrological mechanisms despite what al-Kindi and Albertus Magnus may have said. This we will never know. We can say that ours has approached the *Liber lune* as a suitable companion to other works on astrology and natural philosophy. In addition, the presence of the *Secretum secretorum* in the same volume indicates that the scribe's interests probably lie in the direction of natural wonders rather than what Richard Kieckhefer has described as the 'flamboyantly transgressive' rites of ritual magic.[38]

Scribes and collectors of image magic were a diverse group, a significant number of whom were in regular orders. Medical doctors and those with medical training may have collected the material in some instances for the sake of show or from a theoretical rather than practical interest in it, but also may have been actively interested in image magic from a practical perspective. The alchemists may have been interested in such texts for the sake of the stones as well as the imagery. For the astrologer (whether he was a professional astrologer or doctor) the texts could have been used in the context of professional work, but also as a part of a more general study of the subject. All of this does not preclude a practical interest on the part of any scribe, but it does suggest a group with a broad set of interests and a synthetic, theoretical approach. The treatment of the texts reflects a concern to reproduce them accurately and to identify their sources clearly. If Oxford, Corpus Christi 221 proves to be evidence of a project like that of Thomas of Cantimpré, we may have magical images being used as a means to emphasize the wonders of God's creation. The *Liber lune* in Digby 228 was apparently included in the category of astrological magic despite its dubious ritual aspects. However we interpret these two collections, the vast majority of collections including works on images exhibit a common assumption that magical images are to be related to the natural world. Moreover (and perhaps most importantly) their collectors were an intellectual and mainstream group; their interest in the material as suggested by their books need not have conflicted with a more or less orthodox faith, and this interest existed in the context of mainstream ideas about the functioning of the universe. Finally, despite the apothecary's dilemma, contextual evidence suggests that the vast majority of these texts were not considered by their scribes and collectors as belonging to the same category as the more explicit texts of ritual magic. In the few cases where ambiguities exist, the collections remain strongly informed by natural philosophy and an interest in the wonders of the natural world. With the possible exception of the volumes in Erghome's collection, none can be taken as evidence for a practical interest in more explicit forms of ritual magic.

THE ARS NOTORIA

The Ars Notoria makes up a portion of the magical texts of the Middle Ages quite out of proportion to the small amount of attention it has received. In E.M. Butler's discussion of ritual magic,[39] no mention at all is made of the Ars Notoria. And yet among the surviving manuscripts, texts from this group recur quite frequently. An unsystematic search of modern and medieval European catalogues turns up almost fifty manuscripts which include a text of this genre dating from 1300–1600. In British medieval library catalogues this text is mentioned almost as many times as all other texts of ritual magic put together. To this point I have found seven medieval notices of texts in this genre, which taken together with the surviving manuscripts of British origin or provenance makes a total of ten, possibly eleven, versions.[40] In time more manuscripts may surface, either having been catalogued as *ars notaria* or notarial art[41] (or, as in the case of the *Liber visionum* found in Hamilton, Canada, McMaster University Library, Unnumbered MS, having been thought to be prayer formularies). The continuing significance of the Ars Notoria through the sixteenth century is attested by its condemnation in the indices of Milan and Venice of 1554 as a category parallel to necromancy.[42] It was also printed in the seventeenth century in a Latin edition and an English translation, so it would appear that even in the early modern period it is deserving of more attention than it has received.[43]

More copies of these texts may survive because they did not appear as threatening as the necromantic manuals. Similarly, their apparent harmlessness might have made it less worrisome to catalogue such a book, hence the large number of medieval notices. However, the frequency with which it was discussed and condemned in the later Middle Ages indicates not only that late medieval conceptions of magic included it, but also, because it was so widely understood to be illegitimate, that one might well think twice before cataloguing such a work (in other words, the catalogue entries may not provide an accurate reflection of the number of Ars Notoria texts which exist, or may have existed). A by no means comprehensive list of those who discuss or condemn this text includes Michael Scot, Thomas Aquinas, Peter Abano, Giovanni da Fontana, Nichole Oresme, James the Carthusian, Dionysius the Carthusian, Thomas Ebendorfer, Vincent of Beauvais, Augustinus Triumphus and Trithemius.[44] It would not be hard to expand considerably upon this list, and the frequency of condemnations alone suggests its importance, whatever the relative survival rates may have been.

We have few records of prosecutions for using or possessing a work of the Notory Art[45] as opposed to the relatively frequent occurrence of prosecutions for the possession of works of necromancy, which were frequently associated with seditious plots. This is not surprising as the Ars Notoria posed no threat to anything other than the operator's soul. In addition, the magic itself does not appeal to the prurient interests so often motivating discussions of magic. In part, no doubt, this also explains why the Ars Notoria did not find its way into literary and artistic representations of magical practice, which are taken up almost entirely with conjuring and other forms of more fearsome magic. Representations of necromancers were more often than not a vehicle for discussing hell, the devil, demons, and the immanence of evil and divine retribution, providing a colourful context and plenty of dramatic material. The sources for the Ars Notoria begin to explain why it would not have been of much value or interest in such contexts.

The Ars Notoria ascribes its authority to Solomon, referring to the account in II Chronicles 1:9–12 and II Kings 3:9–13 where God appears to Solomon in *nocte*. Among other things Solomon has asked for, he is granted *sapientia, scientia et intelligencia*.[46] That a wider group of people might expect these kind of gifts from God is suggested by Daniel 1:17 where God endows Daniel and the four children with knowledge and understanding, or Luke 21:15, where Christ promises to endow his followers with wisdom. In the *Dialogus miraculorum* of Caesarius of Heisterbach a priest is given the gift of preaching in his sleep.[47] The commentary on this miracle refers back to the story of Solomon. The Ars Notoria seeks, similarly, the acquisition of knowledge or other related gifts such as rhetorical skills through the use of prayers and figures (*notae*). Although works of necromancy sometimes appear under titles usually associated with the Ars Notoria, the term was generally confined to this relatively more innocent procedure and agenda. Analyses and condemnations of this form of magic similarly restrict themselves to whether it is possible to acquire knowledge or skills through prayers, fasts and figures.[48]

Many works travel under the banner of the Notory Art. The most common in England appears to be the text of Oxford, Bodley 951, a fifteenth-century large folio manuscript (12$\frac{1}{8}$ in by 17$\frac{1}{8}$ in) running to twenty-one folios. It is possible that it was owned by a fifteenth-century monk, Simon Maidestone, of the Abbey of St Augustine at Canterbury, also the owner of several other books in that library none of which betray any interest in magic. One contains Maidestone's copy of a gloss on Paul's Epistle, a *Summa* also from his own pen and a *repertorium biblie*.[49] The text of Bodley 951 involves the use of prayers and 'notes' (*notae*) for acquiring intellectual skills such as the complete knowledge of the arts and sciences, eloquence, memory and so forth. Some of the prayers are supposed to be recited regularly at certain times of the day. All are supposed to be performed under certain phases of the moon and in conjunction with the use of the notes. The notes are similar to necromantic figures of the kind used in conjuring, but unlike necromantic figures, these 'notes' usually take the form of a formalized presentation of a given prayer.[50] In one instance a prayer is written in a thin line of text which spirals out from the centre of a circle to its circumference, which is over twelve inches in diameter.[51] In other cases the prayers are written in complex connected globes resembling cabalist trees. In Bodley 951, half of the surviving pages are taken up with a glossed text and half with fabulously complex images illustrated in colour. The gloss appears to be a legitimate commentary on the text, and there are several similar manuscript versions in England and on the Continent (although they are not always presented in the same formal two-column fashion with a framing two-column gloss).[52] The images in the second half follow the instructions in the text. The prayers themselves consist of angel names and names of God recorded in several languages many of which, according to the text, cannot be translated without losing their efficacy. This text is singular in its size and the complexity of its presentation, but another lengthy version of the Ars Notoria, Sloane 1712, is similarly accompanied by complex colour images.[53] Bodley 951 is now a solitary traveller and, given its size, probably always has been. Sloane 1712 contains two works of the Notory Art, also now unaccompanied by other texts, although there is no indication that they have always been thus. What is clear from both of these manuscripts is that a great deal of time, effort and money was devoted to their production – a clear indication that they were taken very seriously. Certainly no manuscript of a magical text I have ever examined, other than an Ars Notoria, takes as much care with its production as Bodley 951.[54]

There is also a host of other texts with a similar magical agenda and similar procedures which are sometimes referred to as Artes Notorie and sometimes by other titles like *Nova ars*, or *De arte crucifixi* and later, *Ars memorativa*. Many, like Sloane 3008, and the version found in Sloane 513 (the collection of the monk Richard Dove),[55] are quite short, running to only a folio in length. In general terms, these, like the longer versions of the notory art, have to do with the acquisition of knowledge or intellectual skills such as memory, or obtaining visions. In my sample these shorter versions tend to travel in company similar to that of images: works of astrology, alchemy, natural philosophy, mathematics, and in the case of the collection of Richard Dove, monk at Buckfast, physiognomy and chiromancy. Yet there is comparatively little astrological content in any of the versions I have looked at and so the connection with ideas about natural magic is more tenuous than in the case of works of image magic. Certainly Albertus Magnus' criterion that the images used must be of an astrological variety would not be easily applicable in this case. Given that al-Kindi's theories were developed principally to justify the effectiveness of magical incantations they might be applicable here. Yet the verbal formulas are meant to be prayers, and so, unlike al-Kindi's magical words, are not meant to achieve an automatic response. While it is not impossible that these texts were conceived of in similar terms to texts of image magic, this seems unlikely. A more credible interpretation of the evidence would be that these versions of the Ars Notoria interested a group of people similar to those who were attracted to image magic. It is also possible in the case of the shorter versions that the small size allowed the text to be included as a novelty.

At least two versions of this text[56] also appear in the Library of St Augustine's at Canterbury in the collection of John of London and Michael Northgate. As I have noted, Simon Maidestone, owner of Bodley 951, may also be the monk of the same name at Canterbury in the fifteenth century, although this volume of magic does not appear in the catalogue. It would seem that the community of monks interested in magic at St Augustine's identified by David Pingree is somewhat larger than he has suggested, and also that their interests included the Ars Notoria as well as Arabic image magic. Michael Northgate, discussed above, was the owner of Oxford, Corpus Christi 221, which includes a work on image magic and Gregory the Great's *Dialogues*. For the most part his collection reflects the usual accompanying interest in scientific and medical topics, yet his collection of books may reveal another facet of his interests. The catalogue of the Library of St Augustine's also includes among his volumes a codex containing orations extracted from an Ars Notoria. This codex includes a variety of devotional and religious works in addition to several compilations of prayers apparently of a more orthodox provenance. Northgate did not extract these himself as the catalogue ascribes this to Bartholomeus de Ripa Romeo, but the evidence suggests that he may well have been interested in such literature, and so would have had motivations to collect or copy the text himself. The context indicates that Northgate's interest in these texts existed in the presence of considerable devotional zeal, and it would appear that Northgate regarded his active interest in the Notory Art as defensibly orthodox.

This appears to be the case with other occurrences of the Ars Notoria as well. In some cases, like Sloane 3008, the orations were directed to the Virgin.[57] This is a common feature of the Notory Art which sets it apart from works on conjuring, where the figures addressed are generally not exclusively God, angels, saints, or the blessed Virgin. In addition, whereas prayers (which are supplicatory by definition) are used in the Notory Art and necromancy,[58] necromancy principally employs conjurations and incantations to command and constrain the beings it employs. It is interesting to note that prayers to the Virgin and miracles of the Virgin accompany the Ars Notoria in medieval catalogues.[59] Among the existing manuscripts, other revelatory texts of the same genre are also frequently companions to works of the Ars Notoria.[60]

One of the instances of this text which includes a *tractatus de miraculis beate virginis* appears among the books of John of London, a monk of St Augustine's, Canterbury, sometime in the late thirteenth or early fourteenth century.[61] This entry also includes a work on sermons, a work on the cure of leprosy, a Chiromancy, a work entitled *quedam extrauagancia de papis* and Solomon on rings.[62] The Solomonic treatise is a work of images regarded by Albertus Magnus as belonging to the better of the two detestable varieties of image magic, and directly follows the Ars Notoria.[63] This bizarre combination of texts may be taken as indicative of the many contexts in which this text may be found.

To summarize, texts of the Ars Notoria involve complex rites, purifications, confession, drawn figures, and orations or invocations. They purportedly seek results from the benign entities in the Christian pantheon (angels, saints, Christ, Mary, etc.), and astrology plays only a minor role in the ritual practice. Operators of the Ars Notoria generally seek to gain knowledge or skills such as rhetoric and knowledge of languages, and also often seek visions. In comparison to the standard texts on images, the Notory Arts have a decidedly more religious orientation, so that it was possible to extract prayers from that context without fear that they would appear particularly unorthodox. Although an operator might assume the results of the prayers to be automatic, the verbal formulas do not involve the binding of spirits. Finally, there is great concern with ritual procedures such as fasts, confession, observing special times and extensive formulaic prayers. Clearly we are dealing with texts of ritual magic.

How the scribes may have regarded them is somewhat less clear. As the longer versions now tend to be solitary travellers we have no context in which to evaluate them except to say that in this respect they are similar to many other works of ritual magic (like the *Liber sacer*). This may have to do with the fact that such books were consecrated (consecration of the book sometimes required in instructions given to the operator in such texts) and so would be more likely to have been written and preserved as discrete volumes. However, the treatment of these texts in manuscripts does not always conform to the treatment of other works of ritual magic. I have found no examples of necromantic magic where anywhere near the same amount of care was taken with the *mise-en-page*. Among works of ritual magic, the relatively deluxe copies of the Ars Notoria (Bodley 951 and Sloane 1712) are quite singular examples. Finally, these texts rarely travel with works of necromancy.[64] The more frequent companions for the Ars Notoria are the works associated with image magic – natural philosophy, books of secrets, alchemy, divination, and so forth (despite the fact that in terms of operating procedure the Ars Notoria has less in common with them than with less salubrious works of ritual magic). A sizeable portion of Ars Notoria texts also travel with devotional materials, prayers, or saints' lives.

The many contexts in which this text appears may be accounted for by the fact that it appeared less dangerous than necromancy, and thus may have been more frequently copied. Some of the scribes appear to have regarded it as a more or less legitimate and devout work and this would certainly have been an encouragement. The fact that at least five of the owners were monks suggests, at least, a religious environment for the scribes. This may in part account for the instances in which they are found in the company of devotional material such as prayers or saints' lives; but the more explicit religiosity of the texts, the foundation of the idea in the Bible itself, and their focus on revelation would also make this association understandable. The possibility that Michael Northgate regarded his interest in magic and natural wonders as part of a larger project like that of Thomas of Cantimpré may further link the religious and scientific interests. However, it appears likely that an interest in prayer was part of Northgate's motivation for acquiring extracts from an Ars Notoria.

In sum, the Notory Art appears to have been of interest to collectors of image magic and those interested in the natural world, despite the fact that it does not have a great deal in common with the other texts they collected. It was also of interest to collectors of divinatory material, which makes sense as the text could be considered divinatory. Finally, the more explicitly religious or Christian nature of the text corresponds with the religious calling of most of the known scribes or collectors and the devotional works with which it sometimes travels. This feature may well have made the text more palatable to those who would otherwise have limited their interest in magic to material safely within the orbit of natural philosophy.

THE LIBER SACER OR SWORN BOOK OF HONORIUS

Among the most significant magical works in our period is the *Liber sacer*. Two fourteenth-century copies survive[65] and two versions of the work appear among the superstitious works of Thomas Erghome discussed above. The *Liber sacer* stands on a middle ground between the Ars Notoria and works of necromancy for a number of reasons. In the surviving manuscripts it travels alone or in like company,[66] and never travels with works which would indicate a general interest in the natural world. The two volumes of superstitious works collected by Erghome put the *Liber sacer* together with a wide array of magical works including images and also with al-Kindi. As Robert Mathiesen and Richard Kieckhefer discuss the contents of this remarkable book in the present volume I will not analyse them in any great detail. My concern is to demonstrate that this work promotes magic of a highly ritualized character which is very religious albeit unorthodox.

The heart of the book involves an extended set of rituals to achieve the beatific vision. These rituals have more in common with the Ars Notoria than they do with texts of necromancy, although they are more high flown in their goals and have a less firm foothold in scripture. The text involves the same type of extensive orations, some directed to the Virgin and involving the usual kinds of borrowings from liturgical sources.[67] One of the sections of this part can be used for invoking the lower levels of angels which, like demons, can be bound; but there is no trace of the standard necromantic formulas of summoning, binding, and so forth. The introduction discusses the powers of different peoples to work in magic. Jews and pagans cannot conduct successful operations in magic because they are not Christian. Although Jews can bind some spirits 'by the power of the holy names of god spirrites but Jwes (*sic*) because they are nott signed with the sign of god, that is to saye with the signe of the crosse therefore they spirites will nott answere them trewly . . .'[68]

The table of contents of the *Sworn Book* lists ninety-two chapters and includes, in addition to the portion of the book devoted to obtaining the beatific vision, necromantic operations of summoning and binding spirits in addition to magic of a nasty variety (to cause death, destruction, etc.). So although no explicitly necromantic material appears in that portion of the book devoted to obtaining the beatific vision, the author may have regarded necromantic operations as legitimate if not desirable.

Although, as is the case with necromantic works, there is no indication of an interest in *naturalia* or theory in the *Sworn Book*, the text does present itself as a kind of overarching magical approach to the world. In this sense the closest sixteenth-century analogue is Cornelius Agrippa's *De occulta philosophia*. Like the *Picatrix* or Agrippa's *De occulta philosophia*, the *Sworn Book* blends the baser forms of magic with the high-flown goals of contact with the divine. The significance of this text thus lies not only in its somewhat subversive relation to orthodox Christian practice, but also in that it attributes a spiritual value to magical practice in general, and includes necromancy in this category.

NECROMANCY

My last group is made up of those texts more commonly thought of under the heading of ritual magic. The *Liber sacer* or *Sworn Book of Honorius* is the most significant single text to contain necromantic experiments; the *Liber de angelis* is another interesting but discrete text edited by Juris Lidaka in this volume. In some cases, an isolated anonymous necromantic experiment occurs among other non-magical material. For the most part, however, and unlike texts of image magic, this necromantic literature appears in more informal notebooks where the constituent texts are frequently not identifiable by bibliographic means.[69] Like recipe literature, these collections have a fluid, largely anonymous content, the lineage of which would be very difficult to trace. An adequate study of this literature cannot therefore be accomplished from a reading of the texts identifiable by standard bibliographic tags (title, author, incipit, etc.), much less from those texts which ultimately found their way into print.

Whereas works of the Notory Art tend to travel alone or with other works of the Notory Art in larger versions, and frequently appear in short versions in astrological and alchemical texts, works involving conjuring usually travel alone or in like company. A possible explanation for the solitary travellers may be that they were consecrated as part of the process of creating an effective magical book and were thus required to be discrete volumes. The resulting lack of context makes them more difficult to evaluate as codices, but it appears relatively rare for works of necromancy to be collected with other non-magical material. An exception to this rule is the short anonymous necromantic experiment which a fifteenth-century hand has added on the last page of a codex including a geomancy and Chaucer's *Conclusions of the Astrolabe*.[70] A necromantic experiment for seeing spirits in the nails of a boy also appears in the *Commonplace Book of Robert Rynes of Acle* in the company of charms.[71] In both cases, these are isolated examples, not accompanied by other similar magical texts, and so may have been mere curiosities.

For our present examination the necromantic collection is more fruitful for analysis than the single text codex. In Rawlinson D. 252, a fifteenth-century necromancer's collection, a single informal hand has copied a wide variety of short texts in a notebook clearly for personal use. The hand is a rough cursive and the notebook uses only rudimentary textual aids, making it unclear where one text ends and the next begins. Whereas the other texts we have dealt with have consistently identified the author or source of the text, the Rawlinson scribe seems little concerned to do so – from which we might infer that he is more interested in the content of a given piece than its author. There is frequently no obvious coherence to the order in which the texts have been assembled. For example, at one point, with no explanation, the complete text of the first chapter of the Gospel of John appears, with no indications about where or how this may have been used in magical operations.[72] The scribe had no need to give such instructions as the text was intended for personal use and no other reader was assumed.

The bulk of the codex is devoted to conjuring, complete with crude illustrations of pentagrams and other magical figures, lengthy prayers, incantations, and successive operations for summoning, binding and dismissing demons. These procedures involve elaborate ritual performances (such as fasting, preparation of materials or tools, wearing of special clothes, suffumigations, consecrations, exorcisms, conjurations and prayers), and are devoted to the standard goals of finding treasure or stolen goods, detecting a thief, getting spirits to do your bidding, discovering secret information or creating illusions. No

version of the Ars Notoria appears here, although some titles seem to echo
standard titles for Ars Notoria-type texts and may involve similar magical goals.
At one point an 'ars episcopalis' appears, but this is an undoubtedly ironic title
for a work on treasure hunting. The ring of *mercury ad habendam omnem scienciam*
suggests the project of the Ars Notoria, but the ring can also render *victoriam in
omni placito cuiuscunque domii*.[73] A prayer for a vision (162r) turns out to be in aid of
treasure hunting, and a prayer for knowledge in general appears to be a simple
supplicatory prayer and not an Ars Notoria as such (f. 78). A passage describing a
procedure to induce an old bearded man to appear and answer unspecified
questions is the closest this collection gets to the aims of the Ars Notoria
(f. 99r–100r). Given the scribe's overwhelming concern with treasure hunting,
one suspects the questions might have to do with pecuniary rather than
intellectual or spiritual rewards.

Entirely absent are the standard works of images discussed above. One might
reasonably expect texts on images to appear here, especially as they were
generally short and circulated in relatively large numbers. This codex runs to 160
folios and most of the constituent texts are between one and ten folios in length;
many only run to half a page. Raw probability might predict some overlap of
subject matter to occur, in the way that it did in the other codices in our survey.
Moreover, while it is understandable that a scribe might not include a text of
conjuring in an astrological codex, since it would be prudent to hide your
conjuring text, there is no reason not to include a standard text on astrological
images in your collection of conjuring texts if you were interested in such things.
But among the texts in this survey, conjuring or necromantic works are not found
bound together with any other kind of magic (except in the case of Erghome's
collection of 'superstitious' works which, as we have demonstrated, further
confirms the division of ritual magic from image magic). While short sections on
rings or images occur in Rawlinson D. 252, only one does not involve conjuring
and this passage is both heavily abbreviated and uses rather unsophisticated
astrology (f. 80). Interestingly, a similar format and some overlapping passages
suggest that one of the texts involving images in the Rawlinson Collection may be
related to a text which appears in the necromancer's manual edited by Richard
Kieckhefer. It would appear that this codex represents not only a different set of
interests from collections of image magic but perhaps a different set of
manuscript or oral sources specific to ritual magic collections.

The scribe's apparent lack of interest in theory suggests the same. Some
portions of the Rawlinson notebook seek to provide general information which,
in theory, applies to all cases. For example, the scribe provides general
information about astrological conditions, the association of certain planets with
certain days, suffumigations for each day, and days which are not good for
magical operations.[74] Similarly we have 'orationes dicenda[e] in omni opera'.[75]
While the text does not assume a general readership (as is the case with the

necromantic manual edited by Richard Kieckhefer, where the author assumes the presence of a reader other than himself) it does attempt to be systematic. But this does not amount to an abstract, philosophical analysis of the processes which underlie the magical operations such as those that were available to, or provided by, the scribes of image magic. The interest would appear not to be theoretical except insofar as it insists upon the existence of identifiable astrological influences and maintains that the correct astrological conditions must be observed for effective necromantic operation.

Where there seems to be overlapping of subject matter with image magic, this is only in respect to similarity of practice. Some written charms appear, 'goode to bere upon a bedy for many causis . . .' (f. 94r). Where general discussions of astrology occur the astrology is crude and usually in aid of necromantic operations. At one point (f. 62v) a short table identifies the usual shorthand symbols for the planets, but this is the closest this volume gets to the kinds of materials found in books of secrets or works of astrology, astronomy, or natural philosophy. Thus, while there are some magical practices or topics of interest which are roughly identical in both, this necromantic collection has no texts in common with any of the codices showing an interest in images, the Notory Art and the natural world in general.

The common feature of all the elements of this codex is not an interest in the connections between magic, occult properties and astrology, nor yet a particular kind of technique, but rather an overwhelming concern with ritual practices and particular kinds of practical applications. As far as practical application is concerned, there is very little in this collection which does not directly correspond with what we know about professional necromancers in England in the late Middle Ages. The standard professional services included treasure hunting, return of stolen goods, detection of a thief and inflicting damage on someone by occult means. A large number of the texts are also devoted to achieving oracles with the aid of a young boy. The prediction of the future was also a standard service of a magical practitioner and we have many recorded cases of the use of boys for such things.

But it is the ritual itself that seems in some ways the chief attraction of this kind of magic. In particular, the scribes and authors of this material evidently consider contemporary orthodox rituals and more or less credible elaborations upon them as particularly powerful or desirable in magical operations. A formula for confession appears on f. 49, although in this case a concluding section has been added explicitly designed for the protection of a necromancer. A ritual for those with 'dolorem in oculis' would seem out of place in this volume except that it involves the use of a Psalm (perhaps a kind of analogue for a secret of nature in a volume interested in image magic).[76] Various psalms also occur throughout the codex. The chapter of John which the scribe of the Rawlinson manuscript has included was recited at the end of every mass in late medieval England.[77] This and its use in exorcism, not its philosophical tone, provide the context from which it derived its significance and its power for the operator. Since this passage is not contained within one of the constituent treatises on conjuring, but stands on its own, the practitioner has evidently incorporated contemporary religious practices into his magical operations for personal reasons – a kind of borrowing which reveals an active and creative religiosity.

By comparison, texts on images tend to be relatively transparent witnesses to their Arabic or Hebraic sources. Only one similar example occurs in the texts of image magic, where Thomas of Cantimpré records a blessing for a stone. Here, however, we have the repetition of a prior author's suggestion, not the active creation of a new ritual practice. In addition, Thomas did not mean the work to be practical, but rather sought to draw the reader to devotion by the awe it might inspire as a *story* or *report*. What dominates the image magic text is not the ritual procedure, but the occult power in the stone or image. In image magic texts and the codices which contain them, the occult power in the stones or image and the associated frame of interpretation are the centre of focus rather than the ritual procedures. While they might have had religious goals or have inspired religious devotion, they are not the records of personal, albeit unorthodox, religious exercises. To put it another way, where manuscripts of image magic tend to represent the impulse to preserve and analyse, the Rawlinson Collection represents active synthesis and elaboration.

CONCLUSION

Texts of magic exist on a continuum from those in which the ritual features are merely implicit to those which are largely taken up with descriptions of prayers, incantations, suffumigations, ritual gestures, consecrations and so forth. There is no easy way to draw lines between the different kinds of magic texts, or to categorize them one way or another. The categories of magic suggested by the *treatment of these texts by their collectors* is somewhat different. The collections, for the most part, fall into two categories: those witnessing an interest in image magic in conjunction with natural philosophy, astrology, alchemy and magical theory, and those interested in a more explicitly religious, ritual magic, often involving the binding of spirits, which actively incorporated contemporary orthodox religious practice and was, as a result, often more explicitly unorthodox. I do not mean to say that texts concerned with images were somehow secular in comparison. The collections of Michael Northgate and others suggest that a sizeable number of these codices containing works on image magic were brought together in the presence and pursuit of a more or less orthodox faith. It also goes without saying that natural philosophy itself was framed within a Christian perspective and that much of it was motivated by or directed to devotional ends. But affective devotional practices are generally absent from the collections in which texts of image magic occur, while they are actively present in texts and collections of more explicit ritual magic.

While this rule is generally applicable, a few ambiguities remain. We have collectors who owned both kinds of texts. Yet there is no reason why a single person could not maintain an interest in both the theoretical and scientific image magic at the same time as having an interest in the more explicit religiosity or elaborate Christian ritual of necromancy and the Ars Notoria. This may have been the case with Michael Northgate, who collected image magic together with other naturalia in one setting and, in another, orations extracted from an Ars Notoria in a collection of prayers and other devotional material. Most of the shorter versions of the Ars Notoria and some of the longer ones travel in company roughly identical with that of image magic, despite the similarity of the Ars Notoria to necromancy in its preoccupation with ritual. Perhaps as a result of its less threatening goals, the Ars Notoria forms a sort of middle ground. The codicological features of the larger versions are more often like those of necromantic magic, although the Ars Notoria does not tend to travel with necromancy. As already noted, a few necromantic experiments do occur in contexts other than that of necromantic collections; however, we cannot assume that these examples were anything more than curiosities for their readers since they are not generally accompanied by other works of magic which would indicate a more general interest in the subject.

It remains that the common feature of most collections which include the standard Arabic image magic texts is an interest in the natural world and in current issues in natural philosophy. Although some collections including a work of the Notory Art show an interest in natural philosophy, collections of necromantic texts do not. What is particularly interesting about this division between the Christian and devotional impulses of ritual magic and the more theoretical and 'scientific' impulses of image magic is that it dissolved in the hands of the renaissance occultists, who combined the syncretic, explicitly religious flavour and goals of the ritual magic collections with the more theoretical or philosophical orientation of image magic collections. As we move into the sixteenth century, the collections of magical works themselves also betray more synthetic (or perhaps less discerning) impulses.

Notes

1 This paper was in large measure made possible by a Doctoral Fellowship from the Social Sciences and Humanities Research Council of Canada.

2 For the purposes of this paper I limit my discussion to the more radical and illicit forms of magical practice which include transitive and visionary magic. The resulting group of texts are both unambiguously identifiable as magic by most medieval standards and seek to have some concrete effect either on the operator or some other person or thing. I exclude divinatory material recognizing that the dividing lines between magic and divination are frequently indistinct.

3 I use the term 'palaeography' in its very broadest sense, to refer to an integrated approach to all aspects of a manuscript, not merely a study of scripts. See Leonard E. Boyle, *Medieval Latin Palaeography: A Bibliographical Introduction* (Toronto: University of Toronto Press, 1984).

4 This paper draws upon a survey of manuscripts of magical works of British origin or provenance dating from the late thirteenth through the fifteenth century. The paper draws heavily upon collections of material by a single scribe or clearly compiled within the period. Because there is a margin of doubt about how the magical texts were construed, I depend almost exclusively upon texts devoted explicitly and entirely to magical practices. In addition, I do not rely heavily on any codex in which there is not a demonstrable interest in magic (i.e., less than two distinct works on the subject).

My data on manuscript catalogues is based upon a survey of published sources only. Among the richer sources for magical texts are the following. K.W. Humphreys, ed., *The Friars' Libraries* (London: British Library, 1990); M.R. James, *The Ancient Libraries of Canterbury and Dover* (Cambridge: Cambridge University Press, 1903); Mary Bateson, ed., *Catalogue of the Library of Syon Monastery* (Cambridge: Cambridge University Press, 1898); David N. Bell, *The Libraries of the Cistercians, Gilbertines and Premonstratensians* (London: The British Library, 1992); F. M. Powicke, *The Medieval Books of Merton College* (Oxford: Clarendon Press, 1931). I employ shelfmarks from these works.

My current list includes sixty-four codices dating from 1250 to 1600; of these well over half betray explicit magical interests. Among those dating from before 1500, twenty-eight contain magical images, eleven contain works of the Ars Notoria, and eleven other kinds of ritual and necromantic magic.

5 Lynn Thorndike, *History of Magic and Experimental Science* (New York: Columbia University Press, 1923–58), vol. II, p. 835. Hereafter, *HMES*.

6 In this discussion I will not attempt to treat all manuscript occurrences of talismans or seals, but rather confine myself to works which deal explicitly – and preferably exclusively – with images. These may be engraved upon metal disks, or rings, or stones, or stones set in rings. Among the texts are Thebith ben Corath's *De imaginibus*, the *Liber de imaginibus* by Thetel, the *Liber lune* and the Hermetic fifteen stars, fifteen stones, fifteen herbs and fifteen images tract. Not included in this discussion are images moulded from wax, which are a common feature of reports of necromantic operation and occasionally appear in necromantic texts. For a modern edition of the *De imaginibus*, see Francis J. Carmody, *Astronomical Works of Thabit B. Qurra* (Berkeley and Los Angeles: University of California Press, 1960), pp. 167–97. See also Thorndike, *HMES* I, pp. 663–6. For Thetel, see 'Cethel aut veterum Judaeorum Physiologorum de Lapidibus Sententiae' in Jean Baptiste Pitra, ed., *Spicilegium Solesmense* III (Paris: Instituti Franciae, 1852), pp. 335–7. For the Hermetic fifteen star tract, see 'Liber hermetis de quindecim stellis quindecim lapidibus quindecim herbis et quindecim imaginibus' in *Textes latins et vieux Français relatifs aux Cyranides*, ed. Louis Delatte, Bibliothèque de la faculté de philosophie et lettres de l'université de Liège (Liège: Université de Liège, 1942). On engraved gems see Lynn Thorndike, 'Traditional Tracts on Engraved Gems,' *HMES I*, p. 235. For discussions of Arabic image magic see David Pingree, 'The diffusion of Arabic Magical Texts in Western Europe' in *La diffusione delle scienze Islamiche nel medio evo Europeo* (Roma: Accademia Nazionale dei Lincei, 1987), pp. 57–102; and Charles Burnett, 'Adelard, Egraphalau and the Science of the Stars' in *Adelard of Bath: An English Scientist and Arabist of the Early Twelfth Century*, ed. C. Burnett, Warburg Institute Surveys and Texts 14 (London: Warburg Institute, 1987), pp. 133–45; and 'Arabic, Greek and Latin

Works on Astrological Magic Attributed to Aristotle' in *Pseudo-Aristotle in the Middle Ages*, eds. J. Kraye, W.F. Ryan and C.B. Schmitt, Warburg Institute Surveys and Texts 11 (London: Warburg Institute, 1987), pp. 84–96. These articles are reprinted in Charles Burnett, *Magic and Divination in the Middle Ages* (Aldershott: Variorum, 1996). See also, Francis Carmody, *Arabic Astronomical and Astrological Sciences in Latin Translation* (Berkley and Los Angeles: University of California Press, 1956).

7 See, for example, Oxford, Bodley 463, a Spanish manuscript which contains multiple works on astrology in addition to two works on magical images.

8 The examples of Albertus Magnus' *Speculum astronomiae* and Thomas Aquinas' *De occultis operibus naturae ad quemdam militem ultramontanum* should suffice to demonstrate that the debate over the functioning of magical images was taken seriously and had serious philosophical merit in the Scholastic world view. For the *Speculum*, see Paola Zambelli, *The Speculum Astronomiae and its Enigma; Astrology, Theology, and Science in Albertus Magnus and his Contemporaries* (London: Kluwer Academic Publishers, 1992). For the letter of Aquinas, see Joseph Bernard McAllister, *The Letter of Saint Thomas Aquinas De Occultis Operibus Naturae Ad Quemdam Militem Ultramontanum* (Washington: Catholic University of America Press, 1939). See also Charles Burnett, 'Talismans: magic as science? Necromancy among the Seven Liberal Arts' in *Magic and Divination*.

9 al-Kindi, *De Radiis*, eds. M.T. d'Alverny and F. Hudry in *Archives d'Histoire Doctrinale et Littéraire du Moyen Age* 41 (1974), pp. 139–260.

10 Paola Zambelli gives a thorough discussion of the *Speculum Astronomiae* and its intellectual context. She defends Thorndike's position and demonstrates with extensive scholarship that this text is unquestionably the work of Albertus Magnus. For a discussion of the historiography see Zambelli, pp. 1–42. For Thorndike's discussion of the subject see *HMES* II, pp. 692–717.

11 Charles Burnett, 'Talismans: Magic as Science? Necromancy among the Seven Liberal Arts' in *Magic and Divination*, pp. 1–15.

12 Burnett, 'Talismans'.

13 See, for example, London, Institution of Electrical Engineers, Thompson Collection S.C. MSS 3/5, a fifteenth-century Italian manuscript.

14 C.A.J. Armstrong, 'An Italian Astrologer at the Court of Henry VII' in E.F. Jacob, ed., *Italian Renaissance Studies, A Tribute to the Late Celia M. Ady* (London: Faber and Faber, 1960); D.E. Rhodes, 'The Princes in the Tower and their Doctor', *English Historical Review* (1962) 77, 304–6; D.E. Rhodes, 'Provost Argentine of Kings and his Books' in *Transactions of the Cambridge Bibliographical Society* (London: Bowes and Bowes, 1958), vol. II, pt III, 205–11 (Rhodes makes no mention of Society of Antiquaries 39, the manuscript examined here). See also *DNB* (1921) VI, 552; A.B. Emden, *A Biographical Register of the University of Cambridge to 1500* (Cambridge: Cambridge University Press, 1963.), pp. 15–16; and Charles H. Talbot and E.A. Hammond, *The Medical Practitioners in Medieval England: A Biographical Register* (London: Wellcome Historical Medical Library, 1965), pp. 112–15.

15 Pingree, 'Diffusion of Arab Magical Texts', p. 98.

16 Emden, *Biographical Register*, p. 509; John Venn and J.A. Venn, *Alumni Cantabrigiensis* (Cambridge: Cambridge University Press, 1927), I. iv. 27.

17 I have yet to complete a thorough analysis of his works and the other books he owned.

18 Thorndike, *HMES II*, pp. 390–2. See also John B. Friedman, 'The Prioress's Beads "of Smal Coral"', *Medium Aevum* 39 (1970), 301–5.

19 Thorndike, *HMES II*, p. 389.

20 Thomas Cantimpratensis, *Liber de natura rerum* (Berlin and New York: Walter de Gruyter, 1973), p. 5 (91–6).

21 Thorndike wrongly identifies this as the work of Thomas of Cantimpré in *HMES II*, 397. He corrects this error in Lynn Thorndike and Pearl Kibre, *A Catalogue of Incipits of Mediaeval Scientific Writings in Latin* (Cambridge, Massachusetts: Medieval Academy of America, 1963).

22 Pingree, 'Diffusion of Arabic Magic', pp. 95–8.

23 Dan Michel of Northgate, *Dan Michel's Ayenbit of Inwyt or Remorse of Conscience*, ed. P. Gradon (London: Early English Text Society, 1866). Also in a partial modern English translation by A.J. Wyatt, *The Ayenbite of Inwyt or Remorse of Conscience* (London: University Correspondence Press, 1889).

24 I am indebted to Mildred Budney for her expertise on this point.

25 Ashmole 1416; Selden Supra 76; Corpus Christi 125.

26 Dorothea Waley Singer, *Catalogue of Latin and Vernacular Alchemical Manuscripts in Great Britain and Ireland* (Brussels: M. Lamertin, 1928–31).

27 Ashmole 1471; CUL Ff.vi.53; Wellcome 116; and Sloane 1784. For a Continental example see Bodleian, Cannon. Misc. 285.

28 See for example Ashmole 346, f. 164.

29 Ashmole 1471, f. 143.

30 See Digby 194 and Society of Antiquaries 39.

31 London, Society of Antiquaries 39, ff. 21–3.

32 Canterbury, St Augustine's Abbey, 1161, 1170 (=CCC 221), 1275 (=CCC 125), and 1277; Tichfield, Premonstratensian Abbey of St Mary and St John the Evangelist P6, K.III; Isleworth, Syon Monastery B 24; York, Austin Friars A8 375 and A8 383.

33 Humphreys, *The Friars' Libraries*, pp. xxix–xxx. I cite codex numbers from Humphreys.

34 York, Austin Friars A8, 362, 364, 371, 375, 383, 385 and 452.

35 I list the full contents from the catalogue, Humphreys, ed. The bibliographic references derive from Humphreys as well.

York, Austin Friars A8, 362

a. Liber sompniarii Ybin Cyrin' in 8 partibus et pars in cifra (Humphreys identifies this as Achmet (Ahmed) ibn Sirin, *Oneirocriicon*, prob. tr. Leo Tuscus as in Oxford, Bodl. Digby 103; Thorndike *HMES II*, 291–3). b. liber qui intitulatur de iudiciis astrorum (Humphreys suggests this may be al-Kindi). c. 9 ymagines extracte de libro veneris (Humphreys suggests this is *De lapidibus Veneris* of Toz Graecus; see D. Pingree, 'The Diffusion of Arabic Magical Texts', 57–102). d. brevis tractatus quatuor capitulis de sompno et visione (Humphreys identifies as al-Kindi, tr. Gerard of Cremona). e. tractatus de operibus et occultis actionibus naturalium (Humphreys suggests Thomas Aquinas: Thorndike/Kibre, 1280). f. liber Hermetis de celo et mundo distinctus in 6 partes. g. theorica artis magice in 56 capitulis (Humphreys notes that this is a title given to al-Kindi's *De radiis stellarum*). h. flores coniunctionis veritatis geomancie distinctus in theoricam et practicam. i. introductorium ad geomanciam docens terminos artis. k. tractatus de penthagono Salomonis (Thorndike *HMES II*, p. 279ff). l. tractatus ad inclusionem spiritus in speculo. m. opus capitis magni cum aliis capitibus pertinencibus. n. tractatus ymaginum secundum mouimentum planetarum et operacionibus eorum (Humphreys suggests this is possibly *Liber Belemith de imaginibus septem planetarum*; Pingree, 78). o. tractatus ymaginum Gyrgit filie Circis de opere ymaginum distincus in theoricam et practicam. p. Hermes de ymaginibus. q. idem in alio tractatu de ymaginibus. r. tractatus Hyllonii de arte ymaginibus. s. tractatus de nominibus angelorum et effectibus eorum. t. vinculum Salomonis (see k). u. tractatus de valeriana. x. tractatus de spiritu cibile. y. tractatus de capite Saturni. z. liber Honorii diuisus in 5 tractatus (Humphreys suggests this is most likely Honorius Thebensis, *Liber sacratus*: Thorndike *HMES II*, 283–9). aa. tractatus ad habendam loquelam cum spiritu et effectum eternum. ab. aliud opus preciosum ad magnum effectum. ac. liber rubeus qui aliter dicitur sapiencia nigromancie ad experimentum bonum sortis. ae. tractatus Fortunati Eleazari de arte euthontica ydaica et epytologica (Humphreys identifies as Eleazar of Worms or Salomon *De quatuor annulis*; Thorndike/Kibre, *Incipits*, 366). af. tractatus de nominibus angelorum ordine forma et potestate et mansione. ag. tractatus de Floron (On the demon Floron, see *HMES II*, 965). ah. tractatus qui dicitur secretum philosophorum diuisum in 7 partes secundum quod pertractat 7 artes (*HMES II*, pp. 788–91 and pp. 811–12). ai. liber veneris in tres partes diuisus (Humphreys suggests this may be Toz Graecus). ak. liber ymaginum Aristotelis. al. tractatus Hermetis de ymaginibus. am. alius tractatus ymaginum. an. excepctiones horarum a Ptholomeo descripte. ao. fforme ymaginum in singulis signorum faciebus. ap. ffinis artis notorie veteris. aq. ars notoria noua completa. ar. multa experimenta.

York, Austin Friars A8, 364

a. Liber ymaginum lune (most likely *Liber Lune*). b. liber ymaginum veneris. c. liber radiorum (Humphreys suggests this is probably al-Kindi, *De radiis stellarum* which seems very likely). d. liber prestigiorum Alkani philosophi. e. liber sacratus Petri Abellardi (given the contents of this codex, this is most likely the *Sworn Book of Honorius*. Burnett suggests this is potentially an attribution to Adelard of Bath in 'The writings of Adelard of Bath and closely associated works together with the manuscripts in which they occur', in *Adelard of Bath*, p. 195).

36 York, Austin Friars A8, 159.

37 See, for example, Society of Antiquaries 39.

38 Richard Kieckhefer, *Forbidden Rites* (Stroud: Sutton Publishing, 1997), p. 10.

39 *Ritual Magic* (Cambridge: Cambridge University Press, 1949).

40 The catalogue occurrences are: York, Austin Friars A8, 364; York, Austin Friars A8, 362 (includes Ars Notoria and Nova Ars); York, Austin Friars A8, 371; Canterbury, St Augustine's Abbey, 767; and Canterbury, St Augustine's Abbey, 1603; Merton College, 999 (Powicke, 213). The surviving manuscripts are: London, British Library, Sloane 1712 (not of British origin – potentially of medieval British provenance), London, British Library, Sloane 513, f. 192, Oxford, Bodleian, and Oxford, Bodleian, Bodley 951. Thorndike lists Ashmole 1416, f. 123v–124r as a possible Ars Notoria but this seems unlikely. Two sixteenth-century copies are London, British Library, Harley 181 and Oxford, Bodleian, Ashmole 1515.

41 In the case of an indenture 'de libris pertinentibus studio custodis' made between Merton College and Warden Richard Fitzjames, one book is listed as *ars notaria*. The first word of the second folio is given as 'haybala' making it unlikely that this text is on the notarial art. F.M. Powicke, *The Medieval Books of Merton College* (Oxford: Clarendon Press, 1931), p. 213.

42 J.M. De Bujand, *Index de Venise 1549, Venise et Milan 1554*, Index des Livres Interdits, vol. III

(Sherbrooke: Centre d'Études de la Renaissance, 1987), pp. 412 and 434. See also, *HMES*, VI, p. 146.

43 A printed version of an Ars Notoria appears in the *Opera* of Cornelius Agrippa (Lyons: Beringos Fratres, 1620?). For an English translation see *Ars Notoria; The Notory Art of Solomon, Shewing the Cabalistical Key of Magical Operations*, translated by Robert Turner (London: Cottrel, 1657; repr. Seattle: Trident, 1987).

44 Michael Scot, *Introduction to Astrology*, Bodleian 266. f. 2 and 20 v; Aquinas, Summa, Secundae secunda, Quest. 96, Art. I; Peter of Abano, *Conciliator*, Diff. 156 and *Lucidiator*, BN 2598, f. 101r, 'ars dicta notaria fortunati' (Thorndike, *HMES*, II, 903–4); Giovanni da Fontana, S Marco VIII, 72 (Valentinelli, XI, 93), f. 26r. (Thorndike, *HMES*, IV, 171.); Nicole Oresme, *De divinationibus* (Thorndike, *HMES*, III, 420–1); On James the Carthusian, see Thorndike, *HMES*, IV, 287; On Dionysius the Carthusian, see Thorndike, *HMES*, IV, 291–3; Thomas Ebendorfer, Thorndike, *HMES*, IV, 295; Vincent, of Beauvais, *Speculum quadruplex; sive, Speculum maius* (Graz, Akademische Druck-u. Verlagsanstalt, 1964–5) [facsimile reprint of B. Belleri, 1624], III, sviii, 3, col. 1117. Trithemius makes the claim that 'he had written a book giving an occult method by which a person totally ignorant of Latin could learn in an hour's time to write anything he wished in that language'. Thorndike, *HMES*, VI, 439.

45 For discussion of the Ars Notoria and the *Liber visionum* of John of Morigny, see Fanger's essay in this volume.

46 Technically, Solomon asks for *sciencia et sapiencia* and is given *sapiencia et intelligencia*. The *Glossa Ordinaria* overlooks this and uses all three words to designate what God bestowed upon Solomon. The *Glossa Ordinaria* is silent about the issue of acquiring knowledge in this way. *Glossa Ordinaria* ad. II Philo.1–12 (Lyra ed.), 1139–40.

47 Caesarii Hesterbacensis Monachi, *Dialogus Miraculorum*, ed. Joseph Strange (Cologne: J.M. Heberle, 1851) 10.3, p. 217.

48 See for example Aquinas' condemnation of the art (*Summa Theologia*, Secunda secundae, Quaest. 96, Art. 1).

49 Canterbury, St Augustine's Abbey 209, 1616 and 1791.

50 See Michael Camille's essay in this volume for illustrations.

51 Oxford, Bodley 951, f. 9r.

52 Kues, Hospitals zu Cues, 216.

53 The origin of this codex is not likely English.

54 Only Royal 17. A. XLII, a version of the *Sworn Book of Honorius* comes close to these. Robert Mathiesen has suggested that this manuscript was probably written in the sixteenth century.

55 D.N. Bell, 'A Cistercian at Oxford: Richard Dove of Buckfast and London', *Studia Monastica* 31 (1989), 67–87.

56 Canterbury St Augustine's Abbey, 1603, which might be a duplicate copy or entry of Canterbury St Augustine's Abbey, 1538.

57 The relationship of this text to McMaster Manuscript of the *Liber visionum* (Hamilton, Canada, McMaster University Library, Unnumbered MS) bears investigation.

58 In Harley 181, a sixteenth-century codex containing two works of the Notory Art, a short section *contra demones* begins 'Coniuro te vilissimum demonem . . .' (ff. 21r–22r); but this is technically an exorcism to keep demons away during the operations which follow.

59 St Augustine's Abbey, 767, owned by Michael Northgate, includes prayers extracted from an Ars Notoria with other prayers, including prayers to the Virgin, St Appolonius, and the Holy Spirit. St Augustine's Abbey, 1603 might be a duplicate copy or entry of St Augustine's Abbey, 1538. The entries both contain miracles of the Virgin.

60 Sloane 1712 (s. xiii–xv) includes two versions under the name of *Nova ars*, although this is not likely an English manuscript. In a sixteenth-century codex several works of the Ars Notoria are collected together and include *De arte crucifixi* which explains how to get Christ to appear to the operator in a dream and reveal various things. London, British Library, Harley 181, ff. 75r–81v.

61 Canterbury, Abbey of St Augustine 1603. On the identity of this monk, probably known to Roger Bacon, see Montague Rhodes James, *The Ancient Libraries of Canterbury and Dover* (Cambridge: Cambridge University Press, 1903), p. lxxxvii.

62 M.R. James, *Ancient Libraries*, p. 386.

63 *Speculum astronomiae*, 11.23 (Zambelli, pp. 240–1). Thorndike, *HMES*, II, p. 699.

64 A work identified as necromancy appears together with a work on the notary art in an indenture to the library at Merton College in 1483. Given the first word of the second folio (*haybala*) this must be a work of the Notory Art. F.M. Powicke, *The Medieval Books of Merton College* (Oxford: Clarendon Press, 1931), pp. 213–15. The work appears in Erghome's compendium of superstitious works (York, Austin Friars A8, 362) but also appears in another of his volumes (York, Austin Friars A8, 371) with works on natural philosophy and experiments.

65 Sloane 313; Sloane 3854.

66 Sloane 313 and Royal 17.A.XLII are both solitary texts. Sloane 3854, ff. 112–39, may be an exception as it is currently bound with other necromantic works, one of which has been identified as Italian in origin. This version of the *Liber sacer* is written in a single hand, not repeated elsewhere in this collection which now includes seventeenth-century material. Chances are good that this is not a British manuscript and that it was collected relatively late.

67 Royal 17.A.XLII, ff. 29r–31v.

68 Royal 17.A.XLII, f. 8r.

69 The following are the fifteenth-century manuscripts I have examined: Cambridge, University Library, Dd. xi. 45, ff. 134–9; London, Society of Antiquaries 39, ff. 1–17; Oxford, Bodleian, Rawlinson D. 252 (excluding ff. 63–80); Oxford, Bodleian, Rawlinson D. 252, ff. 63–80; and London, British Library, Sloane 3849, ff. 17–19 (possibly sixteenth century). Some sixteenth-century examples are: London, British Library, Sloane 3849, ff. 7–16 and 20–7, and London, British Library, Sloane 3853.

70 Sloane 314.

71 Cameron Louis, ed., *The Commonplace Book of Robert Reynes of Acle; An Edition of Tanner MS 407* (London: Garland, 1980), p. 169. Quoted in Richard Kieckhefer, *Forbidden Rites*, p. 97.

72 f. 35v.

73 f. 80v.

74 ff. 29v–35v.

75 f. 37r.

76 f. 125.

77 Eamon Duffy, *The Stripping of the Altars: Traditional Religion in England* c. *1400*–c. *1580* (New Haven: Yale University Press, 1992), p. 124.

2

THE BOOK OF ANGELS, RINGS, CHARACTERS AND IMAGES OF THE PLANETS: ATTRIBUTED TO OSBERN BOKENHAM

Juris G. Lidaka

Almost forty years ago, in a quick survey of the works by Osbern Bokenham, a fifteenth-century translator, P. Nicholas Toner wrote, 'I have come across only one latin [*sic*] work of Bokenham, which however is not mentioned by any of his biographers, entitled "Liber de Angelis, annulis characteribus et Imaginibus planetarum". Bernard listed it in the famous library of John More, Bishop of Norwich; it is now in the library of the University of Cambridge with the shelf mark Dd XI 45.'[1] Shortly afterwards, M.B. Hackett commented that, 'after examining the manuscript I am of the opinion that this is not an original work of his; rather it was copied by a scribe named Bokenham who may or may not be identical with the Austin friar.'[2] But he did not explain, and the few commentators since then have either just passed along Toner's comment or ignored the work altogether. Most recently, Tony Edwards simply noted, 'I omit from the present discussion the problem of the authorship of the *Liber de Angelis* . . . there ascribed to one "Bokenham"'.[3] So in some work I was doing on Bokenham in general, I needed to decide whether this work – never published and otherwise undiscussed – was by him or not.

In short, Hackett was right: it is not written by Osbern Bokenham, nor is it likely to have been copied by him. That he did not compose it is clear from the text: it begins with an opening inscription *Ad mea principia tibi dico salue Maria, quod Bokenham* [At my beginning, I greet you, Maria, quod Bokenham], which is typical of copyists, but not of authors, and the first section of the work seems clearly ascribed to an otherwise unidentified Messayaac, apparently a transcription of the Hebrew for Messiah. Later, also, there is a reference to burying a brass image of Jupiter *cum oratione subhumacionis ymaginis Solis* [with the prayer of the burial of the image of the Sun] (paragraph [21]); however, since this prayer does not occur in the text, the reference and the omission imply that some portion of the text has not been copied. To these, we can add three passages that explicitly indicate someone as a *compilator* rather than an *auctor* because of departures from sources (paragraphs [11], [18] and [34]):

Omitto nomina angelorum cum carecteribus suis . . . propter certam causam hic scribenda
[For a particular reason, I omit the names of the angels with their characters]
Propter certam causam que me mouit, sigillum Solis & sigillum Lune omisi scribere hic
[For a particular reason that moves me, I left off the sigil of the Sun and the
sigil of the Moon here]
*Hic, autem, propter certam causam que me mouit, carecteres planetarum & signorum
scribere omisi, quod Bokenham* [Here, however, for a particular reason that moves
me, I omitted the characters of the planets and signs. Bokenham].

Exactly what was not copied is now unretrievable, but the general sense here is of
formulae, when taken with the rest of the text, indicating that materials extant in one or
more archetypes have been deliberately not copied here. We will return to the text later.

The manuscript is Cambridge Univ. Lib. MS Dd.xi.45, a herbal and medical
miscellany of the fifteenth century with some relationship to the Sloane Group,[4]
whose contents are summarized in Appendix A (basically the catalogue entry
with a few additions or corrections by me based on an investigation of a
microfilm, on some notes kindly supplied by Linda Ehrsam Voigts, and on a very
short visit at the CUL), with details on quiring and contents' distribution in
Appendix B. A much-discussed letter (between items #11 and #12) helps to place
and date the whole manuscript, though only by association: Angus McIntosh,
calling the letter 'an unsigned draft', notes that the author's staying at 'John Salus
house of Lyn' and his friendship with 'Syr William Cuke preste of Byllesbe'
reinforces the language, placed 'not far north of Lincoln, say in the general
neighbourhood of Market Rasen'.[5] Mary Hamel considers the letter as having
been written somewhere between 1441 (when Cook was still only chaplain in
another document) and 1445 (when Salus is last mentioned in the Lynn records).[6]

Inside this commonplace book, the *Liber de angelis* is #10 in the manuscript,
completely contained within quire 11 and surrounded by other works. In fact, the
environment is such that we must suppose the manuscript remained in the hands of
someone or ones medicinally inclined before and after the *Liber de angelis* was added
to it – works #9 and #11 seem to be written in the same large hand, yet they are
added physically before, after, and thus literally around both the *Liber de angelis* and
the letter. That is, much of quire 11 was blank, and at different times were added
the *Liber de angelis* beginning on f. 134v and the letter on f. 142. After these were in
place, a scribe with a large hand added the miscellaneous notes on the bottom of f.
133v running through 134r, and then jumped over to continue on ff. 140r–144v,
employing the space left around the letter on f. 142. Such medicinal materials, both
preceding and following the addition of the *Liber de angelis* to the manuscript,
indicate the dominant thrust of an early owner's interests, as well as John Moore's.[7]
The precise reason for including this text of ritual magic among the medical works
will no doubt forever elude us, but we may safely assume that it was due to a desire
to know how natural objects may effect certain results in the world.[8]

The scribe of the *Liber de angelis* may be named William Bokenham: the opening and closing scribal notes, of course, name some Bokenham, and the handwriting of the whole matches a *Willelmus* written in the top margin of f. 136r. A William Bokenham is the author of two works on urine in Wellcome MS 408, claimed to be a doctor with a degree from Bologna and a monk at Norwich Holy Trinity (or St Giles),[9] but the claim that he incepted at Oxford in 1479–80 is erroneous.[10] There was also a William Buckenham, DTh, fellow of Gonville Hall, Cambridge, 1488, and Vice-Chancellor of the university 1508–10,[11] but he seems unlikely to have been the scribe here.

The manuscript's contents are quite unrelated to Osbern Bokenham's known interests – he was an Augustinian friar at the convent of Stoke Clare, Suffolk, and probably a Cambridge doctor of divinity. His known works are two translations: the *Lives of Holy Women* and *A Little Map of England*, perhaps to accompany and explain the *Lives*, written for and even at the bequest of several highly ranked ladies. He also tells us he wrote in Latin a life of St Anne, though this has not been found. To him have also been ascribed a translation of *De consulatu Stiliconis*, Claudian's verse political advice; the *Dialogue between a Secular and a Friar*, an original work involving the foundation and history of the convent at Stoke Clare; and even the *Gilte Legende*, a translation of parts of Voragine's *Legenda aurea*, though this last has been rejected hotly by some. This little implies that he is unlikely to have possessed such a book as CUL Dd.xi.45, or that he would have written into it such a text. Rather, he would have objected to its non-Christian use of magic and particularly some of the uses to which the magic is put, such as increasing a wife's sexual desire, or using a kind of voodoo doll to disease or kill.

The *Liber de angelis* is not a single work, but one composed of extracts from at least three, for it falls clearly into at least that many explicit parts, with a digression of several *experimenta*[12] coming from no doubt a fourth work, this digression prompted by a relationship to Saturn via images. The first work, paragraphs [1]–[11], is evidently called the *Liber de angelis* [Book of Angels] and, after a brief introduction, swiftly discusses making rings for the planets in the order Sun, Moon, Mars, Mercury, Jupiter, Venus and Saturn – involving both inscribing the character and name of the angel of each planet on the ring and sacrificing some animal – and the use to which each is put.[13] It closes with a note on the metals to be used for each ring, in the same order but for adding the Head of Draco, whose use had earlier been covered under Saturn. There may be an Arabic background to this text, but more work needs to be done before any certainty or even probability can be claimed.[14]

The second work, paragraphs [12]–[16], is not visually distinguished in the manuscript as it is in the edition below, but the text does seem to call it the *Liber de ymaginibus planetarum* [The Book of the Images of the Planets]. This covers making images, apparently small statues, with inscriptions of names, adds the names of angels and devils related to the planets, sometimes explicitly to be written on the images, and follows generally with suffumigations and conjurations to effect certain ends.[15] These follow in an order like the previous one, but omitting the Moon and Venus: Sun, Mars, Mercury, Jupiter and Saturn. The discussion of Saturn is interrupted by a digression, paragraphs [17]–[25], involving several images, most related to Saturn, but in a different style; this is most notable in the first *experimentum*, which specifies that lead (via an alchemical use of the word 'Saturn') is to be melted into a random shape, while all the rest of the text has the experimenter making specific images. Then follow two love *experimenta*, the first involving a spirit called Zagam (or Zogan, according to the sign or character)[16] and the second apparently an image of the Moon. This digression forestalls any return to the two planets yet to be discussed in this section, the Moon and Venus; the last section of the digression may have been felt to supply or replace the missing discussion, but Venus is unlikely to have been supplied or replaced by the other *experimenta* of the digression.[17]

Finally, the third work here, paragraphs [26]–[33], is also not explicitly marked as such: the *Secreta astronomie de sigillis planetarum & eorum figuris* [Secrets of Astronomy Concerning the Sigils of the Planets and Their Figures], as indicated by its *explicit*.[18] This is a series of discussions following yet a different order – Saturn, Jupiter, Mars, Sun, Venus, Mercury and Moon – because each is attached to what is commonly known as its planetary magic square, and the squares are arranged in order of the size of the grid – 3 × 3, 4 × 4, etc. Each magic square is to be inscribed on a thin metal plate or coin, no doubt as some kind of amulet, though the amulet need not be worn. What makes the squares magic is that the apparently random ordering of digits in columns and rows is not random: within each square, summing each column, each row and each diagonal will produce the same result.[19] Moreover, in those squares with odd numbers of rows, each major diagonal (top left to bottom right) may have a running sequence of numbers: These are detailed in Table 1.

TABLE 1			
Planetary Magic Squares			
PLANET	GRID	SUM	DIAGONAL
Saturn	3 × 3	15	4–6
Jupiter	4 × 4	34	[7–10?]
Mars	5 × 5	65	11–15
Sun	6 × 6	111	[16–21?]
Venus	7 × 7	175	22–28
Mercury	8 × 8	260	[29–36?]
Moon	9 × 9	369	37–45

The squares as presented in the text have many problems. The first is correct, just reversed left to right so the minor diagonal reads as the major ought to (though the direction of the diagonal is perhaps more modern). The second square is also correct, but from the third on the numbers are not correct and the squares seem to have been reversed left to right in general, hence I replaced them with more readily understood squares. The last square was added at the end of the whole work, not at the beginning of the relevant section, perhaps as an afterthought, so I have moved it up to the beginning of its section. As a matter of further information, though I expected the squares with even numbers of rows to continue the numeric sequence in their diagonals, I am assured by a mathematician whose speciality is combinometrics that this has not worked out in practice.[20]

Using magic squares in this fashion is not wholly novel, but does appear to be unusual; Lynn Thorndike has reported only two manuscripts with similar couplings of these squares with the planets in a magical context, ascribed to Ptolemy.[21] The same connection between the planets and these magic squares is used later by Cornelius Agrippa, who called them the *planetarum sacras tabulas* [sacred tables of the planets].[22] However, Bokenham here has not understood the text he was copying, or simply abbreviated it in such a way that the meaning could be misunderstood, viz., he leaves out some words that make clear the design of the square: *Figura Saturni est quadrata et sunt 3* [The figure of Saturn is square and there are 3] lacks the useful detail extracted by Thorndike as the incipit, *Figura Saturni quadrata est et sunt tria multiplacata per tria* [The figure of Saturn is square and there are three multiplied by three]. That is still misleading, but is closer to the mark than a simple *sunt 3*, though both seem equally problematic with the shift from an explicit singular subject to an implicit plural subject in so short a sentence. Not having seen the text ascribed to Ptolomey, I cannot speak as to how closely the remainder of that text may resemble that below, but the size of the grid for each planet is the same in both texts.

In outline form, the whole compilation looks like this:

LIBER DE ANGELIS, ANNULIS, KARECTERIBUS, ET YMAGINIBUS PLANETARUM

Experimentum magistri Messayaac de secretis spirituum planetis

rituals:	rings:
Sun	Sun
Moon	Moon
Mars	Mars
Mercury	Mercury
Jupiter	Jupiter
Venus	Venus
Saturn	Saturn
	Head of Draco

Liber de ymaginibus planetarum
    Sun
    Mars
    Mercury
    Jupiter
    Saturn
digression:
    Vindicta Troie 1 (begins with buying Saturn's metal, lead)
    Dominium super demones (human-shaped image)
    Aliquem abhominabilem facere (marginal identification as Saturn)
    Aliquos discordare (images of Saturn and Mars)
    Maxime reuerencie habere (marginal identification as Jupiter)
    Alicui loco preesse (implied Sun)
    Vindicta Troie 2 (identified with Saturn)
    Ad amorem (Żagam)
    Ad idem (related to Moon)

Secreta astronomie de sigillis planetarum & eorum figuris
    Saturn
    Jupiter
    Mars
    Sun
    Venus
    Mercury
    Moon

The disorganization and arithmetic errors are not the only problems. In addition, there are many stylistic and even grammatical errors: most notably, there are frequent and sometimes senseless shifts of verbs among imperatives, future indicatives, present indicatives, and second and third persons, as well as errors of concord. Some predecessor to the text may have been in French, not Latin, as evidenced by the use of *Oya* (in paragraph [9]) and *'trembler'*, *Anglice 'aps'* (in paragraph [17]). If the translation from French directly to Latin was by a fifteenth-century physician whose reading ability exceeded his translating or composing skills, the errors may well be explicable. There also seem to be several omissions in the text, but the most obvious is in the paragraph where an obviously corrupt reading (here transcribed as *trimi*) occurs [18]:

> *Vt habeas dominium super demones & maxime super Baal . . . fac ymaginem de recente cera ad similitudinem hominis, pedibus distortis. . . . Tercia uero die suffumiga cum herbis thuris, deinde pone sub aqua torrentis per 9 dies. Postea eam de loco trimi cum tribus denarijs diuersarum monetarum.*

[That you may have dominion over the demons and especially over Baal . . . make an image of new wax in the shape of a man, with feet distorted. . . . On the third day, suffumigate with herbal incense, then place under running water for nine days. Afterwards, from that place *trimi* with three pennies of diverse minting.]

At least removal from the water is missing, and a comment later in this paragraph indicates that sprinkling with dove's blood has also been left out somewhere; where the earlier omission of whole discussions of planets may be easily overlooked in the change of topics, here the syntax should draw attention to a serious gap. Reading the word in the gap as *trimi* is possible, but unlikely.

There are more than a few inconsistencies: Michael is an angel of Mercury and an angel of the Moon (paragraphs [14] and [25]); Sariel is an angel of Jupiter and one of Mercury (paragraphs [14] and [15]); Zagam may be named Zogan, or vice versa (paragraph [24]); and the angels of Mars may be Saliciel, Ycaachel and Harmanel, or Samatiel, Casiel and Hermanel, or Salatiel, Taxael and Harnariel (paragraph [13]). The names of these angels and others, moreover, do not match up well with those in Schwab and Davidson,[23] nor the *Picatrix*.

Additional peculiarities abound, but only a few of the more obvious cases will be noted here. The opening section (paragraphs [2]–[8]) frequently does not specify which planet is of concern, leaving this to be noted in the margin, much as if it were first talked about in usual conversational looseness, and only afterwards were the details identified as to which planet is intended, perhaps using the short list of planets with metals and uses at the end (paragraph [10]). Two different *experimenta*, both called *Vindicta Troie*, appear (paragraphs [17] and [23]); the second of these involves suffumigation with 'rotten tin', which may intend stibnite or pond scum (by transference from *stagnum* for pond). The burial of Jupiter's image, mentioned above, is to be done with a prayer referred to but not actually present in the text (paragraph [21]). Finally, one *experimentum* calls for fasting several days with nothing to eat but raisins and bread with honey (paragraph [31]).

In sum, this appears to be the product of a general interest in the *idea* of magic more than in actual use, and to a fair degree the scribe or his predecessor seems light-hearted enough about it not to take many details seriously. I do not wish to imply that Bokenham – Osbern or some other – was excessively serious to the point of being some puritanical stalwart, but just that this text (or these works) of ritual magic, was copied by someone more interested in the idea than in actual application. In this particular case, only a few passages are relevant to medical practice.[24] The text is not unusual for Kabbalistic or other ritual magic texts.[25] In fact, in some ways it does resemble other texts often copied in a medical context, such as Thabit's *De imaginibus*,[26] and in what may superficially appear to be quite different circumstances, such as Provençal Jewish rationalist discussions, working towards a legally and theologically acceptable role for magic in medicine.[27] There may be other texts yet to be found which bear similarities.[28] Over all, the *Liber de angelis* fits rather well in its context of a medical and herbal miscellany, for all these works focus on things to use to alter the present world; however, Osbern Bokenham showed more interest in the next world, and is unlikely to have been either the author or the copyist of the *Liber de angelis*.

Notes

1 P. Nicholas Toner, 'Augustinian Spiritual Writers of the English Province in the Fifteenth and Sixteenth Centuries', *Sanctus Augustinus, vitae spiritualis magister: Settimana Internazionale di Spiritualità Agostiniana, Roma 22–27 Ottobre 1956* (Rome: Analecta Augustiniana, [1959]), 2: 503. In Bernard's *Catalogi librorum manuscriptorum Angliæ et Hiberniæ* (Oxford, 1697) 2.2: 366, this MS is listed as 9381. 195.

2 M.B. Hackett, 'A Note on Osbern Bokenham', *Notes and Queries* 206 (1961), p. 247.

3 A.S.G. Edwards, 'The Transmission and Audience of Osbern Bokenham's *Legendys of Hooly Wummen*' in *Late-Medieval Religious Texts and Their Transmission: Essays in Honour of A.I. Doyle*, ed. A.J. Minnis (Cambridge: Brewer, 1994), p. 167, n. 51.

4 Private correspondence from Linda Ehrsam Voigts; on the Group itself, see her 'The "Sloane Group": Manuscripts from the Fifteenth Century in the Sloane Collection', *British Library Journal* 16.1 (1990), pp. 26–57.

5 Angus McIntosh, 'The Textual Transmission of the Alliterative *Morte Arthure*' in Norman Davis and C.L. Wrenn (eds), *English and Medieval Studies Presented to J.R.R. Tolkien on the Occasion of His Seventieth Birthday* (London: Allen and Unwin, 1962), pp. 231–41, here pp. 237–8. He adds that A.I. Doyle has identified a 'John Salus or Saluz mentioned in the letter as a burgess of Lynn *c.* 1426–45; Salus is mentioned in the Historical Manuscripts Commission's Report on the town archives, *Report* xi, Appendix, Part III (1887), pp. 159–60, 162, 164' (237 n. 2).

6 Mary Hamel, 'Arthurian Romance in Fifteenth-Century Lindsey: The Books of the Lords Welles', *Modern Language Quarterly* 51 (1990), 341–61, here specifically pp. 345–6 and 343.

7 Cf. *DNB* 13: 807: 'satires of the period often refer to his delight in medicine.'

8 Frank Klaassen's contribution to this volume discusses the collection of magic texts by medical doctors, pp. 6–7. General bibliographic introductions to subjects covered by the *Liber de angelis* may be found in *Medieval Latin: An Introduction and Bibliographical Guide*, ed. F.A.C. Mantello and A.G. Rigg (Washington DC: Catholic University of America Press, 1996), specifically Charles Burnett's 'Astrology', Peter Murray Jones' 'Medicine', and Richard Kieckhefer's 'Magic' chapters in this work. For some more on astrology and medicine, see Roger French's 'Astrology in Medical Practice', *Practical Medicine from Salerno to the Black Death*, ed. Luis García-Ballester, et al. (Cambridge: Cambridge University Press, 1994), pp. 30–59.

9 C.H. Talbot and E.A. Hammond, *The Medical Practitioners in Medieval England: A Biographical Register* (London: Wellcome Historical Medical Library, 1965), p. 386.

10 The reference is to H.E. Salter, *Mediaeval Archives of the University of Oxford*, vol. II, Oxford Historical Society 73 (Oxford: OHS, 1921), pp. 326–9, where only a 'Bokyngham' is indicated, and the record is of receipts and payments *de compositione*.

11 A.B. Emden, *A Biographical Register of the University of Cambridge to 1500* (Cambridge: Cambridge University Press, 1963).

12 I use the Latin term here and in the translation, because 'spell' in English lacks the serious intent, 'experiment' is semantically quite different, and the *Dictionary of Medieval Latin*'s 'magical device' is unrepresentative in this context. William Eamon's *Science and the Secrets of Nature* (Princeton: Princeton University Press, 1994) indicates that an 'experiment' was a private activity of trial and error, to uncover a how-to kind of 'secret' (or non-obvious virtue) of nature (cf. pp. 9, 55–8). He uses quotation marks around 'experiment' and 'secret' to remind readers of how medieval and renaissance usage differs from ours, but I shall retain the Latin term itself.

13 The first recourse of information about such treatises with inscriptions is Lynn Thorndike, 'Traditional Medieval Tracts Concerning Engraved Astrological Images', *Mélanges Auguste Pelzer . . . à l'occasion de son soixante-dixième anniversaire*, Univ. de Louvain, Recueil de travaux d'histoire et de philologie 3rd ser. 26 (Louvain: Bibliothéque de l'Université, 1947), pp. 217–74.

14 A good starting point on this is the long survey by David Pingree, 'The Diffusion of Arabic Magical Texts in Western Europe', *La Diffusione delle Scienze Islamiche nel Medio Evo Europeo*, (Rome: Accademia nazionale dei Lincei, 1987), pp. 57–102.

15 These resemble the images, speeches and suffumigations of the *Picatrix* only in general; cf. *Picatrix: The Latin Version of the* Ghāyat Al-Hakīm, ed. David Pingree, Studies of the Warburg Institute 39 (London: Warburg Institute, 1986), pp. 112–37 (III. VII), 140–5 (III. IX), and passim. That the *Picatrix* was not used in the creation of the work or works here is clear at many locations: for example, the *Liber de angelis* suffumigates with human bone to work ill in [23], while the *Picatrix* asserts that burning human bone and flesh is beneficial: *Omnis caro et ossa hominis combusta movent et provocant benevolenciam* (p. 163, III. XI 94).

16 On signs and characters in general, see Linda Ehrsam Voigts, 'The Character of the *Carecter*: Ambiguous Sigils in Scientific and Medical Texts', *Latin and Vernacular: Studies in Late-Medieval Texts and Manuscripts*, ed A.J. Minnis (Cambridge: Brewer, 1989), pp. 91–109. For one set of figures, see the *Picatrix* 64–74 (II. X). Cf. also John B. Friedman, '"Dies boni et mali, obitus, et contra hec remedium": Remedies for Fortune in Some Late Medieval English Manuscripts', *Journal of English and Germanic Philology* 90 (1991), pp. 311–26.

17 Books or works of 'images' seem to have been quite popular, though few have survived until now and fewer have been edited. For example, in addition to those noted by Thorndike, above, we might investigate further several titles donated by John Erghome to the Austin Friars at York, *c.* 1372, as shown in K.W. Humphreys, ed., *The Friars' Libraries*, Corpus of British Medieval Library Catalogues (London: British Library and British Academy, 1990): A8 362c, n–r, ak–am and ao; 364 a–b; 369l; 375a–f; and 383i–n. For Erghome's holdings on angels, see also 362s af.

18 On sigils in general, see Joan Evans, *Magical Jewels of the Middle Ages and the Renaissance, Particularly in England* (Oxford: Clarendon, 1922), pp. 156–66, the appendices, and passim.

19 Modern magic squares need not sum up like this on the diagonals.

20 Ronald D. Baker at my college, the maths department chair. The square here for Jupiter is also that appearing in Albrecht Dürer's *Melencolia I*, where the '15' and '14' on the bottom also represent the date of the plate. In private correspondence, James A. Reeds (of AT&T's Research Labs in New Jersey) has helped me understand the squares and the scribe's errors better; though he suggested that I reverse (left

to right) the 6 and 7 squares in the text so their similarity to the scribe's squares would be more apparent, I have decided to leave them as they are so the whole sequence's major diagonals would be consistent.

21 Corpus Christi College, Oxford, MS 125 and Vatican City MS Ottob. Lat. 1809 (Thorndike, pp. 259–60). Ptolemy is claimed as a source in [18], not a part of this section.

22 Cornelius Agrippa, *De occulta philosophia*, ed. V. Perrone Compagni, Studies in the History of Christian Thought (Leiden: Brill, 1992), p. 310 (i.e., 2: 22). Compagni indicates that Agrippa's source here is a pseudo-Ptolomæus' *Secreta secretorum*, referring to Oxford Corpus Christi College MS 125, ff. 76r–77v. There are some very interesting correspondences with Agrippa's text otherwise, involving the metals used for the plates and the uses to which these are put. More work needs to be done on this *Secreta secretorum* and related texts, as well as with this part of the *Liber de angelis*.

23 Moïse Schwab, *Vocabulaire de l'angélologie* (Milan: Archè, 1989, rpt. from *Mémoires présentés par divers savants* [Académie des inscriptions et belles-lettres, Paris] 1st ser 10.2 [1897], pp. 113–430) and Gustav Davidson, *A Dictionary of Angels: Including the Fallen Angels* (New York: Free Press, 1967).

24 E.g., [28] *si posueris super crus alicuius, pacietur fluxum sanguinis incontinenti* and [31] *si figuraueris figuram istam in speculo calibis, & inspexerit alius qui fuerit paralitus uel qui habuerit spasmum, curabitur. & similiter qui amiserit visum propter coitum.*

25 Personal correspondence from Frank Klaassen for the ritual magic texts, Willis Johnson for the Kabbalistic. Johnson also believes the text either may be not English if this late or may be mid-thirteenth-century, because the comment *cum tribus denarijs diuersarum monetarum* in [18] implies an awareness of different mints producing coins of the same denomination. He added that 'The oath made a few lines later reminds me of Henry III: *per caput regis veri* . . . sounds to me like a response to Henry's favorite oath, "per caput dei"'.

26 This is in Francis J. Carmody's *The Astronomical Works of Thabit B. Qurra* (Berkeley: University of California Press, 1960), pp. 167–97. Main differences, other than uses to which images are put, include Thabit's lack of supernatural beings, suffumigations, and invocations. A text which might seem closer to those edited here, to go by Carmody's information, is in BL MS Royal 12 C 18, ff. 12r–15v (after *De imaginibus* ff. 11v–12r), incipit *Dixit Balenus qui Apollo dicitur: Imago prima fit in prima hora diei* (cf. his *Arabic Astronomical and Astrological Sciences in Latin Translation: A Critical Bibliography* [Berkeley: University of California Press, 1955], p. 73).

27 Dov Schwartz, 'La magie astrale dans la pensée juive rationaliste en Provence au XIVᵉ siècle', *AHDLMA* 61 (1994): 31–55, here 54 – 'La magie astrale reçoit ici une reconnaissance qui légitime son utilisation fréquent en médecine, mais de plus, elle devient un composant théologique important dans les écrits des rationalistes provençaux. Nissim de Marseille, Narboni et Caspi, eux, ne discutent pas le côté halachique de la magie astrale. Cependent, l'integration de la magie dans des conceptions théologiques fondamentales a sûrement contribué au renforcement de sa légitimation légale (halachique) dans la discussion qui a été soulevée.'

28 E.g., Oxford, Bodleian, Ashmole 1494 and British Library, Harley 2267; cf. Evans 170.

29 *Cat.* refers to Lynn Thorndike and Pearl Kibre, *A Catalogue of Incipits of Mediaeval Scientific Writings in Latin*, rev. ed. (Cambridge: Mediaeval Academy of America, 1963).

30 On whom see Talbot and Hammond, pp. 38–9.

31 These + signs are the product of modern collation in the CUL. For this and other information, I am grateful to Jayne Ringrose of the CUL Department of Manuscripts and University Archives, personal correspondence of 26 May 1995.

Note on Plate, Text and Translation

The plate, published by permission of the Syndics of Cambridge University Library, shows ff. 137v–138r of MS CUL Dd.11.45, thus the Zagam (or Zogam) figure and the first two of the magic squares; the text there runs from paragraph [23] to paragraph [27]. The text below, also published with the kind permission of the Syndics of Cambridge University Library, is a fairly diplomatic transcript of what is found in MS CUL Dd.11.45, though I have added some editorial titles where they seemed appropriate, using titles as implied by the text. Because the origin of the text is uncertain and some aspects of the text imply that the text may be a translation from another language into Latin, I have refrained from emending to smooth the text. The only regularization is my paragraphing, punctuation and capitalization, though I have used an ampersand for the text's tironian *et*. This translation has been smoothed for legibility, which also accounts for its repunctuation; however, an eye has been kept on the Latin, which accounts for some roughness of the translation. For both the text and the translation, I have received excellent public and private advice from members of MEDTEXTL, Medsci-L, and Mediev-L, too many to list, as well as from Claire Fanger. Much useful information about the manuscript was supplied by Linda Ehrsam Voigts. Any errors in text, translation, and interpretation are my own.

APPENDIX A

Cambridge University Library MS Dd. Xi.45

Collation: 1^{12} (wants 1), 2^{14}, $3–7^{12}$, 8^{12} (wants 1–4, 6–7, 9–12), 9^{20}, 10^{12} (wants 1–2), 11^{16}, a^{16} (wants 10–16). Trimming has cut away signatures but for the last quire (ff. 145–8 and 150 are signed aj–aiiij and avj, with a alone remaining on f. 151). Pages were numbered after quire 1 lost 2 leaves but before quires 8 and 10 lost leaves.

1. ff. 1–62v. THESAURUS PAUPERUM. Receipts for various complaints. *Cat.* 58.[29]
   Inc. Ad pustulas capitis sanandas.

2. ff. 62v–80v. Uniform with the preceding. 'Quedam capitula Trotule de passionibus mulierum.' *Cat.* 259 has this MS only. *Inc.* Contingit aliquando.

3. ff. 80v–82r. 'Liber de necessariis ad differendum in practica necessaria ad differendum secundum practico. secundum Magistrum R.' *Cat.* 495 has this MS only. *Inc.* Electuaria frigida ad caliditatem curandum competentia.

4. ff. 82r–84v. 'Libellus magistri cardinalis docens purgare quatuor humores.' *Cat.* 971, 3 other MSS. *Inc.* O medice accedens ad infirmum quem nunquam vidisti.

4A. f. 84v Johannes Stephanus, 'De dosibus medicinarum.' *Cat.* 599, 8 other MSS. *Inc.* Hec est ars medicinarum laxativarum simplicium.

f. 89. Part of a treatise or more, uniform in style with the rest. (Quire of ff. 85–96 lost all but ff. 89 and 92).

5. f. 92. A tract, uniform in style, on the human body. *Cat.* 635, 2 other MSS. *Inc.* Homo de humo factus est, constat ex humoribus.

ff. 93–6 and 117–118 are wanting.

6. ff. 94–119. A Latin-English Dictionary of herbs; incomplete; some pages are blank. There are a few philtres and cabalistic signs interspersed on vacant pages (i.e., ff. 112v and 98v).

7. ff. 119–28. Two treatises in Latin, on 'Tenebrositas Visus' and 'Fleobotomia'.

A. ff. 119–21. *Cat.* 1563, this MS only. *Inc.* Tenebrositas visus plerumque.
B. ff. 121–6. Not in *Cat. Inc.* Propositum presentis negotis est breviter tractare in quibus earitudinibus [?] fleobotomia competit.

Besides these two tracts there are miscellaneous prescriptions at the beginning and end of the MS, in Latin (at least two ascribed to Edmund Albon)[30] and English. *Inc.* For a cold stomak. Tak a good quantite of sauge.

8. ff. 129–33. Receipts in English and Latin, some medical, but many for ignis inextinguibilis, volatilis, etc., and other philosophical preparations. *Cat.* 31, this MS only. *Inc.* Ad capiendas aves.

9. f. 134r. This page is a fragment, and utterly irregular.

10. ff. 134v–9. 'Liber de Angelis Annulis karecteribus et ymaginibus planetarum.' A tract on astrology. *Cat.* 1505, which says 'copied or commented on by' Bokenham. *Inc.* Signum admirabile experimentorum dixit Messayaac.

11. ff. 140–4. Irregular Medical Notes, in Latin and English. [These actually run f. 133v–34r, 140r–44v, evidently written after and thus around the *Liber de angelis*, above, and the letter, below, which they cover at a few locations.]

In f. 142, the writing is displaced on account of a copy of a letter, without signature or address, referring to a copy of 'ane Inglische buke cald Mort Arthur'. [An owner's inscription may have been erased on the bottom of f. 144v. The letter is written sideways.]

12. ff. 145–53. An incomplete Latin-English Dictionary of Herbs. Three of the leaves of this part are of parchment. *Cat.* 83, cf. *Cat.* 86 'Alphita' (ed. Mowat, *Alphita* [Oxford, 1887]), p. 5.

APPENDIX B

Details on Quiring					
Quire	Present Folios	+ on Folio[31]	Original Folios	Catch-word	Work
1	1–10	5	12	10^V	1
2	11–24	18	14	24^V	1
3	25–36	31	12	36^V	1
4	37–48	43	12	48^V	1
5	49–60	55	12	60^V	1
6	61–72	67	12	72^V	1–2
7	73–84	79	12	84^V	2–5
8	[85]–[96]		12		5–6
9	97–116	107	20		6
10	[117]–28	123	12		6–7
11	129–44	137	16		7–11
a	145–[60]	153	16		12

THE BOOK OF ANGELS:
TEXT AND TRANSLATION

Ad mea principia tibi dico salue Maria, quod Bokenham

HIC INCIPIT

LIBER DE ANGELIS, ANNULIS, KARECTERIBUS & YMAGINIBUS PLANETARUM

[Experimentum magistri Messayaac de secretis spirituum planetis]

[1] Signum[1] admirabile experimentorum dixit Messayaac & incipit cum adiuncto Altissimi & est mirabile signum & ualde admirandum in quo sunt secreta Altissimi. Per illud autem Iudei operabantur, Caldei, Egipcij, & prudentes Babilonici. Cum igitur operare uolueris, fiat annulus Solis, ex auro fiat, in quo scribantur carecter & nomen angeli solis. & hoc annulus habeatur in omni sacrificio super minore digito sinistre manus. Cartam itaque cum mente curiose & studiose custodire in loco mundissimo, & inuolue in rubeo serico.

[2] & hec sunt opera annuli Solis. Cum itaque secundum annulum Solis die dominice ieiunes usque ad noctem, nocte autem facies sacrificium de quada aue non domestica prope litus aque decurrentis, & cum eiusdem auis sanguine scribe carecter & nomen angeli Solis in carta[2] uirginea, & hanc tecum porta. Et cum uolueris transire de vna terra in alteram, depinge in terra carecter Solis & nomen angeli eius, & statim veniet equus niger qui portabit te vbicumque uolueris. Tene tamen cartam in manu dextera & annulum in manu sinistra.

[3] Sicud prius, habeas carecter & nomen angeli eius[3] & scribantur in annulo, & ieiunes in die Lune quo fit annulus Lune, sicud fecisti in annulo Solis, in quo si operare uolueris continuo, sacrificabis anguillam flumalem, cuius sanguine scribe carecter Lune & nomen angeli eius in pelle tue, & inuolue in pelle anguille & reserua vt cum volueris ut appareat flumen uel arbor cum fructu, scribe in terra nomen angeli & nomen fructus, & uoca angelum carta aperta, & apparebit. Si uis ut non appareat, claude cartam.

[4] De annulo Martis.[4] Fiat sacrificium de aue rapaci intra domum ad ignem,

---

1 *Underlined in red.*

2 *In margin* dicitur 1ᵃ solis.

3 *In margin* dicitur 2ᵃ lune.

4 *In margin* dicitur 3 de marte.

At my beginning I greet you, Maria, quod Bokenham

HERE BEGINS

THE BOOK OF ANGELS, RINGS, CHARACTERS AND IMAGES OF THE PLANETS

[THE *EXPERIMENTUM* OF MASTER MESSAYAAC OF THE SECRETS OF THE PLANETARY SPIRITS]

[1] Messayaac reported an amazing revelation of *experimenta* and begins with one touching the Most High, and it is an amazing revelation, and certainly to be admired, in which are the secrets of the Most High. Moreover, the Jews worked their magic with this, the Chaldeans, the Egyptians, and the prudent Babylonians. When, therefore, you wish to practice magic, make a ring of the Sun (and make it of gold) on which are written the character (magical sign) and name of the angel of the Sun. And this ring should be worn in all the sacrifices on the little finger of the left hand. Also, with a keen and studious mind, keep some paper in a clean place, and roll it in red silk.

[2] And these are the works of the ring of the Sun. When, in keeping with the ring of the Sun, on Sunday you fast until dark, at night sacrifice some undomesticated bird near the shore of running water, and with the blood of this same bird write the character and name of the angel of the Sun on virgin paper, and carry this with you. And when you wish to go from one land to another, write in the dirt the character of the Sun and the name of its angel, and immediately will come a black horse which will carry you whereever you wish. Hold the paper in the right hand and the ring in the left hand.

[3] As before, have the character and name of its angel written on the ring, and fast on the day of the Moon (Monday), on which is made the ring of the Moon, as you did on the ring of the Sun. If you wish to work with it right away, sacrifice a river eel, with whose blood write the character of the Moon and the name of its angel on your skin and roll it in the eel skin and keep it. When you wish a river to appear or a tree with fruit, write on the ground the name of the angel and the name of the fruit, and then call the angel with the paper open, and it will appear. If you wish it not to appear, close the paper.

[4] On the ring of Mars. Sacrifice a bird of prey to the fire in the house, and

et scribe cum eiusdem sanguine in pelle eiusdem nomen angeli & carecteris. Et cum uolueris ut appareant milites armati uel castella uel lubricus ludus, uel ut vincas in prelio, fac carecterem & nomen angeli in terra & aperi cartam & apparebit & faciet que preceperis. & cum clauditur carta recedet & cessabit.

[5] Totum fac ut de alijs,[5] sacrificium fiat de uulpe uel de cato in loco deserto, scribe careterem et nomen angeli in fronte – vinces in omni placito. Tene cartam in manu.

[6] Fac sacrificium de gallo,[6] karetter & nomen angeli scribe in pelle, intelligi, in quo inuoluas denarium, & qociens ipsum donaueris reuertetur.

[7] Fac sacrificium[7] de columba alba viuente, carecterem & nomen angeli eius scribe in pelle [f. 135r] leporis, quod si mulieri ostenderis sequentur te uelociter.

[8] Totum ut supra.[8] Sacrificium de capra inter vepres, carecterem & nomen angeli scribe in percameno veteri. Cum uolueris inter duos odium mittere, eorum nomina in percameno, eodem carecterem & nomen angeli in pelle capre, ut predicatur. Cum uolueris aliquem intoxicare, in eius potu intinge annulum Saturni: cum idem potauerit intoxicabitur.

[9] Nunc de generalibus mandatis restat docere. Annulus Solis in omni sacrificio habeatur, & annulus Febe, in quo nomen angeli ipsius; Febe tam in memoria habeatur quam in opere. & fiat sacrificium in circulo infundali, prius scriptus carecter, & in medio magister dicat: 'Oya,[9] sacrificium tue laudis suscipe', proiciens carnes extra circulum. In qualibet autem operacione, nomen angeli inuocetur & annulus in digito habeatur. Carte uero mundissime reseruentur, nec in noctis tenebris aperiantur nisi operis necessario ingrauerit.

[10] Nunc de annulis. Annulus Solis ad equum & fiet de auro. Annulus Lune ex argento ad fluuium. Annulus Martis ex ere ad uictoriam in bello. Annulus Mercurij ex cupro ad scienciam. Annulus Iouis ex electro ad denarium. Annulus Veneris ex plumbo ad amorem. Annulus Saturni ex ferre ad odium. Annulus Capitis Draconis ex calibe ad toxicandum.

[11] Hoc signum mirabile est experimentum magistri Messayaac de secretis spirituum planetis, secundum mencionem, & sumitur sic. Omitto nomina angelorum cum carecteribus suis (que incipiunt sic: Storax, Abamecta, Paymon, cum ceteris) propter certam causam hic scribenda.

---

5 *In margin* dicitur 4 de mercurio.

6 *In margin earlier* dicitur 5 de ioue.

7 *In margin earlier* dicitur 6 de uenere.

8 *In margin* dicitur 7 de s[aturno] – *the corner of the leaf was damaged and the rest is lost as a result of repairs.*

9 *MS probably* Oza.

10 *Marked and underlined in red.*

write with its blood on its skin the name of the angel and the character. And when you wish for armed soldiers to appear, or castles or mock swordplay, or that you conquer in battle, write the character and name of the angel on the ground and open the paper and it will appear and do as you wish. And when the paper is closed it will stop and go away.

[5] Do all as with the others; let there be a sacrifice of a wolf or a cat in a deserted place, write the character and name of the angel on the forehead – you will prevail in all contests. Keep the paper in hand.

[6] Sacrifice a cock, write the character and name of the angel on the skin, of course, in which you should fold a penny. And no matter how often you give it away, it will return to you.

[7] Sacrifice a live white dove, write the name and character of its angel on the skin of a hare; if you show it to a woman, she will quickly follow you.

[8] All as above. Sacrifice a she-goat among brambles, write the character and name of the angel on old parchment. When you wish to set up hatred between two people, write their names on the parchment, as well as the character and name of the angel on the goatskin, as said above. When you wish to poison someone, dip the ring of Saturn in his drink: when he drinks, he will be poisoned.

[9] Now it remains to teach general mandates. The ring of the Sun should be worn in all sacrifices, and the ring of Phoebus, on which the name of its angel; Phoebus is kept in mind as well as in work. And let there be a sacrifice in a circle traced on the ground, with the character written first, and in the middle the master speaks: 'Hear! Take the sacrifice in your praise', throwing the meat outside the circle. In all these procedures, however, invoke the name of the angel and wear the ring. The papers should indeed be kept clean, nor should they be opened in the dark of night unless required by the needs of the operation.

[10] Now about the rings. The ring of the Sun is for the horse and should be of gold. The ring of the Moon is of silver for the river. The ring of Mars is of bronze for victory in war. The ring of Mercury is of copper for knowledge. The ring of Jupiter is of amber for money. The ring of Venus is of lead for love. The ring of Saturn is of iron for hatred. The ring of the Head of Draco is of steel for poisoning.

[11] This wondrous revelation is the *experimentum* of master Messayaac, concerning the secrets of the spirits of the planets as mentioned, and proceeds in this way. For a particular reason, I omit the names of the angels with their characters (which begin thus: Storax, Abamecta, Paymon, with others).

Liber[10] de ymaginibus planetarum

[12] Primo scribe de ymagine Solis, ymago facta de auro uel de cera pallida, &
fiat hec Sole exeunte in Leone mense Augusti uel quando est in Ariete mensis
Aprilis. Scribe in ymagine nomen angeli eius & nomina angelorum qui positi
sunt super eam, & sunt hij Raphael, Dardaci, Talanasiel. & nomen diaboli qui
tribuit hanc est Barchan, Chatas, Hycandas, Yaciatal. Si uis ligare linguas,[11] fac
ymaginem de predicta re in hora Solis & in signo suo, & dic hanc coniuracionem:

> Coniuro uos angeli qui imperatis carecteribus Solis – Lergeom, et Alleion, &
> Synaynon, & Odymon, & Agmarob, & Aysmarob, Carof Caroli, Loborsomay, Caux,
> Hebenel, Palulnas, Labotapeosy, Saycop, Calacop – qui creauit celos & planetas &
> omnes stellas & fortes ventos [f. 135v] qui uisi sunt inter celam & terram, & non est
> alius creator preter illum, & ipse maior est & excelsior & rex regum. Per illa nomina
> altissima – Dissamata, Hehaha, Sasaha, Lamob, Asiob, Alosy, Maya, Alos – qui scit
> secreta & dirigit rectas. Cito, o tu Raphael, o tu Daniel, o tu Caualasyel!

Omnes isti faciant mente uelle in illa ymagine.

[13] Hanc[12] fac de ere uel de cera rubea in hora Martis, & nomina angelorum
qui mandant fieri sunt ita – Saliciel, Ycaachel, Harmanel – & nomen regis
diaboli qui mandat est Rubeus Pugnator, & tres auxiliatores sui sunt hij: Karmal,
Yobial, Yfasue. Dic istem coniuracionem super ymaginem:

> Coniuro uos, scribas angelorum, qui estis uolantes per etheram – Aynos,
> Gaidis, Scadexos, Ames, Habes, Hayoynois, Mahamtas, Haiaras. Cito o tu
> Samatiel, o tu Casiel, o tu Hermanel; per nomen Bethahamar & quotquot,
> Arnanis & Elcus & Eudelmus, & est alius qui habet nomen placitum. Cito
> Lataleoleas & Prolege, Capaton, & per vnum regem qui imperat stellis et terre,
> & non est preter ipsum, & ipse magnus & ipse altissimus. Cito o tu Salatiel, o tu
> Taxael, & tu Harnariel, pono super Regem Rubeum & super auxiliatores suos!

Et cum ipsa ymagine quicquid uis potes destruere aut discerpere.[13] &
subhumetur in fonte viuo.

[14] Angelus[14] mandans hanc[15] fieri est Michael & Sariel, & nomen regis
diaboli qui mandat hanc fieri est Zombar, & sunt sui auxiliatores Darial &

---

11 *MS* ligᵃs.

12 *Underlined in red; in margin* ymago martis.

13 *MS* discernere.

14 *Underlined in red.*

15 *In margin* ymago mercurii.

The Book of the Images of the Planets

[12] First make an image (talisman) of the Sun from gold or pale wax, and make this with the Sun leaving Leo in August or when it is in Aries in April. Write on the image the name of its angel and the names of the angels which are placed in charge of it, and these are Raphael, Dardaci, Talanasiel. And the name of the devil which bestows it is Barchan, Chatas, Hycandas, Yaciatal. If you wish to bind tongues, make an image of the aforesaid thing in the hour of the Sun and in its sign, and say this conjuration:

I conjure you angels who command by the characters of the Sun – Lergeom, and Alleion, and Synaynon, and Odymon, and Agmarob, and Aysmarob, Carof Caroli, Loborsomay, Caux, Hebenel, Palulnas, Labotapeosy, Saycop, Calacop – who created the heavens and planets and all the stars and the strong winds which are seen between heaven and earth, and there is no creator but him, and he is greater and higher and the king of kings. By these most high names – Dissamata, Hehaha, Sasaha, Lamob, Asiob, Alosy, Maya, Alos – who know secrets and lead aright. Quickly, oh you Raphael, oh you Daniel, oh you Caualasyel!

They should all act willingly in this image.

[13] Make this of bronze or of red wax in the hour of Mars, and the names of the angels who command it to be done are thus – Saliciel, Ycaachel, Harmanel – and the name of the king of demons who commands is the Red Fighter, and his three servants are these: Karmal, Yobial, Yfasue. Say this conjuration over the image:

I conjure you, scribes of angels, who fly through the æther – Aynos, Gaidis, Scadexos, Ames, Habes, Hayoynois, Mahamtas, Haiaras. Quickly oh you Samatiel, oh you Casiel, oh you Hermanel; in the name of Bethahamar and all, Arnanis and Elcus and Eudelmus, and there is another who has a pleasing name. Quickly Lataleoleas and Prolege, Capaton, and by the one king who rules the stars and earth, and there is no other but him, and he is great and he is the most high. Quickly oh you Salatiel, oh you Taxael, and you Harnariel, I put above the Red King and his servants!

And with this image you can ruin or destroy whatever you wish. And it should be buried in a flowing stream.

[14] The angel commanding this to be done is Michael and Sariel, and the name of the king of demons who commands this to be done is Zombar, and his

Faccas. Fac ymaginem de plumbo & scribe in ea illa nomina angelorum & diabolorum qui supra dicat sunt. Fac ipsam in Iunio uel in mense Octobris. Dic istam coniuracionem super ymaginem, & est hec ymago ad odium:

> Coniuro uos angelos per nomen creatoris, qui est altissimus & non habet[16] principem, qui tibi sit equalis, & ipse est Pater Primum & Filius Dei & Spiritus Sanctus & uerus deus trius & vnus. Cito o tu Michael, o tu Sariel, Miriel!

& subhuma istam ymaginem in via per quam transeunt quos vis ad inimicem separare. Ista ymago[17] est ad odium.

[15] Ista[18] debet fieri in hora Iouis. Angeli eius sunt Sariel, Staus, Iucuciel; & nomen diaboli qui mandat hanc est Marastac, qui habet figuram Iouis, & sunt 3 sui auxiliatores Aycolaytoum et Dominus Penarum. Fac ymaginem de ere pallido uel de cera pallida [f. 136r] et tinge ipsam ibidem. Et fac duas ymagines – vnam ad similitudinem viri, alteram ad similitudinem femine – & scribe nomen viri in fronte mulieris & nomen mulieris in fronte viri, & dic istam coniuracionem:

> Coniuro uos angelos per nomen Sophea, Altriman, Haela, Sophea, Crecior, dator & rector malorum, & per illum qui subdit gigantes, viuit & non moritur. Cito o tu Cricios, o tu Faccas, o tu Casfeel, ite & implete quod cupio cum ista ymagine!

Hec coniuracio est ad amorem mulieris.

[16] Scias quod illa[19] est forcior omnibus alijs & debet fieri de plumbo. & angelus qui mandat hanc fieri est in 7 celo & est Cassael, Maxtarcop, & Standalcon. Rex diabolorum qui mandat hanc fieri est Mayrion, Niger uana generabit. Si uis lingnam ligare uel textorum uel balneum, fac ymaginem plumbeam uel ferream. & fiat hec ymago ad modum illius que ligare volueris. Scribe carecterem Saturni & nomina angelorum & diabolorum supradicta. Si uolueris ad lingnam sub terra, pone ipsam in medio urbis uel ruris. Si ad balneum, sub medio hostij. Ad lingnas ligandas in die Martis hora prima diei, vel in die Saturni hora prima diei.

[Vindicta Troie 1]

Experimentum artis ymagice hora matutinali diei sabbati

[17] Eme Saturnum ad voluntatem vendentis, id est ad primum uerbum quod

---

16 *MS* est habet.

17 Ista ymago *underlined in red, in error for* Ista *following.*

18 *In margin* ymago iouis.

19 *In margin* ymago saturni.

servants are Darial and Faccas. Make the image of lead and write on it those names of the angels and demons mentioned above. Make this in June or in October. Say this conjuration over the image, and this image is for hatred:

> I conjure you angels by the name of the creator, who is most high and who has no prince, who is equal to you; and he is the First Father and the Son of God and the Holy Spirit and the true god three and one. Quickly oh you Michael, oh you Sariel, Miriel!

and bury this image in a road over which travel those whom you wish to divide in hatred. This image is for hatred.

[15] This ought to be made in the hour of Jupiter. Its angels are Sariel, Staus, Iucuciel. And the name of the demon who commands this is Marastac, who looks like Jupiter, and his three servants are Aycolaytoum and Lord of Torments. Make the image of pale bronze or of pale wax and dip it in the same place. And make two images – one in the shape of a man, the other in the shape of a woman – and write the name of the man on the forehead of the woman and the name of the woman on the forehead of the man, and say this conjuration:

> I conjure you angels by the name of Sophea, Altriman, Haela, Sophea, Crecior, giver and ruler of evils, and by him who lays low the giants, lives, and does not die. Quickly, oh you Cricios, oh you Faccas, oh you Casfeel – go and fulfill what I wish with this image!

This conjuration is for the love of a woman.

[16] Know that this is more powerful than all others and should be made of lead. And the angel which commands this to be done is in the seventh heaven and is Cassael, Maxtarcop, and Standalcon. The king of demons who commands this to be done is Mayrion, the Black One will create the voids. If you wish to bind wood or weaving or a bath, make an image of lead or iron. And let this image be in the manner of that which you wish to bind. Write the character of Saturn and the name of its angels and devils aforesaid. If you wish to bind to wood under ground, put it in the middle of town or country. If a bath, under the middle of a doorway. For binding wood, on the day of Mars (Tuesday) the first hour of the day, or on the day of Saturn (Saturday) the first hour of the day.

[Trojan Revenge 1]

An *Experimentum* of Magic on the Morn of the Sabbath

[17] Buy Saturn's metal (lead) at the seller's disposition (that is, according to

dixerat, & vadas domum sine loquela. & funde Saturnum nomine ipsius pro quo uel qua hec facis ad suam confusionem. Et cum fusum fuerit iacta in aquam, dicendo 'In nomine Sathan, Samael, proicio hanc ymaginem ut habeat quemdam formam hominis', & dicas super eam hec nomina:

> Gartiraf, Vetearcon, Yron, Artenegelun, Nymgarraman, Laftalium, Oragin, Oclachanos – vt infermetur N,[20] precipio uobis! & in nomine Bilet, regis nomen, quod N sit infermus & tremulet firmiter de febre dura.

Fiet hoc die Martis mane; in eadem hora sume 4 clauos ferri quod percucias cum marcello in arborem que dicitur *trembler*, Anglice *aps*, dicendo supradicta uerba cum nomine suo quem uis infermare. & quando uis ipsum alleuiare de febre, per diem Lune retrahe vnum clauum. Et nota quod claui erunt dissimile. Hoc experimentum vindicte Troie valet.

[Dominium super demones]

[18] Vt habeas[21] dominium super demones & maxime super Baal, qui est magister eorum, qui dat uera responsa & ambigua, quod fit omni die, omni hora, omni [f. 136v] momento, tamen melius est in die Mercurij, Sole occultante, Luna crescente. Igitur illa hora huius diei fac ymaginem de recente cera ad similitudinem hominis, pedibus distortis. Hanc ymaginem asperge de aqua que uertitur cum rota molendini ter die tribus diebus proximis postquam facta fuerit, & illine eam de sanguine nigre galline in fronte, in pectore, & in pedibus. Nono die post, scribe in pectore eius sigillum Solis & in dorso eius sigillum Lune. Tercia uero die suffumiga[22] cum herbis thuris, deinde pone sub aqua torrentis per 9 dies. Postea eam de loco [amove, et asperge cum sanguine columbe, et fac tributum][23] cum tribus denarijs diuersarum monetarum, dicens

> Coniuro uos Baal, Auel, Dariel, Troion, Orion, per creatorem celi & terre, & per eius omnes uirtutes, & per caput regis ueri, & per omnes principes uostros, vt consecretis hanc ymaginem & faciatis ut respondeat mihi ueritatem de omnibus que ab eo quesiero.

& ibi sunt tribus diebus. 3ª uero die veni ad locum illum & iterum asperge

---

20 *Added in margin (later?).*

21 *In margin, rubric* Nota bene.

22 *After expuncted* suffungat.

23 *MS* tⁱmi; *the text is obviously corrupt, and a line may have been lost; the reading is conjectural, based on the text following.*

his first offer), and take it home without speaking. Melt the lead in the name of whatever man or woman for whose ruin you are doing this. When it is molten, throw it in water, saying, 'In the name of Sathan, Samael, I cast this image that it may have some human form', and say over it these names:

Gartiraf, Vetearcon, Yron, Artenegelun, Nymgarraman, Laftalium, Oragin, Oclachanos – I bid you that N may be sickened! And in the name of Bilet, the name of the king, that N be diseased and tremble hard from an intractable fever.

This should be done on the day of Mars (Tuesday) in the morning. In the same hour, take 4 iron nails which you should smite with a little hammer into a tree called *trembler*, in English *aspen*, saying the aforesaid words with the name of the person you wish to disease. And when you wish to relieve him of the fever, during the day of the Moon (Monday) pull out one nail. And note that the nails are dissimilar. This *experimentum* is powerful in the revenge of Troy.

[Power over Demons]

[18] That you may have dominion over the demons and especially over Baal, who is their lord, who gives true replies and ambiguous; this can be done any day, any hour, any moment, but it is best on the day of Mercury (Wednesday), the Sun occluding, the Moon waxing. Therefore in that hour of this day, make an image of new wax in the shape of a man, with feet distorted. Sprinkle this image with water which has been turned with a millstone thrice a day for three days right after it was made, and daub it with the blood of a black cock on the brow, breast, and feet. On the ninth day thereafter, draw on its chest the sign of the Sun and on its back the sign of the Moon. On the third day, suffumigate it with herbal incense, then place it under running water for nine days. Afterwards, remove it from there, sprinkle it with dove's blood, and make it an offering with three pennies of diverse minting, saying,

I conjure you Baal, Auel, Dariel, Troion, Orion, by the creator of the heavens and earth, and by all his virtues, and by the head of the true king, and by all your princes, that you consecrate this image and make it so that it tells me the truth about all that I shall ask of it.

And let it stay there there for three days. On the third day come to that place and

ymaginem cum sanguine columbe, & postea ibi quere ab ea secrete que volueris & dabit tibi responsa uera. Et si moram fecerit in responsione, dic

> Coniuro te Baal per caput regis veri & per Ariel, Dariel, Troion, Orion, vt loquaris mihi ueritatem de cuiuscunquem te interrogauero,

& percute eam cum uirga coruli, & statim dabit tibi responsa. Deinde defer eam tecum & pone eam in domo tua in loco mundo, & secreto pone. & cum uolueris aliquid scire, interroga eam & dabit tibi responsa uera. Hoc secretum alicui noli reuelare, ut sis sapiens[24] super omnes, dicit Tholomeus. Propter certam causam que me mouit sigillum Solis & sigillum Lune omisi scribere hic.

[Aliquem abhominabilem facere]

[19] Cum[25] uis aliquem abhominabilem facere ita ut turpis & fedus & odibilis habeatur, funde ymaginem[26] plumbeam & pone pedes in loco digitorum & econtrario, & uultum tortum, in hora Saturni & eius die. Postea scribe nomen eius pro quo facta est in capite & nomen Saturni planete in pectore, & prius suffumigabis ymaginem horribili & fetido odore, dicens

> O spiritus fulgentissimi Saturni & a[27] superioribus locis descendentes, hunc N. nomine, cuius hec ymago facta est, in lite & odio detradite, tristes, & distorte, inquietantes, eundem, irracundi.

Postea subhumetur humido, horribili, & fetido loco.[28] [f. 137r]

[Aliquos discordare]

[20] Si[29] uis aliquos discordare, fac vnam ymaginem Saturni & aliam Martis,[30] factisque predicto ordine hoc addito: quod ymago vnius teneat lanceam & altera ymago in domo alterius teneat gladium, & vna contra aliam subhumetur. Si[31]

---

24 Sis sapiens *is doubtful, since it seems partly rubbed out; from here to the end of the page the writing becomes a bit irregularly spaced.*

25 C *marked in red.*

26 *In margin* ymago saturni.

27 *Corrected from just* &.

28 *Last half of line taken up with filler.*

29 *Underlined in red.*

30 *In margin* Martis.

31 *Underlined in red.*

again sprinkle the image with dove's blood, and then ask there of it the secrets you wish and it will give you a true reply. And if it makes a delay in response, say.

I conjure you Baal, by the head of the true king and by Ariel, Dariel, Troion, Orion, that you speak to me the truth of whatsoever I shall ask,

and strike it with a staff of hazel, and immediately it will give you a response. Thence carry it with you and put it in your home in a clean place, and put it secretly. And when you wish to know something, ask it and it will give you a true response. Do not reveal this secret to anyone, that you may seem wise over all others, says Ptolemy. For a particular reason that moves me, I left off the sigil of the Sun and the sigil of the Moon here.

[To Make Another Abominable]

[19] When you wish to make another abominable so that he is held to be ugly and deformed and odious, set up a lead image and put the feet in place of the fingers and vice versa, and a twisted face, in the hour of Saturn and on its day (Saturday). Then write the name of the one for whom it is made on the head and the name of the planet Saturn on the chest, and first suffumigate the image with a horrible and fetid odor, saying,

Oh spirit of most resplendent Saturn and those descending from higher places, hand over into strife and hatred this person named N, of whom this image is made, sad ones, and in torment, unquiet ones, the same person, choleric ones.

Afterwards it ought to be buried in a damp, horrible and fetid place.

[To Put Others at Odds]

[20] If you wish that others fall into discord, make one image of Saturn and another of Mars, made in the aforesaid fashion with this added: that the first image holds a spear and the second image in someone else's house holds a sword,

quis aliquem in bello capere uel vincere voluerit, uel ferocissimus uelit esse uel apparere, uel hostes inimici superare, fac vnam ymaginem hora Lune deficiente, fixis genibus, salutem cadenti, & aliam tenens gladium, & nomen eius in capite scribe & Martis in pectore. Postea in panno rubeo inuolue, in quo panno Martis nomen cum sanguine scribe; ymaginem autem alterius debilem & miseram ad pedes reuolue.

[Maxime reuerencie habere]

[21] Si quis maxime reuerencie & dileccionis & benignitatis se uidere uoluerit & habere, hora Iouis & eius die ymaginem[32] fundat ex ere (& hoc secretissime & cum materia mundissima), & nomen suum in fronte ymaginis scribat & nomen planete, scilicet Iouis, in pectore, qua euacuata thuris & bonis odoribus repleatur hanc oracionem, inter hanc non taceat:

> O uos omnes benignissimi spiritus Iouis, adestote! Meque in honorem & dileccionem dei & populi, & maximam potestatem subleuate! & corda potencium & uoluntatem omnium mee uoluntati conuertite!

Quo facto, pannis mundis inuoluatur & in panno sigillum Iouis inpingnatur. & in medio ciuitatis in qua id esse uolueris, fac ut subhumetur cum oratione subhumacionis ymaginis Solis.

[Alicui loco preesse]

[22] Si[33] alicui loco preesse uolueris, fac ymaginem[34] in hora Solis & eius die, deinde scribe nomen tuum in ea & suffumiga conuenienti suffumigacione, & nomen Solis scribe in pectore & in manu signum illius rei super quam preesse uolueris teneatur, & in mundissimo panno inuoluatur, in quo sigillum Solis & Iouis depingatur.

[Vindicta Troie 2]

Experimentum[35] Saturni ad odium inferendum seu ad aliquem infirmandum in aliquo membro siue in toto corpore, & dicitur Vindicta Troie

[23] Accipe[36] ceram inmundam siue vetustate consumptam, & maxime ceram

---

32 *In margin* Iouis.
33 *Underlined and marked in red.*
34 *In margin* Solis.
35 *Underlined and marked in red.*
36 *Underlined in red.*

and one should be buried against the other. If anyone wants to seize someone in war or to conquer him, or to be or to appear very savage, or to prevail over enemy hosts, then, as the hour of the Moon expires, make one image kneeling, life fading, and another holding a sword, and write his name on the head and Mars on the chest. Then wrap it in red cloth, on which you should write the name of Mars with blood; the image of the other, however, roll about its feet, weak and miserable.

[To Have the Greatest Honor]

[21] If one wishes himself to seem and to have the greatest reverence and love and good will, in the hour of Jupiter and its day (Thursday) prepare an image of brass most secretly and with very pure materials. His name should be written on the forehead of the image and the name of the planet, that is Jupiter, on the chest. Purged by incense and sweet odors, it ought to be filled with this prayer, without interruption:

> Oh all you most benign spirits of Jupiter, attend! Raise me up in honor, in the love of God and of people, and in greatest power! And turn to my desire the hearts of the powerful and the wills of all!

This being done, it should be enfolded in clean cloth and the sigil of Jupiter should be painted on the cloth. And in the middle of the city in which you wish this to be, have it buried with the prayer of the burial of the image of the Sun.

[To Rule over Some Place]

[22] If you wish to rule over some place, make an image in the hour of the Sun and its day (Sunday), then write your name on it and suffumigate it with a convenient suffumigation. Write the name of the Sun on the chest, and have its hand hold the sign of that thing over which you wish to rule. It should be wrapped in a very clean cloth, on which is painted the sigil of the Sun and Jupiter.

[Trojan Revenge 2]

The *Experimentum* of Saturn for Delivering Hatred or Disease to Someone in Some Member or in the Whole Body, Which Is Called the Trojan Revenge

[23] On the day of Saturn (Saturday) and in its hour, take foul wax or decayed

funeris, de qua fac ymaginem in die Saturni ac eius hora in nomine illius quem infirmare uolueris uel odiosum uel in desperationem[37] reddere, hoc modo dicendo dum ipsam protrahis:

> O Saturni spiritus fulgentissimi ac potentes, nunc a superioribus locis descendite! O tristes, adestote irracundi inquietantes ipsum N filium C; & in odium & utilitatem descendite, quamdiu hoc simulacrum durauerit creatoris potentia, ipsum N filium C (uel filiam) in nomine cuius nunc istam ymaginem protraho. [f. 137v]

Qua uero protracta viliore modo quo poteris ac turpiore, videlicet wltu tortuoso, manibus loco pedum positis & pedibus econtrario loco manuum, scribatur in fronte eius nomen, in pectore nomen planete, quod est Saturnus, atque sigilla Saturni inter scapulas. Postea suffumigetur vngulis caballinis, soleis antiquis, stanno putrefacto,[38] ossibus humanis atque capillis. Post ipsam, ymaginem inuolue panno funeris & in loco eciam subhumetur horribili, fetido, & inmundo, wltu uersus terram. Uerso quod, si in aliquo membro infirmare uolueris, ligabis ipsius ymaginis membrum panno funeris & infiges acum super spinam, & nomina infirmitatem. Et si uolueris inferre infirmitatem virilem, figas sub ypocondrijs, & nomina infirmitatem. & si uis neci tradere, figas acum super spinam a capite usque ad cor. Et quando curare uolueris ac reddere pristine sanitati, effodias ipsam de terra, & denuda, & acum remoue, & uestigia vnge, & scripturam deleas, & eciam ipsam laua fontis aqua.

Experimentum[39] verum & probatum ad amorem

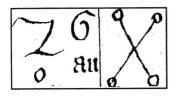

[24] Hinc experimento preest spiritus qui vocatur Zagam & habet tale signum cum carecteribus suis. Accipe 3 columbas & accipe uirgam cedrinam, & fac inde circulum, & post nonam uade ad quadriuium uel ad locum ubi suspenduntur latrones, & defer uirgam tecum & vnam columbam & cultellum album habentem manubrium, & nec eundo nec redeundo nemini alloquare. & sic cum[40] ad dictum quadriuium uel ad alium locum veneris, nigredere circulum & sacrifica columbam dilacerando carnes eius, & sperge per aerem. Inuoca Zagam, qui preest hinc experimento, dicens

---

37 *MS* despurtum.

38 *The text is clear, though the meaning is not.*

39 *In margin, rubric* Nota bene.

40 *MS* cum cum.

with age, and particularly funeral wax, and make an image in the name of the one whom you wish to disease or reduce into hatred or into abhorrence, speaking thus while pulling on it:

> Oh shining and potent spirits of Saturn descend from the higher places! Oh sad ones, attend, wrathful and unquiet, to this N son of C; and, so long as this simulacrum lasts in the power of its creator, in hatred and service descend upon this N son of C (or daughter) in whose name I now pull apart this image.

When it is twisted in as vile and wicked a manner as you can – that is, face screwed up, hands in place of feet and feet contrariwise in place of hands – his name should be written on the forehead, on the chest the name of the planet, which is Saturn, and the sigil of Saturn between the shoulder-blades. Then it should be suffumigated with horses' hooves, old shoes, rotten tin and human bones and hair. After this, roll the image in a funeral swath; it should be buried in a horrible, fetid, unclean place, with its face against the dirt. Regarding this, if you wish to inflict disease upon some member, bind the member of this image in the funeral cloth and thrust a needle along the spine, and name the disease. And if you wish to inflict a disease of virility, stick it under the abdomen, and name the disease. And if you wish to consign to death, thrust the needle in the spine from the head all the way to the heart. And when you wish to cure or to return to full health, disinter it from the ground, strip it, remove the needle, and anoint the feet. You should remove the writing, and also wash it with spring water.

A True and Tried *Experimentum* for Love

[24] In charge of this *experimentum* is a spirit called Zagam and it has this sign with its characters. Take three doves and a cedar staff, and then make a circle. After the ninth hour, go to a crossroads or to a place where thieves are hung, and take the staff with you and one of the doves and a small white knife having a

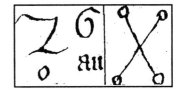

hilt. And do not speak to anyone, neither going nor returning. And thus when you have come to the crossroads or to the other place, blacken the circle and sacrifice the dove, tearing apart its flesh and casting them through the air. Invoke Zagam, who rules over this *experimentum*, saying

O Zagam, accipe columbam istam quam sacrifico tibi!

& postea accipe circulum uirge & res alias quas detulisti & uade domum, & nulli
alloquare. & similiter fac ad uesperam de secunda columba & dic uerba predicta,
'O Zagam' &c. & sic ad completum de 3 columba & dic uerba predicta 'O
Zagam' &c. 3º subiunge 'Rogo te Zagam & omnes socios tuos ut afferas[41] que si
ab aliqua muliere uisa fuerit statim igne mei amoris accensa meam in omnibus
complere uelat[42] uoluntatem'. Hoc expleto, reuertere ad domum tacitus, ut dictum
est. Summo mane, autem, reuertere ubi circulum fecisti & qualemcumque [f.
138r] figuram inuenieris ibi accipe & serua diligenter & munde. Et cum uolueris
ostendere mulieri quam diligis, supra modum te diliget. Nam probatum est.[43]

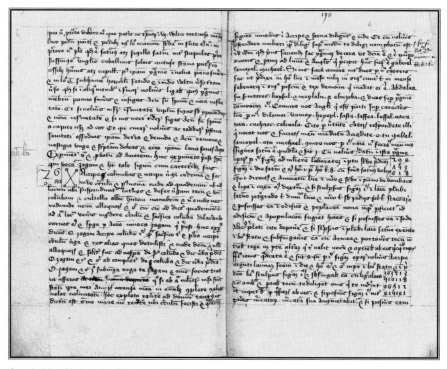

Cambridge University Library MS Dd. 11. 45, ff. 137v–138r.

41 *MS adds several words lined through and mostly illegible; possibly* mihi reliquem futurem depictam.

42 *After expuncted* ualeat.

43 *In margin, in a later hand, scribbles appearing to read* scilicet sic f. litus ddi cucum n habebi, *obscured by
repair to leaf, original corner torn off.*

Oh Zagam, take this dove which I sacrifice to you!

Then take the circle, staff, and other things you brought and go home, speaking to none. And do the same at vespers with the second dove and say the aforesaid words, 'Oh Zagam' etc. Again at compline with the third dove, and say the aforesaid words 'Oh Zagam' etc. At the third, add 'I beseech you Zagam and all your associates that you deliver that which, if seen by any woman, immediately inflames her with the fire of love for me and binds her to fulfill my desire in all things'. This completed, return home silent, as is said. In the early morning, however, return to where you made the circle, and take whatever figure you find there, and keep it diligently and purely. And when you wish to show it to a woman you love, she will love you beyond reason. Indeed, this is proven.

Ad idem quod prius faciendum

[25] Fac ymaginem de cera, vt dictum est, & est ymago amoris & pertinet ad Lunam, & angelus qui precipit hanc fieri est Gabriel, Samayel, Michael. Si uis facere amorem inter duos, per nomen creatoris fac ut predixi in hora Lune in mense Iulij in signo Cancri uel in mense Februarij in signo Piscium. & rex demonum qui mandat ei est Abdalaa, sui seruitores Baysul & Maylalu & Ebuzoba. & dices super ymaginem coniuracionem istam:

Coniuro uos angeli qui estis positi super carecteres Lune per nomen Dilamoi, Vamay, Heyeyl, Sasta, Saffea, Lassal, Uacatara,[44] Cachaoc, Calcaala. Cito per uirtutem creatoris respondete illi qui uocat uos & faciatis meum mandatum. Accedite o tu Gabriel, Samayel, o tu Michael. Coniuro uos per ista nomina ut faciatis meum mandatum in ista ymagine.

[Secreta astronomie de sigillis planetarum & eorum figuris]

[26] Figura Saturni est quadrata & sunt 3. Cum uolueris operare per istam figuram ad mulierem laborantem in partu, scribe predictam figuram in die Saturni & eius hora, id est prima hora uel 8, cum fuerit Saturnus velox cursu, id est directus, & aumentum[45] Lune in Mercurio, & scribe in panno de bombace, &

2	9	4
7	5	3
6	1	8

liga in coxam eius dexteram. & si sculpseris figuram istam in lamina plumbi, Saturno retrogrado uel diminuto lumine & Mercurio, uel sub radijs Solis uel stacionario, & posuisses eam in edificio & populacione noua, nunquam perficietur id edificium & a populacione fugient homines. & si posuisses eam in sede alicuius prelati, cito deponeretur. & si scripseris in plumbi lamina Saturno exeunte in bono statu & subfumigaueris eam cum arinea & portaueris tecum, non timebis regem neque partem alteram qui tibi uelit nocere, & optinebis ab eis quicquid cupis.

[27] Figura Iouis quadrata est & sunt 4. Quando per istam figuram operare uolueris, accipe argenti laminam factam in die & hora eius, & sit Iupiter in bono statu, & in predicta lamina sculpes figuram istam, & subfumigabis eam cum ligno aloes & cum ambrosia, & portabis tecum. Te diligent omnes qui te uiderint, & impetrabis quod quesieris

16	3	2	13
5	10	11	8
9	6	7	12
4	15	14	1

ab eis. & si posueris figuram istam inter pedes mercatorum, mercatura sua augmentabitur. & si posueris eam [f. 138v] in columbario uel in loco ubi apes fuerunt aggregate congregabuntur. & si portaueris tecum fortunatus eris de bono

44 *First two letters uncertain.*

45 *MS* aumientum.

For the Same

[25] Make an image of wax, as said; this is an image of love and belongs to the Moon. And the angel which bids this to be done is Gabriel, Samayel, Michael. If you wish to make two people fall in love, in the name of the creator do as I have said in the hour of the Moon in July in the sign of Cancer, or in February in the sign of Pisces. And the king of demons who commands it is Abdalaa, his servants Baysul and Maylalu and Ebuzoba. And say over the image this conjuration:

> I conjure you angels who are placed over the characters of the Moon, in the name of Dilamoi, Vamay, Heyeyl, Sasta, Saffea, Lassal, Uacatara, Cachaoc, Calcaala. Quickly, by the power of the creator, respond to him who calls you and perform my command. Come, oh, you Gabriel, Samayel, oh you Michael. I conjure you by those names that you fulfill my demand concerning that image.

[Secrets of Astronomy Concerning the Sigils of the Planets and Their Figures]

[26] The figure of Saturn is square and has a grid of three. When you wish to do magic by this figure to help a woman in childbirth, write the figure on the day of Saturn (Saturday) and in its hour (that is, the first hour or eight), when Saturn is fast on course, that is direct, and the Moon is rising in Mercury; write it on silk and tie it

2	9	4
7	5	3
6	1	8

to the right hip. And if you sculpt this figure on a thin piece of lead, with Saturn retrograde or decreasing in light and Mercury, or in the rays of the Sun or stationary, and if you place it in a building or a new inhabitation, this building will never be finished and people will flee from the inhabitation. And if you place it in the seat of some prelate, he will immediately be deposed. And if you write it on a thin piece of lead, with Saturn in a favorable position and falling, and if you suffumigate it with a spider and carry it with you, you will fear neither the king nor anyone else who wishes to harm you, and you will get whatever you wish from them.

[27] The figure of Jupiter is square and has a grid of 4. When you wish to practice magic with this figure, take a thin piece of silver made on its day (Thursday) and hour, and let Jupiter be in a favorable position. And on the piece sculpt this figure, and suffumigate it with aloe wood and ambrosia, and carry it with you. All who see you will

16	3	2	13
5	10	11	8
9	6	7	12
4	15	14	1

love you, and you will succeed in whatever you ask of them. And if you put this figure between the feet of merchants, their business will grow. And if you put it in a dove-cot or in a place where bees are gathered, they will thrive. And if you carry it with you, your fortune will go from good to better. And if you

in melius. & si posueris eam in sede alicuius prelati durabit eius prelacio & non[46] timebit inimicos suos.

[28] Figura Martis est informata bellum & guerras & destruccionem, & est quadrata & sunt 5.[47] Cum uolueris operare per hanc figuram, accipe laminam cupri in hora & eius die cum fuerit diminutus Mercurio vel Lune vel infortunatus uel retrogradus, & sculpes figuram predictam in ea & subfumigabit cum sanguine menstruo, uel cum panno hominis

11	24	7	20	3
4	12	25	8	16
17	5	13	21	9
10	18	1	14	22
23	6	19	2	15

suspensi uel gladio interfecti, uel cum stercoribus murum uel murelegorum. Si posueris in edificio,[48] a quo non complebitur sed heremum relinquetur. & si posueris in sede uel loco alicuius prelati, decolorabitur continue & infirmabitur. & si posueris super mercaturam, destruetur tota. & si socieris predictam figuram sub nomine duorum mercatorum se adinuicem diligencem, cadet inter eos odium. Et si forte timorem de rege habueris uel de alico magno uiro uel de inimicis, uel ad iudicem[49] intrare uolueris, sculpes hanc figuram ut supra dixi, & sit Mars fortunatus directus auctus Mercurio & lumine, & Luna supra, & subfumigabis eam panno serico rubio, & pones cum predictam laminam 1 dragma de cornelio, & fer tecum & uinces in iudicio & bello aduersarios, uel & fugient a facie, uel & timebunt te. & si posueris super crus alicuius, pacietur fluxum sanguinis incontinenti. & si scripseris figuram illam in percameno in die & hora prenotatis, & subfumigaueris eam cum aristologia & posueris eam in loco apum ubi congregabuntur, & fugient apes ab illo loco.

[29] Figura Solis apropriata est regibus & principibus huius mundi, & est quadrata & sex, &

6	32	3	34	35	1
7	11	27	28	8	30
19	14	16	15	23	24
18	20	22	21	17	13
25	29	10	9	26	12
36	5	33	4	2	31

---

46 *Corrected from just* &.

47 *MS figure:*

14	10	12	2	18
20	17	3	2	4
21	17	13	9	5
2	23	19	15	6
8	4	25	16	12

48 *A few words seem missing here.*

49 *MS* uel ad iudicem uel ad iudicem.

place it in the seat of some prelate, his rule will last and he will not fear his enemies.

[28] The figure of Mars is made for war and battles and destruction, and it is square and has a grid of 5. When you wish to do magic with this figure, take a thin piece of copper in its hour and day (Tuesday), when it is falling with respect to Mercury or the Moon, or malefic, or retrograde, and sculpt the figure on it and suffumigate it with menstrual

11	24	7	20	3
4	12	25	8	16
17	5	13	21	9
10	18	1	14	22
23	6	19	2	15

blood, or with the clothing of a man hung or killed with a sword, or with mouse or cat droppings. If you put it in a building, it will not be inhabited but be left deserted. And if you put it in the seat or place of some prelate, he will turn pale continually and will sicken. And if you place it over a business, it will be utterly destroyed. And if you share the aforesaid figure in the name of two merchants who are fond of each other, hatred will fall between them. And if by chance you would be feared by the king or some great man or enemies, or you wish to go to court, then sculpt this figure as said above (with Mars benefic, direct, and rising in Mercury and brightness, and with the Moon above), suffumigate it with red silk, put with it 1 dram of carnelian, and carry it with you – you will defeat your adversaries in court and battle, or they will fly from your face, or they will fear you. And if you put it on someone's shin, it will ease immoderate blood flow. And if you write this figure on parchment in the day and hour noted above, suffumigate it with birthwort, and put it in the place where bees are gathered, indeed the bees will flee that place.

[29] The figure of the Sun is appropriated for kings and princes of this world, and it is square and has a grid of six, and it is the figure of total power.

6	32	3	34	35	1
7	11	27	28	8	30
19	14	16	15	23	24
18	20	22	21	17	13
25	29	10	9	26	12
36	5	33	4	2	31

est figura totius potestatis.[50] Cum uolueris operare per eam, aspice cum fuerit Sol in exaltacione sua hora eius in 5 gradu Arietis, & accipies 6 dragmas auri & facies inde laminam rotundam in die & hora Solis, & subfumigabis eam cum croco & lauabis cum aqua rosacea in qua fuerit muscus & ambrosia, & inuolues in panno serico croceo, & fer eam tecum. Semper continue letus eris & fortunatus in omnibus, & impetrabis quicquid[51] quesieris. & hoc est secretum.

[30] Figura Veneris est quadrata & sunt 7,[52] & est figura fortunata proprie in facto mulieris & in omni dileccione & veneritate. Cum uolueris operare [f. 139r] per istam figuram, vide quod Venus sit in Piscibus, quia ibi est exaltacio sua, aut in Tauro uel in Libra, que sunt domus eius, & sit fortunata & aucta lumine, cursu velox & directa aucta. Gere 7 dragmas argenti puri in die eius & hora, fac

22	47	16	41	10	35	4
5	23	48	17	42	11	29
30	6	24	49	18	36	12
13	31	7	25	43	19	37
38	14	32	1	26	44	20
21	39	8	33	2	27	45
46	15	40	9	34	3	28

laminam & scribe in ea figuram, & suffumiga cum ligno aloes & cum ambrosia & cum mastice, & inuolue eam in panno serico albo, & porta tecum. & quotquot mulieres uidebis te diligunt, & uidebis mirabilia. Et si uir uel mulier tardet multum ad vxorandum, portet eam secum & vxorabitur cito. & si vxor tua uel alia quelibet prima habeat te odio, laua dictam laminam cum aqua fontis uel aqua rosacea & da ei ad potandum, & diliget te & facies quod quesieris. Et si

---

50 *MS figure:*

2	32	34	3	35	6
30	8	27	28	5	7
30	24	15	16	13	23
19	17	21	22	18	14
10	26	12	9	29	24
31	4	2	33	5	36

51 *MS adds* pecie *expuncted.*

52 *MS figure:*

4	35	10	41	16	48	22
29	11	41	17	48	23	5
12	36	18	49	24	6	30
37	19	42	25	7	31	13
20	44	26	2	32	14	78
45	27	2	33	8	39	21
28	3	34	9	40	15	46

When you wish to do magic with it, see when the Sun is in its exaltation in its hour in the 5th degree of Aries, and take 6 drams of gold and make from them a round, thin plate on the day and hour of the Sun. Suffumigate it with saffron, wash it with rose water in which is musk and ambrosia, and wrap it in saffron-coloured silk, and carry it with you. You will then always be continually happy and lucky in all, and you will prevail in whatever you seek. And that is the secret.

[30] The figure of Venus is square and has a grid of 7, and it is a figure of luck proper to woman's matters and all delights and sex. When you wish to work magic with this figure, see that Venus be in Pisces, for there is its exaltation, or in Taurus or in Libra, which are its houses, and that it be benefic and increasing in brightness, fast in its course and rising direct. Prepare 7 drams of pure silver in its day

22	47	16	41	10	35	4
5	23	48	17	42	11	29
30	6	24	49	18	36	12
13	31	7	25	43	19	37
38	14	32	1	26	44	20
21	39	8	33	2	27	45
46	15	40	9	34	3	28

(Friday) and hour; make a thin plate and write on it the figure; suffumigate it with aloe wood, ambrosia, and mastic; wrap it in white silk cloth; and then carry it with you. And all the women you see will love you, and you will behold miracles. And if a man or woman is slow to marry, let that person carry it and that person will soon marry. And if your wife or some other favorite hates you, wash the aforesaid plate with spring water or rose water and give it to her to drink, and she will love you and do as you wish. And if you boil camomile and

decoxeris[53] camamillam & laueris laminam & asperseris aquam illam in locis vbi est discordia uel in locis mundorum, cessabit omne malum; & si asperseris aquam illam in locis ubi mercature sint uel bestie multiplicatur. & si posueris istam figuram in lecto tu habundabis in coitu & diliget te multum vxor tua.

[31] Figura Mercurii est quadrata & sunt 8.[54] Mercurius est ualde uelox in motu & in mutacione, & habet complexionem & naturam omnium planetarum & signorum, & ei attributa sunt anima & virtus & sciencia & sapiencia & philosophia & quadruuium & descripcio. Cum uolueris operare per istam figuram, accipe 8 dragmas puri argenti & fac laminam in hora Mercurij in

8	58	59	5	4	62	63	1
49	15	11	52	53	14	10	56
41	23	22	44	45	19	18	48
32	34	35	29	28	38	39	25
40	26	27	37	36	30	31	33
17	47	46	20	21	43	42	24
9	55	54	12	13	51	50	16
64	2	6	61	60	3	7	57

eius die, quando Mercurius fuerit fortis, directus, uelox in suo cursu, & subfumiga cum ligno aloes, gaziofila,[55] mastice, & porta tecum, & omnia que pecieris impetrabis. & si non poteris habere argentum, scribe in papiro citrino locus argenti & tamen ualebit. Si posueris figuram istam in cathedra alicuius, durabit eius prelacio. & si figuraueris istam figuram in annulo, aut in vitro, uel in pelui, in die Mercurij mane imprimis 7 diebus lunacionis in augmento Lune, & postea delee ueris istam figuram cum aqua munda alicuius fontis & potaueris aquam istam, per tres dies scies quod amittes omnem obliuionem & addisces de facili omnia que volueris. & si figuraueris figuram istam in speculo calibis, & inspexerit alius qui fuerit paralitus uel qui [f. 139v] habuerit spasmum, curabitur. & similiter qui amiserit visum propter coitum. Et si ieiunaueris per 3 dies continuos, quod aliud non comedas nisi tantummodo panem cum melle & vuis passis, & post istos 3 dies istam figuram scripseris in pano serico citrino & subfumigaueris

---

53 *MS* se detoxeris.

54 *MS figure:*

8	79	9	60	61	62	22	1
49	15	54	12	53	51	10	16
41	43	22	21	20	19	47	48
32	34	35	29	28	38	9	15
40	26	17	37	36	30	31	31
17	18	46	45	44	43	23	24
9	52	14	52	13	11	50	56
64	6	3	34	56	5	8	57

55 *For* gariofilo.

wash the plate and sprinkle that water in places of discord or in any places of the world, all evil will cease. And if you sprinkle this water in business places or farms, they will prosper. And if you put this figure in your bed, you will abound in sex and your wife will love you very much.

[31] The figure of Mercury is square and has a grid of 8. Mercury is extremely fast in motion and change, and it has the temperament and nature of all the planets and signs. To it are attributed soul, virtue, knowledge, wisdom, philosophy, the *quadrivium*, and painting. When you wish to do magic with this figure, take 8 drams of pure silver and make a thin plate in the hour of Mercury on its day (Wednesday),

8	58	59	5	4	62	63	1
49	15	11	52	53	14	10	56
41	23	22	44	45	19	18	48
32	34	35	29	28	38	39	25
40	26	27	37	36	30	31	33
17	47	46	20	21	43	42	24
9	55	54	12	13	51	50	16
64	2	6	61	60	3	7	57

when Mercury is powerful, direct, and fast on course, suffumigate it with aloe wood, cloves, and mastic, and carry it with you; you will then succeed in all you pursue. And if you cannot use silver, write on orange paper instead of silver and it will be good enough. If you put this figure in someone's seat, his rule will last. And if you carve this figure on a ring, or in glass, or in a basin, on the day of Mercury in the morning on the first 7 lunar days in the Moon's ascension, and if you wash this figure with clean water from some spring and drink that water, then after three days you will remember all you have utterly forgotten, and, further, you will easily learn all that you wish. And if you put this figure on a steel mirror, and someone who is paralytic or spastic looks in it, he will be cured. And so also whoever has lost his sight due to sexual intercourse. And if you fast for 3 days running, eating nothing but bread with honey and raisins, and if after those 3 days you write this figure on orange silk and suffumigate it with aloe wood, and

eam cum ligno aloes & dixeris tunc 'O dij per uirtutem istius figure ostende mihi hoc N in sompnis' – postea posueris istum pannum sub puluinare tuo quando ieris cubitum – uidebis in sompnis id uolueris. Hoc experimentum est & probatum.

[32] Figura Lune est quadrata & sunt 9.[56] Quando uolueris per istam figuram operare, accipe percamenum & scribe in ea figuram istam in die Lune & eius hora, in augmento eius, & scribe cum incausto ex musco & croco, & sint simul temperati cum aqua rosaceo, & suffumiga illam cum semine cucumerorum & citrillorum. Deinde mitte illam in laminam argenti factam ad modum cane, & porta

37	78	29	70	21	62	13	54	5
6	38	79	30	71	22	63	14	46
47	7	39	80	31	72	23	55	15
16	48	8	40	81	32	64	24	56
57	17	49	9	41	73	33	65	25
26	58	18	50	1	42	74	34	66
67	27	59	10	51	2	43	75	35
36	68	19	60	11	52	3	44	76
77	28	69	20	61	12	53	4	45

tecum. Valet ad petendum omnes res nobiles, & aufert omnem malum. & quicumque habuerit istam penes se non timebit latronem nec aliquod malum. Quando enim volueris aliem expellere de uilla quem odio habes, scribe istam figuram in percameno uirgini ouis, & ex altera parte figurabis figuram piscis cancri cum sanguine galli nigri qui sit decollatus in die Lune, Luna decrescente. & quando totum perfeceris, mitte cartulam illam in aliquo vrceolo paruo nouo, & imple ollam aqua, & dimitte ipsum stare per vnam noctem sub aere. In sequenti die, accipe ollam & dic sic: 'Exeat talis N ab ista uilla uel ciuitate & numquam reuertatur ad illam.' Tunc effunde aquam illam per 4 partes mundi & fiet quod uolueris. Et ut viriliter numquam unebeat, scribe istam figuram in lamina plumbi minuente Luna in die eius & eius hora, & dices sic: 'Ligo enim N[57] ut numquam' &c. & ex alia parte fac ymaginem illius mulieris & post suffumiga eam & inhuma in fossa alicuius ignoti.

---

56 *MS figure, added at bottom by postscript:*

37	78	74	2	1	62	13	54	5
6	38	79	30	71	22	63	14	46
47	7	39	80	3	72	23	55	15
16	48	8	40	81	32	64	24	56
57	17	49	9	91	73	33	65	25
26	58	18	50	1	42	74	34	66
67	27	59	10	51	2	43	75	35
36	68	19	60	11	52	3	44	76
77	18	69	20	61	12	53	4	45

57 *MS* enim N n.

if you then say 'Oh, gods, by the virtue of this figure show me this N in my dreams', after all that put this cloth under your pillow when you go to sleep and you will see in your dreams what you wish. This is tried and true.

[32] The figure of the Moon is square and has a grid of 9. When you wish to perform magic with this figure, take parchment and write on it this figure on the day of the Moon (Monday) and its hour, in its ascent; and write with ink of musk and saffron – both tempered with rose water – and suffumigate with cucumber and watermelon seeds. Then put it on a thin plate of silver made in the shape

37	78	29	70	21	62	13	54	5
6	38	79	30	71	22	63	14	46
47	7	39	80	31	72	23	55	15
16	48	8	40	81	32	64	24	56
57	17	49	9	41	73	33	65	25
26	58	18	50	1	42	74	34	66
67	27	59	10	51	2	43	75	35
36	68	19	60	11	52	3	44	76
77	28	69	20	61	12	53	4	45

of a dog, and carry it with you. It is good for pursuing all noble affairs, and it diverts all evil. And whoever has this in his possession will fear neither a thief nor other evil. Indeed, when you wish to expel from town someone you hate, write this figure on parchment from a virgin sheep, and on the other side draw a crab, using the blood of a black cock beheaded on the day of the Moon, with the Moon waning. When you have done all this, put that card in some new, small pitcher, fill the jug with water, and set it out to stand a for one night in the air. On the following day, take the jug and speak thus: 'May this N depart from this town or city and never return to it.' Then pour the water out to the 4 winds, and it should happen as you wish. And so a man is ever impotent, write this figure on a thin plate of lead with the Moon waning on its day and its hour, and speak thus: 'I bind this N so that never' etc. And, on the other side, make an image of his woman and then suffumigate it and bury it in the grave of someone unknown.

[33] Expliciunt secreta astronomie de sigillis planetarum & eorum figuris.

[34] *Nota a Luna prima ad 14, videlicet ad omnia experimenta, si uolueris ad odium fac sub hora Saturni uel Martis, si ad amorem, pacem, uel concordiam sub hora Iouis, Veneris in eorum potestate, & tunc capient effectus. Hic, autem, propter certam causam que me mouit, carecteres planetarum & signorum scribere omisi, quod Bokenham.*

[33] Here end the secrets of astronomy concerning the sigils of the planets and their figures.

[34] *Note: from the first Moon to the 14th, that is, for all the experimenta, if you wish to act for enmity do it in the hour of Saturn or Mars – if for love, peace, or amity, in the hour of Jupiter or Venus, in their power – and then things will work. Here, however, for a particular reason that moves me, I omitted the characters of the planets and signs. Bokenham*

3

Safe Magic and Invisible Writing in the *Secretum Philosophorum*[1]

John B. Friedman

Late medieval secrets literature includes texts of a theurgic magical cast seemingly intended for a learned and intellectually adventurous audience, but whose content is chiefly an innocuous collection of artisans' technical recipes[2] which would substitute for magic acts chemical or manipulative processes. One such work of this type is the *Secretum Philosophorum* (hereafter called *SP*), composed most likely in England in the third quarter of the thirteenth century.[3] I should like to suggest that the *SP* illustrates the new taste for 'safe' or 'Christianized' magic which seems to result from the popularization of the literature of secrets during the later Middle Ages.

To judge from the eighteen mostly fragmentary manuscript copies,[4] the work attained a modest popularity, particularly in England, and material on dialectic from it is cited several times in the commonplace book of a Syon monk, Thomas Betson, *c.* 1500, and lengthy quotations from the astrological sections appear in a scientific encyclopedia, the *Liber Cosmographiae* (1408) of John de Foxton, who examined a copy of the *SP* in the York Augustinian Library, praising it highly for its cryptic character.[5] A note by an early Lincoln Cathedral Chapter librarian in one fragmentary text of the work names the compiler as George Ripley, the late fifteenth-century author of the *Compend of Alchemy* and similar tracts, but he is surely too late; an Oxford manuscript note assigns the work to Aristotle.[6]

The version of the work I consider here, one of the few complete texts, is that in Trinity College, Cambridge, MS O.1.58, where it forms the first of three volumes, all of the fifteenth century. The manuscript contexts for the *SP* give an idea of the audience for Christianized magic. In MS O.1.58 we also find hermetic treatises on stars and precious stones and a collection of magical recipes for, among other things, obtaining a woman's love through the use of a blue jay's tongue.[7] Another manuscript of the *SP* in Trinity College, Cambridge, MS O.2.40, forms part of a collection compiled and copied in 1492 by William Wymondham, who was an Augustinian canon at the Priory of Saint Peter at Kirby or Kirkby Bellars in Leicestershire. This priory seems to have had an active scriptorium and Wymondham took a special interest in the literature of secrets.[8] For example, in this collection cheiromantic diagrams are juxtaposed with the Kyrie and the Lord's Prayer and a set of instructions for finding out secrets from Hebrew and other exotic alphabets which bears the rubric 'O quam bene dilexi regulas istas in vita mea quod Womyndam quia semper reperi eas veras et nunquam falsas'.[9] Yet another manuscript, Cambridge, Gonville and Caius College MS 413/630 is a four-volume work of which the last two parts, of fourteenth- and fifteenth-century date, are very like the two Trinity codices, containing a phlebotomy by Peter of Spain and an alchemical tract, *Liber Aureus*, followed by briefer recipes for miscellaneous chemical and artists' materials, and the *SP*, and ending with more phlebotomy and urine tracts. Even this volume was once larger, with a physiognomic treatise and various works of Aristotle incorporated.[10] Thus people – both lay and clerical – who would be interested in practical, medical, astrological and similar subjects were also the audience for the literature of secrets.

SP is little known and has never been edited. In 1935, Daniel Thompson claimed he was preparing an edition, but it never appeared, and the work is not mentioned by William Eamon in his study of secrets literature.[11] The only recent treatment is that of Andrew Galloway, who is interested in the riddles it contains rather more than in its theurgic – or faux theurgic – aspect. He sees the treatise as preoccupied with issues of deception and claims that it 'generalizes the principle of deception outward into each of the liberal arts'.[12]

Whether or not this is true, certainly in form and title the *SP* appeals to a learned audience, for its seven-book structure follows the order of the seven liberal arts; each art is the subject of a book which after a preface is subdivided into brief *capitula*. Thus, Book One on grammar is developed through chapters on pigment making of all sorts including many colours not normally used in writing and illuminating. Book Two surveys rhetoric, giving examples of tricks and techniques accompanied by riddles and illustrative verses to help in various verbal problems and situations. Book Three on dialectic treats truth and falsity, with discussions of the five senses and their deception. For taste, we learn how to tell good wine from bad; for smell we learn how it responds to violet water; for sight, we learn all about tricks with mirrors; and for touch, various deceptions.

Book Four on arithmetic, which is quite long, contains a series of *quaestiones* of a simple mathematical type involving formulae, concepts of length and breadth and the like, mnemonic verses for tallying processes and rules for algorithms, and calculating the lengths of musical instrument strings for pitches. Book Five is chiefly practical geometry, with rules for measurements of buildings, towers and fortifications, and contains a discussion of aqueducts illustrated by strongly empirical marginal diagrams. These drawings, in one manuscript, are attributed to a canon Edmund of St Andrews, who made them at Worksop.[13]

Book Six, on music, treats chiefly harmonic proportion from a theoretical perspective, and Book Seven, on astronomy, considers the planets and the constellations with a lengthy discussion of the element of water accompanied by a number of diagrams of experiments to be performed with water in flasks and retorts. It ends with the treatise on magnetism and the compass written in 1269 by Peter Peregrinus de Maricourt.[14]

Yet in spite of its formal academic structure and imposing title, the *SP* is truly a work of popular or middle-class interest. It mixes parlor games and pranks – often of the sort which would have been attractive to Rabelais's Panurge – with detailed recipes of the most mundane sort, many taken from the early ninth-century *Mappae Clavicula*,[15] for how to scrape out parchment once written upon and how to make verdigris.

As I suggested earlier, the *SP* illustrates the intersection of the learned hermetic Latin treatise written for an audience which defines itself through its rejection of a vulgus seeking access to occult knowledge for unworthy reasons with the vernacular artisans' technical recipe collection, which gathers in convenient form the materially valuable knowledge of trades such as gardening, blacksmithing, manuscript illuminating and the like. This dual aim and audience is well seen throughout the work, but nowhere better than in Book One, *De Grammatica*, which is representative of this aspect of the whole treatise.

In a short prohemium, the compiler discusses the work's name and content. 'This book which we have in our hands,' he says, 'is called secrets of philosophers, and is so titled because in it are contained certain secret processes reputed by the vulgar to be impossible of accomplishment. And in the works of the philosophers are found the most important secrets. Contained in this book are certain true secrets of all the arts, because there are seven arts, namely grammar, rhetoric and dialectic, arithmetic, music, geometry and astronomy.'[16]

Incorporating a number of the stock motifs of hermetic literature, but without any indication of what occult truths will be revealed, this prohemium belongs with similar ones to truly hermetic works, which promise to reveal occult wisdom carefully concealed for centuries by sages, or contained in the marvellous workings of nature. The idea that those knowing the seven liberal arts excite the envy of a less educated or refined group is also clear. Indeed, the prohemium would seem to oppose artisans and intellectuals. Thus, those who hope for material gain in manipulating by specific techniques the occult powers of nature for economic or political ends are contrasted with those who contemplate the wonders of nature in a disinterested and speculative way.

Ending his prologue not with the antiquity and majesty of the *artes* and their lofty underlying principles, but with the practical matter of their *ordinatio*, the compiler promises to discuss them one at a time. 'And we will begin with grammar, which is first in order' (f. 1). One might expect some theoretical discussion of grammar, with citations from ancient and late antique writers, like Martianus Capella. Indeed, the grammar section opens conventionally enough in a scholastic fashion: 'Grammar teaches correct writing and speaking, from which it is seen that it is divided into two parts of which the first is speaking and the second is writing.' The compiler, however, quickly strikes a practical note. 'Yet many tricks (*cautela*) should be kept in mind about writing with a pen, namely, that no one can write without the required instrument.'[17] The leap to the utilitarian pen as instrument from the idea of writing and speaking as part of grammar is unexpected and suggests what is to come, the incorporation of recipe literature in a book of an hermetic and magical cast intended to provide 'short cuts' for an audience of students of the arts, which is certainly not a university audience.

What is equally unexpected is the way that the compiler, apparently thinking ahead rather literally to the 'colours' of rhetoric which ought to be featured in the next book on rhetoric, but which, in fact, are not, follows the introduction to the section on proper writing with nine brief articles on the making of illuminators' and scribes' colours, sizing and varnishes. Nor is there further discussion of writing in any stylistic or rhetorical sense.

The second part of Book One, on correct speaking, is considerably more theoretical and intellectually oriented, with a fairly lengthy preface on the arts of speech. It is also illustrated with distichs from unnamed authors introduced by the familiar 'unde versus' formula.[18] But again, in the actual *cautela* to do with speaking, the examples are jejune sample cases in which a hypothetical problem is posed concerning one man with three apples speaking to another man with two apples. Then follows a solution.

Overall, the compiler reveals himself a person of some verbal sophistication and learning, with a fondness for unusual Latin words like 'calibe' for steel and 'dudae' or duds for clothing, and much given to the citation of ancient or quasi-ancient authors in the prefaces to the books. For example, in the preface to the second part of grammar, on correct speech, the writer warns against speaking over much and cites one of the greatest authorities of the literature of secrets, Aristotle in *de Secretis Secretorum*, where in the discussion of kingship he commends brevity to Alexander. This is illustrated with a quotation from the work. In Book Three, on dialectic, as we have seen, the brief preface considers the way one distinguishes truth from falsehood. The author suggests that since this is more often done by the senses than by the rational faculty, it is important to consider the way they can be deceived, and again he supports this idea with a quotation from Aristotle, concluding the preface with the *ordinatio* formula we saw earlier: 'we will talk about the deception of the senses one at a time in order and first we go to the sense of taste'. Yet the first of the *distinctiones* on the senses immediately descends, like the one on writing, to a much more experiential level with a rubric 'how water has the taste and colour of wine' (f. 22v). The contrast of relatively philosophical introductions with the experiential and practical recipes, suggests that the author or compiler may have intended his work for several rather different audiences.

With some of these cautions about the work's internal contradictions in mind, let us consider then the compiler's discussion of the art of writing itself in Book One, *De Grammatica*. For it is here that we actually find the hermetic promise of the work's title fulfilled to a limited degree. Indeed, unlike other portions of the

SP, where the work descends from the abstract to concrete quickly, in the section on writing, we find an opposite movement, for the discussion invokes the kinds of books we have been led by the work's title to expect all along.

Rather than deal with the practical aspects of writing as we find them in some of the fourteenth- and fifteenth-century handwriting manuals, the *SP*'s treatment of writing is devoted to what the author calls 'altering' it for purposes of concealment and willful obscurity. Introduced by a general statement 'On Ways of Altering Writing', seven *distinctiones* touching on magic writing through ciphers[19] and chemicals follow.

The compiler writes in the tradition of high hermeticism when he discusses the purposes of these codes:

> The wisest sorts of men in various secret books alter their writing in order that their words may not be easily read or understood by all. An example is Alkmonute in his books, who treats the seven metals together with the seven names of the planets, calling gold the sun, silver the moon, iron Mars, quicksilver Mercury, tin Jupiter, copper Venus and lead Saturn. And they do this expressly when writing their books so that foolish people having access to these books cannot read the works of the wise and thus vilify the arts which are hidden in these books. And they obscured their books by different kinds of writing.[20]

As with the other prefaces mentioned earlier, the author supports his claims with an *auctor*, in this case an eponymic founder of alchemy, Alkmonute, who is often mentioned in medieval alchemical works and recipe collections of alchemical interest like those on metallurgy. For example, in a late fourteenth-century treatise on metallurgy and the tempering of steels written by an anonymous blacksmith in Nuremberg, we find the author actually fathering his work onto this figure, beginning it 'nv spricht meister alkaym',[21] as he suggests that the magic properties of ram's blood may be transferred to the piece of steel in question during the hardening process. And in Norton's poem *Ordinal of Alchemy*, the author says that this science

> Berith hir name bi a kinge
> Callid Alchymus with-owte lesynge;
> A glorious prince of moost noble mynde,
> His noble vertuys holpe him þis arte to find.
> He serchid nature, he was a noble clerke.[22]

Presumably the *SP*'s author alludes to the tract ascribed to Hermes, the *Secreta*, a work in seven 'books' showing correspondences between the seven metals and the planets. We expect then from our author some information on the occult wisdom or secrets possessed by the philosophers in the course of learning how they have concealed them. But again, as with the prefaces on grammar and dialectic, the leap from the theoretical to the utilitarian is a sudden one. 'Writing,' the compiler notes, 'can be altered in many different ways. One method by which to obscure it is through substituting consonants for the vowels and thus you write the word, giving the consonant which follows the vowel, as for example, write b when you mean a, and f when you mean e and so on, as is shown here: bmfn dkcp xpbks, that is to say, amen dico vobis.'[23] This safe and pious Christian phrase, then, replaces the magical names or theurgic phrases common in truly hermetic or magical works, though we might well expect a more daring phrase to illustrate concealment as an example of the words of Alkmonute and his kin.

The other methods of secret writing can either involve more elaborate substitution schemes, or the use of apparatus. For example, one system uses an ink made of dog gall and phosphorescent wood, which can only be read by night, and another describes a type of 'offset' writing which must be read backwards in a mirror. A last class of recipes in this section seems very far indeed from the pseudo-hermetic character of the work, as these discuss erasing writing from parchment, etching or 'writing' on steel with acid and marking on cloth with wax pencils.

As can quickly be seen, all of the forms of secret writing so far mentioned have relied on mechanical or chemical means rather than magical or theurgic ones. There is nothing in them which could offend the authority of church or state and no hint of dangerous texts which need to be concealed is offered.

Of all these recipes, the only one with a truly occult cast is a description of secret writing combined with the two main types mentioned earlier: a substitution alphabet cipher and a form of chemical writing. As this method promises its practitioner the safe *appearance* of magical knowledge, rather than the dangerous reality of its possession, it is worth examining in some detail. Forming the thirteenth recipe of Book One, *De Grammatica*, it is not privileged in any way over the others either by rubric or by Lombardic coloured initial and indeed is the first of two such recipes: 'Concerning letters which cannot be read except by dust' (f. 13v).

As both substitution alphabet ciphers and chemical writing of various types have already been discussed, this penultimate recipe calls upon the user's careful reading of the previous texts, without which it will make no sense. It differs, moreover, from the other recipes in its self-referential nature, as it shows the compiler hiding secret information by techniques given elsewhere in his book and so is of a level of sophistication considerably higher than what has come before.

The recipe describes a method of invisible writing using dust and urine. The compiler hides the second ingredient by one of the letter shift ciphers he had described earlier, in which each letter of the word in question is replaced by the previous letter of the alphabet.

> Take xskova and write with it on your hand and when it dries nothing will appear at all. When, however, you wish to read it, sprinkle upon the place you have written some ashes or some dust of some sort and rub just a little bit of dust upon the place and then remove the dust and immediately the letters will appear. By this same method you can play a fine prank when seated among your friends. You do it like this. Write in various places on your hand the word 'no' as described above, and let it dry and when you wish to jest, namely to know whether someone is a virgin, sprinkle the dust on the place on which you have written 'no' and then draw the figure of a cross on the dust, and taking care not to let yourself be seen doing it, carefully remove the dust and there will appear the letters of the word 'no' and many onlookers will consider this a magic art and brought about by the sign of the cross.[24]

This recipe must have had its users, as the neatly pen-boxed word 'urina' was carefully placed in the margin opposite the cipher by some later owner or reader of the book. Yet the recipe as an illustration of the sort of knowledge the wise philosophers hid from the vulgar seems a little anticlimactic.

Recipes like this one with its safely vague Christian theurgy remind us a bit of those involving ram's blood in the Nuremberg blacksmith's recipe collection mentioned earlier, or of Gottfried of Franconia, a Bavarian cleric wine-maker and master of orchards near Würzburg, who in his vernacular treatise *Der Pelzbuch*, *c.* 1350, also combined a learned interest in secrets literature and theurgic magic with practical recipes for gardening and grafting. Gottfried's work was translated into Middle English by his friend, an English Benedictine of Westminster named Nicholas Bollard, who also wrote his own treatise on planting and grafting, in which, at the opening, he appeals to the pseudo-Aristotelian *Secreta Secretorum* in a discussion of celestial influence on successful gardening,[25] while in his translation, published as *Godfridus super Palladium* he flirts with theurgy:

> To make that wrytynge or peynture shal ben sene in the corys of the appil. That in alle the kernellis of alle the peches that growyn vpon on tre may be wretyn or coloured what the lest, that the name of the same tre, as *persicus*, may ben wretyn in the kernellis. Putte the kernellis with the skalis in the erthe, & aftyr seuene dayes or mo, whanne the skalis begynne to open, thanne opene the kernells, & in the kernele writ with cinopre, or peynte a word or a marke, what thow wilt, & anon bynde hem togedere aȝen with here skalys, & dyligently berie hem in the erthe aȝen & let hem abyde there tyl they ben treis. In whiche treis, alle the kernellis that come therof shul haue the same sygne.[26]

Interestingly, this text also contains much on the deceptions of wine-sellers with techniques for avoiding them very like those given – without the mercantile emphasis – by the compiler of the *SP*. The quasi-theurgic recipes we have seen indicate a general trend among a certain group of late medieval readers to desire to seem to have the powers of magic without the actual spiritual dangers attendant on using it.

What can be said about the putative audience for a compilation like the *SP*? Though the majority of the work is easily accessible to the Latin reader, and the multitude of diagrams, especially for various processes involving geometry, hydraulics and vacuum, aids such a reader at many points, both writer and reader wish to belong to a group which has transcended difficulty to achieve enlightenment. That the writer is dealing with two different concepts of secrets, one learned and deriving from the eastern magus of Hellenistic antiquity, and the other popular and deriving from the received tradition of craftsmen, may in some ways have been responsible for the ambivalences of his text. Although he does not openly state this, the premise of his various prologues follows the eastern magus idea. He wishes to ally himself and his readers with those who intentionally hide their secrets from unworthy searchers. From antiquity onward, there was a standard set of reasons for why the 'wise' should do this. First was the natural desire of the intellectual to distance himself from the crowd to raise his own esteem. This was well stated by Roger Bacon in the *Opus Majus*, where he notes 'the wise have always been divided from the multitude, and they have veiled the secrets of wisdom not only from the world at large but also from the rank and file of those devoting themselves to philosophy. . . . Hence according to the view of Aristotle in his book of Secrets, and of his master, Socrates, the secrets of the sciences are not written on the skins of goats and sheep so that they may be discovered by the multitude.'[27]

Another equally compelling reason is more practical and is associated with guild protectionism all the way from the humblest artisan to the physician, lawyer and even the priest. Allowing the uninitiated or unworthy to gain access to secrets is undesirable, because ease of access would make the vulgar undervalue or even despise the possessor or practitioner of the wisdom in question and affect his livelihood.

Finally, we can point to a changing intellectual and social climate which provided a ready market for treatises like the *SP*. William Eamon has called attention to the 'proliferation of magical treatises in the thirteenth and fourteenth centuries' and has seen it related to the rise of an 'intellectual proletariat, a group composed of university educated laymen who had failed to find useful or permanent employment. . . . Angered by civil and ecclesiastical structures that denied them preferment, [they] may have been particularly attracted to new ideas. . . . Not only did learned magic give technology a theoretical matrix, it served an important ideological function by promoting the image of the professional engineer as a magus who, with his inventions, manipulates nature's occult forces and gains mastery over the physical world.'[28]

For such an audience the *SP*, with its occasional bows to hermetic authority combined with many practical recipes and diagrams illustrating arcane experimental and measuring procedures, offered a quick way to give the appearance of power and learning, and the chance to earn recognition as a magus by seeming to perform a magic trick with a Christian symbol illustrates the appeal of 'safe magic' to such a readership.

Notes

1 I am very grateful to Julia Boffey, Claire Fanger, Kristen Figg, Juris Lidaka, Lorraine Stock and my colleague Charles Wright for help and suggestions in the course of preparing this paper for publication.

2 On this sort of literature generally see Claudia Kren (ed.), *Medieval Science and Technology: A Selected Annotated Bibliography* (NY: Garland, 1985); William Eamon, *Studies in Medieval Fachliteratur*, Scripta Medieval and Renaissance Studies 6 (Brussels: Omirel, 1982); A. Zimmermann, *Methoden im Wissenschaft und Kunst des Mittelalters* (Berlin: de Gruyter, 1970); H. Roosen-Runge, 'Farben-und Malrezepte in frühmittalterlichen technologischen Handschriften' in E. Ploss, et al. (eds), *Alchimia: Ideologie und Technologie* (Munich: Moos, 1970); and William C. Crossgrove, 'The Forms of Medieval Technical Literature: Some Suggestions for Future Work', *Jarbuch für Internationale Germanistik* 3 (1971), pp. 13–21.

3 See on this work, Dorothea Waley Singer, *A Catalogue of Latin and Vernacular Alchemical Manuscripts in Great Britain and Ireland* (Brussels, M. Lamertin, 1928–31, vol. 2, item 1078, pp. 722–4 and Lynn Thorndike, *A History of Magic and Experimental Science* (NY: Columbia University Press, 1923), vol. 2, pp. 788–79 and 811–12.

4 A convenient list of manuscripts can be found in Rozelle P. Johnson, 'Notes on Some Manuscripts of the *Mappae Clavicula*', *Speculum* 10 (1935) especially Appendix, pp. 77–81.

5 See Richard Kieckhefer, *Magic in the Middle Ages* (Cambridge: Cambridge University Press, 1989), p. 91, and John B. Friedman (ed.), *John de Foxton's Liber Cosmographiae (1408): An Edition and Codicological Study* (Leiden: E.J. Brill, 1988), p. 121 for de Foxton's praise of the *Secretum*. On Betson, see J.E. Wells, *A Manual of the Writings in Middle English 1050–1500* (New Haven, CT: Connecticut Academy of Arts and Sciences, 1980), vol. 7, 'John Gower, Piers Plowman. Travel and Geographical Writings. Works of Religious and Philosophical Instruction', pp. 250–52, who dates the St John's College MS of Betson, *c.* 1500.

6 This is Lincoln Cathedral Chapter Library MS 226, late fourteenth century. See R.M. Thomson, *Catalogue of the Manuscripts of Lincoln Cathedral Chapter Library* (Woodbridge, Suffolk and Wolfeboro, NH: D.S. Brewer, 1989), p. 188. Oxford, Bodleian Library MS Rawlinson D. 1066, f. 25, ends 'explicunt secundum Aristotelem compilator' with a date of 1343.

7 The compilation is described by Montague Rhodes James, *The Western Manuscripts in the Library of Trinity College, Cambridge: A Descriptive Catalogue* (Cambridge University Press, 1901), vol. III, p. 58.

8 See Derek Britton, 'Manuscripts Associated with Kirby Bellars Priory', *Transactions of the Cambridge Bibliographical Society* 6 (1976), pp. 267–70 and 277–84.

9 This manuscript is also described by James, *Catalogue*, pp. 142–4; the rubric appears on f. 144v.

10 See Montague Rhodes James, *A Descriptive Catalogue of the Manuscripts in the Library of Gonville and Caius College* (Cambridge: Cambridge University Press, 1907–14), vol. II, pp. 484–6.

11 For Thompson, see Johnson, 'Notes on some Manuscripts'. A good introduction to the later forms of secrets literature appears in William Eamon, *Science and the Secrets of Nature. Books of Secrets in Medieval and Early Modern Culture* (Princeton, Princeton Univ. Press, 1994).

12 *SP*'s interest in deception was already the subject of a brief study by Bruno Roy, 'L'illusion comme art libéral. Interprétation du *Secretum Philosophorum* (XIIIe S)' in Marie Louise Ollier (ed.). *Masques et déguisements dans la littérature médiévale* (Montreal and Paris: Vrin, 1988), pp. 75–81, a piece not noted by Andrew Galloway, 'The Rhetoric of Riddling in Late-Medieval England: The "Oxford" Riddles, the *Secretum philosophorum*, and the Riddles in *Piers Plowman*', *Speculum* 70.1 (January, 1995), pp. 68–105. Though Galloway claims to be editing the *Secretum*, he also appears unacquainted with Singer's handlist of manuscripts or with Johnson's article cited above, and mentions only sixteen manuscripts, to which he adds Cambridge, St John's College MS 109, ff. 5r–6r and 9r–10r. These folios hardly qualify as 'one incomplete manuscript previously unidentified' (p. 70).

13 This is Oxford, Bodleian Library MS Rawlinson 1066. See Johnson, 'Notes on some Manuscripts', p. 80.

14 See Loris Sturlese and Ron B. Thomson (eds), *Petrus Peregrinus de Maricourt Opera Epistula de magnete* (Pisa: Scuola Normale Superiore Ufficio pubblicazioni classe di lettere, 1995).

15 See Cyril S. Smith and John G. Hawthorne (eds. and trans.), *Mappae Clavicula: A Little Key to the World of Medieval Techniques*, Transactions of the American Philosophical Society n.s. 64.4 (Philadelphia: American Philosophical Society, 1974), pp. 1–128.

16 'Iste liber quem prae manibus habemus vocatur Secretum Philosophorum, et intitulatur illo nomine quia in eo continentur quedam secreta que reputatione vulgari sunt impossibilia, apud philosophos secreta et necessaria. Continentur autem in isto libro quedam secreta diversim arcium verum quia sunt septem artes, scilicet grammatica, rhetorica, dialectica, arsmetrica, musica, geometrica et astronomia.' Cambridge, Trinity College MS 0.1.58, f. 1. All quotations from the *Secretum* will be drawn from this manuscript.

17 'grammatica docet recte scribere et recte loqui ex quo patet quod dividitur in duas partes, ideo de prima parte dicendum est scilicet de recta scriptura. Sunt autem multe cautelas circa scripturam que per pancis sunt note, scilicet quia nemo potest scribere sine debitis instrumentis' (f. 1).

18 Lynn Thorndike, 'Unde Versus', *Traditio* 11 (1955), pp. 163–93.

19 See on this subject, John B. Friedman, 'The Cipher Alphabet of John de Foxton's *Liber Cosmographiae*', *Scriptorium* 36 (1982), pp. 219–35.

20 Quia sapientes habentes quedam secreta in libris suis variant ita scripturam ut licet multi illos libros habeant non tamen sciunt legere nec intellegere verbi gratia Alkmonute in libris suis imponunt septem metalla, septem nomina planetarum, verba gratia aurum vocatur Sol, argentum Luna, ferrum Mars, argentum vivum Mercurius, stagnium Jupiter, cuprium Venus, plumbium Saturnus. Et ideo ita faciunt quia si expresse et distincte scriberent suos libros, tunc unus fatuus habens libros suos posset facere opus unius sapientissimi et sic vilificaretur ars quod est inconveniens obscurant super libros suos in modo scribendi, ff. 9v–10r.

21 The 'Meister Alkaym' recipe collection is edited by Hans-Peter Hils, 'Von dem herten: Reflexionen zu einem mittelalterlichen Eisenhärtungsrezept', *Sudhoffs Archiv* 69 (1985), pp. 62–75. This is Cod MS 3227A, Germanisches Nationalmuseum Nürnberg. The phrase in question appears in Hils, p. 62 and again p. 72. The collection is also discussed briefly in Eamon, *Science and the Secrets of Nature*, p. 86.

22 John Reidy (ed.), *Thomas Norton's Ordinal of Alchemy*, EETS: OS 272 (London: Oxford University Press, 1975), p. 18, II 469–74. In more mundane prose form, Thomas of Bologna wrote a letter to Bernard of Treves on the Philosopher's stone, tracing it to Alkmonute as a legendary founder. See Thorndike, *A History of Magic and Experimental Science*, III, p. 33.

23 Variantur autem scribendi modus multis modis. Uno modo per varietatem vocalem et hoc sic scribe per quilibet vocali litteram sequentem, verbi gratia per a scribe b, per e, f . . . sic deniceps ut patet hic bmfn dkcp xpbks, id est amen dico vobis, f. 10.

24 Accipe xskova et scribe cum ea super manum tuam et cum siccatum fuerit, nichil apparebit in mundo. Cum autem legere volueris, sperge super locum scriptum cineres vel pulverem aliquem et frica parum cum pulvere super locum et dele tunc pulverem et statim apparebit littera. Per illum autem modum potes optime jocari cum sedeas inter socios et hoc sic. Scribe in diversis locis super manum tuum, 'non', et fac siccare et si vis burdare dicendo te posse scire utrum sit virgo vel non, fac eum cum quo vis burdare scilicet sciendo utrum sit virgo, spergere pulverem super locum super quem scribitur 'non' et figure crucem in pulverem et hoc ne percipiatur cautela post depone pulverem, et apparebit ibi scriptum 'non', putabitur autem illud a multis fieri per artem magicam et hoc propter signum crucis, f. 13.

25 See on these two compilers, Gerhard Eis (ed.), *Gottfried's Pelzbuch*, Südosteuropäische Arbeiten 38 (Brünn: Rudolph M. Roherer, 1944); Willy Louis Braekman (ed.), *Geoffrey of Franconia's Book of Trees and Wine* (Brussels: Omirel UFSAL, 1989), p. 30, for the appeal to the *Secreta Secretorum*, and David G. Cylkowski (ed.), 'A Middle English Treatise on Horticulture' in Lister Matheson (ed.), *Popular and Practical Science of Medieval England*, (East Lansing, MI: Colleagues Press, 1994).

26 Cylkowski (ed.), 'A Middle English Treatise', p. 311.

27 Roger Bacon, *Opus Majus*, trans. Robert Belle Burke (New York: Russell and Russell, 1962), vol. I, pp. 11–12.

28 Eamon, *Science and the Secrets of Nature*, p. 69.

4

A Fragmentary German Divination Device: Medieval Analogues and Pseudo-Lullian Tradition

Elizabeth I. Wade

Fifteenth-century Germany produced a large number of manuscripts containing magic texts.[1] One common kind of magical text was the divination device, a text sometimes accompanied by images which was used to foretell the future. The device discussed here appears in Cod. Guelf. 75.10 Aug. 2° in the Herzog August Bibliothek Wolfenbüttel.[2] Though fragmentary, this device (figures 1 and 2) appears to have relied on the randomization and combination of letters of the alphabet as the means of arriving at answers to questions about the future.

It has been suggested by Johannes Bolte that fortune-telling devices of this type would primarily have been employed as entertainment in social settings.[3] The device in Cod. Guelf. 75.10 Aug. 2° would certainly have made an appealing party game and, in addition, the device resonates thematically with the other literary texts in the codex, which may well have served as social entertainment. Yet if this device does not inhabit the codicological environment of the kinds of intellectual magic outlined by Klaassen in this volume, it nonetheless does appear to have appealed primarily to a literate audience, whose more serious tastes possibly also comprised other types of occult writings. I will argue here that there is a need to examine even such apparently innocuous amusements as the fortune-telling device in Cod. Guelf. 75.10 Aug. 2° in the broader context of the traditions of intellectual magic, which were developing in the same period.

Beginning in the thirteenth century, Jewish mystical writings and Arabic scientific and philosophical works became increasingly available among learned Europeans. Magical texts from these traditions played an important role in the development and spread of divination texts in the Middle Ages.[4] The investigation of the elements that make up the device in Cod. Guelf. 75.10 Aug. 2° will take us from the desk of a fifteenth-century scribe living in the Swabian city of Augburg back a century and a half to an important cultural crossroads in the western Mediterranean. In form and function, this device shows a number of interesting similiarities to traditions of Jewish and Arabic magic put to use by

Ramon Lull; and Lull's work in turn provides insight into the principles which may have informed the conception of this device and the composition of its key. Consideration of the device's antecedents not only gives further insight into reasons for its inclusion in the manuscript, but also reveals the device's deeper ties to the European traditions of learned magic.

THE FRAGMENTARY DIVINATION DEVICE IN COD. GUELF. 75.10 AUG. 2°

Upon opening this large paper codex bound in vellum over beechwood boards, the divination device is the first item seen. Part of the device is embedded in the inside front cover of the manuscript. Here, a paper circle is set into a depression about eleven centimeters in diameter.[5] Inscribed upon this surface is a circularly arranged alphabet of twenty-three hand-coloured capital letters (figure 1). 'A' is blue and at the 12 o'clock position; the remainder of the alphabet runs clockwise just inside the circle's edge, alternating pink (B, D, F, etc.) and blue (C, E, G, etc.); Z is red. The small hole in the center of the paper circle was probably made by the point of a compass.

Figure 1. Divination device. Herzog August Bibliothek Wolfenbüttel: Cod. Guelf. 75.10 Aug. 2°, VD.

The second part of the device is a key for the letter 'A' found on the facing leaf which presents twenty-three letter pairs and a brief interpretation for each pair (figure 2). The letters to be deciphered are capitals coloured in blue, pink, red, green and black. The first letter of all the pairs in the key is 'A'; the second letter is another of the twenty-three letters of the alphabet. The pairs are listed alphabetically according to the second letter. A transcription and translation of the key to this article appears in the appendix.

The manuscript contains four other texts: adaptations by Heinrich Steinhöwel of the tales of King Apollonius and of Griseldis, Niklas von Wyle's translation of the story of Guiscardus and Sigismunda, and Johann von Tepl's dialogue between Death and the plowman.[6] Each text treats the vulnerability of humanity to the blows of fortune, and each appeared separately or in other associations before 1468, the year given in the manuscript as the date of their copying. Fortuna and the manner in which humanity copes with her vagaries is treated in the stories of Griseldis, a peasant girl plucked from humble surroundings by a nobleman who marries her and then tests her by putting her to a series of brutal trials; of Apollonius, a young prince tried by shipwrecks and separation from his wife and daughter; and of Sigismunda, a young widow who defies her father by choosing a lover from among his courtiers and proudly faces the punishment she receives. In Johann von Tepl's dialogue *Der Ackermann und der Tod*, a Bohemian farmer challenges capricious Death to a debate. The context of these four works in Cod. Guelf. 75.10 Aug. 2° sharply focuses attention on the theme of fortune's influence, and permits us to see the divination device, the first item in the sequence of texts, as a rubric for the entire manuscript.

Of course, the image of Fortune's wheel had been a favourite literary and artistic image since antiquity. Boethius's descriptions of Fortune in his *Consolation of Philosophy* assured the survival of the image in the Middle Ages, where it was described and depicted in numerous texts and works of art.[7] The fifteenth century in particular saw a renewed interest in Fortune and a concurrent revival of Boethius' work. These two phenomena, the survival of the classical image of Fortune, and a later revival of that image via Boethius and his many medieval readers, informed the design and illustration of a number of late-medieval German manuscripts containing divination devices.[8]

LOT CASTING AND CIRCULAR DIVINATION DEVICES IN ANTIQUITY AND THE MIDDLE AGES

Ursula Hess describes the circular device on the inside front cover of Cod. Guelf. 75.10 Aug. 2° as a 'Buchstabenorakel' or 'alphabet oracle'.[9] 'Losbuch' or 'lot book' is a general term for German divinatory texts dating from at least the thirteenth century. Ancient even in classical times, divinatory practices such as the drawing of lots[10] survived among Christian Europeans in the late Middle Ages and into the seventeenth century.[11]

Figure 2. Key to divination device. Herzog August Bibliothek Wolfenbüttel: Cod. Guelf. 75.10 Aug 2°, 1r.

A large number of manuscripts containing an array of divinatory techniques attests to the widespread knowledge of divination in fifteenth-century Germany.[12] Death personified mockingly mentions eleven kinds of divination in the twenty-sixth chapter of *Der Ackermann und der Tod* (1401).[13] Half a century after Johann von Tepl's dialogue, collections and translations of a variety of mantic writings attest an interest in divinatory practices in southern Germany.[14] In 1456 Johannes Hartlieb, a prominent physician at the court in Munich, completed his *Pŭch aller verpoten kunst*, a polemic against the use of divinatory methods and devices which happens to describe them in great detail.[15] Divination and other magical practices were widespread enough in Germany at mid-century so as to occasion Church inquiry. Leuwis de Rickel (1402–71), also known as Dionysius the Carthusian, conducted an investigation of 'the magical and superstitious practices in vogue' and recorded his findings in *Contra vitia superstitionum*, while on a trip through Germany with the papal legate Nicholas of Cusa (1401–64).[16]

Richard Kieckhefer has noted that popular forms of divination in the fifteenth century 'required active operation of the person foretelling the future' and describes these divinatory techniques as 'experimental'.[17] One such type of German lot book (cgm 312 is an example) employed a complex series of dice throws to guide an inquirer through a series of texts which eventually led to a sought-for answer.[18] Other divinatory techniques found in fifteenth-century German lot books included geomancy and cartomancy – the interpretation of an arrangement of dots and of selected cards.[19]

Johannes Bolte divided German lot books into three categories according to the spirit in which users employed these devices. Some lot books were designed to meet the needs of earnest enquirers, some were meant as entertainment in social settings, and others were characterized by a moralizing bent.[20] Devices in the first category resembled sortilegia in that they employed a series of questions to determine a final prognostication. Devices belonging to the second group used moveable wheels with pointers, dice, or playing cards to arrive at a prediction. The third category included lot books whose oracular utterances tended to moralize. As I have already noted, Bolte placed lot books such as the one in Cod. Guelf. 75.10 Aug. 2° into the second category (the category of party games) because they seemed to call for some action on the part of the enquirer.

The inclusion of moveable disks in some divination devices points not only to a desire to amuse revelers by having them take turns in spinning a disk or other object to discover their fortunes, but also to a fascination with the symbolism of the wheel or circle, an image integral to depictions of Fortune in the Middle Ages. As discussed above, Cod. Guelf. 75.10 Aug. 2° contains four texts in addition to the divination device. The circular divination device in Cod. Guelf. 75.10 Aug. 2° seems to echo the theme of Fortuna present in each of the texts. But is Fortuna's ever-turning wheel the sole inspiration for our divination device?

A discussion of the symbolic use of the circle or wheel in ancient and medieval religion and culture is too vast to be attempted here. We shall therefore concentrate upon magical associations of circles and alphabets in texts. Lynn Thorndike describes one such instance in his discussion of the 'Spheres of Life and Death', a means of divination used in antiquity to discern the fate of the ill which survived into the early Middle Ages.[21] This is his description:

> The so-called 'Sphere' was really only a wheel of fortune, circle, or other plane figure divided into compartments where different numbers are grouped under such headings as 'Life' and 'Death'. Having calculated the value of a person's name by adding together the Greek numerals represented by its component letters, and having further added in the day of the moon, one divides the sum by some given divisor and looks for the quotient in the compartments.[22]

Apparently, the 'Spheres of Life and Death' also made use of a kind of numerology that associated letters with numerical values. Similarly, one aspect of the Kabbalah as it developed in the later Middle Ages, more specifically the practice of gematria, offered students of Jewish sacred texts an elaborate interpretative and contemplative method based on numerology. This method involved calculating the value of words and rearranging letters to see numerically equivalent, but other, profound meanings in words, sentences and texts. Gershom Scholem's study of the historical development of the Kabbalah suggests both an influence of Arab neo-Platonism, as well as the Christian Platonic tradition.[23]

The Middle Ages also witnessed the translation of Arabic texts into Latin and an introduction of Arabic methods of divination into European culture. A comparison of some types of Arabic divination has revealed indebtedness to Greek forms.[24] Charles Burnett observes that the 'earliest translations from Arabic are in the fields of divination, astrology, and those parts of mathematics which prepare the student for these subjects, such as geometry and astronomy'.[25] One work in particular, the *Liber Alchandrei*, includes circular diagrams associated with astrological information and 'number-letter equivalents used in making astrological judgements'.[26] One Arabic writer, Ibn Khaldūn, mentions the use of numbers for the construction of the 'za'iraja', a kind of magic circle associated with letters and numbers.[27] Yet another example of an Arabic form of divination which employs circles is the so-called 'King's Lottery'. This particular method, which is tantalizingly similar to those in some German divination devices, made use of a series of questions, several rolls of dice, and a number of sets of circles to arrive at a prognostication.[28]

Some of the writings by the mid-twelfth-century thinker Bernard Silvestris include works on geomancy and astrology. Geomancy originated in the East and was systematized by Arabic compilers. One of the better known books about geomancy, the *Liber Alfadhol*, is said to date from the ninth-century caliphate of Harun ar-Rashid.[29] This type of divination device came to Europe through contact with the Islamic civilization on the Iberian peninsula, as well as through the work of such twelfth-century translators as Gerard of Cremona and Michael Scot.[30] The astrological and geomantic writings of Bernard Silvestris, especially his *Experimentarius*, were often copied with other kinds of divination devices.[31] Especially noteworthy is the technique ascribed to a 'King Amalricus',

> in memory of that monarch's victory over the Saracens and Turks in Egypt, [which] obtains its key number by revolution of a wheel rather than by the geomantic casting of points, and introduces a trifle more of astrological observance.[32]

One manuscript containing this work (Digby 46) is described by Thorndike as having 'two interlocking wooden cogwheels' which are 'inset inside the thick cover'.[33] Apparently the inside front cover of some manuscripts provided the ideal place for the inclusion of moveable divinatory tools.

The Lullian and Pseudo-Lullian Traditions

The three traditions discussed above, the ancient and Arabic forms of divination and the Jewish Kabbalah, appear to find particular, and, for this investigation, relevant focus in the writings of the Catalan mystic Ramon Lull (1232–1316). Lull's work was described by Pico della Mirandola in the late fifteenth century as an 'ars combinandi', the 'scientia quam ego uoco Alphabetarium revolutionem'.[34] Pico was comparing, according to Moshe Idel, a 'certain brand of Kabbalah, whose main subject is the combination of the letters of the alphabet' to the visual elements in the work of Ramon Lull.

Lull believed that the 'Art' was revealed to him in a mountain-top vision and that its ultimate purpose was to convert the followers of Islam to Christianity. According to Mark D. Johnston, Lull viewed the 'conception of his Art as a programme of theological demonstration alternative to Aristotelian Logic, and basis for redefining Scholastic methods of argumentation'.[35] Lull's art sought to understand the universe through analogy and the apprehension of patterns in creation. Thus his seminal ideas were often depicted visually in the form of diagrams, figures and tables. His art employed rotating circles and diagrams to arrive at combinations of terms. Martin Gardner describes Lull's art as the 'practice of using letters to stand for certain words and phrases so that arguments can be condensed to almost algebraic form'.[36] Lull believed one could formulate and answer any question in any area of human knowledge using his system of notation and combination. Frances Yates has examined Lull's thought and finds that his system effected a synthesis of the so-called Divine Attributes (a neo-Platonic concept) and John Scotus Erigena's 'elementalism', which saw the interrelationship of the qualities of the four elements of fire, air, water and earth as determinants of 'the essential pattern underlying the physical world'.[37]

The similarities in form between Lull's figures and the descriptions of Arabic divination techniques give rise to the question of a possible relationship between them. Lull was born on the island of Majorca in the Western Mediterranean and spent most of his life in the nearby regions of Catalonia, Aragon and Valencia in southern Spain, and Provence and other areas of southern France, as well as in Paris and a short time in Bougie in North Africa.[38] This area was a cultural crossroads influenced by the Islamic states to the west and south and by the French kingdoms to the north. Expansive trade thrived in the area and contributed to the prosperity of Majorcan merchants.[39] Contact with Arab civilization through proximity and trade very likely facilitated the oral and textual exchange of ideas. Lull lived after the era of the great early translators from Arabic to Latin and had the advantage of their work. Moreover, Lull's strong desire to proselytize among the Muslims of North Africa spurred him on to learn Arabic. Later in life Lull urged the church to establish Arabic language schools for Christian missionaries.[40] While Lull mentions only one Arabic author in the course of his almost three hundred works (the logician al-Ghazzali), it is quite possible that he also knew the books of geomantic divination discussed earlier.

As mentioned above, the idea of interpreting letter combinations was also characteristic of gematria, which experienced a particularly fruitful period of study in the thirteenth and fourteenth centuries in the western Mediterranean. According to Gershom Scholem, one of the earliest mystical texts upon which Kabbalists relied, the *Sefer Yezirah* ('Book of Creation') presented 'the world process' as 'essentially a linguistic one, based on the unlimited combinations of the letters. . . . The combination of these basic letters contains the roots of all things and also the contrast between good and evil'.[41] The *Sefer Yezirah* may have been written as early as the sixth century.[42] Similar Kabbalistic works and commentaries on the *Sefer Yezirah* were written in twelfth- and thirteenth-century Germany, France, and later in Spain.[43] The Kabbalistic works of Abraham Abulafia and those of his student Joseph Gikatilla advocated the contemplation of letter combinations as a way to ecstasy and prophecy that is inspired prediction.[44]

Lull's unfamiliar arrangements of letters and shapes put to complicated use in his art apparently puzzled and intrigued those who saw them. He wrote the *Ars brevis* in order to simplify the complex system introduced in earlier works such as the *Ars magna* and, as one writer notes, 'of course, what made it look so alarming was the number and complication of the figures, as well as the letter symbolism'.[45] Apparently the visual component of Lull's art impressed his contemporaries greatly. Gardner writes,

> In Lull's time these circles were made of parchment or metal and painted vivid colours to distinguish different subdivisions of terms. There is no doubt that the use of such strange, multicoloured devices threw an impressive aura of mystery around Lull's teachings that greatly intrigued men of little learning,

anxious to find a short-cut method of mastering the intricacies of scholasticism.[46]

Lull was, in his time and long after his death, a controversial figure. The universities were wary of the method in his 'art' and the church held some of his beliefs in suspicion. His writings may have acquired yet a greater aura of mystery, not to mention notoriety, after having been criticized by the Dominicans and condemned by the church in the late fourteenth century.[47]

A comparison of the circular portion of the device in Cod. Guelf. 75.10 Aug. 2° and one of Lull's 'figures' yields a number of striking similarities. Both the device and Lull's 'A' figure from the *Ars brevis* (figure 3) are circular and are inscribed with the alphabet or portions of it on their circumferences; both the device and the figure make use of colour and possibly of moveable inner circles or parts. The compass prick found on the device in Cod. Guelf. 75.10 Aug. 2° may very likely have served to anchor a pointer or even an inner concentric wheel.

Lynn Thorndike's work and, more recently, Michela Pereira's study have shown that there is a large corpus of works attributed to Lull that surfaced after his death.[48] Lull's writings seem to have inspired others to imitate his style of writing and to use his art in the areas not extensively treated by Lull, such as alchemy, magic and astrology. F. Sherwood Taylor remarks that 'the Lullian works are distinguished by numbers of tables in which the principles, material and operations of alchemy are symbolized by letters of the alphabet and various processes indicated by further combinations of these letters'.[49] Pereira agrees with Yates's view that Lull's 'art' was a unique kind of memory system and finds that the pseudo-Lullian alchemical texts also sought to use Lullian 'figures and alphabets . . . presented as devices for the memorization of the alchemical opus'.[50]

The employment of Lull's art in the area of alchemy indicates a change in the use of his complex figures and tables, a change that may figure in an understanding of the divination device in Cod. Guelf. 75.10 Aug. 2°. Lull himself saw his 'art' as a means of comprehending the whole of creation, its foundation in the Divine Attributes and in its various combinations of elements.[51] After Lull's death others found it only a short step from using his 'art' for demonstrative purposes to applying it prescriptively to alchemy. On the physical level, alchemists attempted to understand and carry out changes in materials by submitting them to intricate procedures. On another level, experiments were conducted in the belief that the controlled manipulation and combination of elements affected forces on a higher plane. An illustration from a fifteenth-century manuscript of 'Lullian Treatises' associates Lull's alphabetical notation with the materials and processes of alchemy (figure 4). The adoption of Lull's art by alchemists imbued it with possibilities for magical application.

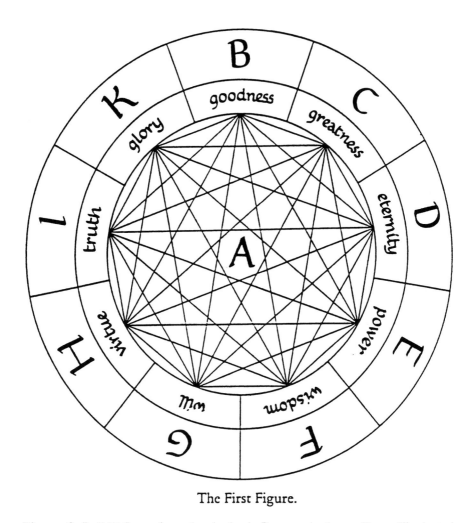

The First Figure.

Figure 3. Lull 'A' figure from the *Ars brevis*. Bonner, Anthony, *'Doctor Illuminatus'. A Ramon Llull Reader.* Copyright © 1993 by Princeton University Press.

A radical example of this line of development appears after the time of our manuscript, that is in the sixteenth century. Giordano Bruno in his work *De umbris idearum* (1582) presents versions of Lullian circular figures in a full-blown Hermetic context, one of which Yates has reconstructed and included in her book, *The Art of Memory* (plate 110). Yates assesses Bruno's accomplishment in the *De umbris idearum* in the following manner:

Bruno's brilliant achievement in finding a way of combining the classical art of memory with Lullism thus rested on an extreme 'occultising' of both the classical art and of Lullism. He put the images of the classical art on the Lullian combinatory wheels, but the images were magic images and the wheels were conjuring wheels.[52]

For Bruno, the figures he created could bring him into contact with higher forces. Such a system which encompassed all areas of knowledge and restored to humanity its once-perfect memory thus conferred power upon its user. Perhaps somewhere here lies the space for the application of what Yates called 'memory wheels' on the one hand and 'conjuring wheels' on the other to the purpose of prognostication.

By the fifteenth century, then, the circle had become a powerful image replete with a range of meaning. Boethius' revival of the figure of Lady Fortuna and her wheel underscored the circle's significance as a symbol of cyclical change and a reminder of humanity's defenselessness in the face of fortune. The translation of Arabic pseudo-scientific and divinatory texts used the circle as an instrument in predicting the future. Kabbalistic writers contemplated letter combinations. The writings of Ramon Lull presented creation as the sum of infinite combinations of the elements expressed visually by a notational system of letters placed upon revolving concentric circles. Lull's system inspired later alchemists and magicians like Bruno to see magical potential in Lull's arrangements of shapes, letters and colours. The device in Cod. Guelf. 75.10 Aug. 2° appears to have an interesting affinity with Arabic divination devices and, more recently, Lullian circular diagrams indebted perhaps to Kabbalistic letter mysticism put to a quasi-magical use.

KONRAD BOLLSTATTER AND THE KEY TO COD. GUELF. 75.10 AUG. 2°

The second element of our device is a key, which was used to decipher letter pairs arrived at by employment of the circle in some manner. Keys similar to the one in Cod. Guelf. 75.10 Aug. 2° appear in two other fifteenth-century manuscripts, ÖNB 145 and BSB cgm 312 (figures 5 and 6).[53] Cod. Guelf. 75.10 Aug. 2° contains the most detailed key of the three and is the only one which deciphers letter pairs. The two other keys bear more resemblance to one another than to the key in Cod. Guelf 75.10 Aug. 2° in that they both present explanations for each letter of the alphabet, but not for letter pairs. Neither key seems to have been accompanied by any figure, as in the case of the Wolfenbüttel codex. The most likely source of inspiration for divination keys of this kind, as we have seen above in the discussion of the 'King's Lottery' and the technique ascribed to 'King Amalricus', is the variety of Arabic geomancies. Such divination devices relied on a series of text sets which were navigated by a certain number of dice

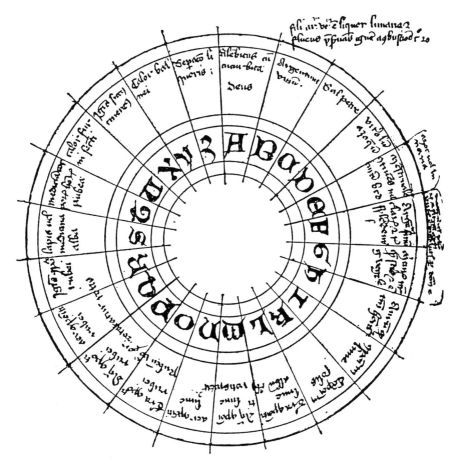

Figure 4. 'Tables of letters and materials of the Art, from a fifteenth-century manuscript of the Lullian Treatises' (Courtesy of Mr. D. I. Duveen). From F. Sherwood Taylor, *The Alchemists. Founders of Modern Chemistry* (New York: Henry Schuman, 1949) p. 112.

throws. Karin Schneider's description of how the devices in cgm 312 were used explains the method.

> As is the case for other texts in the literature of fortune-telling, very precise rules apply for the use of the lotbook. Bollstatter placed these rules ahead of the text itself in a kind of user's guide (f. 120r); using these rules one can still today arrive at an oracle for most of the questions, which have, for the most

part, remained quite relevant. In order to play the divination game, one needs only a pair of dice in addition to the lot book.[54]

In the catalogue of the collection of German manuscripts in the Bavarian State Library, Schneider reports that cgm 312 contains works, including divination devices, copied by a scribe named Konrad Bollstatter.[55] Konrad Bollstatter was also the scribe who, in 1468, completed the manuscript known as Cod. Guelf. 75.10 Aug. 2°. Bollstatter was a Swabian scribe active in his profession from about 1450 to 1482. He lived in Augsburg during the time when the first printers in that city established themselves. Bollstatter's scribal œuvre included not only Early New High German prose fiction such as the texts in Cod. Guelf. 75.10 Aug. 2°, but also a number of divination devices.

The 'alphabet oracle' in the Wolfenbütteler Bollstatter manuscript is incomplete, yet its key resembles the one on the leaf copied by another hand in cgm 312, the manuscript containing Bollstatter's other divination devices. There is, however, enough of the fragment to permit speculation on its appearance in a complete state and how the device as a whole would have been used. My previous study of this device posited the following as a sequence for the employment of the device. One asked a question. The existence of letter pairs necessitated a way of associating two letters. Dice were thrown to determine how to move a pointer and a smaller, inner circle inscribed with letters. Where one chanced to stop, the pointer and the inner wheel placed one letter on the inner wheel in proximity to a letter on the fixed outer wheel – thus yielding two letters. The interpretation of the resulting combination was sought in the key. The first four interpretations for pairs beginning with the letter 'A' found in the key to Cod. Guelf. 75.10 Aug. 2° are: 'A in A means luck and a happy life / A in B means leadership or leadership of the people / A in C means shyness in matters of the heart / A in D means disfavor of a ruler.'[56] This scenario assumes that the device made use of the entire alphabet for the construction of pairs, not just the letter 'A'. As seen above, Lull's circular 'A' figure connects an 'A' in the middle of a circle (which stood for God) with nine letters inscribed upon it. Such a figure yielded a pairing of letters, each of which would begin with an 'A'. If Lullian figures constituted any guide or inspiration, it is possible that since the key presents only interpretations for pairs beginning with 'A', Cod. Guelf. 75.10 Aug. 2° simply had a pointer with the letter 'A' on it affixed to the circle's center. In this case the device would, in its present state, lack only such a pointer and not additional pages in the key.

CONCLUSION

The fifteenth century witnessed a survival and transmission of older divinatory techniques, as well as a reception and adaptation of Lullian images. The circular divination device in Cod. Guelf. 75.10 Aug. 2° bears witness to the processes of

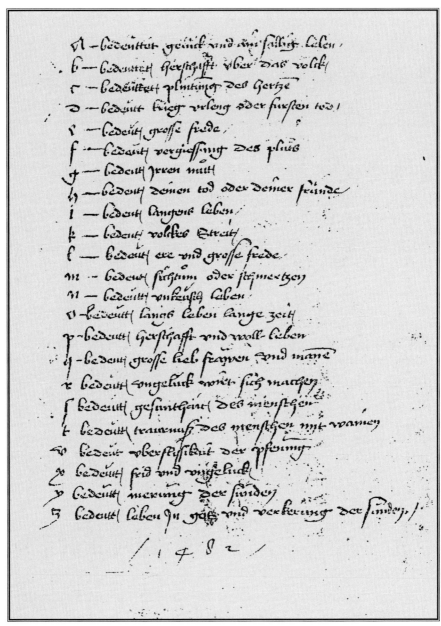

Figure 5. The alphabet key from cgm 312 f. 154v. Courtesy of the Bayerische Staatsbibliothek München.

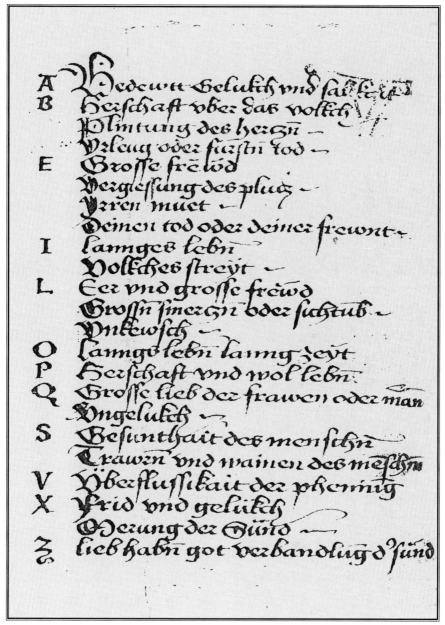

Figure 6. The alphabet key from Cod. 145 (Hübl 209) f. 322v. Courtesy of the Österreichische Nationalbibliothek–Schottenstift.

preservation and recycling in the late Middle Ages. There may yet be more substantial connections to be discovered between Konrad Bollstatter's interest in copying and collecting divination devices and the reception of Lull in mid-fifteenth-century Germany. One of Bollstatter's contemporaries was the bishop and philosopher Nicholas of Cusa, who collected manuscripts containing Lull's works at a time when the Church discouraged discussion of Lull.[57] Toward the end of his life Bollstatter produced an adaptation of Sigmund Meisterlin's *Augsburger Stadtchronik* (cgm 213), which relates the great effect the preaching of Nicholas of Cusa exerted upon the people of Augsburg. Nicholas of Cusa was a thinker of wide-ranging interests. The symbolism of games and the possibility of using them to explore what can be known fascinated him.[58] His work, *De ludo globi* (1463), examined a game based partially on the movements of a ball upon a set of concentric circles.[59] A deeper connection between Bollstatter and Nicholas of Cusa remains, of course, only tantalizing conjecture. Yet the fascination with games, divination and epistemology, which characterizes some of the writing of this period, seems to call for more attention.

In examining each of the components of the fragmentary device in Cod. Guelf. 75.10 Aug. 2°, I have ventured beyond Fortuna symbolism as inspiration for this particular kind of fortune-telling mechanism and tried to place this type of divination device both within the older traditions of Arabic divination and mysticism of the Kabbalah and within the later Lullian and pseudo-Lullian traditions. Clearly the connections between such divination devices and the larger context of occult thinking that surrounded them are many and varied. It is clear that more investigation into the background of the different types of magical practice of the period, particularly with respect to the occult philosophy developing at the same time, is needed. As I have tried to show, the questions that can be put to a divination device such as the one in Cod. Guelf. 75.10 Aug. 2° are more complex and interesting than Bolte's category of 'party games' might seem to allow.

Notes

1 Sotzmann in 'Die Loosbücher des Mittelalters', *Serapeum* 20 (1851), p. 307–8 noticed numerous lot books in fifteenth-century manuscripts during the course of his studies, '. . . so leuchtet ein, dass das XV. Jahrhundert reich an solchen Büchern gewesen sein muss, und wirklich giebt es fast keine Hauptbibliothek in Deutschland, welche nicht eine oder mehrere Handschriften dieser Art aufzuweisen hätte.' [. . . so it becomes clear that the fifteenth century must have been rich in such books and really there is almost no major library in Germany which would not have one or more manuscripts of this kind to present.] All translations appearing in brackets are my own.

2 Ursula Hess describes the manuscript in detail in *Heinrich Steinhöwels 'Griseldis.' Studien zur Text-und Überlieferungsgeschichte einer frühhumanistischen Prosanovelle*, Münchener Texte und Untersuchungen zur deutschen Literatur des Mittelalters 43 (München: C.H. Beck'sche Verlagsbuchhandlung, 1975), pp. 41–3.

3 Johannes Bolte, 'Geschichte der Losbücher', *Georg Wickrams Werke*, vol. 4 (*Losbuch. Von der Trunkenheit, Der Irreitende Pilger*), edited by Johannes Bolte (Tübingen: Litterarischer Verein Stuttgart, 1903), pp. 309–42.

4 Marie-Thérèse d'Alverny presents a thorough overview of this topic in 'Translations and Translators', *Renaissance and Renewal in the Twelfth Century*, edited by Robert L. Benson and Giles Constable, with Carol D. Lanham, Medieval Academy Reprints for Teaching 26 (Toronto/Buffalo/London: University of Toronto Press, 1991), pp. 423–62. The influence of Arabic and Jewish cultures upon the development of European magical practices is discussed in detail by Richard Kieckhefer, *Magic in the Middle Ages*, Cambridge Medieval Textbooks (Cambridge: Cambridge University Press, 1989), pp. 116–50.

5 I am grateful to Professor A.E. Tietjen-Wright for examining the manuscript and for transcribing f. 1r during a visit to Wolfenbüttel, Germany. Thanks are also due Professor Tom Kilton for obtaining a microfilm of the manuscript from the Herzog August Bibliothek in Wolfenbüttel.

6 The Apollonius matter probably dates from the fifth or sixth century AD. See G.A.A. Kortekaas, '*Historia Apollonii Regis Tyri.*' *Prolegomena, Text Edition of Two Principle Latin Recensions, Bibliography, Indices and Appendices* (Groningen: Bouma's Boekhuis, 1984), pp. 116–21. On Steinhöwel's adaptation of the Apollonius tale, see Elizabeth I. Wade, 'History and Fortuna in Heinrich Steinhöwel's *Appolonius*', diss., University of Illinois at Urbana-Champaign, 1995. The Griseldis tale first appeared in Boccaccio's *Decameron*, but Steinhöwel based his redaction on Petrarch's epistolary casting of the material. See Ursula Hess, *Heinrich Steinhöwels 'Griseldis'*. 'Gwiskard und Sigismunda' appeared as Niklas von Wyle's second 'Translatze' in 1463; Wyle used Leonardo Bruni Aretino's tale as his *Vorlage*, although Boccaccio had also included a redaction in the *Decameron*. See *Translationen von Niclas von Wyle*, edited by Adelbert von Keller (Stuttgart: Litterarischer Verein Stuttgart, 1861), p. 79. Johann von Tepl's *Ackermann aus Böhmen*, dates from about 1400 and appeared in numerous South German manuscripts. See *Der Ackermann aus Böhmen*, edited by Günther Jungbluth, Germanistische Bibliothek, vierte Reihe, *Texte* (Heidelberg: Carl Winter Universitätsverlag, 1969).

7 David M. Robinson, 'The Wheel of Fortune', *Classical Philology* XLI (Jan.–Oct. 1946), p. 207. Also, Jerold C. Frakes, *The Fate of Fortune in the Early Middle Ages. The Boethian Tradition*, Studien und Texte zur Geistesgeschichte des Mittelalters 23 (Leiden: E.J. Brill, 1988) and Ann W. Astell, *Job, Boethius and Epic Truth* (Ithaca: Cornell University Press, 1994); Alfred Doren, 'Fortuna im Mittelalter und in der Renaissance', *Vorträge der Bibliothek Warburg (1922–1923) Part 1*, edited by Fritz Saxl, repr. (Nendeln/Liechtenstein: Kraus Reprint Limited, 1967), pp. 71–144.

8 One outstanding example is the collection of lot books in cgm 312. Karin Schneider produced a partial facsimile edition of cgm 312 in *Ein Losbuch Konrad Bollstatters aus CGM 312 der Bayerischen Staatsbibliothek München*, (Wiesbaden: Dr Ludwig Reichert Verlag, 1973) and a transcription of the manuscript in *Ein Losbuch Konrad Bollstatters aus CGM 312 der Bayerischen Staatsbibliothek München. Transkription* (Wiesbaden: Dr Ludwig Reichert Verlag, 1976). For a discussion of the wheels of fortune in the manuscript, see Irmgard Meiners, 'Rota Fortunae. Mitteilungen aus cgm 312', *Beiträge zur Geschichte der deutschen Sprache und Literatur* 94 (1972), pp. 399–414. Michael Schelling examines Fortune's wheel in image and text in 'Rota Fortunae. Beziehungen zwischen Bild und Text in mittelalterlichen Handschriften', *Deutsche Literatur des späten Mittelalters. Hamburger Colloquium 1973*, edited by Wolfgang Harms and L. Peter Johnson, Publications of the Institute of Germanic Studies,

University of London, vol. 22 (Berlin: Erich Schmidt Verlag, 1975), pp. 293–313. Schelling also discusses the presence of rotae fortunae in lot books in general and includes cgm 312 among many examples.

9 Hess, '*Griseldis*', p. 42.

10 One such technique was 'cleromancy', or divination by lots. See Robert Flaccliere, *Greek Oracles*, trans. Douglas Garman (London: Elek Books, 1965) p. 4.

11 Boehm, in his entry 'Losbücher' in the *Handwörterbuch des Deutschen Aberglaubens*, edited by E. Hoffmann-Krayer and Hanns Bächtold-Stäubli, vol. 5 (Berlin and Leipzig: Walter de Gruyter, 1932–3), col. 1,387–8, points out the church's often ambivalent position regarding divination. Despite the church's official position against divination of all kinds, the interpretation of lots was in some cases left to a priest in the belief that a Christian reading was preferable to a pagan or heretical one. Valerie I. J. Flint examines church attitudes and policies toward divination and other forms of magic in *The Rise of Magic in Early Medieval Europe* (Princeton: Princeton University Press, 1992), pp. 87–126. She discerns a remarkable degree of acceptance of some forms of divination in the early medieval church. See also W.L. Braekman, 'Fortune-Telling by the Casting of Dice. A Middle English Poem and Its Background', *Studia Neuphilologica* 52 (1980), p. 3; and Keith Thomas, *Religion and the Decline of Magic* (New York: Charles Scribner's Sons, 1971) pp. 121–4 and 237–44.

12 Johannes Bolte, 'Geschichte', pp. 309–42.

13 '*Geomancia* mit der satzunge der planeten vnd des himelsreifes zeichen auf erden allerlei frage behende verantwurterin; *Pyromancia*, sleuniges vnd warhaftiges warsagens aus dem fewer wurkerin; *Ydromancia*, in wassers gewurke der zukunftigkeit entwerferin; *Astrologia* mit oberlendischen sachen irdisches laufes auslegerin; *Chiromancia*, nach der hende vnd nach des teners kreisen hubsche warsagerin; *Nigromancia*, mit toten opferfinger vnd mit sigel der geiste gewaltige twingerin; *Notenkunst* mit iren hubschen gebeten, mit irem starken besweren; *Augur*, der vogelkoses vernehmer vnd daraus zukunftiger sachen warhafter zusager; *Aruspex*, nach altaropfers rauche in zukunft tuende ausrichtung; *Pedomancia* mit kindergedirme vnd *Ornomancia* mit auerhennen dermig luplerin . . .' [*Geomancy*, the answerer of all kinds of questions posed on earth with the help of the examination of the planets and the zodiac; *pyromancy*, the conjurer of quick and true fortune-telling by fire; *hydromancy*, the revealer of the future by movements in water; *astrology*, the interpreter of earthly events through heavenly things; *cheiromancy*, the pretty reader of hands and the lines on the palm; *nigromancy*, the powerful conjurer of spirits through the fingers of the dead and talismans; *ars notoria*, the Notory Art, with her fine prayers and powerful oaths; *augury*, the soothsayer who tells the future by understanding the speech of birds; *haruspicia*, seeing the future through the smoke of sacrificial altars; *pedomancy*, which using childrens' entrails, and *ornomancy*, which using cock's entrails lays clear the future.] Johannes von Tepl, *Der Ackermann und der Tod. Text und Übertragung*, translation, notes and afterword by Felix Genzmer, bibliography by Wolfgang Mieder (Stuttgart: Philipp Reclam, 1984), pp. 48, 50. The italics are my own. Often the distinction between the 'natural sciences' and what we would call the 'pseudo-sciences' was unclear. This list of divinatory practices is sandwiched between a description of the insufficiencies of the seven liberal arts (with philosophy appended) and of law. The last four practices are Roman and probably found few practitioners in the Middle Ages.

14 Frank Fürbeth has recently re-evaluated the work of Johannes Hartlieb (d. 1468) in *Johannes Hartlieb. Untersuchungen zu Leben und Werk* (Tübingen: Max Niemeyer Verlag, 1992). Fürbeth concludes

that mantic writings previously ascribed to Hartlieb were most likely part of his manuscript collection and not products of his own hand.

15 *Die Kunst Chiromantia des Dr Hartlieb. Ein Blockbuch aus den Siebziger Jahren des 15. Jahrhunderts*, edited by Ernst Weil (München, 1923). *Johann Hartliebs Buch aller verbotenen Kunst*, edited by Dora Ulm (Halle, 1914). Fürbeth ascribes authorship of this work to Johannes Hartlieb. The formulaic self-references present in the work find corroboration in contemporary court documents. (*Johannes Hartlieb*, p. 85.)

16 Lynn Thorndike, *A History of Magical and Experimental Science*, vols 3 and 4, (New York: Columbia University, 1934), p. 294.

17 Kieckhefer, *Magic in the Middle Ages*, p. 88.

18 'Sortes', an early and common type of divination in the Middle Ages, required the participation of the inquirer. Use of 'sortes' involved opening a book, often the Bible, and applying a randomly selected text to a question posed beforehand. An elaborate example of a 'sortilegium,' the 'Sortes Sangallenses' (sixth or seventh century) made use of a succession of dice throws to lead an inquirer through sets of texts. According to Valerie Flint, the 'Sortes Sangallenses' addressed 'every conceivable source of human anxiety requiring a difficult or worrying decision', a feature of many types of divination devices. Flint, *Rise of Magic*, pp. 220–23 and A. Dold and R. Meister, 'Die Orakelsprüche im St. Galler Palimpsestkodex 908 (die sogenannten "Sortes Sangallenses")' *Österreichische Akademie der Wissenschaften. Philosophisch-historische Klasse Sitzungsbericht 225, Abhandlung 4* (Vienna, 1948), pp. 1–115. See also Boehme, 'Losbücher', *Handwörterbuch des deutschen Aberglaubens*, vol. 5, col. 1390. 'Die Berge. . . . Die namen der zwölf vogel. . . .Die namen der zwölf tyre . . .' [The mountains. . . . The names of the twelve birds. . . . The names of the twelve animals . . .]. There are twelve sets of texts in this device. Schneider, *Ein Losbuch Konrad Bollstatters aus CGM 312 der bayerischen Staatsbibliothek München. Transcription*, pp. 145–8.

19 Bolte, 'Geschichte', pp. 309–39.

20 Bolte, 'Geschichte', pp. 310–11.

21 Thorndike, *A History of Magic and Experimental Science*, vol. 1, pp. 682–4.

22 Thorndike, *A History of Magic and Experimental Science*, vol. 1, p. 683.

23 Gershom Scholem, *Kabbalah*, The New York Times Library of Jewish Knowledge, The Jewish Publication Society of America (New York: Quadrangle/*The New York Times* and Jerusalem: Keter Publishing House Jerusalem Ltd, 1974), p. 48. Scholem suggests John Scotus Erigena's *De Divisione Naturae* as a possible source of Christian neo-Platonic influences in medieval Kabbalah.

24 Bächtold-Stäubli, *Handwörterbuch des deutschen Aberglaubens*, vol. 5, 1,394–5.

25 Charles Burnett, 'The Translating Activity in Medieval Spain' in *The Legacy of Muslim Spain*, edited by S. K. Jayyusi (Leiden: E.J. Brill, 1992), p. 1,038.

26 The earliest manuscript of the *Liber Alchandrei* dates from the late tenth century. Burnett, 'Translating Activity in Medieval Spain,' p. 1,040.

27 Burnett, 'Translating Activity in Medieval Spain,' p. 1,040.

28 Bächtold-Stäubli, *Handwörterbuch des deutschen Aberglaubens*, vol. 5, 1394.

29 Gerhard Eis, 'Einleitung', *Wahrsagetexte des späten Mittelalters aus Handschriften und Inkunablen*, edited by Gerhard Eis, Texte des späten Mittelalters 1 (Berlin: Erich Schmidt Verlag, 1956), p. 7 and Bolte, 'Geschichte', p. 288.

30 Lynn Thorndike, *A History of Magic and Experimental Science*, vol. 2, p. 120.

31 Thorndike, *A History of Magic and Experimental Science*, vol. 2, p. 115.

32 Thorndike, *A History of Magic and Experimental Science*, vol. 2, p. 116.

33 Thorndike, *A History of Magic and Experimental Science*, vol. 2, p. 116 and n. 1.

34 Moshe Idel, 'Ramon Lull and the Ecstatic Kabbalah. A Preliminary Observation,' *Journal of the Warburg and Courtauld Institutes* 51 (1988), p. 170. Idel examines the similarities between Lull's 'ars combinatoria' and, using Pico, *Opera Omnia* (Basle, 1582) 180, as a guide, the writings of Kabbalists, such as Abraham Abulafia (1240 after 1292). He concedes that, although these similarities 'cannot stand as definitive evidence of the sources of Lull's theories', he proposes that the Kabbalah influenced 'the technical aspect of his thought' (p. 174).

35 Mark D. Johnston, *The Spiritual Logic of Ramon Llull* (Oxford: Clarendon Press, 1987), p. 2.

36 Martin Gardner, *Logic Machines and Diagrams*, 2nd ed. (Chicago: The University of Chicago Press, 1982), p. 5.

37 Frances A. Yates, *Lull & Bruno*, Collected Essays Volume I (London: Routledge & Kegan Paul, 1982), pp. 78, 81.

38 *'Doctor Illuminatus.' A Ramon Llull Reader*, ed. and trans. Anthony Bonner (Princeton: Princeton University Press, 1985), pp. 9–23.

39 Bonner, *'Doctor Illuminatus'*, p. 6.

40 Bonner, *'Doctor Illuminatus'*, pp. 13, 16.

41 Scholem, *Kabbalah*, pp. 25–6.

42 'Concerning the original and spiritual home of this work, which numbers only a few pages, divergent opinions have been voiced, although to date it has been impossible to come to any reliable and definitive conclusions. This uncertainty is also reflected in the various estimates of the date of its composition, which fluctuate between the second and the sixth centuries.' Gershom Scholem, *Origins of the Kabbalah*, edited by R. J. Zwi Werblowsky, translated from the German by Allan Arkush, The Jewish Publication Society (Princeton: Princeton University Press, 1987), pp. 24–5.

43 Scholem, *Origins*, pp. 34–5.

44 Scholem, *Kabbalah*, pp. 53–4, 180.

45 Bonner, 'Introduction to the *Ars brevis*', *'Doctor Illuminatus'*, p. 291.

46 Gardner, *Logic Machines and Diagrams*, p. 10.

47 Anthony Bonner, 'Introduction', *Selected Works of Ramon Llull (1232–1316)*, ed. and trans. Anthony Bonner, vol. 1 (Princeton: Princeton University Press, 1984), pp. 71–2.

48 Lynn Thorndike, *A History of Magic and Experimental Science*, vols 3 and 4, pp. 619–52 and Michela Pereira, *The Alchemical Corpus Attributed to Raymond Lull*, Warburg Institute Surveys and Texts XVIII (London: The Warburg Institute University of London, 1989), p. 1.

49 F. Sherwood Taylor, *The Alchemists. Founders of Modern Chemistry* (New York: Henry Schuman, 1949), p. 111.

50 Pereira, *Alchemical Corpus*, p. 7.

51 Frances A. Yates, *The Art of Memory* (Chicago: The Unversity of Chicago Press, 1966), p. 178.

52 Yates, *The Art of Memory*, p. 211.

53 Albertus Hübl, *Catalogus codicorum manu scriptorum qui in bibliotheca monasterii B.M.V. ad Scotos Vindobonae servantur* (Vienna: Braumüller, 1899), p. 209. Karin Schneider, *Die deutschen Handschriften der Bayerischen Staatsbibliothek Munchen. CGM 201–350, Catalogus Codicum Manu Scriptorum Bibliothecae Regiae*

Monacensis, vol. 5, part 2 (Wiesbaden: Otto Harrassowitz, 1970), p. 301. My thanks again to Professor Tom Kilton for obtaining copies of these leaves.

54 'Für die Benutzung des Losbuches gelten, wie für andere derartige Texte der Wahrsageliteratur, ganz bestimmte Regeln. Bollstatter hatte diese Spielregeln in einer Art von Gebrauchsanweisung dem eigentlichen Text vorangestellt (Bl. 120r); demnach kann man sich auch heute noch aus dem Losbuch einen Orakelspruch auf eine der meist durchaus aktuell gebliebenen Fragen holen. Man benötigt zu dem Wahrsagespiel außer dem Losbuch nichts als zwei Würfel.' Karin Schneider, *Ein Losbuch Konrad Bollstatters aus CGM 312 der Bayerischen Staatsbibliothek München*, p. 55.

55 *Die deutschen Handschriften der Bayerischen Staatsbibliothek München. CGM 201–350*, p. 301.

56 'A yn A bedeüt glück vnd ain seligs leben / A yn B betüt herrschaft des volcks / A yn C bedeüt plödigkait des herzen / A yn D bedeutt ain mißhellung ains fürsten.'

57 Yates, *Lull & Bruno*, p. 118.

58 Pauline Moffit-Watts, *Nicolaus Cusanus. A Fifteenth-Century Vision of Man*, Studies in the History of Christian Thought XXX (Leiden: E. J. Brill, 1982), pp. 189–223.

59 *Vom Globusspiel. De Ludo Globi*, translated, with an introduction and notes by Gerda von Bredow, Schriften des Nikolaus von Cues, Heft 13, Die Philosophische Bibliothek, Band 233 (Hamburg: Felix Meiner, 1952).

APPENDIX 1

Divination Device in Cod. Guelf. 75.10 Aug. 2°, 1r

Transcription

A yn A bedeútt glúck vnd ain seligs leben.

A in B betüt herrschafft oder herschung des volcks.

A in C bedeüt plödigkaitt des hertzen.

A in D bedeútt ain mißhellung ains fúrsten.

A in E bedeütt fróde der eren vnd gůt wollust.

A in F beteütt außgießung des plůts.

A in G bedeütt herschung des gemüts.

A in H beteútt ain todt sine oder seiner fründ.

A in J beteutt langes leben ains menschen.

A in K beteutt künfftig streytt des volks.

A in L betüt Gross künfftig Ere der lütt.

A in M betüt wetragen oder traurigkait.

A in N beteutt andacht des gemüts.

Translation

A in A means luck and a happy life.

A in B means power or rule of the people.

A in C means shyness of the heart.

A in D means misunderstanding of ruler.

A in E means joy of honour and good pleasure.

A in F means spilling of blood.

A in G means self-control.

A in H means your own death or that of a friend.

A in J means long life of a person.

A in K means future strife among the people.

A in L means great future honour by others.

A in M means sorrow or sadness.

A in N means a devout mind.

A in O bedeutt frölich Syngen vnd Leben.	A in O means joyous singing and life.
A in P betütt frid vnd ain seliges leben.	A in P means peace and a happy life.
A in Q betútt lang leben der frawen oder man.	A in Q means long life of woman or man.
A in R bedeütt uil grosses vnglúck.	A in R means much great misfortune.
A in S beteütt gesunthait des leybes.	A in S means health of the body.
A in T bedeutt traurigkait mit klagen.	A in T means sadness with grieving.
A in U beteútt úberflússigkait des gŭts.	A in U means abundance of goods.
A in X beteütt frid vnd gŭts gelúcke.	A in X means peace and good luck.
A in Y beteútt zükunfftige liebin.	A in Y means future love.
A in Z beteutt vngunst der herren.	A in Z means disfavour of a ruler.

APPENDIX 2

Alphabet Key in BSB cgm 312 f. 154v

Transcription	**Translation**
A – bedeüttet gelück vnd ain sallig leben.	A – means luck and a happy life.
B – bedeüttet herschafft vber das volck.	B – means rule of the people.
C – bedeüttet plintung des herzen.	C – means blindness of the heart.
D – bedeütt krieg vrleng oder fursten tod.	D – means war or death of a ruler.
E – bedeütt grosse freude.	E – means great joy.
F – bedeütt vergießung des pluots.	F – means spilling of blood.
G – bedeütt irren muott.	G – means madness.
H – bedeütt deinen tod oder deiner fründe.	H – means your death or the death of your friends.
I – bedeütt langens leben.	I – means a long life.
K – bedeütt volckesstreitt.	K – means strife among the people.
L – bedeütt ere vnd grosse freude.	L – means honour and great joy.
M – bedeütt sichtuom oder schmertzen.	M – means sickness or pain.
N – bedeütt vnkeusch leben.	N – means unchaste life.
O – bedeütt langs leben lange zeitt.	O – means long life for a long time.
P – bedeütt herschaft vnd woll-leben.	P – means rulership and a good life.
Q – bedeütt grosse lieb frauwen vnd mans.	Q – means great love from women and men.
R – bedeütt vngelück und siech machen.	R – means bad luck and sickness.
S – bedeütt gesundhait des menschen.	S – means good health of a person.
T – bedeütt trawenuß des menschen mit wainen.	T – means sadness of a person with weeping.
U – bedeütt vberflussikait der pfennig.	U – means abundance of money.
X – bedeütt frid vnd gelück.	X – means peace and happiness.

Y – bedeütt merung der sünden.

Y – means increase of sins.

Z – bedeütt leben in got vnd verkerung der sünden.

Z – means a godly life and a reversal of sins.

Reference: Karin Schneider, *Die deutschen Handschriften der Bayerischen Staatsbibliothek München. Cgm 201–350. Neu beschrieben von Karin Schneider. Catalogus codicum manu scriptorum Bibliothecae Monacensis*, tomus V, editio altera, pars II, codices germanicos 201–350 complectens (Wiesbaden: Otto Harrassowitz, 1970), p. 301.

APPENDIX 3

Key in ÖNB cod. 145 (A. Hübl 209) f. 322vb

Transcription

A – Bedeutt Geluckh vnd salikait.

B – Herschaft vber das volkch.
Plintung des herczen.
Vrleng oder fursten tod.

E – Grosse frewd.
Vergißung des plutz.
Irren muet.
Deinen tod oder deines frewnt.

I – Langes lebn.
Volckhes streyt.

L – Eer vnd grosse frewd.
Grossen smerczen oder sichtuß.
Vnkeusch.

O – Lannges lebn lanng zeyt.

P – Herschaft vnd wolleben.

Q – Grosse lieb der frawen oder man.
Vngeluckh.

S – Gesunthait des menschen.
Trawren vnd wainen des menschen.

V – Überflussikait der pfenning.

X – Frid vnd gelückh.
Merung der Sünd.

Z – lieb haben got verbandlung der sünd.

Translation

A – means luck and happiness.

B – power over the people.
blindness of the heart.
war or death of a noble.

E – great joy.
spilling of blood.
madness.
your death or that of a friend.

I – long life.
strife among the people.

L – honour and great joy.
great pain or illness.
unchasteness.

O – long life a long time.

P – power and a good life.

Q – great love by women or men.
misfortune.

S – health.
sadness and weeping of a person.

V – abundance of money.

X – peace and happiness.
increase of sins.

Z – love of God, restraint of sins.

Reference: Albertus Hübl, *Catalogus codicorum manu scriptorum qui in bibliotheca monasterii B.M.V. ad Scotos Vindobonae servantur* (Vienna: Braumüller, 1899), pp. 225–30.

5

VISUAL ART IN TWO MANUSCRIPTS
OF THE ARS NOTORIA[1]

Michael Camille

The images in the two manuscripts that I shall examine in this paper pertain to the widely condemned ritual practice called the Ars Notoria. According to the following account in the *Grandes Chroniques de France*, one version of this was deemed so dangerous that it was burnt.

> And in this same year [1323], there was a monk of Morigny, an abbey near Étampes, who through his curiosity and pride wanted to inspire and renew a condemned heresy and sorcery called in Latin Ars Notoria, although he hoped to give it another name and title. This science teaches the making of figures and designs, and they must be different from one another and each assigned to a different branch of learning. Also, they must be contemplated at particular times with fasting and prayers. And so, after contemplation, the branch of knowledge which one wants to have and acquire through this act of contemplation is bestowed. But one had to name and invoke various little known names, which were firmly believed to be the names of demons. Hence this science disappointed many and many were deceived by it. For nobody using this science had ever gained any benefit or received any fruit. Nonetheless, this monk condemned this science, even though he feigned that the blessed virgin Mary had appeared to him many times, thereby inspiring him with knowledge. And so in her honour he had had many images painted in his book, with many prayers and letters, very richly in expensive colours, feigning that the virgin Mary had revealed everything to him. After these images had been applied to each branch of learning and contemplated, once the prayers had been said, the branch of learning one was seeking would be bestowed. . . . And . . . the said book was justly condemned in Paris as false and evil, against the Christian faith, and condemned to be burned and put in the fire.[2]

For the historian of magic this often-quoted passage raises a number of important issues that are explored in other essays in this volume, such as the relation between the art revived by the monk of Morigny (whom we now know was named John) and the complex variants of the Ars Notoria.[3] For the art historian interested in the relationship between art and magic it suggests a number of broader questions about the importance and function of images in this long neglected type of text. According to the Chronicle account, the images to be included in this version of the Ars Notoria are described as being executed by a trained artist 'in expensive colours'. Whether or not John the monk made these pictures himself remains an open question.[4] What is clear, however, from the Chronicle reference, is that images were extremely important to the practice of the Ars Notoria, both in the old Solomonic version of the art, and in the new version composed by John the monk. Further, with reference to the old art, it is suggested that these images 'must be different from one another' in a way that does not pertain to the usual medieval aesthetic category of *varietas*. The variety of shapes and signs here served a specifically magical purpose. The 1323 condemnation is one of a number of sorcery trials that took place during the early fourteenth century that have been linked to the rise of the 'persecuting society' and the church's increasing hostility to magic.[5] But as Klaassen suggests in his essay in this volume, the type of ritual magic presented in the Ars Notoria seems to have been more widespread than has hitherto been supposed, and appears to have been deemed less dangerous than other forms of magic in this period.[6] This was in part because of its association with orthodox learning, but also, as I shall argue here, because those who developed it were building on a long tradition of using images to communicate complex forms of knowledge. Throughout the Middle Ages the visual and magical arts were intimately intertwined. For example, the instructions contained in the painters' recipe books and technical treatises are closely related to alchemical texts.[7] However, the arts which we are dealing with in the Ars Notoria are not 'fine arts' but the traditional seven liberal arts.

The term 'Notory Art' will make many medievalists think of the marvellously varied personal signs made with the pen that notaries used in the later Middle Ages to authenticate their documents. They might also confuse it with Salatiele's *Ars Notarie*, a treatise on legal shorthand published in a fine 1961 edition.[8] That there are no modern editions of the Ars Notoria is not surprising, considering how enigmatically constructed the *notae* appear to be in the numerous and as yet unpublished manuscript collections. In this short essay I will deal neither with historical origins nor textual questions; I seek rather to understand the Notory Art in the context of medieval visual art and *as* a visual art. Lynn Thorndike, in a chapter in the *History of Magic and Experimental Science* called 'Solomon and the Ars Notoria', describes this text as containing geometric figures and characters thought to have been revealed in a dream by an angel to King Solomon, who was reputed during the Middle Ages to be the wisest of all men and a magician, and to whom was granted *sapientia, scientia et intelligentia*.[9] This immediately places the work in an intellectual and highly literate milieu. Marie Thérèse d'Alverny traced the roots of the Ars Notoria to monastic contexts in the twelfth century and argued that it was linked to the 'sacred names established in the Judeo-

Alexandrine milieu and the *ephesia grammata*, a sequence of vocables unintelligible to mere mortals but which put the magician in contact with mysterious forces'.[10] However it was during the thirteenth-century revival of learned magic, inspired by the influx of translations from the Arabic, that the Ars Notoria began to gain in popularity, along with the newly available Aristotelian and pseudo-Aristotelian works of Greek and Arabic philosophy and the Hermetic Books.[11]

From the beginning of the thirteenth century, those who criticized magic often made reference to its inherently visual nature. For example, William of Auvergne, Bishop of Paris, in his diatribe against various forms of learned magic complained that there was no divinity in 'the angles of Solomon's pentagon' and that the 'rings and seals of Solomon' were a form of idolatry involving execrable consecrations and detestable invocations and images. 'As for that horrible image called the *Idea Salomonis et entocta*,' the bishop went on, 'let it never be mentioned among Christians.'[12] Roger Bacon thought all such books should be 'prohibited by law' and in his *Opus Tertium* of 1267 he named the Ars Notoria.[13] Though not mentioned in the list of illicit magical texts in Albert the Great's *Speculum Astronomiae*, in the chapters on 'the science of images' dealing with engraved astrological signs, he does describe a 'somewhat less unsuitable but nevertheless detestable' use of images 'which is effected by means of inscribing characters'.[14] This suggests that there were clearly many other arguably magical contexts in which figures or characters could be a site of contention. Albert is probably referring here to the production of talismans and amulets under certain planetary influences, a common and widespread way in which image-making and magic converged, but was not describing the Notory Art proper.[15]

With a few powerful exceptions like the pioneer iconographers Aby Warburg and Fritz Saxl, as well as Otto Kurz and Ernst Kris, and a few scholars of the ancient world like A.A. Barb and W. Deonna, art historians have been hesitant to approach the magic of the image.[16] Recent interest in the power of images has begun to address phenomena such as fascination and sympathetic magic, but this research has also tended to functionalize the instrumentality of the object, divorcing the aesthetic from the magical.[17] The Ars Notoria is just one of a number of case studies I want to make of how magic and image-making are inextricably linked and how the nascent notion of art was linked both to forbidden forms of knowledge as well as licit practices in this period. This study can only be preliminary, but of the dozen manuscripts of the Ars Notoria that I have examined in Paris, London, and elsewhere, I have chosen to focus on two here that are not only visual but pictorial. By this I mean that they not only make special use of signs as part of their magical language, but in addition contain figurative elements that help structure the presentation of those signs. They are, in addition, both works by trained artists, as described in the condemnation in the *Grandes Chroniques*. Neither mention Solomon, but they are both examples of the Ars Notoria which utilize complex sets of figures in relation to magical prayers. According to Lynn Thorndike, 'Other works of notory art are listed in manuscript catalogues without name of author. But all alike are apt to impress the present reader as unmeaning jumbles of diagrams and magic words.'[18] Though 'difference' and incomprehensibility are in fact part of their intended effect, I would argue that the complex visual configurations drawn in these manuscripts are less jumbled than this description suggests, and that like all images they are dependent upon earlier models. By examining their sources and divergence from other types of manuscript illustration, art historical methods can help to clarify key issues in the still exploratory history of medieval magic as a system of representation.

Turin, Biblioteca Nazionale MS E.V. 13 (not known to Thorndike) is described as *Notae arte liberalium* and on f. 1, in a later fourteenth-century hand, someone has written Ars Notoria (figure 1). Only slightly water-damaged by the disastrous fire that destroyed so much in the library earlier this century, the codex contains thirty-two folios.[19] The diagrams or schemata called *notae* in the accompanying inscriptions are the work of two distinct illustrators, both North Italian in my view, the second one being a particularly fine draughtsman.[20] They begin on the very first folio under the rubric 'Hec est prima nota grammatice facultatis, sancta et iusta et bona et visa' (figure 1). This opening page of the manuscript presents what looks at first like a very traditional diagrammatic image. The four evangelist symbols in the corners support their traditional Latin tags, and the crucifixion in the centre is highly standardized. The evangelist symbols had been put to magical use since the early Middle Ages, and here they surround long incantatory lists of names, some transliterated from Greek and Hebrew: 'Elym ratam zamaam . . .'.[21] These words are in the tradition of cryptic alphabets known as *ephesia grammatica*, a distortion of *aphasia grammatica*, that is, 'unutterable letters', which are a feature of the amuletic tradition.[22] It looks like a conscious ploy on the part of the designers of this book to have the first and most visible opening seem pictorially so conventional. Concentric circles or *rotae* of this type are commonly used in diagrams of everything from the stars to the attributes of God. In one of the diagrams in the early fourteenth-century English *Psalter of Robert de Lisle*, the four evangelists are placed in the corners, as was customary.[23] The *rota* was a means of organizing material in a diagrammatic way, but other common means were geometrical squares, often used in logic texts, and the ubiquitous trees, or *arbores*. Diagrams are often found in treatises on the liberal arts, and as this manuscript presents itself as a treatise on the liberal arts it is significant that the maker of this manuscript uses diagrammatic techniques in the traditional mode of providing access to rational and ordered learning, but it does so in a very untraditional and ultimately irrational or magical way.[24]

In Robert Turner's 1657 English translation of the Solomonic Art we read, 'Oh almighty God . . . illustrate my mind with the beams of thy holy spirit, that I may be able to come and attain to the perfection of this most holy art . . . that I

Figure 1. Ars Notoria: the first *nota* of grammar. Turin, Biblioteca Nazionale MS E.V.13, f. 1.

might be able to gain the knowledge of every science, art and wisdom and of every faculty of memory, intelligence, understanding and intellect'.[25] The Ars Notoria was in fact well named, being inextricably linked to the conventional notion of *ars* and the seven liberal arts that had structured medieval education from the time of Boethius. It involved the reception of an already inherited and revealed set of visual signs or *notae* that functioned as a meditative and diagrammatic link between the operator and the celestial powers who delivered the knowledge. Whereas much medieval magic involving the inscribing of images or signs and the rituals surrounding them were spells or charms for the usual humdrum list of human needs – love, health and harming one's enemies – the Notory Art was used for a far more elevated purpose than 'to keep bugs out of the house'. Its aim was nothing less than to provide its user with knowledge of all the mechanical and liberal arts in as short a time as possible. Learning the liberal arts in the Middle Ages was a process of arduous and painful education beginning from the childhood stutterings of grammar to the exercises of astronomical calculation twenty years later. The sequence that the arts follow in the Turin manuscript is traditional, beginning with the three language arts of the trivium and continuing to the quadrivial arts. The association of the arts with visual aids or diagrams was not new, and can be seen in the German vernacular treatise *Die Walscher Gast*, where the seven liberal arts are each shown engaged with a material sign, an object (such as the oppositional squares of logic or the Boethian diagrams of music) which was associated with the learning of the art.[26]

The rest of the schemata in the Turin manuscript, however, do not in any way represent the traditional organizing modes of diagrammatic depiction, using neither wheels (*rotae*) nor trees (*arbores*). Nor do they represent religious signs or symbols of the standard type. Indeed the word *figura* (which is the standard term to designate a diagram in Latin texts) is not used to label them; these *notae* are distinguished from the geometric squares of opposition and the trees of Porphyry used in grammatical treatises (and in the whole tradition of iconography associated with the seven liberal arts) precisely in their refusal to be diagrams.[27] They are rather anti-diagrams in the sense that the diagram was used in medieval culture to stratify and inculcate verbal concepts and ideas in an easily memorizable, spatial way.

They are also closely linked to another crucial art of the period – the art of memory. As Michael D. Swartz notes with reference to the social context of the Hebrew Sar-Torah texts in his magisterial study *Scholastic Magic*, 'Considering the importance of memory in both the value system and social structure of ancient Jewish society, we should not be surprised to see magical practices designed for the acquisition of memory'.[28] Although memory can use 'dissimilar figures' or shocking and ugly figures as Mary Carruthers has shown,[29] these strange shapes and striking signs are powerful precisely because of their incomprehensibility. That they are also called *artes memorative* in many manuscripts (for example in the

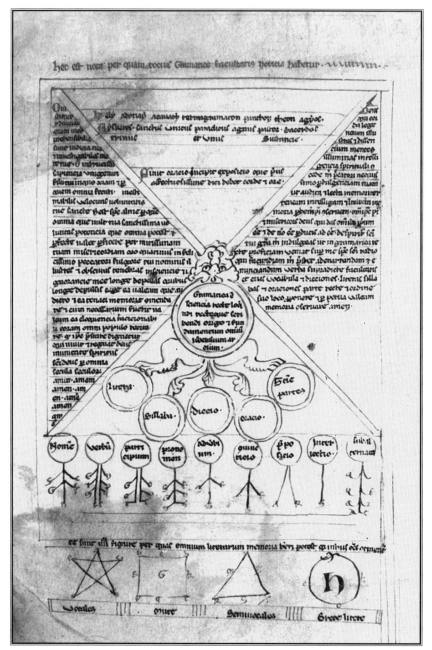

Figure 2. Ars Notoria: the *nota* by which the whole faculty of grammar can be had. Turin, Biblioteca Nazionale MS E.V. 13, f. 6.

second manuscript dealt with here, Paris BN lat. 9336, f. 17v) places these manuscripts in this important tradition of the art of memory. This is underlined in a Cracow manuscript which has a rubric directly describing the link: 'Item vocatur ars memorativa, quia in profundo orationis eius adhibetur memoria.'[30] But if they functioned properly, these images did not need to be memorized in the traditional way, since their magical effect linked the operator directly to the celestial powers responsible for the enhancement of memory.

We can see how this was meant to work by looking at the first of three figures which are *notae* of the art of grammar on f. 6, which opens with the rubric 'Hec est nota per quam totius grammatice facultatis noticia habetur' (figure 2). Divided diagonally by ribbons emerging from the head of a centrally placed beast, the five parts of speech are listed in circles below and nine other grammatical concepts, each with a distinct termination below these. Words are linked with basic geometrical shapes as in the four signs at the bottom of the page, the first, *vocales*, being a five-pointed star.

Grammar, as the first and most elementary of the trivial arts, comes first in the manuscript, as it does in contemporary collections of texts on the liberal arts, such as the one made for Francesco Carracioli, chancellor of the University of Paris, in 1310.[31] The first extant initial in the volume introducing Cicero's *De constructione* on f. 94r is somewhat damaged, but provides us with at least one powerful if conventional image of medieval grammar which makes a good comparison with the Turin page (figure 3). Within the ornate 'Q', it introduces, in visualized form, the 'parts of the sentence' described in the very first sentence here: 'Quoniam in arte expositis libris de partibus orationis.' A female personification of grammar, swathed in blue robes and looking not unlike contemporary representations of the Virgin Mary, holds, like a royal sceptre across her lap, a branch displaying the 'parts of speech'; she points at its stem, *oratio*, meaning 'sentence'. This rod is an extension of grammar's usual attribute, a sometimes heavy club or stick with which she beats her recalcitrant pupils. Touched in viridian green to emphasize the organic metaphor of these 'branches' of learning, the centre of seven buds or petals has been left bare by the illuminator and then filled by a scribe with ornate red capitals, spelling out in much abbreviated form the division discussed in the text below. To the right (from the viewpoint of 'Grammar' herself), the tree branches off into 'congrua', or 'congruous sentences', which can be either 'simplex' or 'composita'. On the left, the branch leads to 'incongrua', or 'incongruous sentences', which can be either 'barbaris' or something else, now unreadable, but which was probably 'inconcinnis(?)'. Note that this, too, involves memorizing a conceptual tree diagram of the parts of speech. It is interesting that the kind of knowledge represented here involves very basic, rudimentary grammatical ideas, suggesting that if the book were to be used by a literate reader, much of it would already be known.

Figure 3. Grammar teaching the parts of speech. Book of the diverse liberal arts, London, MS Burney 275, f. 94.

By contrast, in the Ars Notoria, grammar is not shown being taught by hard work, memorization and discipline. The power which bestows grammar is embodied in a geometrical and verbal form which awaits only the operator's sustained attention. Its structure is not rooted in a symbol of the upward sprouting tree of nature, but in the lower quarters of a lion-like creature. The bestial and maleficent nature of this animal is linked to the astrological and cosmic power of the universe since antiquity, and its tail and legs also point down to the lower regions (fig. 2). Despite the fact that different categories of grammatical knowledge are isolated in little circles (as in the Paris manuscript of the orthodox teaching of grammar), the Ars Notoria diagram is structured with a strict iconic symmetry centred on the animal's mouth. From the time of Carriodorius's treatise on the arts in tenth-century manuscripts and in the neo-Platonic tradition generally, diagrams had been used to distinguish concepts and bodies like the four elements.[32] But divisions like those of the *oratio* labelled in the Turin manuscript are designed to be retained, not as conceptual tools in a process of learning, but as a means of direct access to the celestial powers bestowing knowledge. These shapes were not meant to be representations of grammatical ideas, but were the transcendent means by which these practical and human ideas could be grasped. The basis of the design around a set of pure shapes or forms is also characteristic of alchemical diagrams of the period. In her discussion of the origins of alchemical imagery, Barbara Obrist describes how geometrical forms have an 'ontological rapport with the ultimate truth' without 'the arbitrariness of the linguistic sign and the illusionism of painting'.[33] Normally the relationship between text and image in a medieval manuscript is one in which the image is secondary to, or at least dependent upon the text for its validity and existence.[34] In this case, however, the *nota* (which is neither a text nor a painting in the traditional sense) seems to have priority as the form to be taken in through prayer and ritual practice by its user.

This physical incorporation is hinted at in the design of the *nota* for arithmetic on f. 21, which is encompassed by the fantastically long arms of the rubber-man-like king who turns a somersault at the top of the page (figure 4). This, too, is distinguished from traditional upward-sprouting diagrams of the orthodox learned tradition by its plunging downward thrust, but also relates to the earlier tradition of diagrams such as the *arbores consanguinitates* where the whole scheme is encompassed by a human body (see fig. 8).[35] Also striking are the mask or animal mouths that lock together the vertical and horizontal bars on either side, and the two snakes with balls in their mouths that are entwined symmetrically around the lower frame. While much of the text carefully framed in circular compartments on the page is composed of obscure-sounding magical names like 'Ibra Albrac . . .', in red ink, lower on the page we see something we can still recognize: the ten numerals. These are written out in descending order from X. Arabic numerals appear at this date in other manuscript illuminations, such as the personification

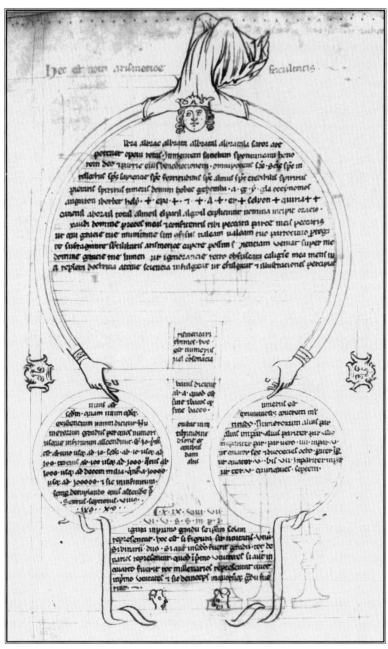

Figure 4. Ars Notoria: the *nota* of arithmetic. Turin, Biblioteca Nazionale MS E.V. 13, f. 21.

Figure 5. *De arithmetica.* Cassiodorus, *Institutiones*, Mantua, *c.* 1330. Paris BN lat. 8500, f. 38.

of arithmetic in Carraccioli's manuscript. We should remember, however, that numbers were also used as magical signs in some quarters, and that the Arabic figures or 'chiffres' (as they were called) were widely distrusted by commercial as well as some learned institutions as radical novelties.[36] That the emphasis is upon the traditional Boethian notion of arithmetic here is significant and suggests an intellectually conservative notion of the liberal arts in this manuscript, despite the radical means of its apprehension. We can contrast this depiction of arithmetic with a conventional one in an Italian manuscript which shows the personification of arithmetic teaching students: here the geometrical forms and numbers are painted clearly alongside, where they represent the substance of the art being taught[37] (figure 5). There is nothing of this type in the Turin image, which uses visual signs not so much to emphasize the boundaries of what can be described and learned, but to indicate the metaphorical grasping after knowledge that is always invisible and beyond.

If the arithmetic diagram seemed very unarithmetical, the *nota geometrie* is not

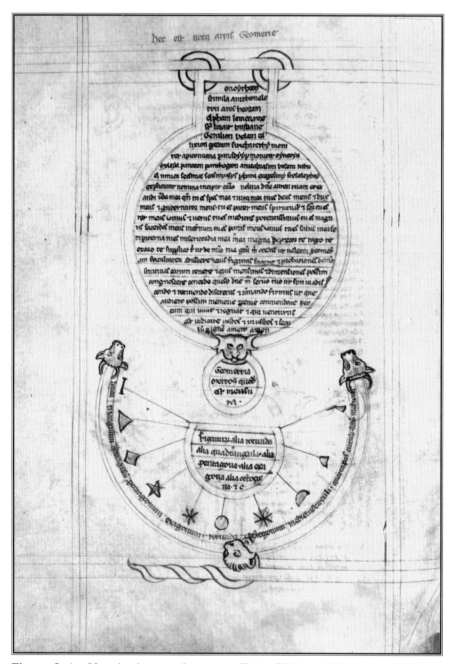

Figure 6. Ars Notoria: the *nota* of geometry. Turin, Biblioteca Nazionale MS E.V.13, f. 16v.

Figure 7. Lion doorknocker from the bronze doors of Hildesheim Cathedral, *c.* 1015.

very geometrical in this manuscript. On f. 16v, the red rubric at the top reading
'Hec est nota artis geometrie' presents a great curved, locked mechanism, once
again articulated through beasts' heads and using serpentine interlacing bands
(figure 6). The circle near the centre encompassing the definition of geometry as
the art of measuring looks like a Romanesque lion-headed doorknocker, similar
to those that had a powerful apotropaic position on the doors of the great
cathedrals[38] (figure 7). The pictorial language of these images, such as the serpent
that makes up the *notae* of dialectic on f. 16, shows that their designer was very
cognizant of the traditional iconography of the liberal arts, but is adapting them
to form a very different kind of image. Most striking is the use of knots or
interlocking ribbon forms, whether in a grid as on the arithmetic page, or in
more complex circular whorls, as at the top of the geometry page. The knot
might be described as the magical visual form par excellence, though here the
designer seems to want to evoke the power of knots to bind and control on a
more than metaphorical level. Like the interlocking circles at the top, these are
forms that had a powerful resonance outside as well as within the context of
ritual magic.

Another important legitimating sign of power used both in magical and other contexts in medieval culture is the sign of the dragon. In traditional diagrams the use of dragons and monstrous heads was not unusual, as can be seen in a famous diagram of the forbidden degrees of marriage in a Parisian manuscript signed by the illuminator Gautier Lebaube (figure 8). Here, however, the monstrous is confined to the margins, whereas in the Ars Notoria it structures the shape and movement of the *nota* itself. The king holding two dragons is a powerful sign of the virile potency of nature; his standing behind the tabular generations is part of his authorizing of its legitimacy as law in a legal manuscript.[39] But the king whose long arm circumscribes the art of arithmetic is not a legitimating sign of power in the same way, although he might have orginated from the same source. What this comparison shows is that it would be wrong to separate images into an orthodox, non-magical realm and an illicit magical one: the two realms are permeable in practice, and of course the illustrator of the Turin manuscript must have provided images for other orthodox works.

Following two interesting diagrams of rhetoric involving half-circles, knots, and lions and dragons biting mouths (which are a common motif in the decorative vocabulary of manuscript illumination here adapted to magical uses), is an unusual page without any text integrated into the image structure, with six swords, three serpents, three candlesticks, and two angels standing over twelve birds. These images can be directly paralleled in other manuscripts of the Ars Notoria, for example Munich, Bayerische Staatsbibliothek Clm 276 (which contains a closely related work, the *Liber visionum*, discussed elsewhere in this volume).[40] The Turin manuscript might have shocked some of those who saw it and certainly its contents were controversial, but its appearance and ordered system seems to suggest an orbit of traditional learning. The second of its two artists is a highly skilled and imaginative practitioner, although it is hard in the absence of more comparative material to know whether these images are copied from an earlier exemplar or are his design. Unlike the McMaster text of the *Liber visionum*, whose devotional aspects partly masked its unorthodox nature, this is less a pseudo-prayerbook than a pseudo-schoolbook. It represents orthodox knowledge obtained by unorthodox means.

Paris, BN lat. 9336, the second manuscript to be discussed here, dates from the fourteenth century and, judging by the more clearly identifiable stylistic features of its illumination, was produced at Bologna, which was a major centre of learning and manuscript illumination.[41] Described with the epithet 'most sacred', this *sacratissima ars notoria* has a longer two-column introductory text on f. 17v, and although it involves the familiar idea of presenting the seven liberal arts through diagrams, it is more complex in its layout and has a quite different format for its diagrams, each called, not a *nota*, but a *figura philosophie*. Like the Turin drawings, the diagrams in the Paris manuscript contain some script, but most of them are

Figure 8. Tree of Consanguinity signed by Gautier Lebaube. New York, Pierpont Morgan Library, MS Glazier 37, leaf 1.

purely visual. The image of rhetoric, with its seven parts organized at the bottom of the page, bears some resemblance in its organization to the image in the Turin manuscript (figure 9). However these images seem far more pictorial and incoherent as signs. The most striking difference between the two manuscripts is the appearance, in the Paris text, of angels in blue and red robes, each holding a small cross. Within the large circle is written the usual list of enigmatic-sounding names.

Angels do not appear in the Turin manuscript, which is inhabited far more by dragon-like monsters. The angels in this manuscript often point to large irregular shapes that contain further shapes that are neither symmetrical nor ordered, but seem like free-associated doodles and jigsaw-like patterns. The figures of astronomy show arcs of stretched out diamond forms filled with circles and smaller shapes. Like the images in the Turin manuscript, these are the work of a professional illuminator (not, as so often in magical texts, the scribe's own efforts). Someone either trained in illumination, or with a good knowledge of techniques, was able to copy these in a large format manuscript with good colours. More than one *figura* can appear on one folio, as on f. 25r, where there are three: the fourth figure of philosophy, which is purely visual, in the form of a triangle surmounted by a circle filled with shapes; the fifth figure, a circle with nine compartments surrounding a text beginning with the phrase 'incipit oratio'; and a sixth figure guarded by four angels, with what appear to be the letters 'm', 'n' and 'o' inside some of the shapes (figure 10). Two of the six figures of astronomy float more freely on the page below texts giving instructions for the proper prayers to be said before them at what intervals of time (figure 11). Here, the elongated diamond shapes appear to become frames themselves; connected by a network of horizontal and vertical bars, they are filled with what look like random squiggles. But these squiggles were probably carefully copied from an exemplar.

Part of the proper ritual effect of the figures, according to the text, comes from their having the correct shape. Their forms are close to those of many images of seals associated with certain demons which appear in later printed grimoires linked with Solomon's name, and on certain talismans.[42] It is common in this manuscript to find angels standing at the four corners of each image, but in the case of the seventh figure of philosophy (figure 12) two male figures are painted within the circles, one upright with his arms crossed wearing a scholar's *biretta*, and the other upside down wearing a crown. On another page where there are no human or angelic figures, the twisting and tentacular terminals of the second figure of philosophy (which should be looked at after the correct perusal of the first according to its rubric), contains only more quirky lines of monumental proportions (figure 13).

The diagrams of the Notory Art were also copied in more unusual contexts. Evidence for this is found in two unexpected places, in both cases in works of

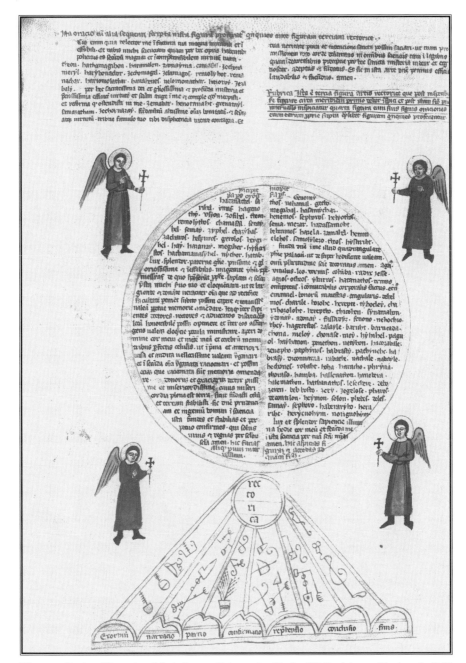

Figure 9. Ars Notoria: third *figura* of rhetoric. Paris, Bibliothèque Nationale MS lat. 9336, f. 23v.

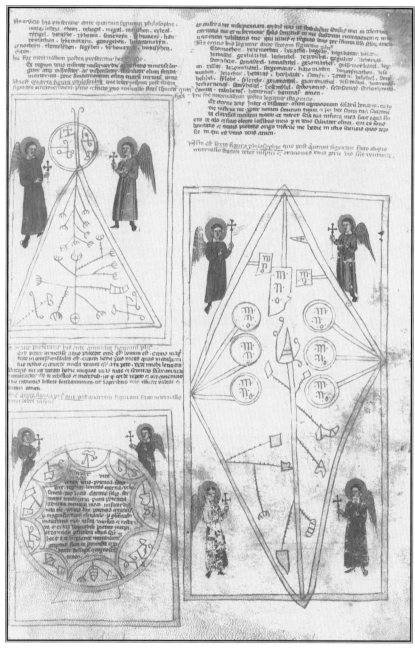

Figure 10. Ars Notoria: fourth, fifth and sixth figures of philosophy. Paris, Bibliothèque Nationale MS lat. 9336, f. 25.

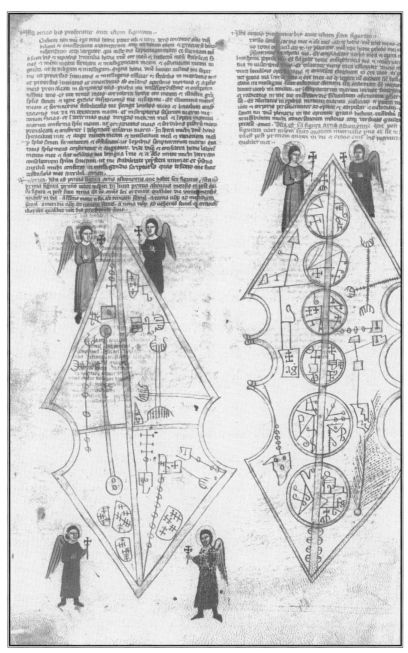

Figure 11. Ars Notoria: two figures of astronomy. Paris, Bibliothèque
Nationale MS lat. 9336, f. 24v.

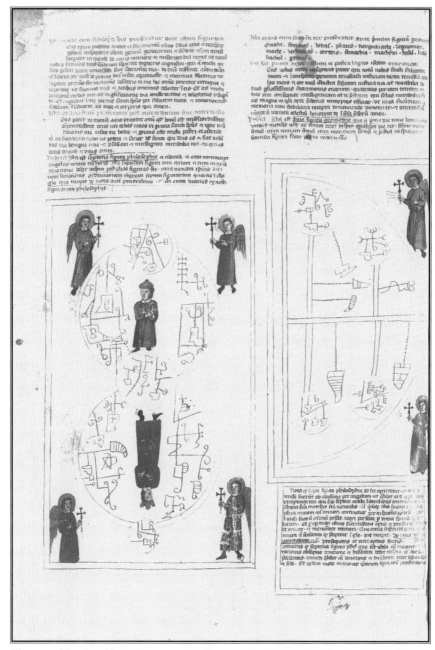

Figure 12. Ars Notoria: seventh figure of philosophy. Paris, Bibliothèque Nationale MS lat. 9336, f. 25v.

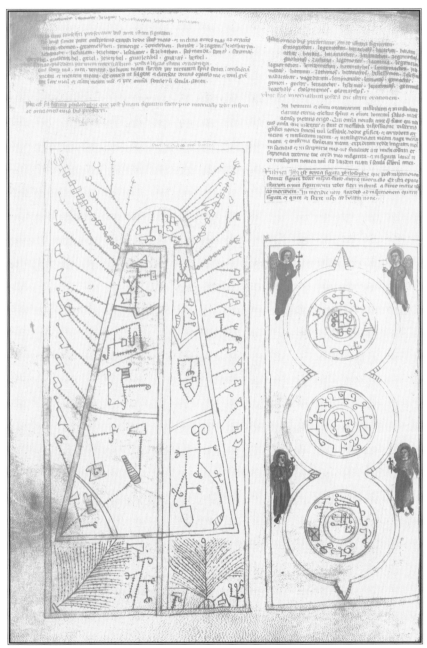

Figure 13. Ars Notoria: second and third figures of philosophy. Paris,
Bibliothèque Nationale MS lat. 9336, f. 27v.

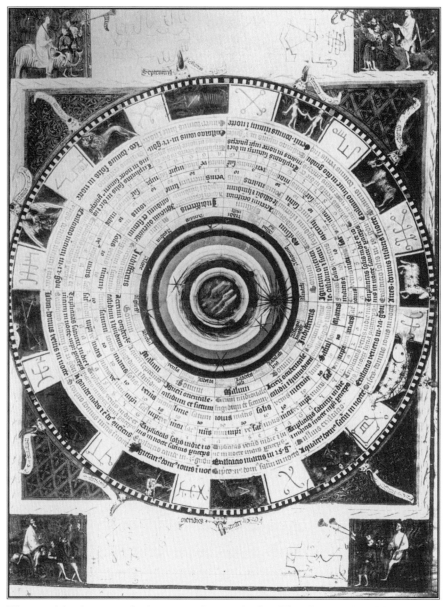

Figure 14. Astronomical manuscript made for King Wenceslas IV. Munich, Bayerische Staatsbibliothek Clm 826, f. 1r. Prague, *c.* 1400.

Figure 15. Detail of the upper frame of a fifteenth-century Florentine cassone panel. Tours, Musée des Beaux-Arts.

much higher quality 'art', which show the importation of these signs as talismanic or magical marks into the margins of art history proper. The first occurs in a beautifully illuminated compendium of astrological texts made soon after 1400 for King Wenceslas IV of Bohemia: Munich, Bayerische Staatsbibliothek Clm 826. On one page showing the concentric universe of spheres and planets, carefully measured in degrees and surrounded by the signs of the zodiac, we recognize the same kind of curvilinear markings and pen-drawn squiggles (on the upper and lower frames, next to trumpet-blowing heralds) as occur in the Ars Notoria texts (figure 14).[43] These are not the same as the pen-drawn symbols of the planets that circle the outer band of this diagram, but are in the same hand, and were perhaps, like them, familiar to the learned astrologers we know were at the Prague court at this date.

Even further afield and less directly linked to the astrological and magical arts, the *notae* of the *Ars Notoria* appear in the frame of a late fourteenth-century Florentine cassone panel in the museum at Tours[44] (figure 15). Art historians have long known of the fashion for inscribing meaningless Arabic letters in Kufic script on the borders of pictures and garments, usually for decorative

Figure 16. Four mechanical arts: Architecture, Painting, Philosophy and Magic. Chartres Cathedral, north transept façade. After 1316?

effect. But this black patterning on the gilt frame seems closer to the wandering shapes in the Bolognese manuscript (figure 14). It represents not the mystery of Arabic words but the sacred aura of the Notory Art. Since cassone panels were part of marriage ritual and nuptial agreements, they are often filled with fertility magic, and these signs which point to a more learned tradition are unusual. I am sure there must be other as yet unnoticed places where these signs were used in liminal sites as protective or powerful. By the end of the fourteenth century these signs, which had links with a whole tradition of image magic, were circulating more widely – widely enough to appear as 'quotations' in what Richard Kieckhefer has called 'the Romance of magic in courtly culture'.[45] These forms must have been appealing outside their learned contexts to have been adapted in this way outside their textual grid. The second and third figures of philosophy in the Bolognese manuscript appear to the modern eye like some Aztec codex or Paul Klee fantasy, but to the medieval observer they probably hinted at more than human ingenuity (figure 13). Asymmetry and almost intentional clumsiness of line are evident in tall pyramidal forms sprouting branches of wonderful variety. On this page these shapes, drawn without rule or compass, have no angels at their corners. There is nothing to compare with these strange forms anywhere in medieval art; but perhaps that is their power.

As other essays in this volume also show with respect to the textual aspects of the practices they consider, the visual aspects of these manuscripts clearly reveal the way in which magical practices are not only intimately connected with, but built out of the very structures of orthodox discourse against which they are so often opposed. It is important to remember that in the encyclopedic sculptural program of the North Transept foreportal at Chartres Cathedral, Magic appears as a personification in a new program of the mechanical arts, probably dating from the early fourteenth century[46] (figure 16). On the left is Architecture holding an architect's rule, followed by Painting drawing on a board. The next pair are Philosophy, who ponders an object of nature, and Magic. The figure representing magic holds a scroll (perhaps indicating his reliance upon inherited texts) and stands on a dragon. Part of an added program of sculptures based on the great scholastic *Mirror* of Vincent of Beauvais, which included the mechanical arts alongside the liberal arts, at the very period of the crackdown against illicit magic, we see the good philosophy on the right side of God and the bad philosophy to God's left. Painting, like Magic, also stands on the sinister side of the pairing. The close juxtaposition of the art of painting and the art of magic, both rejected from the list of the seven liberal arts, should remind us of the manuscripts of the Ars Notoria where we see brilliantly combined the visual and magical arts, in an attempt to provide access to the higher realms of another knowledge from which both were excluded.

Notes

1 This essay could not have been written without Claire Fanger's help and advice on the Ars Notoria tradition. Errors which remain are, of course, my own.

2 Translation by Nicholas Watson in this volume, p. 164. For the original text, see Jules Viard, *Les Grandes Chroniques de France*, 10 vols (Paris: Librairie ancienne Honoré Champion, 1953), vol. 9 (1937), pp. 23–4.

3 For discussion of the Ars Notoria textual tradition see Klaassen's essay in this volume; for John the monk's revision of it as the *Liber visionum*, see Watson and Fanger.

4 Claire Fanger has pointed out that John makes reference in his text to a 'compilation of figures made and published in the beginning by me', which suggests that he could have been responsible. Many authors at this date who conceived of their texts with illustrations would have a hand in devising the pictorial program even if they did not paint the pictures themselves, as in the case of the Dominican Friar Laurent's *Somme le Roi*, compiled in 1272, and the Cistercian Guillaume de Deguileville's *Pelerinage de la vie humaine* in 1333.

5 For other politically motivated and publically celebrated attacks on magic from 1300 to 1360, along with this one, see the discussion in Jeffrey Burton Russell, *Witchcraft in the Middle Ages* (Ithaca: Cornell University Press, 1972), p. 239.

6 Klaassen, pp. 14–19.

7 See Jacques van Lennep, 'Peintres et philosophes' in his *Alchemie: Contribution à l'histoire de l'art alchimique* (Bruxelles: Crédit Communal de Belgique, 1982), pp. 285–909, and Marie-Madeline Gauthier, 'Iris, le peinture et l'alchemiste: di savoir-faire au style', *Colloque International du CNRS: Pigments et Colorants de l'Antiquité et du Moyen Âge: Teinture, peinture, enlumineure études historiques et physiochimiques* (Paris: Diffusions, Presses de CNRS, 1990) pp. 59–70.

8 Salatiele, *Ars Notarie*, ed. G. Orlandelli, 2 vols (Milan: Giuffré, 1961), and Canon J.S. Purvis, *Notarial Signs from the York Archepiscopal Records* (London: St Anthony's, 1957).

9 See Thorndike, *A History of Magic and Experimental Science* (New York: Columbia University Press, 1923–58) vol. II, pp. 279–89. See also Arthur Edward Waite, *The Book of Ceremonial Magic* [London, Rider, 1911] repr. (New Hyde Park, NY: University Books, 1961), p. 22. For the cult of Solomon in antiquity see D.C. Duling, 'Testament of Solomon' in James H. Charlesworth, *The Pseudepigrapha and Modern Research* (Missoula, Montana: The Scholars' Press for the Society of Biblical Literature, 1976), pp. 935–87.

10 Marie Thérèse d'Alverny, 'Récréation monastiques: les couteaux à manche d'ivoire' in *Receuil des travaux offert à M. Clovis Brunel* (Paris: Société de l'école de Chartres, 1955), vol. I, p. 19, and the same author's 'Survivance de la magie Antique' in *Antike und Orient im Mittlealter: Miscellanea Mediaevalia* (Berlin: de Gruyter, 1962), pp. 157–9, which discusses a manuscript from Limoges (Paris BN ms. Lat. 3713), which contains symbols like the 'sceau de Salomon'.

11 Edward Peters, *The Magician, the Witch and the Law* (Philadelphia: University of Pennsylvania Press, 1978) p. 88.

12 *De Legibus*, cap. 27, cited in the Latin original in d'Alverny, 'Survivance de la magie Antique', p. 177. See Pierre Boglioni, 'Peuple et culture populaire chez Guillaume d'Auvergne' in *Mensch und Objekt im Mittelalter und in der Frühen Neuzeit. Leben-Alltag-Kultur International Kongress Krems*, ed. Gerhard Jaritz (Vienna: Verlag der Österreichischen Akademie der Wissenschaften, 1990) pp. 194–222.

13 A.G. Little, *Part of the Opus Tertium of Roger Bacon* (Aberdeen: University Press, 1912), p. 48, and Thorndike, *History*, vol. 2, p. 279.

14 Paola Zambelli, *The Speculum Astronomiae and its Enigma: Astrology, Theology and Science in Albertus Magnus and his Contemporaries* (Dordrecht: Kluwer, 1992), p. 241, and David Pingree, 'The diffusion of Arabic Magical Texts in Western Europe' in *La Diffusione delle Scienze Islamiche nel Medio Evo Europeo* (Rome: Accademia nazionale dei Lincei, 1987), p. 88.

15 For traditions of image magic, see in general Richard Kieckhefer, *Magic in the Middle Ages* (Cambridge: Cambridge University Press, 1990), pp. 75–80, and Christa Habiger-Tuczay, *Magie und Magier im Mittelalter* (Munich: Diederichs, 1992), pp. 241–8; for specialized examples of engraved talismanic images, Lynn Thorndike, 'Traditional Medieval Tracts Concerning Engraved Astrological Images' in *Mélanges Auguste Pelzer* (Louvain: Bibliothéque de l'Université, 1947), pp. 217–74, and Bruno Delmas, 'Médailles Astrologiques et Talismaniques dans le Midi de la France, XIIIe–XVIe siècle', *Archeologie Occitane: Actes du 96e Congres National des Société des Savantes* (Paris: Ministere de l'éducation nationale, 1976), pp. 437–54, and especially Charles Burnett, 'Talismans: Magic as Science? Necromancy among the Seven Liberal Arts' in *Magic and Divination in the Middle Ages* (Aldershot: Variorum, 1976), pp. 1–15.

16 See E.H. Gombrich, *Aby Warburg: An Intellectual Biography* (London: Warburg Institute, 1970); Ernst Kris and Otto Kurz, *Legend Myth and Magic in the Image of the Artist* (New Haven: Yale University Press, 1979); A.A. Barb, 'Birds and Medieval Magic', *Journal of the Warburg and Courtauld Institutes* 13 (1950), pp. 316–22, and W. Deonna, 'Abra, Abraca, la croix talisman de Lausanne', *Genava* 22 (1944), pp. 116–37.

17 David Freedburg, *The Power of Images: Studies in the History of Response* (Chicago: University of Chicago Press, 1989. For fascination, see Frederick T. Elworthy, *The Evil Eye: An account of this Ancient and Widespread Superstition* (London, Murray, 1895); Clarence Maloney, ed., *The Evil Eye* (New York: Columbia University Press, 1976) and G. Lafaye, 'Fascinum' in *Dictionnaire des Antiquités Grecques et Romaines* (Paris: Hachette, 1877–1919), pp. 983–87. For its impact upon medieval art along with a number of instances of erased manuscript images, see the important article by Joaquin Yarza Luaces, 'Fascinum: Reflets de la Croyance au Mauvais Oeil dans l'art médiévale Hispanique', *Razo* 8 (1988), pp. 113–27.

18 Thorndike, *History*, vol. 2, p. 282.

19 Constanza Segre Montel, *I manoscritti miniati della Biblioteca Nazionale di Torino* (Turin: Officine grafiche G. Molfese, 1980), pp. 130–4.

20 Line drawings of a similar form can be seen most usefully in Francesco Gurrieri, *Disegni nei Manoscritti Laurenziani* (Florence: L.S. Olschki, 1979).

21 For the magical use of the images of the evangelist symbols, see J.H.G. Grattan and Charles Singer, *Anglo-Saxon Magic and Medicine* (London: Oxford University Press, 1952), pp. 62–3, and Lawrence Nees, 'A Fifth-Century Book Cover and the Origin of the Four Evangelist Symbols Page in the Book of Durrow', *Gesta* XVIII (1978), pp. 3–8.

22 Theodore H. Gaster, 'Amulets and Talismans' in *Hidden Truths: Magic, Alchemy, and the Occult*, ed. L.E. Sullivan (New York: Macmillan, 1987), p. 146. See also the examples reproduced in Liselotte Hansmann and Lenz Kriss-Rettenbach, *Amulet und Talisman: Erscheinungsform und Geschichte* (Munich: Callwey, 1966), p. 132, and the seals and characters in Waite, *Ceremonial Magic*, pp. 186–219.

23 See Lucy Sandler, *The Psalter of Robert de Lisle in the British Library* (London: H. Miller; New York: Oxford Univeristy Press, 1983) and John E. Murdoch, *Album of Science: Antiquity and the Middle Ages* (New York: Scribner, 1984), p. 61.

24 For *rotae* see Michael Evans, 'The Geometry of the Mind', *The Architectural Association Quarterly* 12/14 (1980), pp. 42–3, and his 'The *Ysagogue in Theologiam* and the Commentaries attributed to Bernard Silvestris', *Journal of the Warburg and Courtauld Institutes* 54 (1991), pp. 1–42; Robert Suckale, 'Thesen zum Bedeutungswandel der gothischen Fersterrose' in K. Klausberg, D. Kimpel, H.J. Kunst, R. Suckale, *Bauwerk und Bildwerk im Hochmittelalter, Anschauliche Beiträge zur Kultur und Sozialgeschichte* (Giessen: Anabas, 1981), pp. 259–99. For diagrams more generally see Jean-Claude Schmitt, 'Les Images Classificatrices', *Bibliothèque de l'École de Chartres* 147 (1989), pp. 311–41; and for their use in traditional schoolroom pedagogy see Karl-August Wirth, 'Von mittlealterlichen Bildern un Lehrfiguren im Dienste der Schule und des Unterrichts' in Bernd Moeller, Hans Patze and Karl Stackmann (eds), *Studien zum städtischen Bildungswesen des späten Mittelalters und der frühen Neuzeit* (Göttingen: Vandenhoeck and Ruprecht, 1983), pp. 256–359.

25 *Ars Notoria: the Notory Art of Solomon shewing the Cabalistic key of Magical Operations, The Liberal Sciences, Divine Revelation, and the Art of Memory, written originally in Latin and now English'd by Robert Turner* (London: J. Cottrel, 1657), p. 2.

26 F. Neumann, *Zucht und Schöne Sitte: Eine Tugendlehre der Stauferzeit mit 36 Bildern aus der heidelberger handschrift Cod. Pal. Germ. 389 'Der Welsche Gast' des Thomasin von Zerclaere* (Wiesbaden: Reichert, 1977), pp. 134–5.

27 See Adolf Katzenellenbogen, 'The Representation of the Seven Liberal Arts', *Twelfth-Century Europe and the Foundation of Medieval Society*, ed. Marshall Clagett, Gaines Post and Robert Reynolds (Madison: University of Wisconsin Press, 1961); Phillipe Verdier, 'L'iconographie des arts libéraux dans l'art du môyen age, jusqu'à la fin du quinzième', *Arts Libéraux et Philosophie au Môyen Age* (Montréal: Montréal Institut d'études médiévales, 1969), pp. 305–55. For the tree of Porphyry and its importance in visual images of the period see Jean Wirth, *L'Image Médiévale: Naissance et developpements (Ve–XVe siècle)* (Paris: Méridiens Klincksieck, 1989), pp. 61–6. For the use of images in late medieval grammar teaching see Monika Asztalos, Jan Oberg, Astrid Stedje and Birgit Stolt, *Die Seligenstäadter Lateinpädagogik* (Stockholm: Almqvist & Wiksell, 1989).

28 Michael D. Swartz, *Scholastic Magic: Ritual and Revelation in Early Jewish Mysticism* (Princeton: Princeton University Press, 1996), p. 43.

29 Mary Carruthers, *The Book of Memory: Memory in Medieval Culture* (Cambridge: Cambridge University Press, 1992) and John B. Friedman, 'Les images mnémotechniques dans les manuscrits de l'époque gothique' in *Jeux de mémoire: Aspects de la mnémotechnie médiévale* (Montreal-Paris: Presses de l'université de Montréal, 1985), pp. 169–84.

30 Quoted in Jerzy Athey, '"Pere la storia dell" ambiente magico-astrologico a Cracovia nel quattrocento' in *Magia, Astrologia e Religione nel Rinascimento* (Warsaw: Zaklad Narrowdwy im Ossonlinskich, 1974), p. 102.

31 London, British Library MS Burney 275. See Michael Camille, 'The Discourse of Images in Philosophical manuscripts of the Late Middle Ages: Aristoteles Latinus' in *Album: I luoghi dove si accumulano I segni dal manuscritto alle reti telematiche*, a cura di Claudio Leonardi, Marcello Morelli e Francesco Santi (Spoleto: Centro italiano di studi sulli alto Medioevo, 1995), pp. 96–110.

32 See Murdoch, *Album of Science*, p. 351.

33 Barbara Obrist, *Les Débuts de L'Imagerie Alchemique (XIVe–XVe siècles)* (Paris: Le Sycamore, 1982), p. 107.

34 For more traditional text/image relationships see J.J.G. Alexander, *Medieval Illuminators and their Methods of Work* (New Haven and London: Yale University Press, 1992), pp. 72–95; and Michael Camille, 'The Book of Signs: Writing and Visual Difference in Gothic Manuscript Illumination', *Word and Image* 1 (1985), pp. 133–49.

35 See the illustration in a manuscript of the *Decret* of Burchard of Worms in Paris, in Avril François, *Dix Siècles d'Enlumineure Italienne* (Paris: Bibliothéque Nationale, 1984), fig. 13, p. 26.

36 On Arabic numerals see Dirk J. Struik, 'The Prohibition of the Use of Arabic Numerals in Florence', *Archives Internationales des Histoires des Sciences* 21 (1968), pp. 290–7; Richard Lemay, 'The Hispanic Origin of Our Present Numerical Forms', *Viator* 8 (1977), pp. 435–68; and Alexander Murray, *Reason and Society in the Middle Ages* (Oxford: Oxford University Press, 1977), pp. 167–80.

37 For this manuscript, with illustrations of the liberal arts accompanying the *Institutions* of Cassiodorus, produced in Mantua, *c.* 1330, see *Dix Siècles d'Enlumineure Italienne*, no. 71, p. 85.

38 For Romanesque doorknockers which obviously have an apotropaic effect, see Ursula Mende, *Die Tüzieher des Mittelalters*, ch. II, 'Bronzegeräte des Mittelalters' (Berlin: Deutcher Verlag für Kunstwissenschaft, 1981).

39 Robert Branner interpreted this figure as the King of France in *Manuscript Painting in Paris During the Reign of Saint Louis* (Berkeley: University of California Press, 1977), p. 72; but for the tradition of having such a figure in diagrams of this type see Hermann Schadt, *Darstellung der Arbores Consanguinitatis und der Arbores Affinitatis* (Tübingen: Wasmuth, 1982).

40 Manuscript cited in Thorndike, *History*, vol. 2, p. 282. I am grateful to Claire Fanger for providing me with photographs of the Munich manuscript for comparison.

41 Listed in Thorndike, p. 282, its amazing images were first brought to my attention by Paola Zambelli. For manuscripts produced in Bologna at this date see F. Filippini, G. Zucchini, *Miniatori e Pittori a Bologna, Documenti dei secoli XIII e XIV* (Florence: G.C. Sansoni, 1947); and G. Orlandelli, *Il libro a Bologna dal 1300 al 1330. Documenti con uno studio su il contratto di scrittura nella dotrina notarile Bolognese* (Bologna: Zanichelli, 1959); and for the style of the miniatures see A. Conti, *La Miniatura Bolognese: Scuole e Botteghe 1270–1340* (Bologna: Alfa, 1981).

42 For similar shapes see Waite, *Ceremonial Magic*, pp. 184–219.

43 Josef Krasa, *Die Handschriften König Wenzels IV* (Vienna: Forum Verlag, 1971), p. 198.

44 Paul Schubring, *Cassoni: Truhen und Truhenbilder der italienischen Frühenrenaissance* (Leipzig: K.W. Hiersemann, 1915), no. 461 (attributed to Neroccio di Bartolomeo).

45 Kieckhefer, *Magic in the Middle Ages*, p. 95.

46 See Sue A. Levine, *The Northern Foreportal Column Figures of Chartres Cathedral* (Frankfurt and New York: Peter Lang, 1984), pp. 121–58.

Part Two

ANGELIC KNOWLEDGE: THE *SWORN BOOK* AND THE *BOOK OF VISIONS*

6

A THIRTEENTH-CENTURY RITUAL TO ATTAIN THE BEATIFIC VISION FROM THE *SWORN BOOK* OF HONORIUS OF THEBES

Robert Mathiesen

INTRODUCTION

My subject is a medieval handbook of ceremonial magic, titled *Liber sacer sive juratus*, that is, the *Sacred or Sworn Book*. (For brevity we shall call it the *Sworn Book*.) This remarkable work is not so much a literary text as a genuine handbook of ceremonial magic. Moreover, it is not just a random collection of miscellaneous spells, but a systematic treatise, the work of a single author.

The author of the *Sworn Book*, who names himself Honorius of Thebes, is clearly one of the ultimate 'outsiders' in the High Middle Ages, a professed and practicing magician. But unlike many of his fellow magicians, Honorius – henceforth I shall take his pseudonym at its face value – is not inclined to lurk silently in the shadows of his age. In his *Sworn Book* he speaks clearly and eloquently not only about the aims and methods of his magic, but also about its necessary place in his world, and he appeals to sympathetic men in power to defend and protect that place.

As he does this, Honorius also explicitly and powerfully challenges the ideological foundation on which the 'insiders' of his age were busily constructing the power and authority of the late medieval church and state in Western Europe. It is because of this challenge, above all else, that the *Sworn Book* merits far more attention from medievalists than it has received in the past – even from those medievalists who would otherwise have very little need to consider the history of medieval magic.

THE SURVIVAL OF THE *SWORN BOOK*

Medieval handbooks of ceremonial magic have survived mostly by accident. Kept hidden by their owners, sometimes destroyed by civil and ecclesiastical authorities, they are rarely discussed in any detail by any medieval author. When they are mentioned at all, they are usually condemned without extensive quotation. Even medieval library catalogues and bibliographies often fail to note their existence, sometimes deliberately.

For example, in the thirteenth century Richard of Fourniville compiled his *Biblionomia*, a detailed catalogue of almost all the 260 manuscript volumes in his extensive library, with tables of contents for the volumes containing more than one treatise. So precise are his indications that one can even see how most of these 260 manuscripts must have been arranged on their shelves. The sole exception is the class of what he calls, 'the secret books, the description of which we do not wish to include in this work'.[1] His deliberate silence is all the more to be regretted since one can see from his list of shelf-marks that these 'secret books' amounted to thirty-six manuscript volumes, and thus comprised a little less than one-seventh of his entire library.[2]

In his introduction Richard de Fourniville says a little more about his 'secret books':

> Moreover, in addition to those of which we have made mention, there is also another class of secret tractates, the profundity of which ought not to be exposed to public gaze. And hence it is not our intention that they be ordered among the aforesaid [other books]; but a secure place ought to be set aside for them, which no one can enter save their proper owner. Wherefore neither is their description included in this book.[3]

Similarly, some 250 years later, Johannes Trithemius carefully excluded all magical texts from his comprehensive bibliography of ecclesiastical writers, *De scriptoribus ecclesiasticis* (1495), the first such work to appear in print. He even omitted all the magical texts that were attributed to well-known writers such as Michael Scot or Peter of Apono, all of whose other works he carefully lists.[4] Nevertheless, Trithemius was well aware of these excluded works, and probably had copies of many of them, for in another work of his, *Antipalus malificiorum*, or the *Antagonist of Sorceries* (written in 1508, but not printed during his lifetime), he gives a careful catalogue of over one hundred such magical texts, with an incipit in almost every case.[5] This catalogue of titles and incipits is often our best reference, and sometimes our only reference, to many of these texts on medieval magic. Thus his omission of all works on magic from his *De scriptoribus ecclesiasticis* shows discretion, not ignorance.

Despite such constraints, as many as six manuscripts of the *Sworn Book*, or rather of parts of it, are known to have survived.[6] All six of these manuscripts happen to be in the British Library. Five of them preserve the original Latin text.[7] They are the following:

Sloane 313	14th c.	parchment	27 ff.
Sloane 3854	14th c.	parchment	ff. 112–39
Sloane 3885	16th c.	paper	ff. 1–25, 58–125
Sloane 3826	17th c.	paper	ff. 58–83?
Sloane 3883	17th c.	paper	ff. 1–25

The sixth offers a partial English version, supplemented by extracts from Agrippa von Nettesheim's *De occulta philosophia libri III* (Cologne: Johannes Soter, 1553) and other sources.[8] Thus the manuscript cannot be earlier than the sixteenth century, although past cataloguers have assigned it to the fifteenth.[9] It is the following:

| Royal 17.A.XLII | 16th c. | parchment | 82 ff. |

Note that two of these six manuscripts are as old as the fourteenth century, which provides us with an extreme *terminus ante quem* for the text. Note, too, that one of these fourteenth-century manuscripts (Sloane 313) was once the property of the famous Elizabethan scholar and magus John Dee, and still bears his distinctive mark of ownership. Later it came into the hands of the dramatist Ben Jonson, who inscribed it 'Sum Ben: Jonsonij liber'.[10]

The *Sworn Book* was first introduced to historians of medieval magic by Arthur Edward Waite in 1898.[11] Not long thereafter it also caught the attention of Lynn Thorndike, who gave a somewhat fuller account of it in 1923, in the second volume of his monumental, *A History of Magic and Experimental Science*.[12] Until recently, most other references to the text rested on the work of these two scholars.

In 1977, however, an English version of the *Sworn Book* was hand-printed and privately published by Heptangle Press at Gillette, N.J., for use by modern ceremonial magicians. A second edition, lithographically reprinted from the sheets of the first, was published by the same press in 1983. This attractive volume was the work of the late Daniel J. Driscoll (*obit* 20 July 1990), who consulted the Latin text in Sloane 313 as he slightly modernized the medieval English version in Royal 17.A.XLII. Mr Driscoll took account of only two of the six known manuscripts, and edited them with a high and arbitrary hand. Yet with all its faults his edition can be of some use to scholars, for it gives them much fuller access to the text than do Waite's and Thorndike's brief summaries.[13]

THE DATE OF THE *SWORN BOOK*

The *Sworn Book* is clearly not a translation from Arabic, Hebrew or Greek, but an original composition in Latin by a person who was fully conversant with the liturgy and ritual of the Roman Catholic Church, as it had developed by the beginning of the High Middle Ages.

The core of the *Sworn Book*, or at least of that part of it which has survived, is a series of seventy-odd prayers, some quite long, which are referred to as a 'Psalter'. This Psalter is directly followed by a shorter text titled 'Litany'. The Psalter and Litany are accompanied by detailed directions for their ritual use (rubrics).

Many of these prayers are wholly or partly in unintelligible language. At first glance they appear to be in pure gibberish, but an attentive reader can recognize deformed Greek and Hebrew words (at least) in some of them. We shall cite a specimen of this kind of prayer below. The remaining prayers are quite intelligible, and some of them are standard Catholic prayers.

As already noted, the author of the *Sworn Book* styles himself Honorius, a son of Euclid and a master or teacher (*magister*) of Thebes. We are probably meant to identify his father Euclid as the famous geometer of Late Antiquity, whose classic *Elements of Geometry* was first translated into Latin in the twelfth century. Thus the *Sworn Book* is a late medieval pseudepigraphon. Despite its pseudepigraphical character, I am convinced that we can determine within fifty years when the *Sworn Book* was composed: sometime in the first half of the thirteenth century.

Although the two oldest known manuscripts of the *Sworn Book* – *Liber sacer sive juratus*, to give it its full title – were copied only in the fourteenth century, an earlier *terminus ante quem* is provided by William of Auvergne, who was Archbishop of Paris from 1228 until his death in 1249, and who makes two very brief references to it in his *De legibus*. In chapter twenty-four of that work, as he condemns various books on magic, William remarks in passing: 'From this same plague of curiosity came forth the accursed and execrable book which is called the *Sacred Book*.'[14] In chapter twenty-seven he is only slightly more informative, as he censures several pseudo-Solomonic magical texts:

> To this sort of idolatry belong those four figures which are called the *Rings of Solomon*, and a fifth which is called the *Seal of Solomon*, and nine others which are called the *Nine Scarabs*. The most execrable consecrations and most detestable invocations, writings, images in all these contain very evident impiety of idolatry. Let Christians not so much as mention that unlawful image which is called the *Idea of Solomon*, nor that book which is called *Sacred* and its works, nor the figure which is called *Mandal* or *Amandel* and its works.[15]

Note that William regards the *Sworn Book* as one of the very worst of all the reprehensible handbooks of magic which he has ever encountered. We shall see below why he might well condemn it more than other works on magic.

A reasonable *terminus post quem* for the *Sworn Book* may be deduced from its Prologue, which responds to an impending attempt by the current Pope – whose name is not given – to obliterate any practice and teaching of magic and to condemn all magicians to death. Such a program first took shape during the papacy of Gregory IX (1227–41), although a perspicacious observer might have seen it coming as early as the papacy of Innocent III (1198–1216).[16] To be sure, trials and executions of magicians become common only during the fourteenth century, but the *Sworn Book* nowhere implies that such trials have already occurred, only that they are foreseen.[17]

In general, one might also claim that what the *Sworn Book* offers on the subject of the Beatific Vision is more readily understood as part of the ferment of theological opinion on that subject during the first half of the thirteenth century, than as a response to the dogmatic pronouncements about it during the fourteenth century.[18]

On the basis of these considerations, I am very much inclined to ascribe the *Sworn Book* to the first half of the thirteenth century, and probably to the Papacy of Gregory IX.[19]

THE PROLOGUE TO THE *SWORN BOOK*

We have already mentioned how the author of the *Sworn Book* – one of the ultimate 'outsiders' in the High Middle Ages, a professed and committed ceremonial magician – delivers an explicit, formidable challenge to the basis upon which the 'insiders' of his century were busily constructing the power and authority of the late medieval church and state in Western Europe. This challenge is given literary form in the Prologue to the *Sworn Book*, but is also implicit in the magical processes themselves which the *Sworn Book* describes.

We shall examine the Prologue first. The text here is based on Driscoll's edition, with normalized spelling and punctuation, and some further corrections (marked by square brackets) based on two of the six manuscripts.[20]

When wicked spirits were gathered together, intending to send demons into the hearts of men, so that they should destroy all things profitable for mankind, and to corrupt the whole world even to the uttermost of their power, they sowed among men hypocrisy and envy, and rooted bishops and prelates in pride. Even the Pope and his Cardinals were affected and gathering themselves together, said to each other: *That [Salvation] which our Lord has given his people is now through magic and necromancy turned into the damnation of all people. For even the magicians are being intoxicated and blinded by the devil and contrary to the order of Christ's Church, and [are] transgressing the commandment of God, which is: 'Thou shalt not tempt the Lord thy God, but Him only shalt thou serve.' And denying the sacrifice due God, they have done sacrifice unto devils and are abusing God's name in the calling of devils. This is contrary to the profession made at Baptism, for there it is said: 'I forsake Satan and all his pomps.' These magicians do not only follow the pomps and works of Satan, but have brought all people, by means of illusions, into errors, drawing the ignorant and such like into the damnation of both soul and body. And they thinking that by this that they should destroy all other sciences, it is right, therefore, to pluck up and utterly to destroy this deadly root and all the followers of Magical Art.*

This is a fair summary of some of the arguments really advanced during the thirteenth and later centuries to justify the severest possible repression of magic.[21] Note that Honorius has immediately gone on the offensive in his Prologue. He makes the extreme and radical claim that the Pope and Cardinals have been led by demons, not by God, to undertake their campaign against magic.

> Moved by covetousness and envy under the similitude of truth, these bishops and prelates through demonic instigation spread abroad false and unlikely stories. For it is not possible that a wicked and unclean man could work truly in this Art; for men are not bound unto spirits, but spirits are constrained against their will to answer clean men and fulfill their requests.

Here Honorius continues to claim that the church's hierarchy is demonically inspired, and is acting from unworthy motives. In addition, he attacks the hierarchy's premise as false: a wicked man cannot truly work magic, he says, but only a man who is clean can overmaster spirits and demons. Since 'men are not bound by spirits', the common opinion that magicians are the Devil's bond-servants cannot be true.

> Yet against our will we have gone about to set forth the principles of Magical Art in the cause of truth. For that cause the Church condemned Magical Art and judged us to death. We, through God's sufferance having foreknowledge of this judgement and knowing that much mischief would follow, thought to seek the aid of spirits, for it was impossible for us to escape the people by our own power.

Here Honorius says that the church's demonically inspired hierarchy now threatens the very lives of the magicians, although all of their efforts have been made 'in the cause of truth', and not just to gratify their own willfulness. Thus the use of any available counter-force can be justified as self-defense. However, the magicians have chosen a more compassionate and prudent response: they have called a council to deal with the problem, as immediately appears.

> Yet we feared a greater danger: the wicked power of the spirits under our command would have destroyed all our enemies at once. Instead we called a general council of all of the Masters of Magic. In this council of 811 masters from Naples, Athens and [Toledo] we chose Honorius, son of Euclid and the Master of [Thebes], where [lectures on] Magic [were] read, to work for us in Magical Art.

The number 811 has a numerological significance that is important for Honorius's argument: it is the numerical value of the Greek magical word IAΩ. (In the Greek alphabet I = 10, A = 1 and Ω = 800.) IAΩ is the most sacred of all God's names, equivalent to the Hebrew Tetragrammaton YHWH, which Jews forbear to pronounce. This number implies that the Council of 811 Magicians acts in God's name, even as the 318 Fathers at the Council of Nicaea showed by their number that they were acting in the name of Jesus and his Cross (300 = T [the Cross] and 18 = IH [an abbreviation for 'Ιησοῦς, Jesus]).[22]

The cities from which these 811 magicians came were famed for magic lore: Naples, where the Roman poet and reputed necromancer Virgil had his tomb; Athens, the seat of all Greek learning; Toledo, where Jews and Arabs freely taught their sciences; and Thebes, the ancient centre of Egyptian magic, whence sprang the magic of the Greeks and the Romans.

> Honorius with the counsel of [an angel named] Hocroël wrote seven volumes of Magical Art, giving to us the kernel and to others the shells. Out of these seven volumes he composed a book of 92 chapters in which is contained the effect of Magical Art. We call this book the *Sacred or Sworn Book*, for in it [are] contained 100 sacred names of God and [it is] thus sacred, for it is made of holy things; and because Hocroël did deliver and show Honorius that it was consecrated by God. The princes and prelates, pacified with burning mere fables and trifles, thought verily that Magical Art had been destroyed.

Here we are told that the work of Honorius was aided by God's angel Hocroël, who guided Honorius as he compiled seven books containing the essence, or 'kernel', of magic. Other works on magic contain merely its 'shells', so that it will not matter too much if the princes and prelates burn them.[23] From this work in seven books Honorius then extracted the ninety-two chapters of the present *Sworn Book*.

> Wherefore we being somewhat moved made this oath among ourselves:
> – that this book is not to be delivered to anyone unless the Master be in danger of death;
> – that only 3 copies will be made of it;
> – [that] it is not to be given to a woman or a minor;
> – [that] the recipient shall be godly and faithful, and tested for one year;
> – [that] this book be restored to Honorius or his successors; and if no one can be found able and sufficient to receive it the Master will bind his executors to bury it with him in the grave, or he must bury it and never reveal its place;
> – [that] scholars of Magical Art will suffer death rather that betray the confidence of their Master;
> – [that] the Master will unite his disciples in concord and love, so that they will always help each other;

    – [that] one will not reveal the secrets of another; and
    – [that] he who works in Magic will keep every article of this oath.
      For this reason this is called the *Sworn Book*.[24]

Finally we see how, in order to keep the *Sworn Book* safe, it is necessary to keep it secret, yet also to hand it down from generation to generation. Its possessor is envisioned as having several disciples, and as many as three magical heirs, and all are to swear this oath. Oaths of secrecy were common in alchemy at least since the fifth century, but I know of none so detailed as this, nor of any other specimen of a magician's oath before the Modern era.

    To sum up the Prologue: the Pope and his subordinates, and likewise the Princes, are doing Satan's work, not God's, when they attempt to eradicate magic. In this matter, at least, *only* the Council of 811 Magicians and their spokesman Honorius are acting with God's authority and under the guidance of his angel Hocroël, for God intends that magic be preserved and secretly handed down in writing.[25]

    The Prologue merely *asserts* this radical claim. To learn how its author could possibly *sustain* it, we must turn to the text of the *Sworn Book*, and particularly to its most elaborate and difficult ritual.

A Magical Operation to Obtain the Beatific Vision

As noted above, the six known manuscripts of the *Sworn Book* seem to contain only part of the whole work. This part describes just two magical operations.

    The second and less interesting of the two operations is a ritual in order to summon an angel, a spirit or a demon to appear and serve the magician. It requires the construction of a magic circle, and is merely one of many such operations found in handbooks of ceremonial magic from Late Antiquity up to our own times, for instance in the *Key of Solomon* (*Clavicula Salomonis*). The variant in the *Sworn Book* does not show any features of great interest.[26]

    It is the first of the two magical operations which is truly remarkable, and which makes the *Sworn Book* so important and interesting even for medievalists who would not otherwise have any reason to consider medieval magic. To the best of my knowledge, this operation has no parallel in any ancient or medieval handbook of magic. It is nothing less than an elaborate ritual to obtain, almost at will, what Catholic theologians term the Beatific Vision, that is, a vision of God Almighty in all His Glory, during which the viewer can (one presumes) even participate to some extent in God's omniscience.[27]

    This ritual is much too long to reproduce here in full; we shall have to be content with a summary description.

    The *Sworn Book* begins its account of this operation with two general observations, the one on angels, the other on men. We are told that angels are either celestial, aërial or earthly, and further that the celestial angels are of two kinds, namely, 'those who serve God only and those who serve God, but will also answer to man'. The former are the nine orders of angels: Seraphim, Cherubim, Thrones, Dominations, Virtues, Powers, Principalities, Archangels and Angels. The latter are the angels of the seven heavens – that is, of the seven planetary spheres – who resemble the angels (spirits) of the air and the earth in this respect. The celestial angels of the nine orders

> . . . will not be constrained by artificial power, for they always stand before the Divine Majesty and are never separated from Its presence.
> Yet because the soul of man was created with them and in their likeness, looking to be rewarded with them, it may [by] the gift and grace of God, while [its] body is still living, behold the Divine Majesty. This knowledge is not to know God as He is, but as Adam and the Prophets knew Him.[28]

Concerning men, the *Sworn Book* then tells us that

> . . . there are three kinds of men who work in Magical Art: Pagans, Jews and Christians.
> Pagans sacrifice to the spirits of the air and earth, but they do not bind or constrain them. The spirits feign themselves to be bound by the words of their law so that they may make them commit idolatry and never turn to the true faith. Because their faith is naught, their works are naught. He who would work after these men must forsake the living God and sacrifice to spirits and idols. For it is faith that works in a man either good or evil, wherefore it is said in the Gospel, 'Faith has made thee safe'.
> Jews do not work to obtain the true vision of God, for by the coming of Christ they lost their preeminence. They cannot come to heaven for the Lord has said, 'He who is not baptized will be damned'. They cannot by invocations bring any work to effect, because they are not alive in Christ. For it is said by the Prophet, 'When the King of Kings and the Lord of Lords comes, your anointing will cease'. But it would not have ceased if they had worked effectively in this Art. Therefore their works are naught.
> Thus only a Christian can come to the Divine Vision and succeed in all other works.[29]

The operation itself lasts for a full twenty-eight days (if I have correctly understood its rubrics). It falls naturally into two parts. The first part, lasting twenty days, serves to purify the operator for the work of the second part, which requires eight days more.[30]

The operation must begin on a Friday. The operator must already be clean in body and soul, that is, he must have washed and put on clean clothes, and he must have truly repented and confessed all his sins. Note that the assistance of a sympathetic priest is required throughout the entire operation. Nowhere does the *Sworn Book* presuppose that the operator himself is a priest, though he must be literate and very familiar with the liturgy and rituals of the church.

The first part of the operation must begin on a Friday and end on a Wednesday. These are days of prayer and fasting. They make extensive use of thirty-seven prayers, so numbered in the *Sworn Book*. About one-third of these prayers are in perfectly intelligible Latin, and some of them are common Catholic prayers. The remaining prayers are not in Latin at all, but are said to be in 'Hebrew and Chaldee'.[31] A few prayers combine this language with Latin.

In addition, the operator must hear a mass of the Holy Spirit every morning and receive the sacrament. This mass has to be celebrated by a sympathetic officiating priest, who is willing to insert several prayers from the *Sworn Book* into the celebration at certain specified points. The operator, too, has other specified prayers to recite while hearing the mass and also before and after he takes communion.

The first three days of the first part of the operation (i.e., Friday, Saturday and Sunday) prepare the operator to learn whether his ritual work will be successful. Eighteen of the thirty-seven prayers are to be said in a specified order three times a day, at Matins, Terce and Sext. Only after finishing these prayers at Sext may the operator break his fast. On Friday and Saturday he may do so with bread and water only, but on Sunday he may also eat fish or meat in moderation. (Other prayers of the thirty-seven may be said by the operator at need, as a defense against his falling into sin. Should he sin nevertheless, then he must confess and fast for seven days.)

Having done all this, on Sunday in the night it 'will be revealed unto you by an angel whether you will obtain your petition or not'.[32] If so, the operator proceeds to the remaining seventeen days of the first part of the operation. (If not, he may start over again next Friday, taking more care in his preparation.)

The ritual for these seventeen days differs from that for the first three days only in two respects. For the first five of the days (i.e., Monday through Friday) no fast is prescribed, unless perhaps the operator is still fasting for some sin committed during the first three days of the ritual. He resumes his fast on bread and water only on Saturday, and continues for twelve days (i.e., through Wednesday). In addition, the pattern of daily private prayer changes somewhat, and becomes more complex. During these seventeen days specified prayers from the *Sworn Book* are to be recited at Terce, None and Vespers, and the choice of prayers to be recited on any given day depends on precisely which day it happens to be in the current lunar month, according to a rather complicated rule. Despite these changes, the operator must continue to hear mass and to take communion every morning, exactly as he did during the first three days. This may be a fearsome obligation, for the *Sworn Book* cautions the operator at this point:

Let him take heed that he receive not the Body of Christ for an evil purpose, for that were death unto him. Wherefore some men have entitled this book, calling it *The Death of the Soul*, and that is true to them that work for an evil intent and purpose and not to have some science or some good thing.[33]

The second part of the operation begins on the very next day (Thursday). For it the *Sworn Book* prescribes thirty-one further prayers, as well as a Litany. These prayers differ sharply from those prescribed for the first part. With only a few exceptions, each of them invokes a Name of God. The Names of God seem to be in Hebrew, Aramaic or Greek, but the rest of each prayer is usually in intelligible Latin.[34]

For the second part of the ritual the operator retires to some isolated place, continues to fast on bread and water, and at Prime, Sext and Vespers recites a much longer set of texts: the Biblical Psalms of David and the Litany with proper prayers following, and then three specified prayers from the *Sworn Book*, each followed by the versicle:

> That Thou by thine immaculate conception, birth, circumcision, preaching, baptism and ascension, O Lord Jesus Christ, vouchsafe to clarify and purge my body, that being washed, I may see Thee with Thy nine orders of angels while yet I live, and that my soul might worship and praise Thee: for Thou, God, art mighty and merciful, who livest and reignest and shalt reign, God in Unity and in Trinity, world without end. Amen[35]

After these three prayers, which are from the first part of the operation, the operator must recite all thirty-one prayers prescribed by the *Sworn Book* for the second part, together with the Litany and ritual which the *Sworn Book* appends to them. This is to be done three times a day for seven days (Thursday through Wednesday), and will occupy a large part of each day.

On the final day of the operation (Thursday) the operator continues this pattern of prayer, but must also clean his chamber, and prepare it for the Beatific Vision. In the morning he is to make a couch of hay, and then strew clean, sifted ashes about it. In these ashes he must write the one hundred Names of God, so that they surround his couch: *Agla* ✚ *Monhon* ✚ *Tetragrammaton* ✚ *Elydeus* ✚ *Ocleiste* . . . [and ninety-five other Names which I omit].[36]

Then he washes himself in 'fair clear water and cold of a spring' while reciting a prayer of lustration.[37] Next he puts on a hair shirt next to the skin, and black clothes over the hair shirt. At Vespers, after the prescribed prayers, he returns to this couch for one long final course of prayer, which I quote in full as a specimen of the whole operation:

> *Zabuather rabarmae iskiros kiros gelon hel tethel nothi imei atethon karex sabaoth sellal chiros opron monigon oriel theos ya.*

God almighty, King of eternal glory, the pleasantries of Whose brightness do fill the heaven and earth, Whom angels and archangels do fear, worship and praise, chanting,

Holy, Holy, Holy, Lord God of Sabaoth,
Heaven and Earth are Full of Thy glory,
Hosannah in the highest;

Who to be Lord over mankind camest out of heaven down to earth;

Orha, Which be Gabriel in the Temple of Jerusalem, Who didst tell Mary of her immaculate conception;

Christus, Who didst show Thyself without spot of corruption in Mary's womb as the sun enters into a glass;

Hospesk, Who madest the dry rod flourish in Joseph's hand;

Gofgar, Who through John the Baptist didst send to the people of Israel testimony and foreknowledge of Thy coming, by preaching those things which were spoken of Thee, of Thy birth as foretold by the Prophets, and Who didst send a light to man sitting in darkness so that they might know of Thy holy coming;

Occynnomos, Who didst send the first star to the three kings, Jasper, Melchior and Balthazar, who came to worship Thee and Thou receivedst their gifts; and [who] showedst them that Thou art both God and man, and showedst them in their sleep by Thine angel the falsehood of King Herod, and Who crownedst gloriously in heaven the Holy Innocents who suffered for Thy name;

Elyorem, Who upon being presented to God in the Temple of Jerusalem by the hands of Simeon, didst show to him that Thou art God, causing him to say,

Now, Lord, let Thy servant depart in peace, for mine eyes have seen the salvation which hath been prepared before the face of all people, a light for the gentiles and the glory of Israel;

Theloy, Who at Cana turnedst water into wine;

Archima, Who for thirty-two years didst preach to the people the Catholic faith, and Who didst make the twelve Apostles perfect in knowledge and grace;

Rabuch, Who for forty days fastedst in the desert and wast tempted by the devil; Who didst forgive Mary Magdalene, weeping at Thy feet and anointing Thee with oil; Who gavest sight to one born blind; Who didst raise Lazarus who was dead for four days; Who didst vouchsafe Thy body to be sacrificed, drawn cruelly, intreated and spitefully judged, blasphemed, whipped with sharp cords, crowned with thorns, nailed to the Cross through Thy hands and Feet, given vinegar and gall to drink, pierced in the side with a spear, laid in a grave, and kept by soldiers – all for us miserable sinners;

By Thy mighty power, and by the sign of Thy Holy Cross with which I now sign myself,
 In the name of the Father ✠ *and of the Son* ✠ *and of the Holy Spirit,*✠
Who brokest the brazen gates and deliveredst Thy friends out of the dark places of hell;

Lord, by the faith which I confess in these Holy Mysteries deliver my soul from the darkness of my body, that I may see Thee with Thy nine orders of angels while yet I live, and that my soul may look upon Thee and praise Thee and glorify Thee.

Thou Who on the third day didst rise from the dead and revealedst Thy resurrection to Mary Magdalene, Mary James, Mary Salome, and to Thy Disciples; Who didst show Thy wounds to Thomas; and [Who] after three days ascendedst into heaven, from whence Thou sent Thy Holy Spirit to Thy Disciples;

Who showedst to Paul Thy Apostle and John the Evangelist Thy secrets;

Who didst open the heavens to Stephen when he was stoned, so he saw Thy majesty with his eyes, saying,
 Behold, I see the heavens open and the Son of Man standing at the right hand of the Power of God;

Who didst grant to Thy martyrs to suffer torments patiently; Who shalt come to judge the quick and the dead with fire,

Look upon me and hear my prayers, that through Thy grace and the power of Thy Holy Names, Thou wouldst vouchsafe to deliver my soul from the darkness of my body and the filthiness of my sins, for in Thee do I end my life,

O my God, ✠ *Stoexhor* ✠ *Ablay* ✠ *Scyystalgaona* ✠ *Fullarite* ✠ *Resphiomoma* ✠ *Remiare* ✠ *Baceda* ✠ *Canona* ✠ *Onlepot,* Who said on the Cross,
 It is finished! [38]

The *Sworn Book* continues, 'Then sleep and say no more, and you shall see the Celestial Palace, and the Majesty of God in his Glory, and the Nine Orders of Angels, and the company of all Blessed Spirits'.[39] This is the end of the ritual and of the magical operation to obtain the Beatific Vision.[40]

THE EFFECT OF THIS MAGICAL OPERATION

Christian theologians and Christian magicians may, if they will, argue with one another whether the ritual prescribed by the *Sworn Book* could ever result in the true Beatific Vision, as that term is defined within Christianity. What cannot be doubted, however, is that a person who scrupulously performs a ritual as complex and demanding as this one, within any religious tradition or none, will often have extraordinary experiences. Whether these experiences are always purely subjective ones, or sometimes have an objective character, need not concern us here, provided we recognize one fact: sometimes experiences that result from such rituals, even if they are completely subjective, have the power to overwhelm their practitioner, whose life can never afterwards move comfortably along its former paths.

The last two centuries have been a period when occult and magical societies have flourished as never before, providing a supportive environment in which one can experiment with the practice of such rituals and investigate their consequences with a modicum of safety; the same period has also witnessed many individual occult and magical experiments. As a result of this unprecedented freedom, there are now many published accounts of the impact which rituals like that in the *Sworn Book* have had on the lives of their practitioners. Although most of this literature has the form of memoirs, nevertheless it suffices in its totality to support the simple claim made above, that complex and demanding ritual practices can wholly unmake and remake the lives of those who carry them out.[41]

The same sort of radical transformation, of course, would surely result from any genuine encounter with the Divine, as the Beatific Vision is defined by Christian theologians. This is why a medieval Christian magician might well have supposed that a ritual such as the one in the *Sworn Book* could result in the Beatific Vision. This is also why such rituals raise a genuine theological issue wherever they are found.

We may leave the theological issue to the theologians, if we like. Even if we do, we must still take note of a considerable body of scientific and academic literature which tries to explain – largely in psychological and physiological terms – just *how* ritual practices and esoteric disciplines are able to produce such powerful experiences in people who follow any religion or none. Here there is no need to survey this field of scholarship, since the reader may consult the several very competent surveys that have already been published.[42]

One paper only requires fuller notice here: Barbara Lex's major article on 'The Neurobiology of Ritual Trance'. In this masterful synthesis of previous work in several fields of scholarship Lex established the existence of a powerful subjective experience – she calls it 'ritual trance' – which results from 'the impact of patterned, repetitive acts on the human nervous system'. She also demonstrates how this experience can be produced by appropriate 'manipulation of universal neurophysiological structures of the human body' and thus 'lies within the potential behavior of all normal human beings'. Particularly noteworthy is Lex's insistence that the *entire* nervous system is implicated in 'ritual trance', not merely or chiefly the brain: in simpler terms, it is an experience of the whole body, not only (or chiefly) the head.[43]

On this basis Lex propounds a number of specific neurophysiological hypotheses, each of which could be tested scientifically. Taken together, her hypotheses provide a framework within which one can easily account for the observed psychological and sociological consequences of ritual, and also for such phenomena as the observed uses of ritual to either heal or harm particular individuals under certain special conditions. Perhaps the most interesting of her hypotheses are the ones about how rituals synchronize biological rhythms, facilitate temporary right-hemisphere dominance in the brain, and result in new patterns of right-left hemisphere integration. If her hypotheses can withstand scientific scrutiny, then they provide all the theoretical support necessary to maintain that some of these 'ritual trances' are among the most powerful of human experiences, and are indeed able to unmake and remake the lives of those who undergo them.

Thus, when the operator has completed all twenty-eight days of the operation prescribed in the *Sworn Book*, he may well have one of these powerful experiences, in which he seems to 'sleep and say no more', and seems to see 'the Celestial Palace, and the Majesty of God in his Glory, and the Nine Orders of Angels, and the company of all Blessed Spirits', just as the *Sworn Book* had promised.[44]

Conclusion

Now we see how Honorius could justify his radical challenge to the authority of the medieval church and state: what he offers is nothing less than a magical operation – in modern terms, if you will, a 'psychotechnology' – seemingly able to put the operator into direct and authentic communication with God, bypassing the hierarchies of church and state alike. Few of the many thirteenth-century intellectual challenges to the authority and power of the church and the state cut as deeply as this one; none cut more deeply.

If magicians could obtain the Beatific Vision almost on demand through the practice of this ritual, then these same magicians could know the will of God more precisely and in greater detail than any Pope or Prince, for the latter, it was conceded on all sides, obtain the Beatific Vision only rarely and in exceptional circumstances, if ever.

If the author of the *Sworn Book* is a typical magician of the thirteenth century, one can better understand now just *why* the church and state began to oppose so strongly any teaching or practice of magic precisely in that century, and maintained its strong opposition for so long afterwards.

One can better understand, too, why William of Auvergne, Archbishop of Paris, regarded the *Sworn Book* as one of the very worst books of magic in circulation. Other books of magic might enable a magician to harm this person or that, but Honorius's work could undercut the foundations of the entire late medieval world.

Though they are hard to track through the following centuries, magical processes to obtain the Beatific Vision must have continued to challenge the authority of church and state for a very long time. On 19 September 1398, the theological faculty of the University of Paris found occasion to condemn twenty-eight errors pertaining to the practice of magic, the last of which was 'that by certain magical arts we can come to a vision of Divine Essence or of Holy Spirits'.[45] Just a few years later, in 1402, Jean Gerson, then the chancellor of the University of Paris, repeated the condemnation in his short treatise *On Errors about the Art of Magic* (*De erroribus circa artem magicam*).[46]

The *Sworn Book* itself continued to be read and copied for many centuries. At the end of the fourteenth century John Gower mentions 'the scole which Honorius wrot' in his *Confessio Amantis*, at the end of an interesting list of magical texts and methods which a lover might use to win his love.[47] The *Sworn Book* is cited in a short treatise, *Magisterium eumaticae artis, sive scientiae magicalis*, preserved in a single fifteenth-century manuscript.[48] From the sixteenth century come the partial English version and one of the five known Latin manuscripts; two other Latin manuscripts of the work were written in the seventeenth century.[49] Although Johannes Trithemius does not, so far as I know, mention the *Sworn Book* anywhere in his writings, he does cite the name of Honorius of Thebes in one of his cryptographic works as the author of a magician's alphabet: 'Here follows the alphabet of Honorius surnamed the Theban, by means of which he concealed his fatuities concerning magic, as Peter of Apono testifies in his major fourth book.'[50] In addition, Giordano Bruno seems to have met with the *Sworn Book* somewhere, for one of the speakers in his *Cabala del cavallo Pegaseo* is a donkey named Onorio, who came from Thebes.[51] Bruno composed this work during his visit to England in 1583 to 1585, where he could have read Honorius's treatise, possibly in the fourteenth-century Latin copy that was then owned by John Dee.

The challenge which the *Sworn Book* delivered to the thirteenth- and fourteenth-century church and state was eventually turned back: its author did not succeed at his chosen task. Yet even an unsuccessful challenge may instruct the perceptive student of bygone ages. So it is with the *Sworn Book* of the unknown thirteenth-century magician who styled himself Honorius of Thebes.

Notes

1 Léopold Delisle, *Le cabinet des manuscrits de la Bibliothèque Impériale* (Paris: Imprimerie Impériale, 1868–81), vol. II, pp. 518–35, at p. 523: '. . . secretorum librorum, quorum descriptionem ad hunc librum nolumus pertinere'.

2 David Pingree, 'The Diffusion of Arabic Magical Texts in Western Europe', *La diffusione delle scienze Islamiche nel Medio Evo Europeo* (Rome: Accademia Nazionale dei Lincei, 1987), pp. 57–102, has identified one of these thirty-six manuscripts (Paris, BN lat. 16204) and has succeeded in determining many of the astrological, alchemical and magical texts that were in Richard de Fourniville's 'secret books'.

3 Delisle, vol. II, p. 521: 'Ceterum, praeter illa quorum fecimus mentionem, est et aliud genus tractatuum secretorum, quorum profunditas publicis oculis dedignatur exponi. Ac proinde non est intentionis nostrae ut inter praehabitos ordinentur; sed eis deputandus est certus locus, neminem praeter dominum proprium admissurus. Quare nec eorum descriptio pertinet ad hunc librum.'

4 Johannes Trithemius, *De scriptoribus ecclesiasticis* (Basel: Johannes Amerbach, 1495).

5 Johannes Trithemius, *Antipalus malificiorum*, book I, chapter III [in Johannes Busaeus, ed., *Paralipomena opusculorum Petri Blesensis et Joannis Trithemii aliorumque* (Mainz: Balthassar Lippius, 1605)], pp. 291–311.

6 Some of the manuscripts preserve a list of the ninety-two chapters into which the entire *Sworn Book* was divided [e.g., BL Sloane ms. 313, ff. 1v–2r]. To judge by this list, the six known manuscripts are far from complete.

7 Samuel Ayscough, *A Catalogue of Manuscripts Preserved in the British Museum* (London: Rivington, 1782), vol. 2, pp. 874, 876, 878–80 [Sloane mss. 313, 3854(9), 3883(1), 3885(1,3,4)]. Edward J.L. Scott, *Index to the Sloane Manuscripts in the British Museum* (London: British Museum, 1904), pp. 261, 473 [Sloane mss. 313, 3854 and 3885]. Sloane ms. 3826 also contains extracts from the *Sworn Book*, according to Arthur Edward Waite, *The Book of Black Magic and Pacts* (London: Redway, 1898), pp. 31–5, or *The Book of Ceremonial Magic* (London: Rider, 1911), pp. 18–22.

8 Cf. Royal ms. 17.A.XLII, ff. 15r–23r, 74r–79v, with H.C. Agrippa von Nettesheim, *De occulta philosophia libri tres*, ed. V. Perrone Compagni, Studies in the History of Christian Thought, vol. 48 (Leiden: Brill, 1992), book I, chaps 43–4, and book III, chaps 24–5; the editor identifies Agrippa's various sources throughout.

9 George F. Warner and Julius P. Gilson, *Catalogue of Western Manuscripts in the Old Royal and King's Collections* (London: British Museum, 1921), vol. II, p. 224 [Royal ms. 17.A.XLII].

10 Julian Roberts and Andrew G. Watson, *John Dee's Library Catalogue* (London: The Bibliographical Society, 1990), pp. 57, 169.

11 Waite, *Black Magic*, pp. 31 ff.

12 Lynn Thorndike, *A History of Magic and Experimental Science* (New York: Columbia University Press, 1923–58), vol. 2, pp. 279–89 [citing five of the six known manuscripts, omitting Sloane ms. 3826].

13 Daniel J. Driscoll, ed., *The Sworn Book of Honourius the Magician, As Composed by Honourius through Counsel with the Angel Hocroell* (Gillette, NJ: Heptangle Press, 1977; repr., 1983).

14 William of Auvergne, *Opera Omnia* (Paris: Pralard, 1674 [facsimile reprint, Frankfurt a/M: Minerva, 1963]), vol. I, p. 70: 'Ex hac eadem peste curiositatis processit liber maledictus et

execrabilis, qui dicitur Liber sacratus.' [I take William's title, *Liber sacratus*, as a variation on *Liber Sacer* or a conflation of *Liber sacer et juratus*.]

15 William of Auvergne, vol. I, p. 89: 'Ad hoc genus idolatriae pertinent illae quatuor figurae quae *Anuli Salomonis*, et quinta quae vocatur *Sigillum Salomonis*, et novem aliae quae vocantur *Novem Candariae* [read: *Canthariae*], quorum omnium execrabilissimae consecrationes et detestabiles invocationes, scripturae, imagines, apertissimam idolatriae continent impietatem. De nefanda autem imagine illa quae *Idea Salomonis et Entocta* [perhaps: *Eutocta*] dicitur, nulla fit mentio apud Christianos; similiter nec de libro quem *Sacratum* vocant nec de operibus eiusdem. Eodem modo neque de figura quae *Mandal* sive *Amandel* dicitur aut operibus eius.'

16 Edward Peters, *The Magician, the Witch and the Law* (Philadelphia: University of Pennsylvania Press, 1978), ch. 4.

17 Norman Cohn, *Europe's Inner Demons: An Enquiry Inspired by the Great Witch-Hunt* (New York: Basic Books, 1975), p. 178, sees in the Prologue a reference to fourteenth-century Papal condemnations of magic, and thus dates the *Sworn Book* to the fourteenth century.

18 Cf. R. Schnackenburg and K. Forster, 'Anschauung Gottes', *Lexikon für Theologie und Kirche*, 2nd ed. (Freiburg: Verlag Herder, 1957–68), vol. 1, cols 583–91, and now Christian Trottmann, *La vision béatifique: des disputes scolastiques à sa définition par Benoît XII*, Bibliothèque des écoles françaises d'Athènes et de Rome, vol. 289 (Rome: École française de Rome, 1995).

19 Thorndike, vol. 2, pp. 279–81, and Peters, pp. 110–12, 117, 119, 124, also assign the *Sworn Book* to the first half of the thirteenth century.

20 Driscoll, pp. 1–4; cf. Sloane ms. 313, f. 1r–v; Royal ms. 17.A.XLII, ff. 2r–4v. I am indebted to Richard Kieckhefer for the brief use of his microfilms of these two manuscripts, which enabled me to correct or emend Driscoll's English text at some places.

21 The statement that magic can 'destroy all other sciences' probably refers to the strange pseudo-Solomonic work in circulation at the time, called *Ars Notoria*, which gives a series of conjurations and magical figures for acquiring an instant mastery of any field of learning, without any need for study. Cf. Thorndike, vol. 2, pp. 281–3, and see essays by Camille and Fanger in this volume.

22 This interpretation of the number of the Fathers at the Council of Nicaea – which is also the number of Abraham's servants who fought with him to rescue Lot from captivity (Genesis 14:14) – is made explicit in Ambrose of Milan's *De fide*, book I, prologue. It is probably implicit in Athanasius the Great's *Epistola ad Afros Episcopos*, chapter 2, where the Fathers at the Council of Nicaea are said to number 318. (Other early sources for the Council indicate that these Fathers were somewhat fewer.) The roots of this interpretation are much older: in the first century CE the *Epistle of Barnabas*, chapter 9, interprets the number 318 of Abraham's servants as looking forward to Jesus and the Cross.

23 Are these 'shells' (*cortices*) perhaps the same as the deceiving and empty *q'lipoth*, or shells, against which the Kabbalah warns?

24 Here the end of the Prologue is marked in the Latin text with *Explicit prologus*, and in the English version with *Finis prologi*.

25 No doubt the name Hocroël is as significant as the number 811, but I have not yet discovered what its significance might be. Gustav Davidson, *A Dictionary of Angels Including the Fallen Angels* (New York: Free Press, 1967), p. 141, suggests that Hocroël is a variant of Hochmel or Hochmael, the angel of the wisdom of God, from a Hebrew root *ḥkm*, 'wise'.

26 Driscoll, pp. 69–72, 87–96, 97–105, 111 (Sloane ms. 313, ff. 19v–27v). For the *Clavicula Salomonis* cf. the arbitrary edition by S.L. MacGregor Mathers, *The Key of Solomon the King* (*Clavicula Salomonis*) (York Beach, ME: Weiser, 1989). More than 100 Western European manuscripts of the *Key of Solomon* have been recorded, which vary greatly among themselves; Mathers consulted only seven of these manuscripts, and minimized the variability of the text. The ultimate source of all these Western European texts seems to be a Greek work, the *Magical Treatise of Solomon* ('Αποτελεσματικὴ πραγματεία Σαλομῶνος), for which see Richard P.F. Greenfield, *Traditions of Belief in Late Byzantine Demonology* (Amsterdam: Hakkert, 1988), part II (esp. pp. 159–63).

27 Driscoll, pp. 7–8, 14, 17–68, printed out of order. To restore the original order (as in Sloane ms. 313, ff. 2v–19v), read pp. 7–8, 20–39, 17–19, 40–57, 60–3, 57–9, 14, 63–8.

28 Driscoll, p. 7.

29 Driscoll, pp. 7–8.

30 Driscoll, pp. 7–8, 20–39, 17–19, gives the first part of the ritual (20 days); pp. 40–57, 60–3, 57–9, 14, 63–8, gives the second part (8 days).

31 Sloane ms. 313, f. 10v; Royal ms. 17.A.XLII, f. 46r–v (not in Driscoll's edition). Unfortunately, I cannot judge whether these prayers are truly in Hebrew or Aramaic ('Chaldee'), or are merely gibberish that sounds like those languages.

32 Royal ms. 17.A.XLII, f. 46r (cf. Driscoll, p. 17).

33 Royal ms. 17.A.XLII, f. 48r, Sloane ms. 313, f. 11r (cf. Driscoll, p. 19).

34 As before, I cannot judge the Hebrew or Aramaic, but the Greek is real Greek, although badly transcribed, and it is clear that the author had some knowledge of the liturgy of the Greek Orthodox Church.

35 Driscoll, p. 61.

36 Driscoll, pp. 63, 14.

37 Royal ms. 17.A.XLII, f. 62v (cf. Driscoll, p. 63).

38 Driscoll, pp. 64–7.

39 Driscoll, p. 67.

40 The same operation, with appropriate changes in certain prayers as indicated in the *Sworn Book*, may also be used to obtain knowledge, or to invoke spirits, or to remit or avoid sins, or to redeem three souls from purgatory (Royal ms. 17.A.XLII, ff. 35r–v, 66r–v; cf. Driscoll, pp. 25–6).

41 The most instructive of all these memoirs, for our purposes, is by William Bloom, *The Sacred Magician: A Ceremonial Diary*, 2nd edn (Glastonbury: Gothic Image,1992). It covers the six months that the author devoted in 1973 to the performance of a similar magical ritual translated and edited by S.L. MacGregor Mathers, *The Book of the Sacred Magic of Abramelin the Mage*, 2nd edn (London: Watkins, 1900). The goal of this latter ritual is not the Beatific Vision, but open communication with one's Guardian Angel.

42 I particularly recommend Andrew Neher, *The Psychology of Transcendence*, 2nd edn (New York: Dover, 1990); Marghanita Laski, *Ecstasy in Secular and Religious Experiences*, 2nd edn (Los Angeles: Tarcher, 1989); and now Jess Byron Hollenback, *Mysticism: Experience, Response, Empowerment* (University Park, PA: Pennsylvania State University Press, 1996), as well as the relevant parts of Charles T. Tart, *Altered States of Consciousness*, 3rd edn (San Francisco: HarperSanFrancisco, 1990), and T.M. Luhrmann, *Persuasions of the Witch's Craft: Ritual Magic in Contemporary England* (Cambridge, MA:

Harvard, 1989). I have also found several things of value in a book of a wholly popular character: J. Finley Hurley, *Sorcery* (London: Routledge & Kegan Paul, 1985).

43 Barbara Lex, 'The Neurobiology of Ritual Trance', *The Spectrum of Ritual: A Biogenetic Structural Analysis*, ed. Eugene G. d'Aquili et al. (New York: Columbia University Press, 1979), pp. 117–51. See also her 'Voodoo Death: New Thoughts on an Old Explanation', *American Anthropologist* 76 (1974), pp. 818–23; and 'Neurological Bases of Revitalization Movements', *Zygon* 13 (1978), pp. 276–312.

44 Driscoll, p. 67.

45 Henri Denifle and Emil Chatelain, *Chartularium Universitatis Parisiensis* (Paris: Delalain, 1886–97), vol. IV, pp. 32–6: 'XXVIIIᵘˢ articulus, quod per quasdam artes magicas possumus devenire ad visionem divine essentie vel sanctorum spirituum. Error.' [Richard Kieckhefer, *Magic in the Middle Ages* (Cambridge: Cambridge University Press, 1990), pp. 170–1, was the first to see in this condemnation a possible reference to the *Sworn Book*.]

46 Jean Gerson, *Œuvres complètes* (Paris: Desclée, 1961–77), vol. 10, pp. 77–90.

47 John Gower, *The English Works*, ed. G.C. Macaulay, The Early English Text Society, e.s., vols 81–2 (London: The Early English Text Society, 1900–1), vol. II, p. 203 (VI: 1331–2). I am indebted to Claire Fanger for this reference. [Gower's list of magical texts (VI: 1311–32) is interesting in its own right. The only known text on which Gower might have based his list is chapter XI of the *Speculum Astronomiae* attributed to Albertus Magnus, but the difference between the two texts is considerable. (See Paolo Zambelli, *The* Speculum Astronomiae *and its Enigma: Astrology, Theology and Science in Albertus Magnus and his Contemporaries*, Boston Studies in the Philosophy of Science, vol. 135 (Dordrecht: Kluwer, 1992), pp. 240–51. If the *Speculum Astronomiae*, chapter XI, is indeed Gower's source, it extends only as far as VI: 1324; even so, Gower will have to have misread *specula* as *spatula* in the title of Toz Graecus's *De quatuor speculis*, and he will have to have drawn on another source for several of his authors, including Honorius. It may be that Gower had seen a manuscript containing all of the magical texts which he mentions, which would be of the same general character the extant manuscript from Richard de Fourniville's library mentioned in note 2 above.]

48 A.M. Bandini, *Catalogus codicum latinorum Bibliothecae Mediceae Laurentianae* (Florence, 1774–8), vol. III, cols 305–8 (ms. 89. sup. 38).

49 These four manuscripts (Royal 17.A.XLII, Sloane 3826, 3883, 3885) were cited and dated in section 2 above.

50 Johannes Trithemius, *Polygraphiae libri VI* (Basel: Johannes Haselberg, 1518), book VI, at sig. q[5]r–v: 'Sequitur aliud alphabetum Honorii cognomento Thebani, cuius ministerio suas in magicis fatuitates abscondit, sicut Petrus de Apono testatur in suo maiore libro quarto.' [I have not been able to identify more precisely the reference to this passage by Peter of Apono. The alphabet in question is also given by Agrippa, book III, ch. 29, who clearly has Trithemius as his source here.]

51 Giordano Bruno, *Cabala del cavallo Pegaseo* ('Paris: A. Baio' [= London: J. Charlewood], 1585).

7

John the Monk's *Book of Visions of the Blessed and Undefiled Virgin Mary, Mother of God*: Two Versions of a Newly Discovered Ritual Magic Text

Nicholas Watson

The *Liber visionum beate et intemerate Dei genetricis virginis Marie* (*Liber visionum*) is a recently identified book of prayers and other materials which has a close relationship with the group of ritual magic texts known as the Ars Notoria.[1] Two manuscript versions of this work will be discussed here: Munich, Bayerische Staatsbibliothek Clm 276 (hereafter Munich) and Hamilton, Canada, McMaster University Library, Unnumbered MS (hereafter McMaster). In the Munich text (indeed in all known texts but the McMaster version, which is the only copy so far identified not to bear the author's name) the *Liber* identifies itself as written by 'frater Iohannes, monachus de Mariginato', who composed the work as a result of a series of dreams inspired by the Virgin Mary, some of which took place between 1304 and 1307 (Prologue; Part I, Second Prologue).[2] The text describes itself as the outcome of Mary's attempts to persuade John to abandon his practice of the *artes exceptive* (magic arts)[3] by teaching a new, holy art instead. It is this art, revealed by Mary in thirty prayers – and in other revelations which apparently took place over some years, many of them mediated by angels – that the text unlocks for prepared readers. These readers are informed that, like John, they can use the prayers (which are directed not only to Mary but to Christ, the Trinity, the orders of angels, and the saints) to gain knowledge of all the seven liberal arts; medicine, philosophy, physics, metaphysics and theology; and both the mechanical arts and the very exceptive arts the *Liber visionum* purports to displace. In the McMaster text (which is a revised version of John's rituals consecrated for the use of one Bernardus, more organized and in certain ways more detailed than Munich), this list is expanded to include almost any item of information about past, present or future that users desire (Quarta Practica).

Although its full genealogy may prove to be more complicated, the *Liber visionum* clearly did have its immediate origin where it claims it does: with John, a monk at the Benedictine monastery of Morigny (near Etampes, east of Chartres in north-west France), writing in the first quarter of the fourteenth century.[4] In the *Grandes Chroniques de France* (which originated at the abbey of St Denis in Paris, and details the major political and ecclesiastical events of the times), there survives a well-informed account of the condemnation, in 1323, of a work by an author from the same monastery. From the account, it is clear that this text is the *Liber visionum*:

> And in this same year [1323], there was a monk of Morigny, an abbey near Etampes, who through his curiosity and pride wanted to inspire and renew a condemned heresy and sorcery called in Latin Ars Notoria, although he hoped to give it another name and title. This science teaches the making of figures and designs, and they must be different from one another and each assigned to a different branch of learning. Also, they must be contemplated at particular times with fasting and prayers. And so, after contemplation, the branch of knowledge which one wants to have and acquire through this act of contemplation is bestowed. But one had to name and invoke various little known names, which were firmly believed to be the names of demons. Hence this science disappointed many and many were deceived by it. For nobody using this science had ever gained any benefit or received any fruit. Nonetheless, this monk condemned this science, even though he feigned that the blessed virgin Mary had appeared to him many times, thereby inspiring him with knowledge. And so in her honour he had had many images painted in his book, with many prayers and letters, very richly in expensive colours, feigning that the Virgin Mary had revealed everything to him. After these images had been applied to each branch of learning and contemplated, once the prayers had been said, the branch of learning one was seeking would be bestowed – and more, for if there were riches, honours or pleasures one wanted to have, one could have them. And because the book promised these things, and because one had to make invocations and write one's name twice in the book, and have a copy of the book personally written for one's own use, a costly matter – otherwise, if one did not have a copy written at one's own cost and expense, it would be worthless – the said book was justly condemned in Paris as false and evil, against the Christian faith, and condemned to be burned and put in the fire.[5]

A shorter account, written in Latin and probably deriving from the *Grandes Chroniques*, survives in the continuation of the Chronicle of Guillaume de Nangis.[6] Neither account quite represents the text in either version discussed here. But there can be no question that we are dealing with the same text, whose condemnation forms a single and apparently not very significant item in the long list of trials and burnings for heresy or magic which make up a good deal of the early fourteenth-century parts of each chronicle. (No information about what happened to John himself is given, although since there is no mention of punishment, it can be suspected that he recanted.) The *Liber visionum* is thus a rare phenomenon: a condemned ritual magic text with a known author and point of origin.

The *Grandes Chroniques* entry provides some insight into the milieu in which the text was written (a milieu in which it was condemned as heretical), and offers an avenue for future research on the text. But our present knowledge of the text's circulation locates the *Liber visionum* and its readers in rather different times, places and contexts. The two copies discovered soon enough to be discussed in this article are both from late fifteenth-century manuscripts, neither of them French and only one of them containing other ritual magic texts. One of these (Munich) originated in Germany and preserves most of what I take to be something close to the original form of the text – although we'll see that the phrase 'original form' may itself have its difficulties – alongside a copy of the Solomonic Ars Notoria and other divinatory and scientific works.[7] The other (McMaster) was possibly copied in Italy and contains all but the first section of a careful revision, presenting the text in much the format of a Book of Hours.[8] Four further copies of varying dates, all of them German or Austrian, have also been identified, thanks in large part to the assiduity of German manuscript cataloguers. The catalogue entries, too, are suggestive of the variety of contexts in which the text appears and the complexity of its history. In two fourteenth-century manuscripts – one of them now in the British Library (copied by Albertus de Judenberga in 1374), the other in a monastic library in Vienna (copied in 1377) – the work is either on its own or part of a collection of closely related texts.[9] In a mid-fifteenth-century copy, originally from a Carthusian monastery (then in the library at Werenigerode, now either lost or preserved in Herne), it is included in what seems to be an inquisitor's collection, with numerous papal bulls and a treatise against the beghards and beguines.[10] This last manuscript, along with an attack on the *Liber visionum* in the *Sopholegium* of Jacobus le Grand (*c.* 1405), which insists on the work's nefarious aims and effects, shows that its heretical origins were not forgotten, despite its extensive, seemingly mainly monastic, circulation.[11]

Finally, in an early fifteenth-century manuscript from Graz, dated 1414, it appears in what is otherwise apparently an orthodox compilation, alongside Honorius's *Elucidarium* and a collection of sermons.[12] This manuscript, which we learned of too late for a detailed account to be included in this volume, but which is the only one of the four manuscripts above cited which I have been able to examine at all, preserves a remarkable prologue containing additional material about the visionary experiences leading to John's composition of the *Liber visionum*.[13] There is evidence (in the form of a scribal instruction apparently accidentally preserved at the opening of Munich) that this prologue was in fact intended for inclusion in the Munich version of the text, but was either lost or omitted. Clearly much information still awaits discovery in this and in the other extant manuscripts. But even at this stage of work on the text – before any systematic search of European manuscript catalogues has been undertaken – it is clear that some of the features of the *Liber visionum* that need to be taken into account are its geographical dispersal, its survival in active use over at least a century and a half, and its presence in a wide array of kinds of manuscript.

Some of the larger issues raised by the *Liber visionum* and its relationship to the Ars Notoria and other forms of ritual magic are addressed elsewhere in this book by Claire Fanger and Richard Kieckhefer. Fanger looks at the rhetorical strategies by which John negotiates his relationship to the condemned Solomonic Ars Notoria, while Kieckhefer examines the *Liber visionum* in the context of parallel Jewish mystical practices. This article focuses narrowly on the *Liber visionum* itself in the two forms in which I have so far been able to study it. The three appendices give a detailed breakdown of the Munich and McMaster texts, aiming to take the reader step by step through the two versions, demonstrating their relationship and the remarkable degree of organization they exhibit, and providing a summary of their contents, so far as these are yet clear. Before this, however, some space must be spared for an overview of the text, to act as a guide to the detailed analysis that follows it and as a preliminary hypothesis about how the *Liber visionum* may have been put together. The overview takes the Munich version as its basis, and operates on the assumption that at least Parts I–III of the Munich text are fairly close to John's original version (although one can be much less confident about Part IV); thus the overview generally speaks of 'John' as the author not only of the prayers but of their rubrics. This assumption is, of course, most vulnerable to the untapped evidence of the four other manuscripts, at least three of which were copied earlier than Munich and which may well complicate or even clarify these findings. (For example, according to the catalogues cited in notes 9–12, some of these manuscripts provide the text with a different incipit, *Nemo cum lucernam accendit sub abscondito eam ponit* – the first words, e.g., of the Graz prologue and a tantalizing array of possible versions and structuring principles.) Despite the rapidity with which our knowledge of this text is evolving, however, I have chosen to present not simply a bald account of the Munich text but a relatively detailed argument as to its make up and the process of its composition. This argument stands to be corrected by further research, but for the present seems to me to offer not only a more lively account but a more cogent one than did my first attempts to present the text in a neutral way.

According to the Munich text, John's composition of the *Liber visionum* was the outcome, first, of the Virgin's persistent attempts to rescue him, second, of a delicate set of negotiations between himself and the Virgin. In the Prologue to the work, and elsewhere, John sketches his seduction by the nefarious *artium et scientiarum exceptivarum* – the magical arts and sciences, elsewhere identified specifically with the Notary Art (Part IV, Discussion ~1, Nota ~4). After the Virgin's initially unsuccessful attempts to lure him away from his passion, and his eventual surrender to her, John ultimately induces Mary to teach him a holy version of the very art he now rejects, by which he can attain 'to the summit of all the sciences and arts' (Prologue).[14] According to Part IV (Discussion ~1, Nota ~5), the history of John and the Virgin's relations also involved the composition of at least one earlier text, now superseded and subsumed by the *Liber visionum* (although the passage is extremely elusive, I have some suggestions to make about this later). The *Liber visionum* itself is at once the fulfilment of the Virgin's promise and an account of this fulfilment, told through prayers, *cogitationes* (meditations), and the rubrics that link them together.[15] In the *Liber visionum*, John can thus present himself not only as the devout servant of the Virgin and of Christ, but as the converted sinner, comparable to Theophilus the apostate[16] (e.g., Part III, Concluding Prayer, i); as the enslaved Israelite, journeying from Egypt to the Promised Land (Part IV, Discussion ~1, Nota ~4); as the mature man, able to ingest spiritual meat and no longer dependent on mere milk (Part IV, Discussion ~1, Nota ~5); and as a successor to Solomon, to whom God revealed the key to wisdom, the Tetragrammaton (Part III, Prayer 30), and also to John's persecuted and finally martyred patron, John the evangelist (e.g., Prologue). While he claims for himself only the infused purity and wisdom that are the rewards for the *opus* his book describes, and refers to himself as the book's *compilator*, rather than *auctor* (Part IV, Discussion ~1, Nota ~5), the authority of the book is taken as all but final. Only a revelation equivalent to the one he received from Mary (admittedly a possible event, according to this text) can justify changing anything in it, including the rubrics (Part IV, Discussion ~1, Nota ~1). Moreover, his story leads him into exalted company. Like Dante in the *Paradiso*, John journeys from earth to heaven, ascending stage by stage through the angelic orders until he attains the court of heaven. Here, he is filled with all wisdom, if not the Beatific Vision itself. By the outset of Part IV, he can thus describe himself as speaking 'with the authority of sacred eloquence and the revelation of heavenly angels' (Part IV, Prologue),[17] responsible as he is for a 'new compilation' (*nova compilatio*) of heavenly wisdom, part or all of which boasts the proud subtitle 'the book of the flowers of celestial teaching' (*liber florum doctrine celestis*, Part IV, Discussion ~2). This book is consecrated by God, displacing the *antiqua compilatio* and all other *artes* as the New Covenant displaces the Old.

The process by which the prayers were received is intriguingly unclear. They are said to be dictated by angels (Part IV, Prologue). But they are also described as composed and tested (*composui et probavi*) by John himself (Part I, Second Prologue), and as licenced by the Virgin (Prologue), who is the true authority behind the book and goal of the *opus* it describes (*experimentum visionis habende*, Part I, Prayer *3). They are almost all in some sense to be thought of as products of a

long series of visionary dreams (the major exceptions are Part I, Prayers *3 and
*7.iii), as is the structure of Parts I–III, and perhaps Part IV. But they are also
described as partly derived from the Ars Notoria and John's earlier attempt to
transcend that work (Part IV, Discussion ~1, Nota ~5), in a process John frankly
calls *compilatio*. Moreover, only three dreams are even remotely evoked
throughout the entire work, and only one (Part I, Prayer *5.iv) explicitly includes
the composition of a prayer; this is said to be by John, rather than being written
to angelic dictation.[18] There is, perhaps, a deliberate refusal in the book to
resolve the tension between the claim that angels or the Virgin spoke the prayers
to John and the fact that in all the prayers it is John who speaks to the Virgin or
the angels. John mouths words which may have been approved in advance by his
interlocutors, but they are still in a real sense his words: this is basic to the book's
fine sense of the dramatic. As a whole, the book creates the impression that the
prayers were approved or confirmed by the Virgin in dreams, and that the reality
of angelic intervention was assumed, more than experienced. The dreams
themselves, where they are alluded to, are used for confirmation and for
addressing specific questions (the function they are also meant to have for users of
the work), rather than for dictation.

This emphasis on the final form of the system described by the *Liber visionum*,
rather than on the process by which it came into being, is unusual at a period
when visionary writers often built their accounts around the exact circumstances
of their experiences, assuming that these circumstances were integral to the truth
of what they saw. John's gender may play a part in his strategies. Like the male
visionaries recently described by Robert Lerner, his concern is with the
production of a formal literary authority that is not dependent on the detailed
revelation of his interior disposition, in the way the authority of women
visionaries tended to be.[19] But the book's lack of attention to the processes of its
composition – beyond the bald outline just described – has three more concrete
reasons. First, we'll see various signs that the *Liber visionum* as we now have it may
be a drawing together of material written over a fairly lengthy period, some of it
before the overall structure of the finished work had been conceived. All too
aware of this history and the threat it poses to his finished work's unity, John was
perhaps anxious to present the final form of his lifework as pellucidly as possible.
Second, John's concern with the final form of the text is of a piece with the
almost total lack of interest in interiority exhibited throughout the *Liber visionum*,
despite the expression of and exhortations to emotion in the practitioner's
dealings with the Virgin. This is a rhetorical religious system, in which devotion
is a performative activity, not a subjective experience, and virtue is achieved and
maintained by ritual means, not grounded in self-examination. John's
relationship with the Virgin is thus formally limited to its public expression – as
often with relations between subject and ruler – and the process by which that
relationship was arrived at is of fairly small importance. The process that matters

is the one by means of which John uses his intimacy with the Virgin to ascend to the knowledge of all the arts and sciences. Finally, despite its narrative cast, the *Liber visionum* is essentially a practical manual, all of whose autobiographical details have to do double duty as a series of instructions for the book's readers, who hope to follow where John has led. Unlike most visionary texts, which emphasize their own singular status and whose value resides precisely in their privileged access to the other world, the *Liber visionum* offers readers a visionary system they can *imitate*; by doing so, they can learn to conduct their own visionary research into the arts and sciences and precipitate their own prophetic dreams. Reading the book of visions (*liber visionum*) is only a preliminary to embarking on the *opus* it describes. Moreover, the aim of the *opus* is itself highly practical. Where other visionary texts purport to act as a bridge between this world and the next, the system described in the *Liber visionum*, for all its connections with the heavenly realm, is firmly anchored in the present life, and the advantages that knowledge of the arts and sciences can bring.

   The *opus* – that is, the exact method by which readers can use the *Liber visionum* to attain to the knowledge it offers – is a major subject of Part IV (now incomplete), and is presented in detail by the McMaster version of the text. Before describing the *opus*, however, it is necessary to say something about the exemplary narrative the *Liber visionum* presents as the basis for its system, and about the formal structure of the text. (This structural analysis leaves Part IV, which consists of various discussions and sets of instructions, aside for the present.) Despite the practical goal of the *Liber visionum* and the book's careful alignment of the reader's progress with John's, this structure is not in the first instance much concerned with the would-be user. Indeed, for all its narrative coherence, it is surprisingly hard to put together as a set of practical instructions. It is true that the prayers (like those in the Ars Notoria) are subdivided into the categories of *generales* and *speciales*, a division which makes practical sense. It is also true that the text is heavily rubricated and subdivided into sections for easy access and cross-referencing. Thus most of the prayers are divided into numbered *partes*, each introduced in the Munich manuscript with its own large capital for easy recognition, and the prayers are grouped in a framework consisting of three books which are also referred to as *partes*.[20] Two of these have their own subtitles: 'The Grace of our Lord Jesus Christ' (Part I, Second Incipit, referring to Part I, Prayers *2–7, also called 'The Book of Mary the Virgin'); and 'Prayers to God or to the Blessed Virgin Mary' (Part II, Incipit). Yet this subdivision into three parts has less to do with the type of prayer each part contains or the use to which they are to be put than with the underlying narrative of John's progress. Part I, which consists mainly of *generales*, contains at least one 'special' prayer (Prayer *5), while Part III begins with a series of *generales* similar to those found in Part II before the *speciales* that are its principal purpose. We will see why this subdivision works later, but it would have been logical to divide Parts II and III at Part III, Prayer 20 (the end of the *generales*), had John's main concern been to make his text accessible to users.

The numbering of the prayers also submits to narrative, rather than practical exigencies. Here, John has evolved a system in which the prayers written or used before the Virgin gave permission for the book to be written (i.e., the prayers in Part I, here numbered as *1–7; see Prologue) are numbered separately from the 'thirty' prayers which occupy the book proper (Parts II–III). That is, Part I uses one (internally intricate) numbering system, while Parts II and III together use another. This makes cross-referencing much harder than it would otherwise have been. Moreover, it takes some dexterity on John's part to arrive at the symbolic number thirty. He does this only by subdividing a single huge prayer to the orders of angels in Part II into nine (see Part II, Prayers 2–10, concluding rubric); by including more than one prayer with no number (e.g., Part III, Prima Oratio and Concluding Prayer); and by allowing the numbered prayers to be of highly uneven length. Single parts of some prayers are longer than other complete numbered prayers; the shortest of these (Part III, Prayer 13) is less than a hundred words long. There is a theoretical justification for all John's numbering decisions: each numbered prayer, at least in Parts II–III, can be understood as a rung in the ladder that leads him from earth to heaven or ignorance to knowledge. It is clear that John does not equate length with efficacy; like both pseudo-Dionysius the Areopagite in the *Mystical Theology* and Geoffrey of Vinsauf in the *Poetria nova*, he indeed regards brevity as having special power (see Part I, Prayer *7.iv, rubric).[21] But the numbering of the prayers remains another area in which John consciously subordinates the practical working out of the *opus* to the demands of his spiritual autobiography, insisting his readers understand the system he describes as the story of his own exemplary journey before they are allowed to begin appropriating it for their own use.

This journey is perhaps best thought of as having four largely distinct stages, respectively described in Part I, Part II, Part IIIa (Prayers 13–20) and Part IIIb (Prayers 21–Concluding Prayer). I am going tentatively to nickname these stages Conversion, Purgation, Illumination and Union; the last three titles deliberately evoke a text whose narrative outline resembles that of the *Liber visionum*, which it is just possible John was aware of as a model, Bonaventure's *De triplici via* (*c.* 1260).[22] The first stage, Conversion, is ostensibly described in a series of seven prayers (Part I, Prayers *1–7), whose lack of clear narrative direction and complicated numbering system suggest two hypotheses. First, actual (as well as exemplary) autobiography here lies close to the surface. Second, this part of the *Liber visionum* retains traces of a former existence as part or all of an earlier work by John. Indeed, Conversion is a much less important theme in the prayers themselves than should, formally, be the case. After the Prologue's account of John's involvements with the forbidden arts and the Virgin's rescue attempts, the prayers in Part I are introduced as written 'before I had licence to compose the present book' and in order to gain permission to do so (Part I, Prayer *1, rubric).[23] Since the Prologue has just described John seeking Mary's permission to write the book just after his second and final renunciation of the *artes exceptive*, we are presumably meant to see Part I as staging the process of his full recuperation, as John wrestles with the Virgin and she with him. Certainly, both the Prologue and Part I present a common picture of a world beset with diabolic persecution; John several times identifies himself with his patron, John the evangelist, drawing on the language of Revelation 1–3 to portray his role as a visionary writer in apocalyptic terms. Yet there turn out to be different things going on in this somewhat confusing part than this outline suggests.

Formally, the seven prayers in Part I are said to correspond to the days of the week; most of them incorporate a number of *cogitationes*, some on the life of Christ and the Virgin, others on scenes which John himself presumably dreamed or imagined. This seven-day structure is referred to again in Part IV (Discussion ~6.i), in which these seven prayers make up the first week that the *opus* users of the *Liber visionum* are meant to perform. After Prayer *1, which is addressed to Christ and is carefully organized as an introduction to the entire *Liber visionum*, most of Prayers *2–7 consists of addresses to the Virgin. (It is this portion of Part I that bears the title 'The Grace of our Lord Jesus Christ'.) These addresses circle around her first visionary appearance to John (Prayers *3–4), the manner in which he sought to gain (Prayer *2) and exploit (Prayers *5–6) this experience, and his gratitude to her and his special intercessors, St John and Mary Magdalene, for her favours (Prayer *7). Some of these prayers fit this exemplary narrative snugly. Prayer *2, for example, names Mary with all her many names, reminding her of her powers at the outset of John's dealings with her; Prayer *6 is a fierce set of demands for help (and, in the McMaster version, for special revelations; Opus I.vi). Others, however, are included only because they were apparently important to John at the time. Prayer *3, most of which consists of the Office for Christmas Day, is said to be a 'suitable' prayer in its place, because John said it when the Virgin appeared to him in sleep, not because it makes any request for such an appearance. The other prayer in Part I not written by John (Prayer *7.iii, to Mary Magdalene, said to be written by Peter of Fontaines) has a similarly loose relationship with the part's central themes, and contributes to a corresponding feeling of looseness in the argument of the part.[24]

Most interestingly, however, there is ambiguity about what it is the Virgin bestows on John. Is it, as the first Prologue states, her permission to write the *Liber visionum*? Or is it, rather, the visionary appearances themselves? Behind the forward-moving narrative of John's progress towards learning the arts and sciences lies another narrative. Here, John set out to evolve a narrower system for precipitating and interpreting dreams of the Virgin – a system of divination which he intended to be used to gain specific items of information or help in specific situations. I take this to be, in part, an early form of the developed *opus* described by the *Liber visionum*. At the centre of this system is a type of dream in which an image of the Virgin is transformed into the likeness of flesh, speaking to the dreamer and indicating certain truths by her posture. This dream is alluded to in outline in Prayer *5.i, with the rubric 'this is that holy and wonderful part of the prayer that nobody should say unless the most blessed, the Virgin Mary, has transformed her stone or wooden or other image before the one who prays'.[25] But we are not given detailed instructions how to operate the system, even in the further allusions to it in Part III (Prima Oratio, following Prayer 28) and Part IV, although two passages of the latter certainly describe this system (Discussion ~1, opening and Nota ~8), while a further passage may do so (Discussion ~1, Notae 4–5).[26] This is because the prayers in Part I that make up this system have been partially adapted to a new role as the story of John's commissioning by the Virgin (and, potentially, that of the would-be user's commissioning too; see McMaster, Opus I, concluding rubric). That is, while John continued to consider this divinatory system important, it has been formally subsumed into the larger structure of the *Liber visionum*.[27]

Yet it has not been subsumed without leaving a number of traces. These help to render the ostensible argument of Part I as loose and sometimes confusing as it is. Yet they are clearly meant to be noticed. First, rubrics like the one referred to above, which insist that certain prayers can only be said under specific personal conditions, are in clear tension with the rubrics that align each prayer with a day of the week. The former could belong to an earlier phase of the text (see also Prayer *5, concluding rubric), and certainly suggest that sections of it have multiple uses. Second, Prayer *1, which carefully evokes the entire *opus* that is to follow, is self-evidently not a product of the time before John designed the book, but belongs to a late phase of its composition (like the Concluding Prayer at the end of Part III, which it parallels). Third, Prayer *1 is followed by a Second Prologue, which gives the various prayers that follow a new title (and assigns them, probably not the *Liber visionum* as a whole, the date 1304–7); this, too, may itself imply that Prayers *2–7 formed part or all of an earlier work which has been incorporated into the *nova compilatio*. Fourth, several of the prayers are also assigned multiple numbers, one set beginning with Prayer *1, another with Prayer *2. Prayer *2 is called 'the second prayer, and the first of the Book of the Virgin Mary', while Prayer *4 is actually categorized as 'the fourth day, the third prayer, but the second concerning the blessed Mary'.[28] This last is almost impenetrable, but I think must suggest that the previous prayer, Prayer *3 (the Christmas Office), was not included in the earlier version of this part of the text. It is clear, at least, that John wishes to make what he considered important distinctions between the prayers in Part I. All these pieces of evidence, as well as the general sense in which Part I fails to do what its introductory rubric says it will do, suggest that in Part I, Prayers *2 and *4–7 (at least) we may have a section of an earlier work composed before John had conceived the design of the

Liber visionum as a whole. Incorporated into the structure of the *Liber visionum* by being made into a prolegomenon to the rest of the work, John has interestingly refused to erase the traces of its original existence. Moreover, he has faced challenges adapting the old material to its new context. He has added two items he did not write himself (Prayers *3, *7.iii), a practice he follows nowhere else in the work; and he has allowed what should have been the climax of the part, Mary's agreement to his writing project, to go by almost unnoticed. Even without reference to the Ars Notoria material John says he uses as a source, at least part of the *Liber visionum* is apparently indeed a 'compilatio'.[29]

Part II, Purgation, is fortunately nothing like so complicated as Part I, although the fact that it seems to have its own title, 'Prayers to God or the Blessed Virgin Mary', could suggest it also had an earlier, independent existence. This part is structured as a long, repeating single prayer (reckoned as Prayers 1–12 in John's developed system). A brief address to God (Prayer 1) acts as a prologue to prayers to each of the orders of angels in turn (Prayers 2–10), interspersed with summarizing prayers to each group of orders, as well as to the saved (Prayer 11), and to the Virgin, queen of angels (Prayer 12). There are some difficulties following the system of cross-references used in the Munich text to indicate what to say when. But these are very efficiently presented in the McMaster version, and I assume the original to have been fully worked out. What the prayers do (after the opening prayer to 'Deus, potentissimus triumphator') is to draw John, a baptized and purified Christian, to the attention of each order of angels in turn, and to enlist its aid: 'open the doors of justice for me', 'rise up, rise up, rise up everyone I have named', 'come, come, come, all holy angels', begin a few sections of the prayer (Prayers 2–10.i–iii).[30] Exactly what is asked varies from order to order, but the aid requested is for purification and amplification of the faculties of the soul and for various kinds of knowledge, each appropriate to the order from which the request is made.[31] The subsidiary prayers to the groups of angels (lower, middle and upper) act only to repeat and confirm the prayers they follow. All the prayers end by asking for help after death. The final one, to Mary, amplifies this concern for salvation into a prayer that defends the work's religious utility, against those 'authorities' who maintain that the kinds of knowledge John is after are not relevant to salvation. This prayer insists that to bestow this knowledge upon him will be 'to the praise and glory of the holy Trinity, and you, and all the heavenly court, and useful to the holy Catholic church', as well as to his own eternal soul and the souls of others (Prayer 12).[32] Part II, all of whose prayers are listed as *generales*, thus anticipates in broad brushstrokes the much more detailed requests for renovation and illumination to be made in Part III. By its end, all the benign spiritual powers in the universe, human, angelic and divine, have been drawn into the drama of John's search for knowledge, while the Catholicity of this search has been explained and defended, enlisting the church's aid as well.

So far, the implication of my nicknames for the early phases of the *Liber visionum* (Conversion and Purgation) – that the work has some structural relationship with mystical thought – may seem too hopeful. This relationship is clarified, however, by the great scene with which Part III begins. Set in the court of heaven, as described in the Book of Revelation, this dramatized sequence of prayers is strongly reminiscent of another such scene, composed at almost the same time, in the later cantos of Dante's *Paradiso*. At this stage of the *Liber visionum*, the reader is told, one must not simply be wise, chaste and clean of sin – a prerequisite for practising every part of the *opus*. Rather, it is necessary to be 'most wise and most chaste, as though standing rapt above every angelic creature in mind and spirit, before the door, above the hierarchies of heaven, before the Judgement-seat of Christ' (Part III, opening rubric).[33] Fully participating in a drama which, it is implied, enacts a situation that has happened to John in reality, the practitioner now speaks to God on bended knee 'with fear and trembling' (*cum timore et tremore*), as the prayers begin that supposedly effect real change in the hearts and minds of those who say them. Only here, standing before the throne of God, does it become fully clear that the two previous parts of the *Liber visionum* have been arranged as a careful progression, each representing different stages of a soul's journey from earth to heaven. Part I, with its *cogitationes* on Christ and the Virgin, corresponds to the early phases of the spiritual life. Here the soul, uncertain of its direction, is still preoccupied with carnal reality and must be kept from sin by meditation on Christ's humanity and other easily digestible forms of spiritual 'milk'. There is a good deal in common between the emotional rhetoric of several prayers in Part I (e.g., Prayers *5–6) and that of mystical texts written to cater to this phase of the soul's existence: texts such as the *Stimulus amoris* by the late thirteenth-century Franciscan, James of Milan, which are much concerned with meditative exercises of the type exemplified by the *cogitationes* in Part I.[34] Part II, on the other hand, ostensibly represents the shift from this corporeal mode of thinking to what Augustine calls intellectual vision. Here, the soul detaches itself from the world and ascends, stage by stage, to heaven, following a route taken by St Paul in II Corinthians, Scipio in the *Somnium Scipionis*, and in different ways by a host of mystics and saved souls (including, again, Dante).[35] An early prayer in Part III describes John's ascent in Part II as that of a soul 'passing by degrees through all the orders of the celestial army, praying and contemplating' (Prayer 15.i).[36] And although John's purpose in ascending to heaven – to gain access to systems of knowledge – may seem more worldly than spiritual, we saw that the ending of Part II insists to the Virgin herself that this is not so, but that the true purpose of any user of the *Liber visionum* must be holy. By associating the structure of knowledge as closely as possible with that of the divine realm, Part III elaborates this argument at length by indicating that the structure of knowledge as the medieval academic curriculum presented it is itself holy. Not only does each of the angelic orders and group of the saved have its own attribute, corresponding to an earthly human attribute (in Parts II and IIIa), but in the climax of the *Liber visionum* (Part IIIb), the nine orders are identified with the nine sciences (the seven liberal arts, philosophy and theology). It will be clear that this is not a mystical work by any current definition of this vexed term,[37] but it can at least be said that John is anxious to exploit the structural analogies between his project and certain kinds of mystical thought.

In the *Paradiso* (cantos 30–3), Dante undergoes various experiences in the heavenly court before he is fit to gaze directly at God, in whom all the scattered leaves of the book of knowledge are gathered together (33.85–7). So it is here with John. He must begin Part III by knocking at the door of heaven for admission: 'O open to us the way of the just! Behold me, John, your servant, standing outside at the door of the dispensation of your mercy!' (Part III: Prayer 13).[38] Then, after a longer preliminary prayer to Mary, God, the orders of angels and the saved, he must undergo a prolonged process of inner renovation, as he addresses a series of petitions to Christ and the denizens of his court, and is illuminated with inner light in the process (Prayers 14–20). Only then is he at last allowed to appeal to God and each order of angels to have knowledge infused into his soul, an experience that is this text's nearest equivalent to mystical union (Prayers 21–30).

The preliminary prayer sets the scene by its careful invocation of many of the principal figures who live in heaven: Mary and the angels, now invoked from the seraphim down to the angels (not the other way around, as in Part II); the four evangelists, invoked as the four beasts of Revelation 4: 6–8; and the patriarchs, prophets and holy fathers, fifteen of whom are mentioned by name. 'Lord, who shall dwell in your tabernacle?' (*Domine, quis habitabit in tabernaculo tuo?*) asks John of himself and all these figures, reciting the psalm which, in its demands for purity, could be taken as the very definition of the life of the elect Christian (Psalm 14). Six specific petitions – which are interestingly still listed as *generales*, not *speciales* – follow in the next six prayers. (The first is addressed to the Trinity, Mary and the angels, while the rest are mainly spoken to Christ, but as in Part II there is a good deal of structural repetition between the prayers.) These six prayers request, respectively: 1) salvation, defined as the overcoming of temptation, the guarding of the soul, and the reception of divine grace (Prayer 15.i–iii); 2) the renovation of the bodily senses and the faculties of the mind or soul so that they may transcend the natural order (Prayer 16); 3) understanding of what is revealed (Prayer 17); 4) the ability to retain all revealed knowledge in the mind (Prayer 18); 5) the ability to declare it eloquently and with mental agility (Prayer 19); 6) stability and fortitude in all the above (Prayer 20). Through these prayers, the petitioner is seemingly returned to the state of sinless perfection that characterized humankind before the fall, when humanity was 'an immaculate mirror of the majesty of God' (*speculum sine macula maiestatis Dei*; Prayer 15.ii). This state also characterized the life of Christ, whose full humanity was revealed in his miraculous ability to transcend nature. Christ's miraculous existence is a constant reference point in most of these prayers (e.g., his ability to give sight to the man born blind from birth, Prayer 16.ii), and it is he who is expected to 'renew' this same existence in the petitioner, and do so now. 'In this time' (*in hac hora*), is a constant refrain in requests for illumination or knowledge throughout Part III, after not being used at all in Parts I and II. For it is here that the series of preliminary stages through which John must pass at last gives way to the realization of his desires: a realization that occurs at the very moment when, properly prepared, he utters them clearly before those who have the power to help.

After the six petitions, we arrive at the requests for understanding of the arts and sciences which constitute the *Liber visionum*'s ostensible central purpose, and its closest approach to the Ars Notoria. This sequence of prayers (Prayers 21–30) is so well-ordered that it needs relatively little by way of introduction. All the prayers address Christ and the Virgin, as well as the angelic order associated with each branch of learning; all of them also link the various requests to events in Christ's life and the days of creation (Prayers 21–7). Each prayer is constructed as a dramatic sequence in three broad stages. First, requests are made, in considerable detail and often in several parts. Second, the angels and the powers they represent are asked to reside with the petitioner or else to teach him the information he seeks. Finally, Christ and the Virgin are asked to bring this about. With a fine sense of heavenly politics, only the lowest orders (Angels and Archangels, the messenger orders) actually convey the information and remain on earth with the petitioner. The other seven orders, who never leave their places in the celestial court, instruct him through the mediation of their junior colleagues. Otherwise, the symmetry between the different prayers is fairly complete, to the extent, indeed, that the prayers repeat much material and contain many cross-references. The nine orders, along with groups of the saved associated with each order, are invoked in order to acquire each of the seven liberal arts, with philosophy and theology. John's interest in rhetoric, which the prayer to the Thrones interestingly associates with government, not simply with poetic composition, gives a certain specificity to this prayer; this specificity is matched only by the prayer for philosophy or physics to the Cherubim, which is also much concerned with issues of government. Otherwise each art receives more or less equal billing. Other arts not included in this structure, especially medicine and the mechanical and exceptive arts, form the topic of a brief digression (Addendum, following Prayer 27), which explains how the prayers can be adapted to learn these also. Yet, falling just before the prayer to the Cherubim (Prayer 28) – who are associated not only with philosophy and physics but with knowledge in general – even this digression respects the linking of academic discipline and angelic order so important to the *opus*. Finally, these nine prayers are followed by two concluding prayers: the last numbered prayer (Prayer 30), to

Christ and the Father, which requests all knowledge; and a lengthy unnumbered prayer to the Virgin, which parallels the opening prayers of Part I (Prayers *1–2) and evokes several others in Part I, not least in its reintroduction of the apostle John (Concluding Prayer, iii). This 'general' prayer is introduced by a rubric that instructs the user to 'conclude your meaning thus in the blessed Mary' (*conclude sic intentionem tuam in beata Maria*), suggesting both an aesthetic and a prudential reason for this ending to Part III. Linking Mary with all the arts and sciences in turn, the prayer implies (what is not obviously true) that her praise is the ultimate goal of the entire *Liber visionum*, just as the power of her intercession has been partly instrumental in causing it to come into being.

The only peculiarity of the second half of Part III is a single prayer, here situated after the prayer to the Cherubim (Prayer 28), which is also addressed to the Virgin. This prayer states that its proper place is the very beginning of the *Liber visionum*, although various copies place it elsewhere through caution (Prima Oratio, opening rubric).[39] This prayer, which is specifically designed to precipitate visions of the Virgin, is crucial to the divinatory aspect of the *Liber visionum* which is most clearly present in Part I and out of which I hypothesized the *opus* as a whole may have grown. In copying it, the Munich scribe (or his exemplar) may have drawn on a different exemplar from the one used for much of the rest of the text, since in this phase of Part III the petitioner is twice referred to as Luca. If so, this hypothetical second text was a consecrated copy of the *Liber visionum*, written out by or for an individual in the way the *Grandes Chroniques* entry describes and the McMaster text exemplifies.[40] The importance accorded the divinatory and visionary aspect of the *opus* is clear in the trouble that has here been taken both to include this prayer and to hide it. Since the achievement of visions is the focus of a good deal of the earlier discussions in Part IV, and recurs constantly in the McMaster text, it seems likely that John and his readers considered this mode of 'Marian divination' to be one of his major contributions to the Ars Notoria tradition, and a much more important part of the *opus* than the formal structure of the *Liber visionum* suggests. Whether or not my map of the development of the *Liber visionum* is correct, this aspect of the *opus* was never left behind.

This, then, is the shape of the first three parts of the *Liber visionum* as Munich preserves them. (As we'll see, the prayers, though not the rubrics or structure, are preserved in essentially similar form and order in the McMaster version.) It is a structure which at every level betrays its author's desire for order, formal completeness and eloquence 'without prolixity', as the prayer for rhetorical brilliance made to the Thrones has it (*absque prolixitate*, Prayer 23.iv). Indeed, it is a structure that, at least after the complexities of Part I, is so coherent as to constitute quite a helpful mnemonic guide to the arts and sciences its users hope to acquire.[41] With the possible exception of the *figure* and/or depictions of the Virgin the *Grandes Chroniques* describes as part of the original text, this is not a system that has any place for the unknown names or incomprehensible diagrams which seem to be crucial to the Ars Notoria in its other forms. On the contrary, full lucidity appears to have been John's goal almost throughout.

By contrast, the incomplete Part IV, described in its opening rubric as the *pars practica* and final 'general' part of the book, is frankly a mess, a collection of short notes, many of them autobiographical in nature, loosely structured as a series of discussions ostensibly concerned with the practice of the *opus*.[42] We have to hope that Munich preserves an incomplete and heavily corrupted version of something that was originally much clearer. If it does not, then John wrote only notes towards this part, and did so in such a way that many of the urgent things he had to say about his own history as writer and visionary would be incomprehensible except to those who already knew it. There is a great deal of interest in this part: about the requirement to write the book out for oneself in order to use it, changing nothing on the way, not even the rubrics (Discussion ~1); about the process of preparing to read the book, by contemplating its images and writing them in the book of the heart before reciting the prayers (Discussion ~2); on saying the canonical office before saying the prayers, and where, when and how to say them (Discussions ~3–6); and on the history of the work's composition and its relationship to the Ars Notoria (Discussion ~1, much of which I have sadly found incomprehensible). But analysis of other manuscripts of the *Liber visionum* is so likely to clarify our picture of this portion of John's text that detailed speculation as to what it tells us at this stage is pointless.

The single most helpful section of Part IV is actually the incomplete Discussion ~6, in the midst of which the Munich text breaks off in mid-page. For it is from this discussion that we learn both how the prayers were actually to be said and how the McMaster version came into being. Taking the seven-prayer structure of Part I (itself based on the canonical office) as its model, this discussion divides the *opus* into eight 'weeks' of prayers. The instructions for only three of these have survived, but these correspond exactly to the structure of the McMaster text. Here, the Prima Operatio (corresponding to Munich, Parts I–III) is divided not into three parts but into nine (rather than eight) Opera.[43] Although these Opera are of uneven length and there are some peculiarities to the structure, I think we can thus assume the McMaster text to represent John's wishes for the practice of the *opus* quite closely. The McMaster text (the beginning of which is unfortunately missing) omits almost all the rubrics found in Munich, largely destroying the narrative of a visionary progress implied by the *Liber visionum*. Instead, it contains a series of detailed instructions as to the correct performance of the *opus*, which focuses especially on the gestures the petitioner is to make in the course of praying. In the Secunda Operatio, which has a loose structural correspondence to Munich's Part IV, it also presents sustained discussions of the *opus* which have no parallels in Munich and which provide the clearest possible picture of the *Liber visionum* actually in use. Unfortunately, the relationship of this portion of the text to anything written by John the Monk is not yet clear. The McMaster version does allude to the author of the original work (e.g., Opus I.vi and closing rubric), although never by name; perhaps it once had a prologue explaining the text's genesis. But in focusing so clearly on the *opus* at the expense of the narrative aspects of the *Liber visionum*, the redactor responsible for the McMaster version has simplified the double structure of the original, flouting John's insistence on preserving his *ipsissima verba* (in Part IV, Discussion ~1) in the very process of interpreting John's wishes for the *opus* with obvious care. If the Virgin told him to do this in a dream, the surviving portion of the text does not say so.

As a consecrated text, written by or for a certain Bernardus in 1461, lavish as a Book of Hours in its use of pictures (in Opus 1) and rubrication – although hardly as lavish as John's original, according to the *Grandes Chroniques* – McMaster acts as an extremely helpful interpretive guide to the Munich version. Where Munich refers obscurely to *figure* and *ymaginationes*, McMaster contains a series of illustrations of the Virgin (apparently heavily touched up and needing more expert treatment than I can give them), and regularly refers its user to the need to practice the *opus figurarum*. (Unfortunately, the explanation of how this *opus* was meant to work seems to have been in the lost opening portion of the text.) Where the Munich version is often unclear in its instructions about how given prayers are to be said, especially where repetition is involved, McMaster is always clear. Where Munich is written in a crabbed hand with many abbreviations and very many textual cruces – as though the text's history has involved passage through the hands of someone who sorely needed the infused knowledge of grammar it offers – McMaster is easy to read and lucid. It preserves several passages not found in Munich but surely authentic, most notably a fierce attack on the Virgin's tardiness in responding to the prayers (Opus 1.vi), as well as fuller versions of certain prayers which may be the result of editorial amplification. Its very full instructions as to the gestures and postures the supplicant is to perform bring the *opus* to dramatic life in a way Munich does not. In the Secunda Operatio, it even provides instructions for the writing and consecration of new copies, which allow us to reconstruct the process by which this very book has been made, and the prayers and incense offered up for it, in brilliant detail (Secunda Operatio, Prima et Secunda Practica, Quarta Practica x). Where it seems clearly to be adding material, it does so with a high order of intelligence. At the end of the first Opus, for example, practitioners are instructed not to continue until they have had a 'good dream' allowing them to do so; if Opus I does not produce a dream on the first attempt, it must be repeated until it does (Opus 1, closing rubric). This rubric helps make sense for practitioners of the prayers in Opus I – the prayers by which John tells us he sought permission to write the book (Munich, Prologue) – by recasting them as prayers by which practitioners seek Mary's permission to embark on the *opus* proper. The rubric is also helpful in keeping the dual goals of the *Liber visionum* – the attainment of knowledge in the general way through the angels, and the acquisition of a means of divining answers to more specific questions through the Virgin Mary – in balance with one another, suggesting the McMaster reviser has given thought to this duality. In short, while McMaster shows revealingly little interest in the meaning of the prayers, or at least in their place in a narrative (as distinct from a ritual) framework, its presentation of the *Liber visionum* is indispensable for our understanding of the text.

The most interesting parts of McMaster for our purposes, however, are the places where it is furthest from the Munich version, and perhaps also from the writings of John the Monk, notably in its Secunda Operatio. Here we see how, in one textual tradition at least, the practical benefits offered by the *Liber visionum* have tended to win out over what I tentatively called its 'mystical' aspects. Although it is important to recognize the devotional and metaphysical urges that continue to be implicit in the book, the attainment and retention of certain kinds of specific knowledge and power are given far more detailed treatment than the acquisition of all the arts and sciences. Perhaps this is for the simple reason that the *Liber visionum* was in practice less good at delivering the universal knowledge it claimed to provide than at helping practitioners believe they had attained more limited goals. At the outset of the Secunda Operatio, the whole of the Prima Operatio (corresponding to Parts I–III of Munich) appears as a mere preliminary to the making and consecration of a ring of power, and the consecration of the book the practitioner has copied and then used (Prima Operatio, closing rubric). (In the Tertia Practica, it becomes clear that the Prima Operatio also has to be repeated once a year, one Opus for each month, during the whole of the practitioner's life, to retain its power.) This ring has various uses, notably in precipitating divinatory dreams from Mary (Quarta Practica ii–iii), in winning disputations or expounding texts with eloquence (Quarta Practica iv), and perhaps for dispersing evil spirits (Quarta Practica vii). Since the ring is innocuous looking (inscribed with the image and the names of Mary and Jesus), portable, and consistently paralleled with the book (with which it is to be kept hidden most of the time, Prima et Secunda Practica iii), it perhaps represents a concentration of the energies found in or released by the book. It also functions as a sign of the practitioner's special relationship with the Virgin (much like the wedding rings worn by nuns). Even here, though, where the singularity of the practitioner's state of life is so important, there is an emphasis on the communal benefits that must be kept in mind if ring and book are to be used successfully. Only visions whose meaning is publishable for the benefit of the community can be expected from the Virgin (Quarta Practica i), who conveys information through word, gesture and posture (Quarta Practica ii), and whose meaning is so important that it must be written down and given again if it is forgotten (Quarta Practica iii, vi). In light of this insistence on the Christian purpose of the *opus* (even where it can be adapted for gaining victory over one's opponents or learning the exceptive arts, Quarta Practica iv, ix), it is not surprising that, appended to the *Liber visionum* in the McMaster manuscript, we find another, apparently orthodox, text. This is a rare liturgical office to *Sapientia* based on the writings of Henry Suso, which is itself followed by a set of prayers to do with memory, and seems to have travelled with the *Liber visionum* in this textual tradition.[44] Despite its concern for secrecy and its use of religious devotion for ends that are in some cases hard not to define as private (and thus inherently suspect), this version of the *Liber visionum* remains thoroughly committed to its own Catholicity.

Notes

1 The identification of the text, which Claire Fanger and I are in the early stages of editing, was a collaborative effort involving myself and Claire Fanger, with an invaluable early tip from Richard Kieckhefer. Claire transcribed more than half the Munich copy, and has saved me from numerous errors in the Latin; remaining errors, of which there are certainly a number, are my responsibility. I am also indebted to Frank Klaassen, who helped me find (or in one case found himself) three further manuscripts of the work; to Father Peregrin Barres at the Hill's monastic microfilm library, St John's, Minnesota, for helpful responses to my enquiries; to Deborah Schlow, who made a preliminary transcription of the McMaster text; to Scott Westrem, who examined the Munich manuscript of the *Liber visionum* for me and wrote detailed notes on its composition; to the University of Western Ontario and the Social Sciences and Humanities Research Council of Canada, who have funded my work on the text; and to the Bayerische Staatsbibliothek in Munich and the William Ready Division of Archives and Research Collections, McMaster University Library, Hamilton (Canada), for permission to consult and quote from manuscripts in their keeping.

2 See Appendix B. References to the *Liber visionum* in this article are to the analytic summaries in the appendices, rather than directly to the manuscripts. Appendix A provides a summary overview of both texts; Appendix B, an analysis of the Munich text; Appendix C an analysis of the McMaster text.

3 For the term 'exceptive arts' see Claire Fanger's article in this volume, p. 238, n. 22.

4 For Morigny, founded in 1095, see *La Chronique de Morigny (1095–1152)*, ed. Léon Mirot, 2nd edn., Collection de textes pour servir à l'étude et à l'enseignement de l'histoire (Paris: Librarie Alphone Picard et fils, 1912). Morigny seems to have been influenced by, but not to have directly participated in, the Cluniac reform.

5 'Et en cest an meismes, fu I moine de Morigni, I abbaïe emprès Estampes, qui par sa curiosité et par son orgueil voult susciter et renouveller une heresie et sorcerie condampneé, qui est nommée en latin Ars Notoria, et avoit pensé à lui bailler autre titre et autre nom. Si est celle science telle que elle enseigne à faire figures et empraintes, et doivent estre differentes l'une de l'autre et assigniées chascune à chascune science; puis doivent estre regardées à certain temps faiz en jeunes et en oriosons; et ainsi, après le regart estoit espandue science, laquelle en ce regart on vouloit avoir et acquerir. Mais il convenoit que on nommast et appellast aucuns noms mescogneus, lesquiex noms on creoit fermement que c'estoient noms de deables; pourquoy pluseurs celle

science decevoit et estoient deceuz; car nul n'avoit onques esté usant de celle science que aucun bien ou aucun fruit en eust raporté; noient moins ycelui moine reprouvoit ycelle science, ja soit ce qu'il fainsist que la benoite Vierge Marie li fust apparue moult de foiz et aussi come li inspirant la science; et pour ce, à l'onneur de li il avoit fait plusseurs ymages paindre en son livre avec plusseurs oriosons et caractères très précieusement de fines couleurs, en disant que la Vierge Marie li avoit tout revelé,+ lesquelles ymages appliquées à chascune science et regardées après les oroisons dites, la science que on requeroit estoit donnée; et plus, car fussent richesces, honneurs ou delices que on vousist avoir, on l'avoit. Et pour ce que le livre prometoit telles choses et que il escouvenoit faire invocacions et escrire II fois son nom en ce livre, et faire escrire le livre proprement pour soy, que estoit cousteuse chose, autrement il ne li vaudroit riens s'il n'en faisoit I escrire à ses couz et à ses despens; à juste cause fu condampné ledit livre à Paris et jugié comme faux et mauvais contre le foy crestienne, à estre ars et mis ou feu.' *Les Grandes Chroniques de France*, ed. Jules Viard, vol. 9 (Paris: Librairie ancienne Honoré Champion, 1937), pp. 23–4 (my translation). At the + sign, one manuscript adds a further sentence: 'Et avoit en ce livre VII ymages paintes qui représentoient les VII sciences que l'en voloit savoir; et part tel regart l'en la savoit' (Paris, Bibliothèque nationale MS fr. 10132, f. 406).

6 *Chronique Latine de Guillaume de Nangis de 1113 à 1300 avec les Continuations de cette Chronique de 1300 à 1368*, ed. H. Géraud, 2 vols (Paris: Jules Renouard, 1843), vol. 2, p. 50. Both this and the previous reference are derived from Henry Charles Lea, *A History of the Inquisition of the Middle Ages*, 3 vols (New York: Russell and Russell, 1955, vol. 3, pp. 436–7 (originally published 1887). The only other modern references to the *Liber visionum* I have found, outside library catalogues, are in Lynn Thorndike, *A History of Magic and Experimental Science*, 8 vols (New York: Columbia University Press, 1923–58). Thorndike mentions John or the text several times without apparently connecting these references, e.g. vol. I, p. 282; vol. III, p. 21; vol. IV, pp. 278–9; some of his information seems to have been derived from Lea.

7 Munich, Bayerische Staatsbibliothek Clm. 276 is a composite fifteenth-century manuscript, put together from three or four different parts and still in its medieval binding. It was probably assembled for, and perhaps by, the bibliophile Dr Hartmann Schedel of Nuremberg, its earliest known owner. In the early seventeenth century it was in the library of the dukes of Bavaria. The binding entitles the book 'Liber appollonij artis notorie. Liber visionis beate virginis . . . Geomancia et ars Alchimie etc.' The *Liber visionum* is in Part I of the manuscript, immediately after the Ars Notoria, and is written in the same, mid-fifteenth-century hand as the rest of the part.

8 Hamilton, Ontario, McMaster University Library, Unnumbered MS is a small mid-fifteenth-century paper and parchment book dated 1461 by the scribe (perhaps 'Bernardus'), and written in a 'bastard gothic' script; from the style of its illustrations, and from internal references, it may be Italian, though this has yet to be confirmed. The binding is modern, probably made for the untraced bookseller from whom McMaster University purchased the manuscript in the 1970s, and bears the title 'Prayer Book'. Owned by a Monsignor Aotti, who signed the book perhaps in the eighteenth century (on what was already clearly, f. 1r., after the original first quire of the book had been lost or destroyed), it contains the *Liber visionum* with addenda as detailed in Appendix C below, and a seventeenth-century Office of the Angels, written on paper and bound in at the end of the volume. This was the first copy of the *Liber visionum* to be found.

9 British Library, Additional 18027, contains a 'Liber apparicionum et visionum B. Marie Virginis' (f. 2r.), attributed to John, Monk of Morigny. This is apparently divided into three works or sections: the *Liber apparicionum* (=Munich, Part I??); 'Liber beate Virginis Marie, qui Liber Florum celestis doctrine appelatur' (f. 15. b) (=Munich, Parts II–III??); and 'Liber figurarum beate Marie Virginis gloriose, de nova compilacione' (f. 71v.) (Munich, Part IV does not seem a likely parallel: there is a *Liber figurarum* among the ritual materials included in the Graz text; both manuscripts are unfortunately without figures.) Vienna, Schottenkloster, MS Scotensis-Vindobonensis 61(140), begins 'Incipit liber apparicionum et visionum beate et intemerate et sanctissime virginis Marie Dei genitricis, alma Maria procurante et eciam revellante et supremo Deo concedente. Incipit liber beate virginis gloriosissime Marie qui Liber florum celestis doctrine appellatur. . . . Nemo cum lucernam accendit sub abscondito eam ponit' (f. 1r.), gives the date at which it was copied as 1377 (f. 106), and apparently has internal references to two dates of composition, 1304–7 and 1315. The last folios in the manuscript (ff. 107–56) contain a variety of closely related works: 'Oraciones bone et utiles ad memoriam, intelligenciam et facundiam retinendam' (ff. 107–31); 'Orationes de passione domine' (ff. 131–9); and a text, 'Experimentum probatum et verum ad intelligendas omnes artes', with a further text on memory (ff. 140–56). See *Catalogus codicum manu scriptorum qui in bibliotheca monasterii b.m.v. ad scotos vindobanae servantur*, ed. P. Albertus Hübl (Vindobanae et Lipsiae: In aedibus Guilelmi Branmüller, 1899), pp. 74–5.

10 This manuscript, from the Carthusian house at Salvatorberg, contains the *Regimen principum* of Egidius Romanus, a series of papal bulls, two treatises against heresy ('Tractatus novus compositus per dominum cardinalem s. Sixti contra hereticos impugnantes sanctam paupertatem Christi et discipulorume eius', and 'Concertacio Felicis, cantoris Thuricensis, cum beckardo quodam super ocio suo et ne elimosinas percipiat et similiter contra Lulhardos et Begwinas etc.') and the *Liber visionum*. The *Liber visionum* is described in terms extremely suggestive of its importance: 'Liber qui dicitur Flos celestis doctrine, sed in re vera magisterio dyaboli confectus, et est liber omnino superstitionibus plenus. Cuius acutro, quamvis mentiatur se voluisse vitare perniciosam artem notoriam sive notorie, tamen videtur eam magis fallaciter et occultius tradidisse ad decipiendum simplices ex magisterio dyaboli, cum per dulcissima orationes et supplicationes etc. quasi per mel venenum aspidum et mortiferum propinet. Quare nullus lector superstitionibus hic traditis insistat nec acquiescat, nichilominus tamen hic huiusmodi materia colligata est non ut discatur, sed ut, quomodo multi miserabiliter et dampnabiliter decipiuntur callidissime per dyabolum, videatur.' For this description, see *Mittelalterliche Biblotheksataloge Deutschlands und der Schweiz . . . Zweiter Band, Bistum, Mainz, Erfurt*, ed. Paul Lehmann (Munich: C.H. Beck'sche Verlagsbuchhandlung, 1928), pp. 425–6; no folio numbers are given.

11 Thorndike vol. 4, pp. 278–9. The *Sopholegium* survives in various MSS and early printed editions, according to Thorndike, including MS Geneva 994, and BM Arundel 229 (MSS) and BM.IB.243, an incunabulum. Jacobus's discussion forms part of Book I (e.g., Geneva ff. 23v–27r.).

12 Graz, University Library MS 680, part of which was copied by one Jacobum de Villaco, baccal. in artibus in 1414. The *Liber visionum* is on ff. 94r.–154v.: 'Incipit liber apparicionum et visionum b. et intemerate et s. virg. Marie Dei genitricis, alma Maria procurante et eciam revellante et supremo Deo concedente. Incipit liber b virg gloriose Marie qui liber florum celestis doctrine appellatur. . . . Nemo cum laternam accendit sub abscondito ponit eam' (almost identical to the Vienna MS described in the previous note, and, like that text, apparently complete). For this reference, see *Die*

Handschriften der Universitätsbibliothek Graz, ed. Anton Kern, 3 vols (Leipzig: Otto Harrassowitz, 1942), pp. 410–13.

13 For a brief outline of this prologue see the Appendix to Fanger's article.

14 '. . . impetravi apud beatam virginem gloriosam Mariam ut unum librum, nomine suo, si sibi placeret conponebam, per quem de spiritis antiquis erroribus ad culmen scienciarum et artium ego, et quicumque ipsum haberete et operaretur, attingere posset'.

15 There are no figure or pictures of the Virgin in Munich, but scattered references imply that they were included in earlier copies, as the account in the *Grandes Chroniques* suggests.

16 On Theophilus the apostate, see Valerie I.J. Flint, *The Rise of Magic in Early Medieval Europe* (Princeton: Princeton University Press, 1991), pp. 344–7. John's history as one who gave his loyalty to the Virgin, only to lapse back into evil practices until recalled to his senses, closely parallels the story of Theophilus as told by Paul the Deacon.

17 '. . . auctoritate sacrae eloquentiae et revelatione angelorum celestium'.

18 For the others, see Part I, Prayer *5, and Part IV, Discussion ~1, Nota ~5.

19 John the Monk's deployment of the trope of the vision bears comparison with the three male visionaries discussed by Robert Lerner in a recent article, Joachim of Fiore, Robert of Liège (i.e. Rupert of Deutz), and Arnold of Villanova: see 'Ecstatic Dissent', *Speculum* 67 (1993), pp. 33–57. The autobiographical prologue in the Graz manuscript, however, seems in part to be an exception to these observations.

20 See Appendix A for a diagram of the structure of Munich.

21 See Geoffrey of Vinsauf's remarks about *abbrevatio* in *Poetria nova*, lines 690–735, translated as *The Poetria Nova of Geoffrey of Vinsauf*, by Margaret F. Nims (Toronto: Pontifical Institute of Mediaeval Studies, 1967), pp. 40–2; and chapter 1 of pseudo-Dionysius's *Mystical Theology*, in *Pseudo-Dionysius: The Complete Works*, trans. Colm Lubheid, Classics of Western Spirituality (Mahwah, NJ: Paulist Press, 1986).

22 *Opera omnia sancti Bonaventurae*, various eds, 10 vols (Quarrachi, Collegio S. Bonaventurae 1882–92), vol. VIII, pp. 3–27.

23 'Istas vero orationes usque ibi [i.e. Part I, prayers *2–7] iam consequeram antequam liber presentis conponendi licentiam habuissem et per ipsas dictam licentiam impetram Deum et enim impet[trat]ive seu etiam generales.'

24 I have not yet found any other clear reference to Peter of Fontaines (or Fontfroides?).

25 'Hec est clausula illa sancta et mirabilis que nunquam debet dici donec beatissima scilicet virgo Maria transformaverit ymaginem suam lapideam vel ligneam sive aliam coram orante.'

26 The long treatment of this system of divination in the Quarta Practica of the McMaster version is extremely helpful, but may not be by John the Monk. See Appendix C.

27 See also Part IV, Discussion ~1, opening rubric, which distinguishes between the *magnus liber*, which contains the prayer 'O rex regum' and the other prayers in Part I, and the *nova compilatio*, whose composition is unclear (except that it certainly includes Part IV), but which may be the name John gave to Parts II–IV. However, it would be unwise to hang too much on Part IV's discussion of the versions and revisions of the *Liber visionum* at this stage.

28 'Sequitur oratio secunda et prima de Liber Maria virgine'; 'feria 4a et oratio tertia, set 2a de beata Maria'.

29 Munich's Part I and its hypothetical earlier version thus have the following relationship:

Part I:	Hypothetical Earlier Version:
Prologue:	Opening Prayers from Prologue (?)
	Prima Oratio (see Part III, after Prayer 28)
Prayer *1: Sunday	
Second Prologue:	Prologue (entitling work and dating to 1304–7)
Prayer *2: Monday	Prayer #1: Invocation of Mary (not to be said in a state of sin)
Prayer *3: Tuesday (Christmas Office)	
Prayer *4: Wednesday	Prayer #2: Praise (said only after visionary dream of Mary)
Prayer *5: Thursday	Prayer #3: Glory (said only after Mary's visionary transformation)
Prayer *6: Friday	Prayer #4 (?): Help (said only when sinless and in great need)
Prayer *7: Saturday	Prayer #5 (?): Thanks (a composite prayer from several sources)

If the 'hypothetical earlier version' existed, it is also possible that it included Prayer *3.

30 'Aaperite michi portas iustitie'; 'Surgite, surgite, surgite omnes prenominati'; 'venite, venite, venite omnes sancti angeli'.

31 For the angelic orders and the 'powers' they represent, see the classic discussion by pseudo-Dionysius in his *Celestial Hierarchies* (see *Complete Works*, trans. Lubheid). For an account contemporary with John the Monk, see Hugh of Strasbourg, *Compendium theologicae veritatis* in *Opera omnia sancti Bonaventurae*, ed. A.C. Peltier, 15 vols (Paris: Vives, 1864–71), vol. VIII, pp. 60–246, II.xii–xxi (pp. 95–100).

32 'Ad laudem et gloriam sancte Trinitatis et tuam totiusque curie celestis et sancte ecclesie katholica utilitatem . . .'.

33 'Qui vero in omni libros debes esse sapiens et castus et mundus, a criminalibus et a criminis mundanorum expers soli Deo solummodo placere cupiens, animo sis sapientissimis et castissimis et quasi stans raptus super omnem angelicam creaturam mente et spiritu ante hostiam super celestis ierarchie, ante tribunal Christi . . .'.

34 See *Opera omnia sancti Bonaventurae*, ed. Peltier, vol. XII, pp. 631–703.

35 For 'intellectual vision', see Augustine, *The Literal Meaning of Genesis*, trans. John Hammond Taylor, Ancient Christian Writers 41–2 (New York: Paulist Press, 1982), book XII. For Paul, see 2 Corinthians 12: 1–4, often elaborated by academic theologians and writers of apocrypha such as the *Visio Pauli*. For the *Somnium Scipionis*, see Macrobius, *Commentary on the Dream of Scipio*, trans. William H. Stahl (New York: Columbia University Press, 1952).

36 ' . . . gradatim transiens per omnes gradus militie celestis orando et contemplando'.

37 For a discussion of the term and its history in modern scholarship, see Bernard McGinn, *The Foundations of Mysticism: Origins to the Fifth Century*, vol. I of *The Presence of God: A History of Western Christian Mysticism* (New York: Crossroad, 1991), Appendix: Theoretical Approaches (pp. 265–343).

38 'O aperi nobis viam iustorum! Ecce, ego Iohannes, servus tuus, foris stans ad hostium dispensationis misericordie tue.'

39 'Haec enim est huius artis vel lib[ri] prima oratio, set ad cautela ante orationem philosophie (et in quibusdam aliis libris ante orationem gramatice) situatur; ultima enim est generalium et prima specialium seu singularium . . .'.

40 The opening rubric to the Prima Oratio actually refers to 'other copies' of the *Liber visionum*,

allowing the inference that Munich is here drawing on more than one exemplar. But another explanation is possible. The *Grandes Chroniques* states that copyists of the *Liber visionum* had to write their own names in the work twice; if so, it follows that, on all the many other occasions on which John's name appears in the text, they were transcribing his name, instead of substituting their own: a good system for reconciling the need to personalize the *opus* with the equal need to preserve John's name. Since the name 'Luca' does appear only twice in Munich, this could be the system in operation here and could also explain why prudence (*cautela*) has displaced this prayer from its original position at the beginning of the text. (But note that in the sole consecrated copy so far examined, McMaster, the name 'Bernardus' occurs throughout, and the only references to John are indirect and not by name.)

41 For background to the mnemonic features of the *Liber visionum*, see Mary Carruthers, *The Book of Memory: A Study of Memory in Medieval Culture*, Cambridge Studies in Medieval Literature 9 (Cambridge: Cambridge University Press, 1990).

42 'Incipit prima practica; qualiter sit operandum per orationes predictas, vel quibus diebus sit dicenda ad consecrationem predictarum scientarum, inveniandam consequendam et fruendam, et vocatur practica perambula et generalis huius libri pars ultima.' From this rubric, it seems that Part IV may originally have been followed by a Part V, a second *pars practica* focused on *speciales*. See also Part IV, Discussion ~6, opening rubric.

43 See Appendix A for a schematic breakdown of the McMaster text and its relation to Munich. Note that the ninth Opus, not mentioned in Munich, is created by subdividing a long single prayer, a subdivision that could have been made largely for symbolic reasons, to make the number of weeks equal that of the orders of angels. McMaster's Quarta et Ultima Practica iv indeed refers to part of the Opus VIII prayer as the 'ultima oratio', suggesting that the creation of Opus IX as a separate 'week' may have been a relatively late development.

44 *The Cursus de eterna Dei sapientia*, appended to the *Liber visionum* in the McMaster manuscript is an office based on Henry Suso's *Horologium sapientiae*. See the edition printed as an appendix to the edition of the *Horologium sapientiae* by Pius Kunzle (Freiburg/Schweiz: Universitätsverlag, 1977), pp. 606–18; I have not yet had an opportunity to compare the McMaster and the printed versions of this text. (I owe this information, and the identification of the *Cursus*, to Barbara Newman.)

APPENDIX A

Structural Analyses of Two Texts of the Liber Visionum

GENERAL STRUCTURE OF THE MUNICH AND MCMASTER TEXTS

Munich:		**McMaster:**
Part I:	Prayers *1–7 (*generales*): Mary, Christ	**Operatio I**, **Opus I**: seeking a vision
Part II:	Prayers 1–12 (*generales*): God, angels, souls, Mary	**Opus II**: *orationes de essentia*

Part IIIa: Prayers 13–20 (*generales/petitiones*):
    God, angels, heavenly court
    [Prayers 13–16]   **Opus III**: renovation of senses
    [Prayers 17–20]   **Opus IV**: renovation of mind
Part IIIb: Prayers 21–30 (*speciales*) for
    knowledge: angelic orders/God/Mary
    [Prayers 21–7: Angels to Thrones]   **Opus V**: 7 liberal arts (*speciales*)
    [Addendum on medicine]   [see *Pars practica* IV]
    [Prayer 28: Cherubim]   **Opus VI**: natural philosophy
    [*Prima Oratio*, for visions: Mary]   [see Opus I]
    [Prayer 29: seraphim]   **Opus VII**: theology
    [Prayer 30: God   **Opus VIII**: all knowledge
    [final prayer to Mary, a)]
    [final prayer to Mary, b)   **Opus IX**: thanksgiving,
                              confirmation
Part IV: *Pars practica* (differs from McMaster) **Operatio II, Pars practica
                              I–IV
                              Cursus de eterna Dei
                              sapientia** [office based on
                              Suso's *Horologium Sapientiae*]
                              **Oratio pro scientia
                              Adipiscenda** [series of prayers
                              for memory]

APPENDIX B

Analysis of Munich Clm 276

(Prayers are underlined and numbered; the thirty prayers given in Parts II–III are numbered separately from those in Part I, which are numbered *1 etc.; prayers unnumbered in the text are given as ~1 etc. *Cogitationes* in Part I and the Discussions and Notes in Part IV, all unnumbered in the text, are also given as ~1 etc. Major prayer incipits are in bold face, quotations from prayers are underlined; rubrics and other discussions are italicized; *cogitationes* are underlined and italicized. These conventions do not necessarily correspond to rubrication practice in the manuscript. In offering a preliminary transcription of the passages excerpted below, capitalization and punctuation is modern, i/j have been normalized as i, consonantal u/v as v, and medial c/t has been rendered as t (since these letters are often hard to distinguish); other peculiarities of spelling have been retained. Doubtful words or phrases are followed by an asterisk*, emendations are noted, but deletions in the manuscript are not.)

Opening and Prologue: *Incipit liber visionum beate et intemerate Dei genetricis virginis Marie* [f. 48r.1]; contains *cogitatio* ~1: <u>*cogita hic quod tu sis in itinere paradisi*</u>; unnumbered prayers ~1–2: (~1) <u>Ave Maria</u> (three brief parts: <u>Ave Maria</u>; <u>Sancti Spiritus</u>; <u>In nomine patris</u>); (~2) <u>Ioth: Deus intellectus</u>, headed *oratio sequitur cum figura que indagatione et placatione totius scripture dicenda est semper cum ymaginatione figure* [i.e. the Tetragrammaton, invoked in the course of this prayer]; this begins by interweaving two syntactically distinct prayers, one invoking God: <u>Ioth: Deus intellectus et intelligentie . . . He: Deus perfecte reminiscentie et memorie . . . Vau: Deus rationis et eloquentie . . . Het: Deus stabilitatis, perfectionis et perseverantie, fons totius gratie, sapientie, scientie et prudentie</u>; the other a poetic prayer to Christ: <u>Ihesu Christe vite principium . . .qui per crucis patibulum . . .per passionis obitum . . .vita factus es omnium</u>; followed by <u>te invoco . . .</u>

   Prologue, [f. 48r.1], autobiographical details, instructions and warnings to readers: *Ego, frater Iohannes, monachus de Mariginato, particeps in tribulationibus vestris* (Revelation 1:9) . . . *Ego . . . in preteritis temporibus artium et scientiarum exceptivarum sectando fui sepius involutus, et ab hiis tenebris ignorantie per sacras revelationes . . . ex parte beate et intemerate gloriose virginis Marie et sanctorum angelorum Dei, [n]olentes* [MS 'volentes'] *me per ignorantia[m] condempnare quasi per quedam temporis spatium ad suam misericordiam revocare.* But John relapsed, *non credendo sacras revelationes . . . esse ex bono spiritu*, until recalled by three signs [f. 48r.2]: *primo per vocem spiritus minando me . . .; secundo verberationes spirituales in presentia ipsius in sompnis michi crudeliter illata . . . et ad hoc non credidi omnibus set potius hesitam . . .; tertio . . . persecutiones temporales et corporales.* Then, *quasi de gravi sompno evigilans*, he repented his sin, and *impetravi apud beatam virginem gloriosam Mariam ut unum librum, nomine suo, si sibi placeret conponerem, per quem de spiritis antiquis erroribus ad culmen scientiarum et artium ego et quicumque ipsum haberet et operaretur attingere posset. Et cum hec multotiens quesivissem, tandem illa beata virgo Maria . . . apparens in sompnis, predictum librum et conponendi modum tantummodo de 30 orationibus finibus ut iam in visionibus superius ostensum et michi lic[entiam]* [MS reads 'licitiam'] *contulit et concessit.* Prologue ends [f. 48v.1] with appeal to readers to keep book carefully, and with directions for its use: information for *operantes* found at the end (see Part IV); formal numbering of the prayers begins at *[De]us potentissime triumphator* (f. 53v.2, opening of Part II).

Part I: *generales (1):* after Prayer *1, Prayers 2*–*7 said to have been written before Mary gave permission for John to write the book and in order to gain that permission [f. 48v.1]: *Istas vero orationes usque ibi* [i.e. prayers *2–*7] *iam composueram antequam liber presentis conponendi licentiam habuissem et per ipsas dictam licentiam impetram Deum.* Prayers *1–*7 equated to days of week, Sunday to Saturday (see f. 49r.2, etc.).

Prayer *1: O Rex regum [f. 48v.1], to Christ, headed *oratio prima generalium que est oratio laudis ad dominum nostrum Ihesu Christum, que dicenda est bis in die, scilicet mane et sero, cum gratia Christi ex[er]cetur, quam ego, frater Iohannes, cum divino auxilio, ad* *augmentum gratie, composui, et est oratio prima Liber beate Marie virginis gloriose; cogitationes* ~2–11; four parts:

i) O Rex regum, *cogitationes* ~2–8: *cogita hic quod tu videas incarnationis Christi anunciationem et dic:* O Maria res (~2); *cogita hic quod tu videas Christi nativitatem et dic:* O quam felix (~3); [f. 48v.2] *cogita hic quod tu videas passionem domini nostri Ihesu Christi;* O quam medici[n]abilis (~4); *cogita hic quod tu videas resurexionem Ihesu Christi:* O quam fortis (~5); *cogita hic quod tu videas ascensionem Ihesu Christi et dic:* O quam miraculosa (~6); *cogita hic quod tu videas Spiritum Sanctum descendente[m] super appostolos et dic:* O quam sancta (~7); *cogita hic quod tu videas Deum in trinitate regnantem et dic:* O quam felix (~8).

ii) O dulce mi Domine, *cogitatio* ~9, headed *secunda pars orationis: cogita hic quod tu videas Deum inter septem candelabra sicud beatus Iohannes eum vidit in appokalypsi in principio visionum suarum* (see Revelation 1–2).

iii) Creator omnium rerum, *cogitatio* ~10, headed *tertia pars orationis: cogita hic ut in secunda quod videas inter candelabra.*

iv) [f. 49r.1] Veni creator Spiritus, *cogitatio* ~11, headed *quarta pars orationis ad Spiritum Sanctum: cogita hic quod tu videas Spiritum Sanctum in columbe specie de celo super te descendentem et dic hanc orationem sequentem.*

Second Incipit and Prologue [f. 49r.2]: autobiographical details, warnings: *Incipit liber qui Gratia Domini Nostri Ihesu Christe nuncupatur, per quem si devote dixeris in intimo cordis . . . gratiam Christi et eius gloriose et intemerate genitricis virginis Marie et sanctorum angelorum consequeris et adepisceris, et multa secreta que non licet homini loquere* (2 Corinthians 12:4) *tibi manifestabuntur. Ego frater Iohannes monachus has orationes conposui et probavi, et in veritate eas testificor eas esse veras* (John 21:24). *Liber iste inceptus fuit anno incarnationis domini 1304, et finitus anno domini 1307, et hoc quantum ad orationes tantummodo.*

Prayer *2: O excellentissima [f. 49r.2], to Mary, headed *oratio prescripta die Domenico dicatur* (see Part IV, Discussion 6). *Sequitur oratio secunda et prima de beata Maria Virgine, que feria secunda* [Monday] *debet dici, et est contra temptationes carnis; cogitationes* ~12–15; four parts:

i) O excellentissima, *cogitatio* ~12, headed (after incipit as above) *cogita hic quod tu videas eam devote.*

ii) [f. 49v.1] Virgo, virga, flos, nubes, *cogitatio* ~13, headed *hec sunt nomina beate Marie virginis gloriose: cogita hic quod tu videas ymaginem ipsius Marie virginis.*

iii) Et presta michi tantum virtutum, *cogitatio* ~14, headed *finiunt nomina Marie et sequitur ipsorum expositio efficacia et conclusio: cogita hic quod tu videas ut prius et dic ista.*

iv) [f. 49v.2] O pulcherrima mulier dulcissima, *cogitatio* ~15, headed *hec est tercia pars orationis predicte et est oratio spiritus sive beate anime* [refers to previous section?]. *Cantus ad beatam Mariam, et nunquam debet dici inmortali peccato existendo: cogita hic quod tu sis in celo et quod tu videas reginam gloriosam et dic hanc oratio[nem].*

Prayer *3: Ave Maria gratia plena, *cogitationes* ~16–22, Office for Christmas day, headed [f. 50r.1] *feria tertia* [Tuesday], *oratio tertia, quam ego non componi; set hic tamen convenienter coloravi, hanc enim orationem dixi quando primum apparuit mihi beata virgo Maria in sompnis et quotiens desidero ut mihi appareat: ipsam, dico, ipsam est experimentum visionis habende, cum suis similibus.* <u>*Cogita hic quod tu videas ymaginem beate Marie tecum loquentem in qua ecclesia*</u> [*cogitatio* ~16] **quidam vero profert** *eam cum missa celebratur, dicas eam cum suis partibus . . . et scias quecumque digna seu licita petieris inpetrabis. Finita autem missa, prosterne te ante crucifixum et dic que secuntur . . .* <u>*Et cogita hic quod tu sis in celo cum angelis ante Deum*</u> [*cogitatio* ~17]: *quo finito, dic iterum*; [f. 50r.2] *hec sunt partes dicende postea dicas officium <u>Puer natus</u>*; six/seven/eight parts:

i) <u>Ave Maria gratia plena</u> [f. 50r.2] followed by <u>Gloria in excelsis</u>, followed by mass for Christmas day as described in rubric: introits, collects, lessons.

ii) [f. 50v.2] <u>Ora pro nobis sancta Dei genitrix</u>, headed *postea dicas istas preces sequentes.*

iii) <u>Deus qui hanc sanctissimam noctem</u>, *cogitatio* ~18, headed <u>*hic cogita quod tu videas Christum nascentem ex utero virginis Marie et quod sit nox*</u> *et dic hanc tertiam partem.*

iv) <u>Da nobis quis Domine</u>, *cogitatio* ~19, headed *quarta pars orationis: <u>cogita hic quod tu videas Christum natum, iacentem in presepio</u>*

v) <u>Deus qui salutis eterne</u>, *cogitatio* ~20, headed *quinta pars orationis: <u>cogita hic quod tu videas Christum adorari a te, sicut in apparitione a tribus magis</u>*, *et dic orationem beate Marie ut hic sequitur.*

vi) <u>Ihesu, pie Ihesu</u>, *cogitatio* ~21, headed *sexta pars orationis: <u>cogita hic quod tu videas Christum suspensum in cruce</u> et dic.*

vii) <u>Illumina quos domine Deus</u>, *cogitatio* ~22, headed *oratio ad Patrem et Filium et Spiritum Sanctum: <u>cogita quod tu videas sanctam Trinitatem</u> et dic*, with a further *Oratio ad Patrem*: <u>Salva nos, omnipotens Deus</u> (neither is numbered; the latter could be seen as part viii).

Prayer *4: Ave salve gloriosa Domina [f. 50v.2], to Mary, headed *feria 4a* [Wednesday], *et oratio tertia* [i.e. of *Liber Maria virgine*, which begins with Prayer *2], *set 2a de beata Maria, quam ego frater Iohannes composui postquam prima vite apparuit mihi beata virgo Maria in memoria illius visionis specialiter, et nunquam debet dici nisi ipsa beatissima virgo in sompnis apparuit*; *cogitationes* ~23–8; four parts:

i) <u>Ave, salve gloriosa Domina</u>, *cogitatio* ~23, headed (after incipit as above) <u>*cogita hic quod tu intras aliquam ecclesiam a parte meridiei.*</u>

ii) [f. 51r.1] <u>O Maria domina mea</u>, *cogitationes* ~24–6, headed *secunda pars orationis istius; <u>cogita hic quod tu videas in eadem ecclesiam virginem gloriosam cum beate Iohanne in humana specie vestitis candidis adornatus</u>*; at [f. 51r.2] <u>cuius amplexus requies</u>, headed <u>*cogita hic quod tibi videantur amplecti a virgine gloriosa*</u> *et dic hunc orationem*; at <u>cuius visus ardens</u>, headed <u>*cogita hic quod tibi arriderat sancta virgo Maria.*</u>

iii) <u>O sancte Iohannes</u>, *cogitatio* ~27, headed *tertia pars orationis, ad beatem Iohannem ewangelistam; <u>cogita hic quod tu videas beatem Iohannem stantem in eadem ecclesiam iuxta latus virginis Maria [sic] ad amplectantem [sic] et cum te loquentem</u> et dic ut sequitur.*

iv) <u>O Domina dominarum</u>, *cogitatio* ~28, headed *quarta pars orationis; <u>cogita hic quod tu videas in eadem ecclesia Virginem gloriosam tecum loquentem</u> et dic hanc orationem.*

Prayer *5: Gloriosa flos celorum [f. 51v.2/52r.1], to Mary and God, headed *incipit tertia oratio generalis et specialis ad glori[os]am virginem Maria, feria* [i.e. *quinta*? Thursday]; *cogitationes* ~29–32, four parts.

i) <u>Gloriosa flos celorum</u>, *cogitationes* ~29–30, headed (after the incipit above) <u>*cogita hic quod tu videas ymaginem beate Marie in ecclesia ubi vis*</u> *et dic orationem hanc*; at [f. 52.r.2] <u>O Maria mater Christi</u>, headed *hec est clausula illa sancta et mirabilis que nunquam debet dici donec beatissima scilicet virgo Maria transformaverit ymaginem suam lapideam vel ligneam sive aliam coram orante*; at <u>O Maria stella maris</u>, headed *<u>cogita hic quod tu videas Virginem gloriosam in celo sedentem ad dextram filii sui Ihesu Christi.</u>*

ii) [f. 52v.2] <u>Deo patre filioque</u>, *cogitatio* ~31, headed <u>*cogita hic sanctam Trinitatem*</u> *et dic hanc secundam partem orationis predicte.*

iii) <u>Gratias tibi ago domine Ihesu Christe</u>, headed *tertia pars ipsius orationis que dicitur gratiarum actio post quamlibet visionis dicenda quam dedit nobis beata virgo Maria et divine precepit.*

iv) <u>O Revelatrix omnium secretorum</u>, *cogitatio* ~32, headed *quarta et ultima pars ad exprimendum propositum vel quid vis petere, ante omnes scriptu[r]arum orationes dicenda; et vocatur Oratio proposite, quam ego, Iohannes, in sompnis composui; <u>cogita hic quod tu sis in celo coram domina nostra</u>, et dic 'O revelatrix' et postea dic 'Ave Maria' sicud Feria tertia*; this concludes with *hic exprime petitionem* (a chance for petitioner to make personal requests).

Prayer *6: Surge beatissima [f. 52v.2], to Mary, headed *feria sexta* [Friday]; *oratio vel invocatio beate Marie Dei genetrix [sic] et gloriose virginis Marie et omnium angelorum; cogitatio* ~33; four parts; concludes with warning rubric *prescriptam orationem nemo presumat dicere nisi in neccessitate positus et sine peccato mortali* [f. 53r.2].

i) <u>Surge beatissima</u>, headed (after incipit as above), *cogita hic quod tu videas angelum Dei loquentem et cum voce tube.*

ii) [f. 53r.1] <u>Surge, surge, surge, dulcissima</u>, headed *secunda pars orationis.*

iii) <u>Scio enim domina mea</u>, headed *tertia pars orationis.*

iv) <u>Moveat te ad hoc illa beatissima humanitas</u>, headed *quarta pars orationis.*

Prayer*7: Gemma resplendens [f. 53r.2], to Virgin, John, Mary Magdalene, headed *die Sabbati; oratio ad beatem Iohannem ewangelistam; cogitationes* ~34–7; four parts.

i) <u>Gemma resplendens</u>, *cogitatio* ~34, headed (after incipit as above) <u>*cogita hic quod tu videas ipsum*</u> [John the evangelist] <u>*in habita iacobita*</u> [i.e., in the habit of a pilgrim to Compostella] <u>*in quedam ecclesia iuxta virginem gloriosam*</u> *et dic hanc orationem.*

ii) [f. 53v.1] <u>Si propter multitudinem peccatorum meorum</u>, *cogitatio* ~35, headed *secunda pars orationis; <u>cogita hic ut prius</u>.*

iii) <u>O lampas fulgida inter choros</u>, *cogitatio* ~36, headed *tertia pars orationis ad beatam Mariam Magdalenam, pro impetranda gratiam apud Virginem gloriosam; <u>cogita hic quod tu videas sanctam Mariam Magdalenam</u>; et hanc conposuit Magister Petrus de Fontibus.*

iv) [f. 53v.2] <u>Ave et gaude virgo Maria mater</u>, *cogitatio* ~37, headed *quarta et ultima pars orationis, quam dedit michi quidam qui erat de prima apostolorum* [possibly John the evangelist, visiting John the monk in sleep?], *et quamvis sit brevis est tamen efficacissima; <u>cogita hic quod tu videas virginem Mariam in celo</u> et dic orationem breve sequentem.*

Part II: *generales (2)* prayers to angelic orders and faithful dead, flanked by prayers to God and the Virgin; headed [f. 53v.2] *finit huius liber gratia Christi pars prima. Incipit 2a, que introitus* orationum ad Deum sive ad beatam virginem Mariam nunccupatur;* contains Prayers 1–12.

Prayer 1: Deus potentissimus triumphator [f. 53v.2], to God, headed *Ista oratio antequam aliquam descriptis [sic] dicatur; sive sit ad Deum sive ad beatam Virginem, semper dicatur oratio prima ad Deum*; repeats Tetragrammaton, asks help with <u>orationes mee, cogitationes, figure et imaginationes, preces, laudes, devotiones et affectiones</u>; Prayer 1 is repeated before each of Prayers 1–12 (see Part IV, Discussion 6.ii).

Prayers 2–10: O vos omnes spiritus sancti angeli [f. 53v.2], repeating prayer to angelic orders, headed *oratio ad angelos et ad suos equales in memoria habenda* (with similar headings to different orders later); prayers work through orders in turn, with *additiones* appropriate to each order, and further repetitions of the sequence addressed to lower, middle, upper orders: Angels (2), Archangels (3), Virtues (4), *inferiores*; Powers (5), Dominations (6), Principalities (7), *mediores*; Thrones (8), Cherubim (9), Seraphim (10), *superiores*. Subsections of prayers, as given in Prayer 2:

i) <u>O vos omnes spiritus sancti angeli</u> [etc.]

ii) <u>Aaperite michi portas iustitie</u>, headed *secunda pars orationis private et omnium orationum sequentium.*

iii) <u>Surgite, surgite, surgite omnes prenominati</u>, headed *tertia pars prefate et omnium aliarum sequentium invocatio*, with a parallel appeal <u>venite, venite, venite omnes sancte angeli</u> [etc.].

iv) <u>Videlicet</u>, headed *petitio ad angelos* [etc.]: *additiones* addressed to each order, requesting: memory (2), [f. 54r.2] eloquence (3), intellect (4); *ad spiritum medium ierarchie*: perseverance (5), all particular sciences (6), all knowledge generally (7); *ad spiritus superioris ierarchie*: understanding of written texts (8), poetic ability (9), [f. 54v.1] understanding of philosophical writing (10).

v) <u>Et post huius vite fragilis</u>, headed *additio generalis in fine cuiuslibet.*

In Prayer 3, a second version of <u>O vos omnes</u> apparently supercedes that to the

angels [f. 54v.1] and interjects a new *secunda pars ipsius orationis et additio aliarum ad angelos sequentes*, <u>in nomine illius</u>, but then refers back to earlier prayer with rubric *cum finires ad angelos dic etiam de aliis ut versum est supra, semper accipiendo verbum nostrum vivus cum maximo dolore et angustia plenus*, and the key phrases [f. 54v.2] <u>Apperite michi portas; Surgite surgite; Videlicet . . . et post huius vite</u> *et ut supra*. Prayers 4–10 then refer back to this second version, as do the prayers to the *inferiores, mediores, superiores*, which add their own *additiones/petitiones*, using the <u>Videlicet</u> formula, plus a further subsection (used only in these three repetitions and Prayer 11), <u>Auxilio* in omnibus</u> [f. 54v.2]. Sequence concludes with rubric explaining numeration [f. 55r.2], *finiunt orationes ad omnes spiritus celestes qui generales vocantur proprie. Notandum vera est quod inter illas 9 generales (sive 9 conputando a prima, que ad Deum) quasdam specialiter intitula 9 generales, que quidem ita intytulare non dicuntur numerando ad orationes, set potius recapitulationes predictarum orationum, que quatuor sunt* [I count only three], *ut superius apparet particularas ipsarum* [f. 55r.2].

Prayer 11: Beati estis sancti Dei [f. 55r.2], headed *oratio generales ad omnes sanctos et sanctas Dei post predictas dicenda*, to all saints: patriarchs, prophets, evangelists, apostles, innocents, martyrs, confessors, holy virgins, widows, *continentes*; organized like Prayers 2–10, concluding *omnia ut supra dicta sunt de generalibus*.

Prayer 12: O gloriosa Regina angelorum [f. 55v.1], to Virgin, headed *hec oracio proximi et consequenter inmediate dicatur hec oratio de beata et gloriosa Dei genitricis Maria, que est oratio 12, et finis istius secunde partis istius libri*; organized like Prayers 2–10 until the <u>Videlicet</u>, where a passage added [f. 55v.1–2] about the text's Catholicity: <u>Scio, domina, scio quod ista prenominata que peto secundum auctoritates quorundam non proprie pertinere ad salutis beatitudinem consequendam quia 'non est bonum multa scire sed potius beatum bene vivere'; tamen primi motus et principaliter sunt studii bene vivendi, et sic per consequens causa felicitatis eterne et celestium premiorum; et idcirco ad ipsam</u> [f. 55v.2] <u>impetrandam a domino nostro Ihesu Christo filio tuo sis in adiutorium meum et quod ab ipso merear exaudiri ad laudem et gloriam sancte Trinitatis et tuam totiusque curie celestis et sancte ecclesie katholica utilitatem et ad gloriam perpetue beatitudinis anime mee et aliarum multarum animarum . . .</u>

Part III: *generales (3)* (incorporating *petitiones 1–6*), *speciales*, headed [f. 55v.2] *omnia ffinit huius libri pars secunda. Incipit pars [tertia]. Qui vero in omni libros debes esse sapiens . . . et castus et mundus, *a criminalibus et a criminis mundanorum expers soli Deo* solummodo placere cupiens, animo sis sapientissimis et castissimis et quasi stans raptus supra omnem angelicam creaturam mente et spiritu ante hostiam super celestis ierarchie, ante tribunal Christi, ante primam summi iudicis et potentiam divinam ac vite eterne ymaginem. Dicendo sic primo istam orationem te habeas in manibus conpilosis et genibis flexis cum timore et tremore*

[f. 55v.2]; contains introductory prayers to God and Mary (Prayers 13–14), *petitiones* to the beings surrounding the throne of God (Prayers 15–20), *speciales* to each of the nine orders (21–9) and Christ as word (30) asking for knowledge; an *addendum* on medicine; a special prayer (*prima oratio*) for visions; a concluding prayer to Mary.

Part III a): Generales (3)

Prayer 13: Domine, domine, domine [f. 55v.2], to Christ, headed *oratio tertia et decima*; John waits outside the divine court asking to be let in: O aperi nobis viam iustorum! Ecce, ego Iohannes, servus tuus, foris stans ad hostium dispensationis misericordie tue.

Prayer 14: Sancta Maria virgo, caritas Dei, amor Dei [f. 55v.2], to Mary and each of the angelic orders from Seraphim down (each address headed *ad Seraphim dic* etc.), invoking each by its qualities: Seraphim as charity (and other qualities), Cherubim as wisdom, Thrones as justice, Principalities as victory, Dominations as rule, Powers as power, Virtues as healing [f. 56r.1], Archangels as revelation, Angels as messengers. *Additio* to the blessed spirits follows; then, after heading *denique surga de statu iunctis manibus extento capiti ad celum quasi mirando, addas hac et dic*, Domine quis habitabit in tabernaculo tuo (Psalm 14). Apostles, associated with the Seraphim, invoked; then God, after heading *denique iterum genibus flexis et manibus conplosis cum timore et reverentia divinam maiestatis tali modo salutes*: Ave, domine Deus, rex eterne . . . Gloria tibi Trinitas equalis. All angels invoked using part of Part One, Prayer *3, with heading *denique ad omnem militiam celestem que finita addas et in prima parte lib[ri] invenies*, Cantemus Domino . . . *sic in prima parte huius lib[ri] scribitur ubi invenies totum scriptum*. Then, after heading *deinde addas hec*, Te Deum. Finally, prophets and church fathers, associated with the Cherubim, after heading [f. 56r. 2] *hoc dicto* [Te Deum etc.] *submissa voce, quasi faciendo silentium addas que secuntur*, invoked and listed. Prayer invokes the aid of the whole of heaven in what follows.

Prayer 15: Pia almiflua, trina Dei omnipotentis [f. 56r.2], to God and angels, headed *incipit prima petitio, de salute anime. Ad Deum patrem ad superandas omnes temptationes; dicenda cum timore genibus flexis manibus complosis; et est oratio quindecima*; for purity and release from evil influences; four parts.

    i) Pia almiflua, introducing John to Trinity and God the Father (compare Part Two, Prayers 2–12), as one who gradatim transiens per omnes gradus militie celestis orando et contemplando.

    ii) Sapientia Dei patris incomprehensibilis, to Christ, headed *secunda pars orationis ad filium, per cura misericordie et custodia anime, et est invocatio vite eterne sive appellatio divine potenti[e] qua finita sine intervallo dicas hanc orationem sequentem*; subdivided into three sections: the second, Sancta Maria virgo, headed *tunc, quasi faciendo silentium submissiori voce dicas ad beatam virginem Mariam*, prepares direct address to humanity of Christ in third, <u>Ihesu pie, ymago vite</u>, headed *in hac hora hoc dicendo iterum oras ad Christum, dicendo.*

iii) [f. 56v.2] <u>Gratia ineffabilis, ardor inextinguibilis</u>, to Holy Spirit, headed *hac secunda parte finita, tertia[m] partem addas que secuntur, et est ad Spiritum Sanctum ad impetrandum eius gratiam nunc et in perpetuum amen.*

iii) <u>Angeli et archangeli</u>, to heavenly court (arguably a separate, transitional prayer), headed *Tunc dic ad totam curiam celestem*, asking for help <u>in hac hora</u>.

Prayer 16: Summa inextinguibilis et ineffabilis [f. 57r.1], to God, headed *secunda petitio in qua fit invocatio divine dispentionis ad in nominandum quinque sensus corporis que metas nature transcendit, et est oratio sedecima eiusdem decem sunt partes*; for renovation of senses and mental faculties, in preparation for *speciales* (Prayers 21–30); ten parts.

i) <u>Summa inextinguibilis</u>, introductory section listing senses and faculties and invoking (in what seems to be a separate, unnumbered, section of this prayer) Mary, the apostles and the martyrs, asking <u>sitis mihi adiutores et rogetis Deum pro me in hac hora</u>.

ii–ix) <u>Domine Ihesu Christe, Deus superne</u>, headed *denique dicas hec nomina ad Deum*; repeating prayer, in which separate appeals for sight (ii), hearing (iii) [f. 57r.2], smell (iv), taste (v), touch (vi), eloquence (*facundia*, vii) [f. 57v.1], memory (*reminiscentia*, viii) and reason (*ratio*, ix) are prefaced in turn by this invocation of God's *nomina*.

x) <u>Deus visus, Deus auditus</u>, headed *generalis oratio predictorum est pars ultima prefate orationis et recapitulatio*, also said after repeating <u>Domine Ihesu Christe</u>; conclusion returns to Prayer 14, with rubric [f. 57v.2] *denique submissiori voce dic hec nomina*, <u>Sancta Maria; omnis ordo totius Seraphim etc.</u> *scripta sunt in secunda oratione* [i.e. of Part Three], *usque ad illum locum* <u>Domine, quis habitabit</u>.

Prayer 17: O lumen clarissimum et inextingwebile [f. 57v.2], to Christ, headed (after rubric above) *oratio intellectus, tertium petitio promittens**, general prayer for infusion of Holy Spirit to prepare soul to receive knowledge; three subsections, the second, <u>Angeli, archangeli</u>, as in Prayer 15.iv), the third, <u>Deus lumen anime</u>, similar to the opening of Prayer 16.ii–ix).

Prayer 18: Memoria incomprehensibilis [f. 58r.1], to Christ, headed *quarta petitio ad memoriam et remeniscentiam promerenda[m], que est oratio decima octava et consequenter dicatur*, for retention of infused knowledge; three subsections, the second, <u>Angeli, archangeli</u> as above, the third, <u>Deus memorie</u> parallel to <u>Deus lumen anime</u> above.

Prayer 19: O fluentissime fons totius sapientie celestis [f. 58r.], to Christ, headed *hic flecte genua et dic quod sequitur*, for eloquence and mental quickness; three subsections, the second as above, the third [f. 58r.2], <u>Deus fons scientie et sapientie</u>, parallel to <u>Deus memorie</u> etc. above.

Prayer 20: O turris bellicosa [f. 58r.2], to Christ, headed *sexta petitio ad stabilitatem perseverantiam intellectus memorie et eloquentie et ad fortitudinem, que est oratio vicesima et generalium ultima,* for stability in memory, intellect and understanding; as with Prayer 16.x), conclusion returns to Prayer 14, <u>Sancta Maria, omnis ordo totius Seraphim</u> *que secuntur que scripta sunt in secunda oratione usque verbi,* <u>Domine quis habitabit</u>.

Part III b): Speciales
Prayer 21: Gloriosa memorabilis et iocunda inconprehensibilis [f. 58r.2], to Christ and Angels, headed *finitis generalibus, incipiunt specialia . . . et est oratio vicesima prima,* knowledge of grammar; six parts (four numbered).

i) <u>Gloriosa memorabilis</u>, Christ addressed as all-knowing, asked <u>Respice hodie super me famulum tuum Iohannem . . . ut mittere digneris de gloriosissimo et tremendissimo habitaculo tuo super me Spiritum Sanctum intellectus ad intelligendam scientiam et artem grammatice et eius partes; Videlicet, ut plenariam cognitionem subitaneam et perfectam omnis ipsius artis diciones obtineam declarandi; per illud ineffabile miraculum per quod tu, Deus, sine virile semine sed mistico spiramine in utero Virginis es conceptus</u>; knowledge of grammar, through miracle of Mary's conception.

ii) <u>Videlicet, ut plenariam cognitionem subitaneam congruam</u>, headed *ad se[cu]ndam partem, ut omnium omnino* grammatice et dicionum conveniens ordinatio habeatur,* preceded by repetition of <u>Gloriosa memorabilis</u> until <u>Videlicet</u>; knowledge of ordering speech, through star that led the magi.

iii) <u>Videlicet ut plenariam cognitionem subitaneam . . .ipsius artius regularum congruam ordinationum divisionis asignationem habeam cognoscendi</u>; headed *ad tertiam partem ut congrua regularum grammatice assignatio ordinate divisionis habeatur;* knowledge of rules, through miracle at Cana.

iv) <u>Spiritus sancte intellectus, gaudium angelorum, robur patriarcharum</u>, headed *ad quartem partem de facundia et facultate ipsius argumento et dic;* summing up prayer: ability to articulate eloquently one's knowledge of grammar and perpetual memory of same, through miracle of creation of heaven and earth on first day.

v) [f. 58v.2] <u>Angeli intellectus, angeli memorie, angeli facundie</u>, headed *denique dicas ad angelos;* lists names of angels and asks them to stay with petitioner.

vi) <u>[C]lementissime filii Dei</u>, preceded by <u>rogo ut vos dimmitat quod veniatis</u> and headed *Denique rogo Deum ut dimittat venire angelos;* asks God for his permission to have angels come to petitioner, <u>per intercessionem beate Marie virginis</u>.

Finally, part v) is repeated twice, part vi) once: *denique repite bis, usque ad illum locum que sic rogo ut supra, et postea tertiam vicem, addas iterum bis* <u>Clementissime fili Dei domine</u>.

Prayer 22: Deus in te superantium [f. 58v.2], to Christ and Archangels, headed *oratio 22 ad dialecticam ut facundiam argumentandi habeatur*; knowledge of dialectic; five parts (three numbered).

i) <u>Deus in te superantium</u>, Christ addressed as all-distinguishing, request for infusion [f. 59r.1] <u>in animam meam Spiritum Sanctum fortitudinis ad rationandum et capiendam scientiam et artem dyaletice et eius partes; Videlicet ut cognitionem . . . facundiam et eloquentiam mellitam ignitam et [in]superabilem in ipsa arte habeam argumentandi</u>; eloquent arguing, through Christ's undoing of the fall on the cross.

ii) <u>Videlicet ut cognitionem plenariam subitaneam . . . rationabilem</u>, headed *ad secundam partem, ut industria [respondendi] habeatur in dyalectica*, preceded by repetition of <u>Deus in te superantium</u>; reasoning power, through Christ's redemption of souls from hell.

iii) <u>Spiritus sancte fortitudinis, archangelorum gloria et solacium prophetarum</u>, headed *ad tertiam partem de facundia et facultate artis dyalectice, dic solummodo* [i.e. not repeating <u>Deus in te superantium</u>, which this partly parallels]; ability to articulate knowledge of dialectic including <u>orationes, propositiones, locos et sillogissimos</u> through division of waters on second day.

iv) [f. 59r.2] <u>Archangeli fanthasie, archangeli intellectus, archangeli memorie</u>, headed *tunc stans in pedibus dic ad angelos et archangelos*; lists names of archangels, asks them to be with petitioner and maintain knowledge of dialectic and ability to discern true from false.

v) <u>Domine Ihesu Christe filii Dei</u>, headed *tunc rogo Deum ut concedat et permittat archangelos ad te descendere, dicens*, citing Raphael's appearances to Tobit, Gabriel's to Mary, <u>per intercessionem beate Marie</u>.

Finally, part iv) is repeated twice, part v) once: *denique dic iterum bis*, <u>archangeli fanthasie</u> *usque ad illum locum* quem sic rogo, *et postea tertiam vicem addas iterum bis* <u>Domine Ihesu Christe</u>.

Prayer 23: O altitudo Sapientie [f. 59v.1], to Christ and Thrones, headed *oratio 23 ad rhetoricam ut continuus ornatus locutionum et competens et floridus habeatur iugiter* [f. 58r.2]; knowledge of rhetoric; seven parts.

i) <u>O altitudo Sapientie</u>, Christ addressed as judge and bringer of peace, through his division of light from darkness on the first day; <u>Videlicet</u>: request for <u>Spiritum Sancti consilii</u> to teach rhetoric, through Christ's descent into hell.

ii) <u>Videlicet ut plenarie . . . possim discernere . . . inter indicia iusta et iniusta, ordinata et inordinata, vera et falsa</u>, headed *ad secundam partem, ut indicia iusta et iniusta, ordinata et inordinata, vera et falsa discernantur*, preceded by repetition of <u>O altitudo Sapientie</u>; request for justice, through Christ's harrowing of hell.

iii) <u>Videlicet ut plenarie . . . officia et causas et personas . . . disponeram</u>, headed *ad tertiam partem, ut officia et causas et personas competenter et composite disponere scias*, preceded by repetition of <u>O altitudo Sapientie</u>; request for discernment, through Christ's raising of the dead.

iv) <u>Videlicet ut plenarium perfectum atque velocem veracem ingenio sis . . .</u> [f. 59v.2] <u>et . . . in ipsius artis omnibus absque prolixitate</u>, headed *ad quartam partem, ut intellectus et facundia ipsius artis omnibus operibus absque prolixitate habeatur,* preceded by repetition of <u>O altitudo Sapientie</u>; request for rhetorical sweetness without excess, through Christ's resurrection appearance to Mary Magdalene.

v) <u>Spiritus sancte consilii, thronorum dignitas</u>, headed *ad quintam partem de facundia et facultate artis rethorice, dicas hoc quod sequitur solummodo* [not repeating <u>O altitudo Sapientie</u>, which this partly parallels]; ability to articulate knowledge of rhetoric as defined in i–iv), and <u>incipere, narrare, petere, confirmare, conprehendere et concludere omnia quecumque dixero sive scripsio</u>. Additional passage concerning articulation of whole *trivium* (not paralleled in Prayers 22–3): <u>Aperi, Domine, cor meum, mentem meam et cerebrum perfectum tribus cellulis, ut prima vel anteriori parte, omnia visa et audita velocissime [possim] ymaginari</u> [grammar]; <u>in secunda, omnia ymaginata ratiocinari possim</u> [dialectic]; <u>et que rationata sunt, ultima, perpetue conservere memoria valeam, que inter sapientes, rectores, doctores discretos . . . locum honorabilem optinere et intra eos assistens valeam loco eloquencie pocula ministrare</u> [rhetoric]; <u>et qui celum et terram tuam prudentia fundasti et stabilisti, ita ingenium meum et sciencia triviali fundare digneris ut super illud recordabile quadriviale philosophie pallatium mirificum edificare valeam</u>; through gathering of waters, emergence of dry land and germination of seeds on the third day.

vi) <u>Sancti et gloriosissimi spiritus thronorum</u>, headed *nunc stans super pedes dic ad thronos*; lists names of Thrones and asks them to have Angels and Archangels teach rhetoric to petitioner; there follows [f. 60r.1] *tunc invoces angelos et dic ut supra in grammatica*, <u>Angeli intellectus</u> etc., repetitions of Prayer 21.v), 22.iv), partly recopied, but with crossreferences as Prayers 21.vi) and 22.v) are also woven in, with some repetitions as in these earlier prayers.

vii) [f. 60r.2] <u>Sancti patriarchi Adam, Abraham</u>, headed *denique adde hec nomina; hec est pars generalis ad pulsuum*, list of patriarchs, prophets, apostles, evangelists invoked to aid in learning.

Prayer 24: Mirabilis Deus [f. 60r.2], to Christ and Powers, headed *finit trivium de philosophia rationale; incipit quadrivium, de philosophie naturale; oratio 24a ad arismetricam*; knowledge of arithmatic; three parts.

i) <u>Mirabilis Deus</u>, to Christ as maker of number, weight and measure, that he send his <u>Spiritum Sanctum scientie</u> to teach petitioner arithmetic; <u>Videlicet</u> that whole art of numbering be revealed, by Christ's division of bread before two disciples in Emmaeus after his resurrection.

ii) <u>Spiritus sancte scientie, celsitudo potestatum et martirum victoria</u>, headed *ad secundam partem de facundia ipsius arismetice et facultate, dic hoc solummodo*, to articulate knowledge <u>ut vere et perfecte scientiam et possim numerare, addere et subtrahere, mediare, duplicare, multiplicare, dividere progredi, radices invenire et ipsas extrahere et fractiones facere materialiter et formaliter</u>, by the miracle of God's proper arrangement of sun, moon and stars on the fourth day.

iii) <u>Sancti et gloriosissimi spiritus potestatum</u>, headed *tunc in pedibus dic stando ad potestates*; lists names of Powers and asks them to make Angels and Archangels teach arithmetic to petitioner; repetition of Prayer 24.vi), with variations: *hoc dicto, dicas omnia sicud dictum est supra in rhetorica, excepto quod ubi invenitur scriptum* <u>officio fungentes tronorum</u> *loco illius dices* <u>officio fungent[es] potestatum</u>, *excepto et quod tu non dices illa nomina* <u>Sancta patriarcha</u>.

Prayer 25: Gloria summa [f. 60v.1], to Christ and Virtues, headed *Oratio 25a ad musicam et ad eius partes et sequitur oratio ista*, knowledge of music; three parts.

i) <u>Gloria summa</u>, Christ addressed as <u>perpetua iocunditas ineffabillium gaudiorum . . . et concordia omnium discordantium</u>, asked for knowledge of music; <u>Videlicet ut plenarie et perfecte omnem naturam proportionum . . . et ad omnem cantum omnes voces et sonos ad decentem et ad suavem concordiam sciam et valeam concordare</u>; by Christ's arrival, through locked doors, among his disciples after his resurrection.

ii) <u>Spiritus sancte pietatis virtutum, sublimitas confessorum</u>, headed *ad secundam partem de facundia et facultatis ipsius musice dicas illud solummodo*, to articulate knowledge of music [f. 60v.2], <u>ad . . . intelligendam et eloquendam . . . omnem [musicam], mellitam, metricam naturalem et omnium vocum sive sonorum earum relatam multitudinem . . . sciam et valeam contemplare</u>, through creation of fish and birds on fifth day.

iii) <u>Sancti et gloriosi spiritus virtutum</u>, headed *tunc stans in pedibus dic ad thronos* [error for *virtutes*]; lists names of Virtues, then refers back to Prayer 24.iii), <u>ego rogo vos etc.</u> *dic omnia alia quemadmodum supra dictum est in arismetrica, excepte hic quod ubi invenies 'arismetice' dicas hic 'musice' et ubi invenies 'potestatum' tu dicas hic 'virtutum' et* <u>Sancti patriarche</u> *non dices*.

Prayer 26: Summa et incomprehensibilis [f. 60v.2], to God the Father, Christ, Dominions, headed *oratio 26 ad geometriam*, knowledge of geometry; three parts.

i) <u>Summa et incomprehensibilis</u>, to Creator God and Christ, awesome measurer of creation, implored through *Spiritus sanctis timoris* for knowledge of geometry; <u>Videlicet</u> measuring, by Christ's mercy in saving Peter when he was unable to walk on the water.

ii) <u>Spiritus sancte timoris, honor dominationum, sanctarumque mulierum continentia</u>, headed *ad secundam partem de facundia et facultate ipsis artis; dic solummodo hoc*; asks Christ, <u>in quo non est residuum vel superfluum set omnis ratio et mensura invenitur</u>, for knowledge [f. 61r.1] <u>ad sciendam intelligendam et</u>

mensurandum omnem geometriam altimetram, planimetram atque
confinimetram et omnes earum partes, ut ipsam valeam adiscere, docere et eius
figuras facere et divisiones cognoscere et proporcionaliter omnia mensurari, and
retention of this knowledge, by the creation of animals and the making of
humankind on the sixth day.

iii) Sancti et gloriosi spiritus dominacionum, headed *tunc stans in pedibus et ad
dominaciones dic hanc orationem*; lists names of Dominations, then refers to previous
prayers.

Prayer 27: Eternalis potestates [f. 61r.], to Christ and Principalities, headed
oratio 27a ad astronomiam sive ad astrologiam et ad eius partes, knowledge of
astronomy/astrology; four parts.

i) Eternalis potestates, to Christ qui celestium profunditatem secretorum
misteriorum tuorum a sapientibus et prudentibus huius mundi abscondisti ut
parvulis mansuetis ydoneis revelares and who has lit the world with the stars and
planets since the fourth day, that Spiritum Sanctum sapientie teach
astonomy/astrology; Videlicet ut plenarie . . . cognoscere possim stellas, planetas,
signa et cursus ipsorum considerare, et eorum naturas scire et ex eis veraciter
iudicare, by the eclipse that occurred at the time of Christ's Passion.

ii) [f. 61r.2] Lux mundi et Deus pater immense, Pater eternitatis, largitor
sapientie et scientie ac totius gratie spiritus sancti sapientie sanctorum
heremitarum et monachorum . . . domine Ihesu Christe, spera intelligibilis cuius
centrum ubique circumferenciam nusquam, headed *ad partem secundam de facundia
et facultatis ipsius artis*; asks Christ ut habeam notitia elementorum et contemplare
sciam et possim meatus stellarum et firmamentorum, et circulorum
revolutionem, ventorum vires, et omnium predictorum naturas presciam et
prevideam ut preteritorum, presentium et futurorum sciam, by God's rest on the
seventh day.

iii) Sancti gloriosi spiritus principatum, headed *tunc stans in pedibus stans et ad
principatus*; lists names of Principalities, then refers to previous prayers as before,
with exception below.

iv) Sancti martires Christi, after instructions to substitute 'Principalities' for
'Dominions' in repeating prayers, adding this prayer; invokes aid of martyrs,
confessors, widows/*continentes*, and holy monks and hermits (equivalent to the
four angelic orders invoked in Prayers 25–8).

Addendum: De physica sive de arte medicine [f. 61v.1], headed *finiunt
orationes ad omnes artes sciendas*; passage on how to adapt prayers above to learn
medicine/natural science: *verum de physica sive de arte medicine nichil tetigimus hic, scias
de ipsa quia proprie pertinet ad spiritus virtutum; verum si ipsam scire volueris, dicendum et
faciendum est quemadmodum dictum est in musica*, with exceptions listed and two new
Videlicet passages for first two parts of prayer, the second running, Videlicet

omnem artem physicam et medicinam cognoscam, omnes virtutes herbarum lapidum et arboris, avium, piscium et omnium reptilium, et 4 elementorum complexiones hominum et naturas regionum et qualitates ipsorum et motus corporum celestium et omnium istorum habita notitia perfecta, pocula salutis infirmis valeam ministrare. Then instructions on other arts: *Aliomodo potest scire medecinam vel phisicam per 7 artes liberales, quia omni indiget; similiter, si scire volueris de aliqua alia arte, utpote de methaphisica vel exceptiva vel virtutum propertates, ipsius vel ipsarum nominabis etiam discretionem tuam et nomina illa in orationibus ubi volueris sub quibus continetur artibus predictis.*

Prayer 28: Altitudo divine consilii [f. 61v.2], to Christ, God the Father, Cherubim, headed *oratio 28a*, for physics/philosophy (consistently confused here) and metaphysics; five parts.

i)–iii) <u>Altitudo divine consilii</u>, to Christ and the Father, that <u>Spiritum sanctum tuum sapientie et intellectus, consilii, et timoris super me, de sancta sede magnitudini tue qui cor meum et animam meam purificet, mundet, accendat, illuminat, doceat, dirigat, exerceat, gubernet, regat, inhabitat, custodiat, protegat, visitat et defendet omnibus diebus vite mee, informet, instruat me omnem physicam amen.</u> Then alternatives offered: *si de physica naturali vel de methaphisica scire volueris, dicas:* <u>Ut plenarie . . .,</u> by Christ's miraculous ascension into heaven; but if ii) *de philosophia morali volueris scire, dic iterum* <u>O altitudo</u> *etc. et pro isto vocabulo 'philosophia naturali' dic 'morali';* then follows variant version of the <u>Videlicet</u> prayer (headed *ad secundam partem*), emphasizing <u>omni philosophia yconomica vel yconica.</u> After heading *ad tertiam partem*, a third <u>Videlicet</u> prayer emphasizes <u>omnem sensum mon[a]sticum yconomicum et polliticum.</u>

iv) [f. 62r.1] <u>Spiritus sancte sapientie et intellectus consilii et timoris, excellentia cherubin speciose,</u> headed *ad quartam partem de facundia et facultate philosophie moralis, et dicas hoc quod sequitur,* sums up i)–iii), as with earlier prayers.

v) <u>Sancti spiritus gloriosi cherubin,</u> headed *tunc stans in pedibus dic ad cherubin,* with names of cherubin from <u>cherubin fantasie</u> to <u>cherubin doctrine,</u> including all liberal arts and physics, with the mechanical and exceptive arts: <u>cherubin omnis discipline, cherubim monastice, cherubin yconomice, cherubin politice, cherubin omnis sensus morali, cherubin lanaficii, cherubin theatrice, cherubin fabrilis, cherubin venatorie, cherubin agriculture, cherubin navigationis, cherubin nigromancie, cherubin geonegia, cherubin aeromantie, cherubin pigromancie, cherubin cyromancie, cherubim geomancie, cherubim geonegie, cherubin ydiomatice, cherubin omnis artis.</u> End of prayer, <u>Ego rogo vos,</u> refers back to previous prayer (*ut supra dictum est in astrologia*).

Prima oratio: Alpha et omega virtus [f. 62r.2] (unnumbered prayer ~3), prayer for visions given out of sequence, headed with explanation as to its proper place, and reasons for inserting it here: *Explicit philosophya naturalis. Hec oratio* *sequens semper ad visiones habundas in hac arte prima, post* <u>Ave Maria etc.</u> *que est in principio libri scripta sicut* [f. 48r.1] *proferri. Similiter, quando operatur per totum corpus huius artis, primo profertur et non in repetitione partium artium proferri debet;* all the other prayers are to be said in order, but this should be said first, and has only been placed here out of caution: *haec enim est huius artis vel lib[ri] prima oratio, set ad cautela ante orationem philosophie (et in quibusdam aliis libris ante orationem gramatice) situatur; ultima enim est generalium et prima specialium seu singularium; ipsa enim est omnium orationum prohemium et experimentum generale, que omnia generalia et specialia mirabiliter et efficaciter audiuntur et memorie retinentur, et eius sunt due partes, quorum prima est ad Deum, 2m ad Virginem gloriosam.* Prayer is named the first prayer of the entire book: *oratio prima huius libri, qua cognoscuntur generalia, que prima pars huius orationis;* two parts.

   i) <u>Alpha et Omega, virtus altissimi,</u> to Christ, with a variant on Prayers 2–10.i): begins <u>Ecce ego Iohannes . . . rogo te . . . ut hodie michi . . . in sompnis cum beata et intemerata genitrice tue virgine Maria apparere, et mecum loque me docendo digneris; et eandem quam et Salomoni tribuisti sapientia, michi quoque famulo tuo Luce toto desidero</u> . . . etc. (see note 40).

   ii) [f. 62v.1] <u>Consolatrix omnium desolatorum,</u> headed *secunda pars ipsius orationis, ad virginem gloriosam Mariam,* to Mary, who (in a lengthy autobiographical relative clause) <u>amicis tuis te fideliter petentibus multotiens in sompnis apparuisti et appares eos quos de quesitis nominibus consulere voluisti et consulis, et petita conferere consuevisti, que [licentiam] petenti componendi orationes istius lib[ri], et isti in sompnis apparens, non suis meritis set tua gratia ad distructionem omnium errorum fallacis inimici per artes</u> *[MS reads 'partes']* <u>exceptivas pullulatorum et omnium aliorum et maxime ad condempnationem et destructionem nephandissime Artis Notorie reprobate condempnate frig . . .</u> *[illegible]* <u>et eciam detestate et tribuisti et misericorditer concessiste et eas conportas cum figuris et ymaginationibus a Deo pie de verbo ad verbum sibi in sompnis revelasti una cum anullo perfectionis, et ipsius scientie institutionibus novis postea plures eidem apparens in sompnis, et aprobasti testata fuisti et etiam collaudando firmasti, sic dans orationes, figuras, anullum et institutiones huius scientie secundum quod adeo sunt institute a nobis, et ab angelis, et a te ipso de licentia nostra institute ratificatus gratificatus, laudamus, approbamus et confirmamus et admittimus in salutem omnium credentium bone voluntatis: Ego, Luca</u> . . . there follows prayer that Mary will appear in sleep again, and protect from all evil influences.

Prayer 29: Flos divini [f. 62v.2], to Christ and Seraphim, headed *explicit philosophia naturalis* [see rubric for f. 62r.2, <u>Prima oratio</u>], *incipit philosophia contemplativa; Oratio 29, ad theologiam et ad eius partes et sensus, sequitur; ipsa haec in sua debita forma,* for theology; seven parts.

   i) <u>Flos divini,</u> to Christ, <u>in cuius manu sunt stella 7 et candelabra 7 et lampadum 7,</u> for seven gifts of Spirit and instruction in theology. <u>Videlicet ut per</u>

Spiritum Sanctum tuum scientie, headed *tunc verte faciem versus occidentem et flexis genibus et dic*; knowledge of sensum historicum, through miracle of Pentecost.

ii) Videlicet ut per tuum Spiritum Sanctum consilii, headed *ad secundam partem; dic iterum* Flos divini *etcetera, usque* videlicet; *et loco illius dicas versus aquilonem illam*; knowledge of tropological/anagogical sense.

iii) [f. 63r.1] Videlicet ut Spiritum Sanctum intellectus, headed *ad tertiam partem versus orientem; dic iterum* Flos divini *usque ad* videlicet *et loco eiusdem dic illud*; knowledge of allegorical sense.

iv) Videlicet ut Spiritum tuum Sanctum sapientie, headed *ad quartam partem versus meridiem; dic iterum* Flos *usque* videlicet, *tunc dicas hoc*; knowledge of anagogical/tropological sense (apparently same request as in part ii).

v) Spiritus Sanctus sapientie, intellectus, consilii, fortitudinis, scientie, headed *ad quintam partem de facundia et facultate theologie, dic solummodo*; knowledge of all theology.

vi) Sancti gloriosissimi spiritus, altissimi seraphin, headed *tunc stans in pedibus dic ad seraphin*, whose names correspond to the seven gifts of the Spirit, as well as seraphin altitudinis, seraphin similitudinis, seraphin signaculi, seraphin ymaginis, seraphin impressionis etc. Ego Iohannes rogo vos headed *omnia dic ut supra in philosophia morali, excepto* . . . etc.

vii) Sancta et gloriosa virgo Maria super choros angelorum exaltata, headed *Et postea sine intervallo dic*; list of virgin martyrs and prayer for their aid in attaining theology.

Prayer 30: Verbum in principio et verbum apud Deum [f. 63v.1], to Christ and the Father, headed *oratio 30a que est finis orationum et [im]plementum ipsa et est ad omnes scientias* [f. 63r.2–v.1]; for all knowledge; no formal subdivisions. Prayer makes much of John's sin and God's grace, and invokes Tetragrammaton five times, once repeating part of unnumbered prayer ~iv) [f. 48r.1].

Concluding Prayer: Ave Maria virgo gratiosa [f. 64r.1] (unnumbered prayer ~4), headed *denique conclude sic intentionem tuam in beata Maria et dic hec 3em; conclusio generalis omnium orationum et singulares addenda est*; praise/prayer to Mary; three parts.

i) Ave Maria, virgo gratiosa. Mary equated with her prefigurations (tu es virga Aaron . . . Hester humilis . . . Judith pulcherima, a long list), praised in the imagery of the Song of Songs (compare Prayer *5). This culminates in [f. 64v.1] tu es grammatice congruus intellectus, dyalectice vera memoria argumenti, rethorice eloquentie ordinata, libra geometr[i]e, collectio arismetrice, concordia musice et consideratio astronomie et philosophie cognitio, theologice contemplatio, artium mechanicarum scientia operatio, exceptivarum admirationis inpetrationis, et omnium virtutum retributio . . . Ecce, Domina et amica vera, ecce cum auditorio tuo completus est liber tuus a fratre Iohanne monacho, de licentia tua et voluntate compositus et factus et ad honorem filii tui domino nostro Ihesu Christo et tuum et totius curie celestis et in salut[em] anime mee et omnium ipso fruentium et utentium bono meo. This becomes a prayer to conserve the book: et nunc, Domina et amica . . . vigila super verbo tuo . . . ut non permittas orationes tantas istius liber a me dictas et pronuncciatas annullari . . . set tu que Theophilum apostatum exaudisti et precibus eius aquievisci ipsum que misericorditer a laqueis dyaboli librasti, exaudies me et acceptas habeas orationes meas (this last a structural echo of Prayer *2.i), f. 49r.2–v.1). This prayer formally ends, Exaudi, exaudi, exaudi, O alma et sanctissima virgo Maria, amen.

ii) [f. 64v.2] Benedicat te gloriosissima virgo Maria anima mea, headed dicans [?] omnia et conferas de peccata.* Explicit ergo ultima hiis dictis, sine intervallo adde invocationem beate Marie que scribitur in prima particula huius libri que incipit sic, Surge beatissima . . . [i.e. Prayer *6] usque in fine tertiam partem, et ultimam huius orationis dicas, que est laus [sancte] beate Virginis; prayer for Mary's aid in the future.

iii) Te Deum laudamus, Spiritus Sanctus a patre procedens, to Holy Spirit, Mary, apostle John, headed completo opere dicas dicas [sic] istud canticum per totum eo dicto*, dicas dicas [sic] hec verba; three subsections: the Te Deum; a prayer Gratiam tuam quesumus, headed de domina nostra oratio; a prayer Sic domine quesumus beatus Iohannes apostolus et ewangelista, headed collecta de sancto Iohanne; final short prayers (Benedicamus domino, Deo gracias, etcetera). Ends with rubric ffiniunt orationes beate Marie virginis de ademptione omnium scientiarum et artium.

Part IV: generales (4) (or prima practica), headed incipit prima practica; qualiter sit operandum per orationes predictas, vel quibus diebus sit dicenda ad consecrationem predictarum scientiarum, inveniendam consequendam et fruendam, et vocatur practica perambula et generalis huius libri pars ultima; incomplete theoretical and practical discussion of the book's use and rationale; divided into unnumbered discussions, some incorporating notae.

Prologue [f. 65r.1], headed Hic incipit prologus; repeats phrases from opening prologue [f. 48r.1], recalling John's rejection of his antiquis . . . erroribus and commitment to Christ and Mary. Part IV concerns the opus described by the rest of the liber. First instruction is to maintain the practice of saying the Office and, if possible, the Office of the Virgin.

Discussion ~1 [f. 65r.1], headed qualiter debet operari ibi qui vocatur predictam corpus huius scientie, vel non presens* sed solummodo ad habendam visio[nem]; discussion of practicing the opus, beginning with an account of writing the book out: faciat primo scribere 7 orationes cum prohemio que in principio magni libri sunt, scilicet O rex regum etc . . . et denique totam presentem novam compilationem prout usque in finem; in practice, mostly a series of unnumbered notae describing the book.

i) **Nota ~1**, on not changing what is written here: nota quod nichil debes agere *minuere vel mutare de omnibus que scripsimus tam in orationibus quam in figuris, ymaginationibus et institutionibus, nisi a Deo vel Virgine gloriosa tibi prius fuerit divinitus inspiritum, id est revelatum.*

ii) **Nota ~2** [f. 65r.2], on need to fast before making any great request *in hac scientia.*

iii) **Nota ~3**, *nota quod omnia huius scientie sicut data sunt ita fiant.*

iv) **Nota ~4**, on the book's relationship to the Ars Notoria: *item nota quod tam in compositione orationum quam institutionum huius scientie nos spoliasse vasis aureis et argenteis (id est verbis divinis et bonis), Egiptum (id est Artem Notoriam), et ditasse Ebreos (id est fideles et sanctos operationes huius scientie)*; warnings concerning the devil's attempts to avenge himself; then a question, *queret aliquis quare compilatio figurarum facta et edita in principio a nobis non valuerit* [or 'voluerit'?] *vel non potuerit confirmari*: important discussion of work's composition.

v) **Nota ~5**, how the *nova compilatio* was prefigured early on; begins *nota quod ista nova compilatio fuit presignata, quod futura erant a principio antiquis* [f. 65v.1] *compilationis argumenta cuiusdam visionis; set non intelleximus donec ipsa nova compilatio fuerit completa.*

vi) **Nota ~6**, *nota quod exercentes istam scientiam primi sciant in veritate adventum autem Christi et fortius omnibus eadem resistant.***

vii) **Nota ~7**, on saying the prayer O potentissima *sicut dicendum est de ea in prima practica* (prayer is not found in the Munich text, so note may refer to a later, missing portion).

viii) **Nota ~8**, on Mary's visionary appearance in the form of an image of wood, stone, metal.

ix) **Nota ~9**, headed *nota de comendatione istius scientie*, how the knowledge offered here transcends speech: *nota quod in recomendatione istius scientie mirabilis deficiunt omnes lingue viventium.*

Discussion ~2 [f. 65v.2], headed *de libro interiori et exteriori quod dicendum sit in principio*, on preparing the self to read the book: *primo in corde tuo describitur debes ymagines summe contemplationis studio depingere, in fide, spe, caritate orationes notare, et ita huius lib[ri] materialis invenies efficaciam et effectum*; instructions on how to internalize the Tetragrammaton prayer (unnumbered prayer ~2, [f. 48r.1]), by imagining it as a ring; more on relation of *antiqua compilatio* and *nova compilatio*, and a new title for the book, *Liber florum doctrine celestis*, with defence of its Catholicity and account of its completion.

Discussion ~3 [f. 66r.2], headed *de fide, spe, caritate operantis et de mensa [recte 'missa'?] celebranda ante inceptionem operis*, on the interior disposition the practitioner needs to have, and the need to say mass before beginning.

Discussion ~4 [f. 66r.2], headed *quo die incipiendum est hec opus et in quo loco* etc., on where and when to practice the *opus*, with instructions for using chapels or private rooms.

Discussion ~5 [f. 66v.1], headed *in qua hora incipiendum sit hoc opus*, on beginning the *opus* by rising before dawn, saying the penitential psalms, creeds etc.; a prayer headed *oratio de misericordia peccatorum et remissionem inpetrandum*, beginning <u>Deus qui proprium es misereri</u> (unnumbered prayer ~5).

Discussion ~6 [f. 66v.2], headed *ista intelligenda solum debeat in prima practica et non de secunda subsequenti: qualiter debeat operari per hunc librum sacramentos sine illi qui sunt in officiis constituti*, concerned with how to integrate the saying of the Office with the prayers in the book, saying them morning, noon and evening and dividing the book into eight (not nine?). This division is then detailed in what must once have been eight or nine successive subsections:

i) headed *de primo opere prime practice quod dicatur inpetratum aliorum, seu per ambulum et qualiter sit operandum*, the prayers for the first week, corresponding to Prayers *1–*7 (Part I).

ii) headed *de secundo opere quod dicitur auxiliatum sive inpetratum qualiter sit agendum*, prayers for the second week, corresponding to Prayers 1–12 (Part II).

iii) headed *de tertio opere quod dicitur salutatem sive preparatum sensuum anime et corporis ad suscipiendum quesita*, corresponding to Prayers 13–14 in surviving portion of text (probably Prayers 13–18 in the subsection as a whole, since this is the case in the McMaster version).

APPENDIX C

Summary Analysis of McMaster Unnumbered MS

(Prayers are underlined, rubrics italicized, considerations italicized and underlined, indications of major structural divisions in bold face. Other conventions used are the same as for the Munich text, although where possible punctuation here reflects the detailed manuscript punctuation.)

Prima Operatio
Opus I: [O excellentissima, famosa, gloriosa] [f. 1.r: modern foliation; an earlier foliation gives this as f. 15], illustrations ~1–, *considerationes* 1–19: closely parallels Munich: Prayers *2–7; originally seven parts, only six [ii–vii] surviving.

i) [ff. 1–14 of earlier foliation] See notes on Opera VII and IX for clues to some of the contents of this part, which may have consisted not of the prayer <u>O rex regum</u> [Munich: Prayer *1], but of the prayer <u>Alpha et Omega</u> [Munich: Part III, Prima Oratio], unless both were included.

ii) <u>O excellentissima</u> [f. 1v.; Munich: Prayer *2], *consideratio* ~1, illustration ~1, headed ¶*Incipit opus ferie secunde*; ¶*Flecte genua, cum devotione* [second prayer of Opus I], after full-page illustration of Mary [f. 1r.]. At f. 2v., rubric, ¶*Hic exprime supplicationem quam desideras*; ¶*Cogita quasi tu Mariam in celo vidisses* [Munich: *cogitatio* ~14]: <u>O pulcerima mulier, dulcissima Virgo</u>. Ends with prayer not in Munich: [f. 4r.] <u>Gratias tibi ago, omnipotens Deus, qui hodie fecisti pulcram speram firmamenti, quod celum vocari voluisti</u>, followed by rubric ¶*Opus figurarum sequitur totum ut supra.* ¶*Illa oratio* <u>Ante secula</u> *dicenda est antequam vadatur dormitum.*

iii) <u>Puer natus</u> [Munich: Prayer *3] [f. 4r.–v], *considerationes* ~2–6, illustrations ~2–3, headed ¶*Tunc sequitur opus ferie tertie et accessus cum horis canonicis, ut dictum est.* ¶*Et ponitur officium nativitatis domini nostri Yhesu Christi, scilicet,* <u>Puer natus est nobis</u> *et cetera, totum legendo vel cantando.* ¶*Et si non poteris habere presbiterum, tunc* [f. 4v.] *lege officium met,* sicut orationes statim post accessum. et dic.* . . . At f. 6v., ¶*Considera quod* <u>Christum vides natum de Maria</u> [Munich: *cogitatio* ~18]; ¶*Considera quasi Christum videre iacentem in presepio.* [Munich: *cogitatio* ~19]; at f. 7r., ¶*Considera quod Christum adores sicut tres magi, et dic collectam* [Munich: *cogitatio* ~20]; ¶*Cogita quod Christum vides pendere de cruce. Flecte genua.* [Munich: *cogitatio* ~21]; ¶*Considera sanctam Trinitatem* [Munich: *cogitatio* ~22]. Ends with prayer not in Munich: [f. 7v.] <u>Gratias ago tibi, omnipotens Deus, qui hodie fecistis maturata gramina et herbas quasque in sua specie florentes . . .</u>, and two illustrations: ¾ page of Mary reading as Holy Spirit descends to her as a dove [f. 7v.]; full page of Christ's Ascension [badly scrubbed, f. 8r.], both with instructions to illustrator at foot of page [cursive script]: *hic ponatur figure beate Marie cum oliva et super columbam, and hic ponatur figura ascentionis Christi cum* . . . [illegible]; final rubric [f. 8v.], *Sequitur opus figure ut supra per totum. Dic iterum antequam vadas dormitum. hanc orationem:* <u>Ante secula</u>.

iv) <u>Ave, salva gloriosa</u>. [Munich: Prayer *4] [f. 8v.], *considerationes* ~7–13, illustrations ~4–5, headed *Opus quarte ferie sequitur inde. Et primo dicendus est accessus cum horis canonicis, ut supra.* <u>*Considera quod transis in unam ecclesiam circa meridiem*</u> (Munich: *cogitatio* ~23). At f. 9r., <u>*Considera quod in eadem ecclesia virginem et sanctum Iohannem evangelistam cum Maria in albis vestibus, Iohannem in una veste unius peregrini Iacobite. Inclina*</u> [Munich: *cogitatio* ~24]; f. 9v., ¶*Hic considera quasi in ac* Maria te amplexum haberet* [Munich: *cogitatio* ~25]; ¶*Considera quod te Maria inspiciat* [not in Munich]; f. 10r., ¶*Cogita quasi arideret te Maria* [Munich: *cogitatio* ~26]; ¶*Cogita quod vides sanctum Iohannem stare iuxta Mariam a latere et tecum vel ad te loqui, et dic* [Munich: *cogitatio* ~27]; f. 11r., ¶*Cogita quod Maria loquitur tecum, et dic* [Munich: *cogitatio* ~28]; f. 12v., final rubric, ¶*Opus figurarum sequitur inde per totum ut supra. Dic iterum illam orationem.* <u>Ante secula</u> *antequam vadas dormitum*, and two illustrations: ½ page of Virgin and child with tree and dove; full page [f. 13r.] of Pentecost, Holy Spirit descending on Mary, seated on dais [with kneeling apostles surrounding] as dove/tongues of fire; f. 13v., prayer [not in Munich]: <u>Gratias ago tibi, omnipotens Deus, qui hodie solem, lunam, stellas fecisti et eis mundum illustrasti</u>.

v) <u>Gloriose flos celorum</u> [Munich: Prayer *5, deferring part of i until end of

Opus I, omitting iv, but see note on Opus VII below] [f. 13v.], *consideratio* ~14, illustrations 6–7, headed *Sequitur opus ferie quinte. Et primo dicendus est accessus cum horis canonicis ut supra. ¶Cogita quasi videns ymaginem Maria in una ecclesia ubi tu vis. Sede.* At f. 16v., *Hic considera sanctam Trinitatem* [Munich: *cogitatio* ~31]; closing prayer [not in Munich]: [G]ratias tibi ago, omnipotens Deus, qui hodie in aques pisces et in aere volatilia creasti, followed by half-page decoration [leaf motif] and two full-page illustrations: Virgin teaching Christ, with pelican on tree behind [f. 17r.]; Coronation of Virgin, Father and Son placing crown on her head, irradiated by Holy Spirit as dove above [f. 17v], both with instructions to illustrator at foot of page [cursive script, partly cropped and illegible]: *hic pona figura****; hic ponatur alia figura **** [mostly illegible].

vi) Surge, o beatissima virgo Maria [Munich: Prayer *6] [f. 18r.], *consideratio* ~15, illustrations ~8–9, headed *Sequitur inde opus ferie sexte. Et primo dicendus est accessus cum horis canonicis scilicet*. ¶Considera quasi angelum Dei tecum loquentem in voce tube.* At f. 18v.–20r., long section not found in Munich, e.g.: O potentissima imperatrix et virtuosa virgo. *inclina.* Maria, ubi est potentia tua et virtus tua? . . . O datrix et revellatrix excellentissima, ubi est doctrina et revellatio tua? . . . ubi sunt promissiones tue michi facte? Ubi est memoria tua?, followed by questions about intelligentia, elloquentia, intellectus, verborum, fantasia, reminiscentia, sapientia, ratio, oppinio, scientia, artes liberales, artes exceptive, artes mechanice, artes virtututive, and Ubi est ymaginis tue talis mutatio quam consuevisti facere coram operantem in arte hac quando in somnis volebas loqui cum illo [a reference to John the Monk], and a series of Numquid questions; addition ends with rubric, *Respice sursum in celum coniunctis manibus, et dic* [f. 20r.]. At f. 21r., ends with prayer [not in Munich], Gratias tibi ago, omnipotens Deus, qui hodie fecisti iumenta et reptilia et bestias terre ac hominem rectum ad tuam simillitudinem dando ei liberum arbitrium et universe terre dominium . . .; rubric *Sequitur hic opus figurarum* etc.; followed by half-page decoration [leaf motif] and two full-page illustrations: Virgin and Child with raven in fruit tree behind [f. 21v.]; Virgin standing on the moon with Child [f. 22r.].

vii) Gema resplendens [Munich: Prayer *7] [f. 22v.], *considerationes* ~16–19; headed *Sequitur opus diei Sabbati. Accessum die primo et horas canonicas, ut supra. ¶Considera quasi videres Iohannem evangelistam stare penes Mariam in una ecclesia in una veste peregrinali Iacobite rogando pro te et quod ipse se inclinate super te. Sede.* At f. 23r., ¶Considera ut prius et quod Maria tecum loquitur penes Iohannem; f. 23v., ¶Cogita ac si videres Mariam Magdalenam penes Mariam rogantem pro te, et dic.; f. 24r., ¶Considera quasi videres Mariam in celo, et dic* [Munich: *cogitationes* ~34–7]. At f. 24r., ends with prayer [not in Munich], Gratias ago tibi, [omni]potens Deus, qui die septimo ab omni opere quod patraras quievisti et ob hoc ipsum sanctificans eidem benedixisti . . .; rubric, *Sequitur inde opus figurarum* etc.

Opus I ends with long rubric and prayers [f. 24v.]: *¶Non si est quod post diem septem ex desiderio istius operis non habebis bonam visionem in somnis, per illas tu habebis* *licentiam ulterius precedendi in hoc opere. Tunc resume primam operationem. Et resume tam sepe et totiens quousque impetrabis unam bonam visionem. ¶Ecce, quando tu habebis unam bonam visionem, tunc habundabis cum magno gaudio ex parte visionis. Si autem est mala et dyabolica, tunc eris ex timore destructus. Et ergo non credas statim visioni. Post bonam visionem quando evigillabis, tunc dic cum suspiriis infra scriptam orationem, scilicet,* <u>Gratias tibi ago, domine Yhesu.</u> *inclina.* <u>Et beatissima virgine matri.</u> *inclina.* <u>tue Marie et omnibus sanctis angelis et ellectis Dei, quia michi, indigno peccatori Bernardo, tua sacramenta et tua secreta miserabiliter revellasti.</u> *¶Sed post hec quando surexisti dic statim illa orationem. ¶Inclina.* <u>O Maria mater, que dominum concepisti . . . que erga</u> [f. 25r.] <u>compositorem huius libri et me tantam gratiam inpendiste . . . quod coram illi et me transformasti ymaginem tuam et mutasti in carnis simillitudinem</u> [this last refers to and repeats the part of Munich: Prayer *5.i omitted in I.v above; further reference to John the Monk]. Then final rubric [f. 25r.]: *¶Nota, in quali forma se manifestat, hoc debes bene notare. Et deinde debes dicere istam orationem,* <u>Ave, salve,</u> *et istam orationem invenis ferie quarta* [i.e. Opus I.iv above] *cum suis particulis, et dic hanc ad gratitudinem. Explicit primum opus.*

Opus II: Deus potentissime triumphator [f. 25r.–v.] [Munich: Part II, Prayers 1–12], closely parallels Munich, although presentation is clearer, with repetitions clearly indicated. Four parts.

i) <u>Deus potentissime,</u> headed *Secundum opus in die Dominica et ferie secunde secundum unum modum, alias quod hore canonice precedant* [f. 25v.], *ut moris est, vel contineat vel postulat. ¶Primo die accessum per totum, ut supra. ¶Iste sunt orationes de essentia.* Prayers to Angels, Archangels, Virtues, and all three at once. Ends [f. 28v.] *Sequitur figure opus,* as with Opus I.

ii) <u>Deus potentissime,</u> headed *¶Opus ferie tertie et ferie quarte sequitur inde sicut quod hore canonice precedent et accessus. ¶Ad potestates dic istam orationem.* Prayers to Powers, Dominions, Principalities, and all three at once. Ends [f. 29v.] as with Opus I.

iii) <u>Deus potentissime,</u> headed *¶Hic sequitur opus ferie quinte et ferie sexte. Ita quod hore canonice et accessus precedat sicut prius* [f. 29v.]. Prayers to Thrones, Cherubim, Seraphim, and all three at once. Ends (f. 31r.) as with Opus I.

iv) <u>Beati estis sancti Dei</u> [Munich: Prayer 11] *consideratio* ~20, headed *¶Sabbato dic opus diei huius. Ita quod hore canonice precedant ut supra, et dic* [f. 31r.]. Prayers to saints and Mary. At f. 31v., <u>*Cogita quod vides Mariam in celo et dic scilicet* O gloriosa regina</u> [Munich: Prayer 12]. Ends [f. 33r.] as with Opus I.

Opus III: Domine, domine, domine [f. 33r.] [Munich: Part III, Prayers 13–17], headed [f. 32v.–33r.] *¶Explicit secundum opus. ¶Et sequitur tertium opus.* Seven parts, each opening with repetition of <u>Deus potentissime</u> [after canonical hours] and closing with a variation on the instruction *Fiat hoc opus bina vel trina vice in die. ¶Sequitur inde opus figure* [f. 35r.]. Correspondences to Munich as follows: *feria* i)/Munich: Prayers 13–14; *feria* ii)/Munich: Prayer 15; *feria* iii)/Munich: Prayer

16.i)–vi); *feria* iv)/Munich: Prayer 16.vii [with repetition of opening of 16; here *fantasia* replaces Munich's *facundia*]; *feria* v)/Munich: Prayer 16.vii [with repetition of opening of 16]; *feria* vi)/Munich: Prayer 16.viii–ix [with repetition of opening of 16]; *feria* vii)/Munich: Prayer 16.x.

Opus IV: O Lumen clarissimum [f. 41r.] [Munich: Part III, Prayers 17–20], headed ¶*Explicit tertium opus.* ¶*Incipit quartum opus.* Four parts, incorporating *ferie* i)–ii)/Munich: Prayer 17, *ferie* iii)–iv)/Munich: Prayer 18, *ferie* v)–vi)/Munich: Prayer 19, *feria* vii)/Munich: Prayer 20.

Opus V: Gloriosa memorabilis [f. 43v.–44r.] [Munich: Part III, Prayers 21–7], headed [f. 43v.] ¶*Explicit quartum opus.* ¶*Incipit quintum opus, ita quod in ipso habet habet* [sic] speciales orationes.* ¶*Et primo Ad Gramaticam. Item die Dominica* etc. Seven parts, one for each liberal art [as in Munich; details of what prayers asks for sometimes differ, as do lists of martyrs, prophets etc., but prayers and repetitions are basically the same]; after feria iii), rubric *Explicit id quod spectat ad illas tres artes. Et incipiat hic quod spectat ad alias quatuor Artes* [f. 50v.].

Opus VI: Altitudo divini [f. 56v.] [Munich: Part III, Prayer 28; note that the Addendum: *de physica sive de arte medicine,* is deferred until Quarta Practica viii, f. 73r.], headed ¶*Explicit quintum opus.* ¶*Incipit sextum opus.* ¶*Item in die Dominica, ad Methaphysicam.* Divides the topic as follows: *Ad physicam naturalem et supernaturalem; Ad physicam moralem et monasticam; Ad Iconomicam; Ad politicam.* Entire prayer is repeated each day of the week.

Opus VII: Flos divini [f. 58v.] [Munich: Part III, Prayer 29: note that Prima Oratio, <u>Alpha et omega</u>, is not included here; but see the note in Opus IX below], headed *Explicit sextum opus. Incipit septimum, ad Theologiam.* As in Munich, the four senses of Scripture are invoked facing in the four directions.

Opus VIII: Verbum in principio [f. 61v.] [Munich: Part III, Prayer 30, Concluding Prayer i], headed as previous prayers, with addition *Item hic sequitur una oratio que valet ad omnes artes.* As in Munich, prayer includes several references to the Tetragrammaton. Concluding prayer, <u>Ave Maria</u>, preceded by rubric *Hec sequitur affluens oratio. Inclina sedendo* [f. 63v.].

Opus IX: Benedicat te gloriosissima virgo [f. 67r.] [Munich: Part III, Concluding Prayer ii–iii with coda], headed as previous prayers; includes a prayer, <u>Placeat tibi</u>, not found at this point in Munich, but referred to in Part Four [Munich, f. 66r.1]: [f. 67v.] <u>Placeat tibi, domine sancte pater, omnipotens eterne Deus, et beate Marie. inclina. virgini, et vobis omnibus sanctis angellis et electis Dei, opus quod agressus sum et legi et dixi de literature cognoscenda</u>

scientia et prestetis ut michi proficiat ad suscipiendam sapientiam et omnem scientiam sive artem in salutem corporis et anime mee [f. 68r.] in vitam eternam. Amen. After this, there follows a coda to the opus parallel to that at the end of Opus I: *Ultimo opere sic finito, roga beatam virginem Mariam que ipsa velit tibi revellare per visionem utrum tu debeas facere anullum per magisterium, et librum tuum in quo laborasti consecrare. ¶Et ista supplicatio sic debet fieri lege post primam orationem primi operis* Alpha et Omega [Munich: Prima Oratio i]; *omni dic* O Revellatrix omnium secretorum [Munich: Prayer *5.iv] . . . *Sequitur iii* oratio[nes]* O Consolatrix *Et* O Excellentissima [Munich: Prima Oratio ii, Prayer *2/McMaster, Opus I.ii] . . . *Et* Surge beatissima [Munich: Prayer *6/McMaster Opus I.vi] . . . *Ulterius non est vis seu necesse ut labores in figuris nisi vellis facere ex devocione, set debes horas tuas canonicas legere. Et ultimum opus debes exhercere donec habeas bonum visionem seu aparitionem. ¶Et postquam habebis bonum visionem debes secundum istum modum* [f. 68v.] *consecrare anullum et librum.*

Secunda Operatio

Prima et secunda practica [not marked as such, but see incipit to Tertia Practica below] [f. 68v.] [no equivalents to any passage of Munich have been discovered throughout Secunda Operatio except a few noted], headed ¶*Explicit prima operatio. ¶Et incipit secunda huius libri hic. ¶Dummodo post generales, vis venire ad speciales scintinos** [although the prayers from Opus V onwards are also referred to as *speciales*]. *Tunc fac fieri anullum aureum, ita tamen quod tres partes sint de auro et quarta sit argentea.* Further instructions on the quality of the metal, then on the ring's design: *Fiat ergo anullus . . . habens incircuitu latitudinem in quo exterius sculptura sit ymago beate virginis Marie, stando cum filio suo, tenens eum in brachiis, et quatuor cruces: una super capud et una sub pedibus, et in utraque latere una, et hec tria nomina* Maria. Mater. Yhesu.

Instructions follow on consecration of the ring and the book: *Quo facto in una die Dominico hora primarum debes stare in capella vel oratorio cum uno turibulo, cum bono thure vel mastice. Et dic ante altare et coram ymagine beate Virginis habentis infantem. Et pone anullum cum libro super altare vel ad unum alium locum purum qui sit altus in eodem* [f. 69r.] *oratorio.*

i) Prayers for the book: Ave Maria, virgo gloriosa [from Opus VIII/Munich: Concluding Prayer i], Surge, O beatissima [Opus I.vi], and a new prayer [somewhat related to Ave Maria, virgo gloriosa]: Deus via veritas est de terra nata . . . Ego servus tuus, Bernardus, humilis famulus oro supplico et *tunde* deprecor et invoco te, hodie et nunc, ut sicut in monte Synay legem in tabulis lapideis propria manu et digito scripsisti et eam sanctificasti et sanctificatam Moysi in salutem populi Israellitici dedisti, ita librum istum in salutem omnium eo fruentium, et omnia que in ipso sunt scripta specialiter in salutem mei Bernardi . . . [f. 69v.] Second part of the prayer exorcises evil magic: [P]urifica et asperge omnia et fantasmatha nocturna removeat artes magicas et delusorias . . .

ii) Prayers for the ring: [f. 70r.] *Pro confirmatione anulli dic istam orationem* Domine sancte pater, omnipotens eterne Deus . . . Ego Bernardus, misera creatura . . . Deprecor oro peto . . . Et concedas michi gratiam tuam specialem multiformamque quotienscumque dicam vel proferam orationes istius libri et figuras videbo, et annullum perfectionis portabo loco et tempore prout est in hoc libro institutum sicut promisisti . . . Ego Bernardus deprecor et exoro quod secundum formam et consuetudinem huius scientie sancte a Deo et a te ipsa per procurationem tuam revellatum velis michi apparere.

iii) Confirming the consecration ritual: [f. 70v.] *Eodem die Dominico ad vesperas fac simillimodo ut prius et debes repetitionem et dicere* Ellevatio manuum mearum sacrificum vespertinum, *et mittas librum cum annullo super altare iacere vel in alio loco alto puro et quod permaneat secretum. Post septimum die nisi ullam certam visionem habueris quod sunt consecrate et confirmate tunc adhuc non debes cessare benedicendo set non incensationem facere nec aspergere . . . Nota quo facto dum liber et anullus confirmati et consecrati sunt debes venerari tanquam reliquias et debes conservare in loco puro, qui sit occultus et non publicus.*

Tertia practica [f. 70v.], headed ¶*Explicit secunda pratica* [sic]. ¶*Incipit tertia pratica que scripta est inferus regulis qui a te oportet promissionem sancte Marie tenere, promittere et agere, et facere immaculatum vite tue*; numbered rules for keeping Mary to her promises: 1) read prayers [f. 71r.], *sine opere figurarum*, from Opus I; 2) be chaste and devout; 3) every Saturday, pray the *cursum de beate Virgine* [i.e. the Office of the Virgin]; 4) say certain prayers to the angels on Sundays etc.; 5) eight months of each year for the whole of your life, starting *a quo mense vel die inceperis secundum executionem huius libri et eius confirmationem et anulli huius solvere*, repeat Opus II–IX, one each month in order; the other four months can be taken off [f. 71r.–v.]. [Presumably, this is how you maintain both the knowledge already gained from initial practice of the opus and the possibility of acquiring further knowledge.]

Quarta et ultima practica [f. 71v.], headed ¶*Explicit tertia praticha* [sic]. ¶*Incipit quarta et ultima. que stat inferus notabillibus quia secunda prefata oportet te procedere ad spiritualia scrutinia*; instructions for seeking visionary information from Mary.

ii) Two types of *scrutinia* [f. 71v.–72r.]: ¶*Prima sunt generalia et possunt revellari; secunda sunt specialia, et illa non tenentur revellari si spectant ad personam illam cui revellantur*, since some heavenly secrets are not meant to be known: examples include *si velles scire declarationem corporis Marie*, or, in the present, *si velles scire utrum esset bonum peregrinare, pugnare vel vindicare*, or, in the future, *utrum deberes ditari vel statim mori*. Visions must be communally useful.

ii) Asking Mary for information: ¶*Hiis partis et operatis sciendum est quod quando talem perscrutationem desideras perscrutari a Maria in somnis, quia Maria est magistra in hoc opere et perscrutatio illa in specialitate solummodo pro te est. Tunc dicas devote antequam vadas dormitum* Alpha et omega *etcetera cum suis partibus, et* Consolatrix *et dic etiam* O Revellatrix, *ut habetur in Primo opere* [see the coda to Opus IX for these prayers, originally found in Opus I.i]; to sleep with the ring: *Et teneas annullum in digito et* *dum evigillaueris in nocte tunc iterum resume* <u>O Revellatrix</u> *Et fiat hoc tam diu die natu que quousque tibi visio fiat*; then thank Mary. Note the position of her image in your dream: *Et in visione debes notare ymaginem modos et verba, et dic etiam illam orationem* <u>Ave, salve</u> *cum suis particulis* [Opus I, *feria* iv; see also Munich: Prayer *4, which nobody should say unless the Virgin appears to them in sleep, according to rubric] [f. 72r.].

iii) First of a series of further notes on visions and the use of the ring and the book: this on the need to watch closely and write things down: ¶*Ulterius* [f. 72v.] *debes dilligenter notare omnes visiones et ymagines, tempus et horam quando et pro quo tibi Maria revellata est, et scribas incidentias adventuum et presentiam persone, utrum aliis res illas debeas revellare.* [See Opus I, closing rubric.]

iv) On the need to prepare properly if Mary is to visit you freely, and on prayers to be used in conducting a disputation: ¶*Ulterius debes scire quod Maria non libenter te visitat dum iacueris in lecto in nocte, set quando oraveris matutinem et iterum vis dormire . . .* But when certain things are to be the topic of an exposition or disputation [*quasi legere vel disputare de ambabus* * *legibus*], e.g. astronomy or mathematics, then the prayers for that day need to be said on the day itself, using the *considerationes* and the *opus figurarum* as well as the words.

v) Grace can be sought by repeating <u>O Revellatrix</u> in front of an image of Mary [f. 73r.].

vi) Instructions for prayers to be repeated if you forget your visions: *si obliviscaris visionem . . .* ¶*Tunc fac ut prius dictum est in Tertia regula* [possibly the third *ulterius* passage, i.e. subsection v) of this *quarta practica*?] [f. 73r.].

vii) Prayer to disperse evil spirits: <u>Precepit tibi dominus noster Yhesus Christus quod hinc recedas per ipsum Yhesum Christum . . . et per beatissimam uirginem Mariam, et per istum librum et anulum in hoc consecratum, et per septem ymagines ipsius</u> [possibly the four crosses and three names inscribed on the ring? or the seven *figure* said to be included in the *nova compilatio* in Munich, Part IV, Discussion ~2?]; further brief prayers against diabolic temptation [f. 73r.–v.].

viii) Instructions for learning a single art: *Etiam tunc poteris operari ad unam artem solummodo*, by beginning with Opus I then skipping straight to that art; instructions for studying medicine [close to Munich: Part III, Addendum] [f. 73v.–74r.].

ix) Further arts which can be learned by this method, although not included in the trivium and quadrivium: *sicut in mechanicha vel exceptiva* [close to Munich: Part III, Addendum]. *Scias etiam quod opus illud ab initio usque ad finem poteris exhercuere cum adiutorio Dei et Marie, in medio anno si diligens et devotus fueris* [f. 74r.].

x) A vow to be taken by anyone wishing to recopy the book: ¶*Ulterius quicumque petierint a te hunc librum rescribendum, dum coram te vel coram presbitero vel coram multis qui ad hoc sint competentes et valent promittere sive iurare coram ymagine Marie in hunc modum, scilicet*: <u>Ego, nomen Christianus, famulus sive famula Yhesu Christi, ex meo libero arbitrio et voluntate propter salutem anime mee promitto omnipotenti Deo et</u>

beate Marie virgini et omnibus sanctis et electis Dei quod ego hunc librum volo met rescribere, vel per alium fidelem sub nomine meo, et secundum hoc librum et institutiones suas volo facere et agere, et eundem librum aliis honestis Christi fidelibus et quicumque a me petent amicabilliter geretis pro Deo omnimodam, et declarabo sub forma iam expressa et prescripta, Amen. [f. 74r.].

xi) [f. 74v.] A table of the Gifts of the Spirit, the Cardinal Virtues, the Theological Virtues, the Seven Liberal Arts, the Seven Exceptive Arts [Pyromancy, Aeromancy, Hydromancy, Necromancy, Gyromancy, Geomancy, Geonegia], the Seven Mechanical Arts.

xii) A prayer to the Trinity, apparently intended as the explicit to the Secunda Operatio and the book as a whole: [f. 75r.] O vera summa sempiterna Trinitas . . . tibi laus et iubillatio, tibi gratiarum actio, per omnia secula seculorum. Amen.

Cursus de eterna Dei sapientia [f. 75r.], headed *Incipit cursus de eterna Dei sapientia. Quicumque desiderat sapientiam eternam familiarem sibi sponsam habere dum ei has horas cottidie devote legere.* No break in manuscript. For this work, based on Suso's *Horologium sapientiae*, see note 44: an Office to wisdom. The hymns mostly consist of parts of the poem *Dulcis Ihesu memoria* [written in thirteenth-century England], although the ending of the hymn here differs, and the *lectiones* include the prayers: O Sapientia eterne splendor glorie [f. 75v.]; O Reffugium meum et liberator meus [f. 76v.]; Deus, qui per choeternam sibi sapientiam hominem [f. 77r.], etc. No echoes of Munich, despite the common interest in *sapientia* and devotional imagery; the *Cursus* postdates the *Liber visionum* by more than half a century.

Oratio pro scientia Adipiscenda [f. 80v.]: a series of prayers for wisdom, mostly general in nature, several of them with some relationship to prayers in Opus I–IX and the Munich text.

i) Lux mundi Deus immense, pater eternitatis [f. 80v.]: opening related to the Prayer for Astronomy [Opus V, *feria* vii/Munich: Part III, Prayer 27], and is structured along generally the same lines as the prayers for the arts, although it is safely general.

ii) [f. 81r.] Domine Deus incomprehensibillis, invisibillis et immortabilis.

iii) [f. 81v.] Vita omnium creaturarum visibillium et invisibillius Deus.

iv) Rex regnum dominantium, Deus infinite misericordie [f. 81v.].

v) [f. 82r.] [apparently beginning is missing, no break in manuscript] et exitum sensuum meorum et cogitationum mearum.

vi) Te queso, Domine, mundi conscientiam meam splendore luminis tui [f. 82r.]

vii) Memoria incomprehensibillis, sapientia incontradicibillis [f. 82r.]: perhaps modelled on Opus IV, *feria* iii–iv)/Munich: Part III, Prayer 18.

viii) [f. 82v.] Deus omnium que es meus Deus.

ix) Omnipotens sempiterne Deus et misericors pater [f. 82v.]; unfinished.

x) [f. 83r.] <u>Deus immense, pater eternitatis a quo procedit</u>.

xi) <u>Deus totius pietatis autor et fundamentum</u>. This ends <u>Rex eterne iudex et discretor omnium agnitor scientarum bonarum. Instruere me hodie propter nomen sanctum tuum, et per hec</u> [f. 83v.] <u>sacramenta sacra glorifica mentem meam, ut intret scientia tua sicut aqua in interiori mea et sicut oleum in ossibus meis; per te, Deum, salvator omnium. Amen</u>. *1461 die xxviii mensis novembris*. After this, a new item apparently begins, opening <u>Hec est quedam missa de passione Christi</u>, left incomplete at the foot of the page, the last medieval folio in the manuscript.

8

PLUNDERING THE EGYPTIAN TREASURE: JOHN THE MONK'S *BOOK OF VISIONS* AND ITS RELATION TO THE ARS NOTORIA OF SOLOMON

Claire Fanger

The Ars Notoria of Solomon is a late medieval ritual text whose goal is to strengthen the operator's memory, eloquence, understanding and perseverance, and to obtain knowledge of the seven liberal arts, all of which are sought in various sequences of prayers and rituals, and directly infused into the operator via angels and the holy spirit. Its characteristic features, those at any rate most marked out in condemnations, are its *notae* or figures,[1] which provide focal points for meditation while the prayers are being said, and its long prayers involving strings of obscure words or names (*verba ignota*) according to the text derived from a mixture of Greek, Hebrew, Chaldean and (in the medieval versions of the text) Arabic. Though extant in numerous manuscripts and much condemned by medieval theologians, little information about the Notory Art is to be found in modern studies outside the present volume, and a good deal remains to be discovered of its origins and history. I will shortly attempt to give a brief account of precisely how much (or little) is presently known of the Solomonic Ars Notoria, but to begin with I want to give some indication of the order of magnitude by which our knowledge of this ritual practice has been increased by the discovery of John the Monk's *Liber visionum* in Munich, Bayerische Staatsbibliothek Clm 276 (discussed elsewhere in this volume by Nicholas Watson, whose synopsis of the Munich text I will be referring to thoughout, and Richard Kieckhefer). Another manuscript of this text (Graz, University Library MS 680), which we learned of too late for a thorough account of its contents to be included in these essays, promises to deliver still more information along the same lines. The Graz text includes a remarkable autobiographical Prologue with an unexpectedly detailed account of John's visionary experiences leading up to his composition of the *Liber visionum*. Though we have not yet transcribed it, I include a synopsis of the contents of this Prologue as an appendix to this article, since even in summary it clarifies much that is described more briefly or allusively in the Munich manuscript.[2]

Even in the Munich text, John gives moderately detailed autobiographical information about his visionary reception of the *Liber visionum*, which is itself a revised and enhanced version of the Solomonic Ars Notoria. What is unusual and interesting about this text is that John was, by his own admission, originally a practitioner of the Solomonic form of the art. The *Liber visionum* thus offers us a unique opportunity to read about a condemned practice from the viewpoint of one of its practitioners – a man who, though he condemns the Solomonic Ars Notoria (astutely, necessarily and conventionally) at the time of writing the *Liber visionum*, did not always do so. Indeed, even where he condemns the text, his voice – unlike that of Thomas Aquinas (as we must presume), or other theologians who condemned the Ars Notoria – is the voice of experience.

At the outset John represents himself as a visionary. As Watson shows, however, he is a visionary of an unusual sort: though he is versed in the standard rhetoric of mystical experience and uses it freely, he has a quite unconventional focus on ritual practice as a means of obtaining visions (a focus which could with justice be called theurgic), and he appears rather confident of his own opinions (or at least the efficacy of his own prayers). He is clearly as well a writer by vocation (by which I mean, there are a sufficiency of references to other things he has written or compiled that we can assume the *Liber visionum* is not his first or only book). Further, from what we can deduce of his other writings with the information presently at our disposal, these writings are no more of a conventional mystical or devotional sort than the *Liber visionum* itself.

But if John was not quite like the visionaries you might expect to find in the early fourteenth century, he is not quite the sort of sorcerer you might expect to find either. Unlike Honorius of Thebes, pseudepigraphic author of the *Liber sacer sive juratus* discussed by Robert Mathiesen in this volume, John the Monk was not quite so much of an outsider as to argue against the condemnation of magic itself, or even against the condemnation of the Solomonic Ars Notoria. Indeed he is fairly astute about the theological problems represented by the Ars Notoria and addresses some of them in his work (it is noteworthy that he was so confident of his resolution of these difficulties that he felt no need of a pseudepigraphic cover for his own revision of the text). Equally unlike the majority of sorcerers represented in medieval literary sources, and in many trial records as well, John does not wear the aura of a crass manipulator, nor of a loser, tool or fool. In him we do not see reflected any of the better known types of medieval amateur or professional magician (the cleric who scries in children's thumbnails, the diviner paid to seek out hidden treasure, or the summoner of demons, of the sort reported, slightly later, to have led astray Gilles de Rais). By the time of writing the *Liber visionum* at any rate, John the Monk is an educated man, rhetorically adept and much given to complicated biblical allusions, conscious of the dilemma of his attraction to the Ars Notoria, and conscious of reasons for which it might be condemned. Though the *Liber visionum* came to a bad end in one sense (burned at Paris in 1323 as a heretical and sorcerous document, as recorded in the *Grandes Chroniques* entry translated by Watson in his essay in this volume),[3] John's rituals also continued to be practiced for the next hundred and fifty years (as witnessed by their survival in Hamilton, Canada, McMaster University Library, Unnumbered MS, a consecrated text of John's rituals dated 1461).

So John the Monk was simultaneously an insider and an outsider, a Christian occultist with a visionary bent, or a Christian visionary with an occultist bent. He is the writer of a text which (like the Solomonic Art itself), was viewed simultaneously (though perhaps not by the same people at the same time) as most sacred, and most unlawful. John gives a reasonably plausible account of himself caught, as it were, between the sacred and the unlawful, and his attempts to mediate the two; and though the *Book of Visions* doubtless contains as much fiction as any autobiography, it is nevertheless manifestly more nearly a picture drawn from life than we find in the account of the origin of the *Liber sacer*. For all these reasons, this text is probably the most important window into the life of the fourteenth-century operator of a condemned ritual text yet to have been discovered. It is likely to alter many aspects of our understanding of both orthodox and seditious varieties of ritual practice in the later Middle Ages, and deserves our careful attention.

ARS NOTORIA TEXTS AND MANUSCRIPTS: CURRENT KNOWLEDGE AND LACUNAE

Most of my essay here will be concerned with John the Monk's relationship to the Solomonic Ars Notoria, so far as it may be deduced from his account in the text of the *Liber visionum* found in Clm 276, with notes to the Graz text in places where my argument is likely eventually to require further development based on its information. In order to understand the intellectual context in which John was working, however, it is necessary to know something of what the Solomonic text contained, and the terms on which it was so widely condemned.

Obtaining information about the textual traditions of the Ars Notoria is a tricky business, since the relation even between the known texts calling themselves Notory Arts is almost entirely unexamined. Outside the pertinent essays in this volume, the bulk of the published secondary information about the Solomonic Ars Notoria is still contained in Lynn Thorndike's *History of Magic and Experimental Science*.[4] Thorndike cites seventeen manuscript texts (or potential manuscript texts)[5] of the Ars Notoria, ranging between the thirteenth and seventeenth centuries,[6] with the majority being fourteenth and fifteenth century. Most of these are held in British libraries, with the exception of three in the Bibliothèque Nationale in Paris, and three in the Bayerische Staatsbibliothek in Munich. Of these latter, one is Clm 276, which also contains John the Monk's *Liber visionum* directly following a full text of the Solomonic Ars Notoria (with figures) in the same hand. Two important deluxe Ars Notoria manuscripts unknown to Thorndike, of the fourteenth and fifteenth centuries respectively, are Turin, Biblioteca Nazionale MS E.V. 13 (discussed by Camille in this volume) and Oxford, Bodley MS 951 (discussed by Klaassen). Two early printed editions of the Solomonic text also exist: one is a Latin edition found in the *Opera* of Agrippa von Nettesheim published *c.* 1600 in Lyons;[7] the other is an English translation of the text from the Agrippa *Opera* done about fifty years later by Robert Turner.[8]

This list of extant texts, while incomplete, does serve to give a rough idea of the chronological range and geographic diversity of occurences of the Ars Notoria. However, a number of things still remain to be investigated about the Latin textual tradition. There has never been any systematic count of manuscripts of the Ars Notoria, and it may be noted that the bulk of the manuscript work that has been done so far relies principally on holdings in British libraries (which means that the number of surviving manuscripts altogether, and in particular the number in Continental or North American libraries, is still unknown). There is no modern edition of the Ars Notoria, and the relation of the seventeenth-century text (found in Agrippa's *Opera* and the Turner translation) to the medieval manuscript tradition remains to be examined. Though the fifteenth-century text found in Clm 276 is easily recognizable as a form of the early modern one,[9] this text itself bears signs of being a compilation of more than one text (or more than one form of the text), and it seems likely that the earliest witnesses to the Ars Notoria will turn out to look different in some respects from those later versions I have been able to examine.

The extent to which the earlier forms of the Ars Notoria may have been similar to the later versions may be gathered indirectly from certain features of the Solomonic Art which are preserved in the *Liber visionum*. Though John's Latin prayers are both more orderly and more elaborate than those of the Solomonic text; and though he has carefully excised all the prayers involving *verba ignota*; and though direct quotations from the Solomonic text are conscientiously kept to a minimum, nonetheless John's revised text shows clear ties to the Solomonic original in its structure, its aims and its use of technical vocabulary. In order to give a more concrete picture of what John has added to, and omitted from, the Solomonic text, I offer the following brief outline drawn chiefly from the early modern editions of the Ars Notoria, with some comparison to the fifteenth-century text in Clm 276.

The structure of the Ars Notoria evident in this late Solomonic text can be broken down into roughly three main parts.[10] The first section, which I will call Part I, appears to be a conflation of what may once have been separate ritual and discursive texts.[11] It is explained that the ritual text is in two parts, of which the first part treats the 'generals', the second the 'specials'. The 'specials' (it is immediately explained) are the seven liberal arts, and the prayers for taking them. The 'generals' (as it only becomes clear toward the end of this part), are the faculties which must be strengthened prior to the taking of the liberal arts themselves: memory, eloquence, understanding and perseverance, and the prayers concerned with those. Part I then slides without warning or heading into the ritual text (the prayers for the generals), interspersing these prayers with commentary on their transcendental qualities, special powers and other possible uses. All the generals involve Latin prayers though some have prayers which use *verba ignota* also.

Part II is the portion of the ritual practice devoted to prayers for the taking of the 'specials' (the liberal arts), with some digressions, and some comments also of an expository nature, but not nearly as many as we find in Part I. Prayers for the liberal arts are arranged in order, starting with the trivium, moving to the quadrivium and ending with philosophy and theology. There are different numbers of prayers for each art, some having only one prayer, some several. All the arts involve Latin prayers, though some also use *verba ignota* prayers as in Part I. It is here in Part II that the 'notes' or figures come into play most prominently; instructions regarding the notes are given at the beginning of each prayer and it is emphasized that if the wrong figure is used the prayers will have no effect. In the manuscript texts which include these notes or figures, the notes tend to be clearly labelled as 'prima de grammatica, secunda de grammatica' and so forth, so the operator is not left in doubt about which figure is correct.[12]

What I am terming Part III is called, in the text, the 'Ars Nova'. Here follow ten prayers which it is suggested were transmitted to Solomon by different angels at a different time from the prayers in Parts I and II. These prayers are said to rectify any problems the operator may have had with the preceding rituals, and marvellous virtues are attributed to them. For the most part, however, the prayers of the 'Ars Nova' involve reiterations of the requests for memory, eloquence and understanding that were already requested in Part I. Indeed there is much cross-referencing between Parts I and III: the same *verba ignota* prayers are used in both, and in fact some of these are given only in abbreviated form in Part I, but written out in fuller form in Part III. It seems possible that Part III, the 'Ars Nova', was originally a deviant version of Part I which was separately circulated for a while and then eventually tacked onto another complete text as an appendix; however, this must remain speculation until further manuscript evidence is gathered.[13] After the ten prayers of the 'Ars Nova' there follows a miscellany of ritual instructions about such things as fasting, confession and almsgiving, consecration of the figure of memory, consecration of place, further instructions on uses of the prayers, and so forth, loosely tied together and with no visible conclusion.

Structurally, John the Monk's *Liber visionum* most precisely reflects Parts I and II of the Solomonic art. Part II of the *Liber visionum* is equivalent to Part I of the Solomonic art (the ritual texts being comprised in both cases of prayers for the

taking of the generals: memory, eloquence, understanding and perseverance)
while Part III of the *Liber visionum* is equivalent to Part II of the Solomonic art
(where we find the prayers for the taking of the specials: the seven liberal arts,
listed in order, and culminating in philosophy and theology). The terms
'generals' and 'specials' are preserved by John, and the language of the prayers is
similar to the language of the prayers in the Ars Notoria of Solomon (though
John's prayers tend to be longer and more elaborate, and John excises the prayers
involving *verba ignota*, as already mentioned).

   There would seem to be no obvious equivalent to the 'Ars Nova' in the Munich
version of the *Liber visionum* though John's Part IV, as preserved in the Munich
text, does involve a number of miscellaneous notes and ritual instructions of the
sort that trail after the 'Ars Nova'. The McMaster text also contains, at the end of
the prayers for the specials, a set of operations for consecrating a ring and the
book containing the *Liber visionum* (which must be copied and personalized with
the operator's name).[14] No copy of the Solomonic Ars Notoria that I have seen
includes instructions for the making of a magic ring (though this does not mean
that such texts do not exist).

   Part I of John's text involves the only real innovation on the principles of the
Ars Notoria, as it consists of a set of 'cogitationes' or visualizations accompanied
by prayers to the Virgin. The goal of these prayers and visualizations is for the
operator to acquire in sleep a vision of the Virgin herself, who will at that point
(all ritual instructions in Part I having been correctly performed) concede divine
permission to perform the next operations of the *Liber visionum* (that is, the
operations of John's revised version of the Ars Notoria). In doing this, the
operator follows in John's own footsteps, for even as the operator uses Part I to
obtain the Virgin's permission to perform the rest of the Art, so John himself
wrote the prayers of Part I in order to receive permission to write the prayers of
Parts II and III, which at some points he claims were divinely handed onto him
by the Virgin.[15] It may be noted here that the part of the *Liber visionum* that John
claims to have been divinely transmitted is the part that most closely imitates the
Ars Notoria, rather than the divergent ritual materials that precede and follow it.

   From the structure of the *Liber visionum*, and from certain remarks John makes
passim, we can deduce that the Solomonic Ars Notoria text to which John had
access at the turn of the thirteenth and fourteenth centuries incorporated the
terms 'generals' and 'specials', and that it arranged its ritual materials as the later
versions do, with the prayers for the generals coming first and the prayers for the
specials coming second. It is possible also to deduce something about the features
of the Solomonic Ars Notoria which were deliberately exluded from the *Book of
Visions*. In the Prologue to the Graz text, John describes the Ars Notoria which he
first looked at, and from this description we know that it was a deluxe version,
with figures done in colour; he states that it included the prayers in 'Latin, Greek,
Hebrew, Chaldean and Arabic' (which are the languages of the prayers

mentioned in the Solomonic text in Clm 276). There are no figures in Parts II and III of John's text,[16] and save for a certain prayer which incorporates the tetragrammaton, he has used no words in any language but Latin. John's exclusion of the prayers involving *verba ignota* are clearly the result of a deliberate policy on his part, the reasons for which will shortly be seen.

THEOLOGICAL DIVAGATIONS: TERMS ON WHICH
THE ARS NOTORIA WAS CONDEMNED

Another indirect but significant source of information about the practice of the Solomonic Art occurs in the form of medieval condemnations.[17] A revealing treatment of the Ars Notoria is found in the *Summa Theologiae* of Thomas Aquinas in the context of a *Quaestio* on superstitious observances (2a–2ae, q. 96). Of the four articles in this *Quaestio* devoted to practices Thomas considers superstitious, the first is concerned with a condemnation of the Ars Notoria specifically. Part of Thomas's argument – the section of the article beginning *respondeo quod* – is recapitulated verbatim (along with other matter lifted without alteration from *Quaestio* 96 of the *Summa Theologiae*), in the *Speculum Morale*, a continuation of Vincent of Beauvais' widely circulated encyclopedia the *Speculum Maius*.[18] It may be deduced both from the specific content of Thomas' discussion, and the fact that it was thought worthy to anthologize by the pseudo-Vincent, that the practice of the Ars Notoria was reasonably well known by the second half of the thirteenth century.

Because Thomas initiates his discussions of topics in the *Summa Theologiae* in good scholastic fashion by listing arguments with which he does not actually agree (*objectiones*), Thomas' treatment of the Ars Notoria is both more specific and more informative than many other medieval condemnations of this practice. The most interesting part of Thomas's treatment in this case occurs in his preliminary *objectiones*, which are not in fact recapitulated by the pseudo-Vincent, and that look very much like arguments that may actually have been put forward by practitioners or defenders of the Notory Art at the time of Thomas's writing. In brief, the *objectiones* are these: firstly, that the observances of the Ars Notoria are not themselves evil, either as to the practice (since they consist of fasts and prayers) or as to ends (namely the acquisition of the sciences, which are not evil in themselves); secondly, it is written in Daniel 1:17 that 'to the children who abstained God gave knowledge and discipline in every book, and wisdom', and the Ars Notoria similarly attains its effects through abstinence; and thirdly, that even if it were the case that the Ars Notoria obtained results through demons this would be no sin, because demons know scientific truths, which are subject to human knowledge, and therefore it is not unlawful knowledge (knowledge proper to God alone) which is obtained from them.

Viewed as a potential practitioner's argument in favor of the Notory Art, this final objection seems a somewhat touching one in its desire to protect and defend the scope of human knowledge as good in itself (to the point where it almost becomes possible to defend demons as acting in the public interest when they provide information about the sciences). As will be seen, John the Monk's defense of his own version of the Ars Notoria similarly relies very strongly on his notion of the potential utility and even holy necessity of the knowledge thus obtained (though he never suggests that any of it might be demonically derived, any more than the Solomonic Ars Notoria itself does).

In fact, Thomas, too, has a strong sense of the benignity and utility of human knowledge in general,[19] though he advances various arguments against the ritual means of its acquisition supplied by the Ars Notoria. The part of the article beginning *Respondeo quod* (in which Thomas outlines the ground of his own opinion), consists of an argument (derived from Augustine's *De doctrina christiana*) condemning the Ars Notoria for its use of figures and unknown words – the unknown words being assumed to receive their efficacy from demons (that is, from the human/demonic consensus as to their meaning); he alludes in passing also to Augustine's condemnation of theurgy in the *De civitate dei*. (This is the portion of the text recapitulated by the pseudo-Vincent, and the commonest type of argument to be voiced against the Notory Art.) Finally, Thomas pits himself against the individual *objectiones*, replying to objection one, that although knowledge in itself is a good thing, the operator of the Ars Notoria acquires it by undue means (that is, the ends are not owed to the means, or owed unnaturally, due means being the natural one of diligent study); to objection two, that the abstinence of the boys referred to in Daniel 1:17 was a matter of refusing to eat the meat of gentiles, not abstinence for the sake of receiving knowledge (in other words the knowledge was an incidental reward for behaving properly, not the end sought for through the fast); and to objection 3, that entering into fellowship with demons is wrong whether demons know about the sciences or not.

The terms on which Thomas condemned the Ars Notoria are unsurprising; his emphasis on Augustine is in keeping with his own habits of thought and in keeping with the terms of most condemnations of magical practices generally in this period. What seems more surprising is the fact that Thomas appears to be so well informed about the Ars Notoria: he is clearly acquainted not only with the general appearance of the text, with its magical diagrams and macaronic prayers (visual features of the deluxe versions likely to have been common knowledge, known to anyone who had heard about the text at all), but also with the fact that it claims to be a holy practice without danger of sin; that it seeks earthly knowledge; that it defends this knowledge as a good thing; that it legitimates itself on Biblical grounds; and that it attains its effects through the apparently licit means of fasting and prayer – ideas which are all framed in the text of the Ars Notoria, and likely to have been important to the practitioners. If Thomas had not actually read through an Ars Notoria text, there seems ample indication here that he had talked to other people about it, and that at least some of these people had found sufficient reason for defending it as a benign practice.

Another condemnation of the Solomonic Ars Notoria important for our purposes is the one found in the entry for the year 1323 in the *Grandes Chroniques*, quoted by Watson and Camille. This entry refers not only to the better known Solomonic form of the Art, but also to John's own revised version of the text, which it is forced to condemn on slightly different terms. Against the Solomonic Art we find advanced the Augustinian argument already familiar through Thomas Aquinas' writing, here in a slightly less erudite and more commonplace form: the Ars Notoria required one to call upon 'various little known names, which were firmly believed to be the names of demons'. As has already been noted, however, John condemns the Solomonic form of the Ars Notoria, and the prayers involving *verba ignota* have all been excised from his own text; thus the *Grandes Chronique* entry gives a separate list of reasons for the condemnation of John's text (all unrelated to the use of *verba ignota*). The reasons for the condemnation of the *Liber visionum* in particular were as follows: not only does John's text promise learning, but also 'if there were riches, honours or pleasures one wanted to have, one could have them. And because the book promised these things, and because one had to make invocations and write one's name twice in the book, and have a copy of the book personally written for one's own use, a costly matter – otherwise, if one did not have a copy written at one's own cost and expense, it would be worthless – the said book was justly condemned in Paris as false and evil, against the Christian faith, and condemned to be burned and put in the fire.'[20] The key theological points are less clear here than they are in Thomas' characteristically lucid treatment, but they seem to hinge on the fact that John's text promises not knowledge alone but also other earthly rewards of more dubious value (riches and pleasures); that its practice involved what appeared to be superstitious observances (such as writing one's name twice in the book); and finally that the *Liber visionum* was expensive to produce and to operate, making it an elitist practice out of keeping with the essentially public-spirited principles of Christian doctrine. (This last looks like an indirect counter to John's own claim that the book would be useful to the salvation of souls.)

Taken together, the terms of these condemnations serve as important indicators of the intellectual atmosphere in which John the Monk's version of the Ars Notoria was composed. Certainly by 1304, the year in which John began working on the *Liber visionum*, ideas about the Ars Notoria would have been fairly well developed, and arguments were undoubtedly circulating among the cognoscenti, not only in condemnation of the practice, but also in its favor. Two things in particular may be noted about the relation between the condemnations and the condemned texts themselves: one is that there appears to be more interaction (on the level of theory and ideas), between the practitioners of literate magic and the spokespersons for orthodox discipline than modern historians are normally in the habit of assuming. The second is that there appears to be more knowledge of theology on the part of those who engaged in occult practices (as well, perhaps, as more knowledge of occult practices on the part of those who condemned them), than modern historians are normally in the habit of examining. As other essays in this volume also demonstrate, the most important condemned texts of ritual magic frame themselves both in terms of, and against, the orthodox ideas about ritual thought and procedure. John's own *Liber visionum* is a key witness to this ongoing dialogue between the occult arts and divine science. And John's private relation to the Solomonic text, as it may be deduced from evidence in the *Liber visionum*, shows all the complexity one might expect from a writer with a strong personal stake in the knowledge to be obtained from the Art (and a certain investment in the ritual practice on its own account), who was yet reasonably well informed about the dangers of the practice and the theological reasons for its condemnation.

JOHN SPEAKS FOR HIMSELF

John's Prologue to the *Liber visionum* in the Munich version of the text provides what initially seems to be a fairly straightforward account of his relation to the Solomonic Ars Notoria.[21] As will be seen, however, his narrative is complicated by passages later on which appear to cast much of what happened earlier in a more ambiguous light. It becomes clear only gradually that the Ars Notoria is not merely a practice that John has escaped by transcending, but in some sense itself a rung on the ladder to heaven. It is a very low rung of course; the practice of the Ars Notoria, which is also identified in the Prologue with the 'exceptive arts',[22] appears to constitute the entire content of John's 'ancient error' – an error he must repent before proceeding to the more sacred form of the art delivered him by the Virgin. However, in terms of the theological allegory in operation, the Ars Notoria comes to appear more or less as the equivalent of earthly knowledge itself – something inadequate for salvation on its own terms, but arguably important to salvation just the same. From John's perspective his 'error' in relation to the Ars Notoria is thus not (or not simply) as Aquinas would have it, the acquisition of knowledge by undue means, and the trafficking with demons that results from this; rather, his error was constituted chiefly in an undue reverencing of earthly knowledge. The Ars Notoria is thus represented more or less as a *means of study*, rather than a means of bypassing study to attain the ends of study; hence John's salvation is certainly not a question of denying or renouncing the practice utterly, but rather of achieving the correct relation to it – a relation of moderation, in which the practice of the Ars Notoria is continued, but with a renewed focus on divinity and the virtues necessary to living well. In the end, John's redemption by the Virgin is not merely his own redemption, but also a redemption of the practice of the Ars Notoria itself.

In the Prologue to his work, John describes the experiences of visions, suffering and eventual conversion which led him to the composition of this book. I will quote from the Prologue at some length, since the experiences he describes are complicated by certain passages at the end of the book, and it is ultimately necessary to read both in conjunction.

> I, Brother John, a monk of Morigny . . . was often involved in the past in chasing after the exceptive arts and sciences; and from these shadows of ignorance by means of sacred revelations and spiritual transformations on the part of the blessed and undefiled glorious Virgin Mary and of the holy angels of God, who, not desiring to condemn me for ignorance, as it were recalled [me] for a certain space of time to their mercy. But afterwards tempted by a certain delayed insufflation,[23] and with that temptation swiftly prevailing – as it were hesitating, not believing that the holy revelations and changes to come would be from a good spirit, I hastened like a dog who returns to his vomit, as it were knowingly, to those arts which I had [once] called upon in ignorance, to the detriment of my soul, and alas persisted in contumely of the creator. But He desires not the death of the sinner, but rather that he might be converted and live; for me as for the fly in the uttermost part of the river of Egypt He mercifully hissed the hiss of His grace: first through the voice of the spirit warning me that I would endure much suffering on account of the things I presumed to do which were against him; second that spiritual beatings would be cruelly inflicted in his presence in my sleep – and at this point I did not believe in every respect, but rather hesitated. And since not even fear of God recalled [me] from evil, he constrained [me] with the disciplines of persecution, or of the promised suffering. Third, the same God [by means of] temporal and corporal persecutions recalled even me from the aforesaid unlawful errors – not according to my merits but mercifully according to his grace. I knew through the advent of these persecutions in sleep that all the things which I had previously seen or heard spiritually were indubitably true. [f. 48r, columns 1–2; Watson synopsis Opening and Prologue][24]

Thus far John's narrative is of a relatively predictable sort: a sinner wandering in errors identified with the 'exceptive arts', John is recalled by God's grace in a manner that is not clearly explained but relies on 'revelations and spiritual transformations'.[25] However, John goes on to declare that he did not believe in these first revelations. He returns to the old error of his ways, and is again recalled, this time more severely (and explicitly) through 'spiritual beatings' which take place during sleep. The content of the revelations would appear to be, roughly put, that the exceptive arts are unlawful, since he mentions that with his second lapse he does 'knowingly' what he did 'ignorantly' in the beginning (suggesting that prior to the revelations he may have assumed the 'exceptive arts' were licit.)[26] With the second set of revelations by his own account he truly repents and lays aside the old errors for good. The next paragraph, however, suggests an attitude to the aforesaid errors which is more complex than the first part of the narrative might seem to declare:

> But because the principle cause of my seduction in the aforesaid matter was that, seduced by error, I believed that I could attain to the height of all knowledge through those exceptive sciences and arts, which could not be done in a good way, I sought from the blessed and glorious virgin Mary that I might compose, if it pleased her, one book in her name, through which I and whoever had it and worked it would be able to reach from old errors of spirit to the height of arts and sciences. [f. 48r, column 2; Watson synopsis Opening and Prologue][27]

It is of interest that the request for permission to author a new book in the Virgin's name is undertaken *because* the principle cause of his error was the Ars Notoria: by this, John suggests that he is seeking not merely a better way to attain 'the height of the arts and sciences' but indeed a salve specific to the wound, a means of atoning for and transcending his previous error as well as a means, ultimately, of accomplishing the same end in a good way. John further suggests that his seeking of this book is in the public interest, as it will enable not merely him, but whoever works with it, to reach 'from old errors of spirit to the height of the arts and sciences'. Clearly John anticipates the involvement of others in the same type of wrongful acquisition of earthly knowledge, in exceptive errors for which they also will need a cure. It seems the Virgin saw the force of this argument (or were her instructions to perform this service already part of the divine plan?) John continues:

> And when I had sought these things many times at length the blessed virgin Mary appearing in sleep . . . conceded permission to me for the aforesaid book and conferred the means of composing it within the bounds of only 30 prayers, as have now been shown already in visions. I began the work of confessing this book in order that she might appear below, and I brought it to a conclusion with the help and support of the Virgin herself. [f. 48r, column 2; Watson synopsis Opening and Prologue][28]

This final sentence contains the first indication of the two-part structure of the ritual text, in which the first prayer cycle is made up of prayers composed by John himself (before he received his permission from the Virgin to write the book), in order to invoke the divine aid by means of which the subsequent prayer cycle was completed – a stage-by-stage process which the operator is intended to follow to reproduce the sequence of permission and visions obtained by John himself. As I noted earlier, it is in fact the *second* part of the text – that is, the divinely transmitted part, rather than the part composed by John himself – that owes most in structure, approach and language to the original Solomonic text.

The question remains open of why John perceived this new book (or 'new compilation' as he sometimes terms it), the designated goal of which would be to attain to 'the height of the arts and sciences', to be an appropriate antidote for one whose previous error had been involvement in the 'exceptive' version of the Ars Notoria. Since John's own revelation avowedly came in a vision from Mary and the holy angels of God, perhaps we may be allowed to wonder whether these divine entities condemned the text on the same terms that Thomas Aquinas had, or whether they said something different. Did John in fact know or understand Thomas' reasons for condemning the Solomonic text?

On balance it seems to me likely that the angels were familiar with some of Thomas' arguments, but not perhaps all of them. It seems clear that they eschewed the 'verba ignota', which have been excised from John's text; but either they did not consider the Ars Notoria an undue means of obtaining learning, or were not awfully particular about methodologies. John offers a partial explanation of what may have been at issue here in his conclusion to the cycle of prayers petitioning Mary for permission to write the book. Here he addresses the Virgin:

> I know that, according to the authorities on certain matters, those previously named things which I seek do not properly pertain to the blessedness of salvation which ought to be sought, because 'it is not good to know many things, but rather blessed to live well';[29] nevertheless the first impulses and beginnings of living well are studies,[30] and thus by consequence the cause of eternal felicity and celestial rewards. And therefore be my helper in obtaining this from our lord Jesus Christ, your son, and hearken to what I may deserve to obtain from him to the praise and glory of the holy Trinity, and yours, and of the whole celestial court, and the utility of the holy Catholic church, and to the glory of perpetual beatitude of my soul, and of many other souls, through the grace and operation, the omnipotent power and admirable dispensation of the holy and undivided Trinity, and through your most powerful and gracious help, amen. [f. 55v, column 1; Watson Synopsis Part II, prayer 12][31]

In this prayer John shows a clear awareness of the indictments of excessive regard for earthly knowledge occurring in both Biblical and patristic sources; at the same time he is most keenly conscious of a need to hold this idea in balance with the high regard for learning which is emerging elsewhere in increasingly distinctly articulated forms in late thirteenth- and early fourteenth-century writings.[32] While he begins by denying that the type of knowledge he seeks is relevant to salvation ('according to the authorities') he nevertheless proclaims that the book for which he hopes to get permission (and by implication the knowledge to be obtained through it) will contribute the eternal beatitude of his soul, and of other souls, and be useful to the Catholic church. Since his admission that 'it is not good to know many things' occurs in reference to his request for the new book (the *Liber visionum*) it remains difficult to tell whether the terms on which his involvement with the old Solomonic Ars Notoria was condemned by the angels may have been the same or different. However, it seems safe to say that insofar as John shows himself to be concerned with the risk of vice in this text, his principal anxiety is not over the possibility that he may be using 'undue means' to procure knowledge, nor yet the possibility of demonic intervention in the delivery of that knowledge. Rather his chief worries are over the potential dangers connected to intellectual curiosity and the risk of tempting God.[33] These concerns are manifest not only in the passage above, but in warnings reiterated passim throughout the text not to say the prayers of this text 'presumptuously' and his defenses of these prayers in and of themselves as being without danger of sin or temptation (by which he clearly means both the danger of tempting God, and the tempting of one's own soul that may be incurred thereby). In the Second Prologue, for example, he writes: 'here begins the book . . . by means of which if you speak it devoutly in your inmost heart the effect will follow, with no tempting and no marvelling and without sin of any criminal things', and again, 'beware lest you say these prayers in temptation or presumption, because there is sin in temptation and presumption'.[34]

Of the devil's role in his own enlightenment John has some quite interesting things to say near the end. His reflections on the devil follow on the heels of (and seem to be induced by) his most explicit avowal that he has drawn on the Ars Notoria as a source for this text:

> Again note that in composition both of the prayers and arrangements of this science, we have despoiled 'Egypt' (that is the Ars Notoria) of the 'vessels of gold and silver' (that is the good and divine words) to enrich the 'Hebrews' (that is to say the faithful and holy operations of this science). Because in composing this we have extorted many things from the Ars Notoria (and not unrighteously did we do it: when my Lord himself ordered the Hebrews going out of the first land to despoil the Egyptians, so also it was permitted to us on going out of the Ars Notoria and transcending to this science to seize spoil and enrich this one – for the devil revealed to us the wickedness of the Notory Art, and through these precepts we withdrew despoiling it) for that reason the devil, seeing himself deceived and deluded, molested us much in visions and did many injuries. But beyond this he was unable to do anything, since God did not permit it: he was always forced to flee confounded. We have written this so that if it happens to our successors that he appear in sleep, or that someone sense him in some other way, they should not fear, for he always flees

confounded and cannot do any evil if it is not permitted by God; and God does not permit him to bring upon you anything but in a quantity you know that you can sustain. And therefore he ought not to be feared, and you ought not to flee from him. [f. 65r, column 2; Watson Synopsis Part IV, Discussion 1, Nota 4][35]

It is clear at least that Brother John and the devil are not strangers to one another, though John adopts a form of rhetoric which seems designed astutely to deflect the possible charges that the devil might have played any role in handing on the *Liber visionum* itself. Using the familiar 'spoliatio aegyptionis' topos, John casts himself metaphorically as a righteous Hebrew, deceiving and triumphing over the devil like Christ himself. By claiming that he has retrieved only the 'good and divine words' from the condemned text, John becomes able to write as though he had been obeying God's command *throughout* his experience with the Ars Notoria (not unlike Christ during the harrowing of Hell); for we now see that even when John was ignorantly involved in the exceptive Solomonic practice, and before he was recalled from his error by Mary, his involvement proved to be in fulfillment of a divine purpose. He was ordered to withdraw, but to withdraw with the valuables in his pockets: a thing he could not have done had he never deviated from a life of holy innocence.

The devil, then, is cast as John's adversary, just as he is God's adversary. Using a motif familiar from the lives of the desert saints as well as the Biblical narratives of the trials of Job and the temptations of Christ, John withdraws from the world (i.e., the magic arts) and describes the torments inflicted upon him by Satan as though they were more directly the result of his attempt to live a life of holiness than his involvement in illicit practices. Perhaps concerned that he should even appear to be vaunting the divine blazon on his soul, John assures us that he passes on this information only for the public good, in order that his successors should not fear the devil's pranks, for Satan, too, must bow to God's commands.

It is at this point that John's original narrative of his lapse and redemption (as set out in the Prologue) begins to become complicated by his new claims. Earlier, John spoke explicitly of divine torments and 'spiritual beatings', experienced during sleep, which were sent by God for the purpose of deterring him from the error of the exceptive arts. Here he speaks of the devil, who molested him 'in visions' and did him many injuries, because he was extorting the 'good and divine words' from the Ars Notoria. The Graz Prologue leaves us in no doubt that all the visions which involved corporal and spiritual torment were experienced during the time when he was actually using the Solomonic Notory Art. While his reference to the idea that the devil 'cannot do any evil if it is not permitted by God' suggests that God is to be viewed as the indirect agency even behind the demonic torments, nevertheless a distinction that initially seemed important is here being obscured: why was he being tormented? Was it in punishment for his presumption, as he suggests in the Prologue, or as a text of his fidelity, as he seems to suggest here?

Even the Graz Prologue does not give a clear answer to this question (though it is possible that other materials in that text will clarify the issues involved) and frustratingly, what follows in this autobiographical epilogue is vexed by obscure and ambiguous locutions. From the passages which follow (the Graz and Munich texts show only minor differences here), it would seem that John continues to insist to a rather surprising degree on the innocence and even, ultimately, the divine motivation of his initial 'ignorant' involvement with the rituals of the Solomonic Ars Notoria.

Immediately after telling his reader not to recede from the devil, John makes reference to 'a compilation of figures made and published by us in the beginning'.[36] It is unclear what this 'compilation of figures' is, at what point (or at the beginning of what) it was made, or whether it was intended for inclusion in the *Liber visionum* or not. The fact that it was published 'in the beginning' (whatever this may really mean) suggests at least that it may have been prepared before this text, and separately circulated. There are no figures, diagrams or drawings associated with the *Liber visionum* in Clm 276[37] (John refers at one point to a figure in the form of a ring associated with 'the prayer of investigation of Scripture' – but that figure does not seem to be included in this manuscript). Tantalizingly, however, the condemnation in the *Grandes Chroniques* refers to images which John included in his books – chiefly, it would appear, images of the Virgin – but these images involved (as the *notae* in the Solomonic text do) 'prayers and characters,' or so the Chronicle states.[38] The McMaster text does include a number of fairly conventional images of the Virgin, but these pictures have no characters or prayers on them anywhere currently visible.[39] In addition, the McMaster illuminations would all seem to be for use with the visualizations or 'cogitationes' of the first prayer cycle (that is, the prayers composed by John himself), rather than the part of the text transmitted by the Virgin Mary – the part of the text which, as already noted, shows the most direct influence of the Solomonic Ars Notoria.

There remains some chance that the unexamined manuscripts will actually contain the figures that may have been intended for use with this text. However, for the moment, I would direct the reader's attention to the way this reference to 'a compilation of figures made and published in the beginning by us' suggests John had some sort of public life even prior to the composition of the *Liber visionum* – that he was writing, compiling and even circulating other works, to however small an audience, either during the period of lapse after his first set of revelations, or possibly even earlier, at the time when he was occupied with 'chasing after the exceptive arts'.[40]

A little farther on, John refers again to an 'antiqua compilatio' as well as 'nova compilatio'. As he goes on, it becomes clear that the 'nova compilatio' refers to the *Liber visionum* itself (or at least to the second cycle of prayers in the *Liber visionum* which were transmitted in visions from the Virgin):

> Again note that this new compilation was prefigured, because the future arguments of this vision were [there] from the beginning of the old compilation, but we did not understand [this] until the new compilation was complete. In that vision we sought to know if we were to compose the book to the end, and the Blessed Virgin, smiling, answered 'no' – and she spoke truly, even though on the literal level – although [then] we interpreted what she said of the visions in the old compilation in another manner, nevertheless [we interpreted them] well, because it is plain that we did not finish this book, but God himself, and the Blessed Virgin Mary. [f. 65r, column 2 and v column 1; Watson synopsis Part IV, Discussion 1, Nota 5][41]

Here the 'antiqua compilatio' is referred to, not (apparently) as a collection of figures, but as another ritual text, also claiming a visionary basis, and written before 'this book' in a manner that 'prefigures' it. By saying that 'God himself and the Blessed Virgin Mary' were responsible for the completion of 'this book', John suggests that the old compilation is in some manner the origin (perhaps a preliminary draft?) of this one.

Nicholas Watson has argued for the possibility that the 'antiqua compilatio' refers to an initial draft of Part I of the ritual text (that is, the prayers accompanied by meditations designed to invoke the Virgin). At least some of the prayers of Part I show signs of having goals not directly related to the project of the *Liber visionum*, and the more detailed account in the Graz text shows that these prayers were indeed composed after John's redemption from his entanglements with the magic arts, but before the project of the *Liber visionum* had been fully conceived. It is indeed likely, as Watson suggests, that John had originally intended them to form a separate book. However, it is not absolutely clear that the 'antiqua compilatio' refers to this project, and indeed the following paragraph contains some suggestion that the 'antiqua compilatio' may refer to a set of extracts drawn more directly from the Solomonic Ars Notoria than the materials of Part I seem to have been. A couple of words in this passage seem to require emendation to make any sense, so in these instances I simply report the manuscript reading in brackets, rather than translating:

> In the beginning of this knowledge the blessed Virgin gave us milk to drink, that what she placed in my mouth with the milk of spiritual grace might be sufficiently signified by her holy breast – by giving me milk showing that I was to this point a youth. And therefore she permitted me to touch on this science and to move through it wheresoever I desired playing with a boy, my lord Jesus Christ [*curpilota voluntatis*][42] making and discovering whatever figures I was

able, and the arrangements of those things to be said. And all things that were mine as a boy I would have lamented with tears of dismissal or renunciation for this holy science. By the lord himself, Jesus Christ, and by the blessed Virgin herself it was confirmed, whence we collected all these things from the old compilation. But because I have grown now and become more mature in knowledge, now that selfsame Virgin gives me no more milk but food to eat. And so they cannot touch me more [or][43] but the arms of virtue extend and another touches me, namely the Virgin, saying to me 'wherefore am I unwilling, when it is pleasing', handing on to me and revealing those figures and their operations in such a way that not my will but God's and the Virgin's must be done and even confirmed. From all these things therefore it is clear that this science was designated in prophetic visions, as it were announced in miracles, and foreshadowed by figures and riddles. [f. 65v, column 1; Watson synopsis, Part IV, Discussion 1, Nota 5][44]

This tantalizing paragraph cannot be fully explicated without more information than is presently at my disposal, but it may be deduced, at least, that the 'old compilation' did include both 'figures and operations'; that these figures were both 'made and discovered' (in other words it is suggested that the 'compilation' is not merely a collection of John's own writings, but was extracted, at least in part, from some other source); and finally that John feared that he would have to let go 'this holy science' as a mere childish diversion, but that the figures and operations were recovered and reaffirmed by God and the Virgin.

The reference to John's 'spiritual boyhood' is obscure, at least in part because we do not know when this paragraph was written; it may or may not have been a part of the original text which was condemned and put into the fire in 1323. The number and variety of manuscripts already uncovered makes it seem likely that John went on to re-copy and revise the *Liber visionum* (from memory or from notes) after it was burnt; thus the 'spiritual boyhood' may well refer simply to the time before the burning of the original copy of the book – a possibility which seems to find corroboration in the suggestion that 'they cannot touch me more' because 'another touches me, namely the Virgin'. The condemnation in the *Grandes Chroniques* asserts that the burnt text included figures which related to each branch of learning, which makes it sound as though the condemned copy may have been more visually similar to the Solomonic Ars Notoria than any copy presently in our possession. Certainly, as I have already shown, the redactions of the *Liber visionum* already available to us show the influence of the Solomonic text in many aspects of its structure and arrangement, and John has explicitly acknowledged that he has drawn 'good and divine words' therefrom. It is tempting to speculate that the 'antiqua compilatio' included a collection of images drawn from or inspired by those in the Solomonic Ars Notoria, and with a similar function. However, unless (or until) we uncover a copy of John's text which includes these figures or images we cannot be certain. (I might add that much seems possible today that did not seem possible yesterday; we can only keep looking and hope.)

What then of the condemnation of the *Liber visionum*? Was it justified? And why was John's ritual text – which condemned the Solomonic art explicitly, and which made a very real attempt to correct its problems – singled out for burning? I have already suggested that John was either unfamiliar with, or unconcerned with, Thomas Aquinas' argument that the Ars Notoria used 'undue means' to obtain learning. John's worries over the Ars Notoria, as evinced both by what he states about the Solomonic text, and what he excises from it, have largely to do with the unknown names, which can be linked to demonic involvement in the effects of the art, and the temptation to pride and curiosity which can accompany the too-greedy acquisition of knowledge.

It seems unlikely, however, that the theological oversight implicit in his neglecting to counter the 'undue means' argument was a primary cause of the burning of John's book. We remember that the portion of Thomas Aquinas's argument which is anthologized in the pseudo-Vincent's *Speculum Morale* does not include the mention of undue means, or any of Thomas' more particular arguments against the Notory Art, so it is likely that these points would have been less well known than the principle terms of condemnation on the ground of unknown names and the possibility of their demonic use. It may be noted also that 'undue means' is not brought up in the Chronicle entry, suggesting that it was not a matter of wide concern. As to the theological matters that *would* likely have been of wide concern (the temptation to curiosity and pride, the unknown names, the possibility of demonic involvement in the transmission of knowledge) all of these have in fact been addressed, in some cases with considerable subtlety, by John in his revision. My point is that John's *Liber visionum* is, among other things, part of an active and ongoing theological conversation about an occult ritual practice, in which he argues that the practice of the Ars Notoria (if not the Solomonic text itself) is defensible. His arguments are framed partly in terms of his own direct visionary experience, and partly in terms of Biblical and doctrinal authorities. From this perspective, the *Liber visionum* is a project perhaps more similar in its aims to that of the explicitly revisionist *Liber juratus* than the *prima facie* evidence would suggest.

The relative success of John's project may be measured in part by the preservation of his text in other copies, in part by the comparative triviality of the grounds on which it is recorded to have been condemned in the Chronicle entry. The terms of this condemnation seem fundamentally less well informed than Thomas's condemnation of the Solomonic text, and all the charges brought against it are potentially refutable as concerning secondary aspects of the text rather than the primary principles of the practice. (Did it in fact request honours, riches and pleasures? Did it include superstitious elements? And was it in fact elitist? It would be possible to argue against all of these charges using evidence from within the text.) The real reasons for the condemnation of John's book were likely essentially political in nature. John refused to keep the *Liber visionum* a secret. Indeed, he seems rather to have advertised his connection with it (indisputably he does so within the text itself, and may have done so orally as well); he declares his prayers to have been delivered by divine revelation, and even proclaims the utility of his book to other souls and to the Catholic church. His followers may have been no more inclined to hide their involvement with the practice than he was, for John suggests at one point (in the instructions contained in Part IV)[45] that while the operator should take due measures to find quiet and solitude when saying the prayers, one ought not hide them or seem to be performing them in secret. All of these things would have marked John as nuisance, even if he did not have a previous history of involvement with magic and with the Solomonic Notory Art in particular (which he did, and which he also admits in his text).

If the John the Monk's confidence in his *Liber visionum* made him a nuisance in his own day, we can only be grateful for it now, for it is precisely his own certainty of the divine authority behind the text that made possible his openness about the project, his willingness to append his name to it, and to tell us the story of what had happened to him when he composed it. We have only begun to work on the information that this makes available. Research on the Solomonic Ars Notoria, too, is still in its infancy. While much remains to be done and much remains to be discovered about these texts, it should be clear at least that the condescending dismissal of the Ars Notoria as 'one of the more obtuse of the grimoires' (as one recent writer puts it)[46] needs re-evaluation, considering its impact on John of Morigny and those around him. By pure fiat, after seven hundred years of obscurity, the *Liber visionum* has been rediscovered, an unexpected windfall from the *arbor scientie*. For myself, I can only say that I am awed at the way this information has tumbled into my hands.

Catch.

Notes

1 Discussed elsewhere in this volume by Michael Camille.

2 Some other manuscripts of John's text, unearthed, but as yet unconsulted by us, are cited in Watson, notes 8–11. The other manuscripts appear to include the Graz Prologue.

3 The burning of Ars Notoria texts would in fact seem to be rather unusual, though its verbal condemnation was not.

4 Lynn Thorndike, *A History of Magic and Experimental Science*, 8 vols (New York: Columbia University Press, 1923–58). Scattered references to the Ars Notoria and its condemnation are to be found throughout the *History*; the most concentrated information about the text is in vol. 2, pp. 279–89. It may be noted that Thorndike sometimes has a less firm grasp of the manuscript texts than it may appear. His information pertaining to the *Liber visionum* is particularly unreliable. He

refers to John's text in Clm 276, but was apparently unaware of its nature, describing it as follows: 'In one manuscript at the close of the *Golden Flowers* of Apollonius are prayers which one "brother John Monk" confesses he himself has composed in the years 1304–1307.' (*History*, vol. 2, p. 282). This information about John Monk's prayers is found in the catalogue. However, even the visual appearance of the manuscript makes it clear that John's work is not an addendum to the *Golden Flowers*, but a separate text, commencing with an elaborate capital on a new folio, and with a blank folio between it and the *Golden Flowers*. Thorndike continues, referring to the sixteenth-century manuscript Paris, Bibliothèque Nationale 7170A: 'In a later manuscript we find his prayers described as given to him by the blessed God and as "perfect science".' This is also catalogue information. However, the two folios of the manuscript in question, though they refer to John, and describe an Ars Notoria type practice, do not contain the same prayers (John's lengthy text would not in any case have fit into two folios, however compressed), and indeed differ significantly from them in the rituals prescribed. The 'perfect science' would appear to be a later pseudepigraphic contribution to John's œuvre, of little interest except in revealing that John's name continued to carry weight in the sixteenth century. Thorndike also does not connect the work of John the Monk in Clm 276 text with the later condemnation (by Jacobus Magnus, and also cited in the *History*, vol. 4, p. 279) of an Ars Notoria written by 'John, a monk of Chartres' and beginning 'Ave gratia'. Information found in Thorndike's *History* not already corrected by material in this volume should thus be treated with caution; nevertheless it remains a point of reference simply due to the paucity of other published materials.

5 Not all the manuscripts cited by Thorndike represent the full text of the Solomonic Art (also called 'The Golden Flowers of Appolonius') exemplified, e.g., in Clm 276 and Bodley 951. As Klaassen notes (pp. 16–18) there is an abundance of Ars Notoria 'short texts' – that is, texts which an author or compiler may have labelled as an 'Ars Notoria', but whose relationship to the full Solomonic text appears somewhat notional. Some (like the one in BN 7170A which occurs just prior to the prayers attributed to John the Monk) profess to do more or less what the full length Ars Notoria claims to do (i.e., deliver memory, eloquence and intellect) and in similar language but via very much abbreviated rituals, perhaps originally drawn from the Solomonic Ars (though it is hard to tell, the text in this case being only about two folios). Others (like the 'De arte crucifixi' in London, British Museum MS Harley 181) contain short rituals with similar goals but with different prayers and ritual methods. These texts (in fact like the full length Ars Notoria), have never been systematically studied.

6 Thorndike, *History*, vol. 2, notes to pp. 280–3. Of the texts listed, at least one is questionable: Clm 19413 contains a text called 'Three Formulae of Solomon' which according to Thorndike 'might turn out to be a notory art' (*History*, p. 281, n. 6); he dates it to the tenth or eleventh century. However, the date spread of the other manuscripts listed by Thorndike, along with the texts cited by Camille and Klaassen, makes it somewhat unlikely that a text recognizable as the Solomonic Art existed before the twelfth century.

7 Agrippa, *Opera* (Lyons, Beringos Fratres, conjectural date 1620); micro-facsimile, Landmarks of Science, New York, Readex Microprint, 1974, pp. 603–60. The Ars Notoria is included as part of a compendium of materials circulated with the spurious 'Fourth Book of Occult Philosophy'. Note that the printed facsimile of Agrippa's *Opera* (2 vols, Hildesheim and New York: Georg Olms Verlag, 1970)

is of an earlier edition (also by Beringos Fratres, conjecturally dated at 1600), and though it contains other materials circulated with the fourth book, it does not contain the Ars Notoria.

8 *Ars Notoria: the Notory Art of Solomon Shewing the Cabalistical Key of Magical Operations, the Liberal Sciences, Divine Revelation, and The Art of Memory* . . . (London: J. Cottrel, 1657). There is a facsimile edition put out by Trident Books (Seattle, 1987). Turner's translation is very close to the Latin of the Lyons edition of Agrippa's *Opera*, even down to the headings, which do not occur in the fifteenth century Ars Notoria in Clm 276, and break up the text rather differently. Neither the Latin edition nor the Turner translation include the figures or *notae*.

9 There are indeed some differences which should eventually be helpful both in sorting out the ambiguities of the later text and tracing its history. Overall, the later text shows a tendency to abbreviation. The most radical differences between the fifteenth-century text and the early modern text are found in the area of the prayers involving strings of words which purport to be in a mixture of Greek, Hebrew and Chaldean. In the seventeenth-century text, these name-string prayers seem generally to be shorter (sometimes much shorter), and to involve in some cases quite different names than occur in the fifteenth-century version (the 1657 Turner text is here identical, letter by letter, with the text published in Agrippa's *Opera*). Some of the differences between medieval and early modern versions are probably accounted for by differences in transliteration from Greek or Hebrew (on f. 1r, col. 2, the medieval text in Clm 276 has a gloss in Hebrew letters in the margin, which would seem to indicate that a user somewhere along the line was familiar with Hebrew); however, not all of the variations can be accounted for by differences in transliteration, as the deviation between the two texts is simply too wide. While the Latin portions of the text do not seem to be grossly different in medieval and early modern versions, the early modern text has a number of rather confusing internal references to 'chapters' which are not marked in the text's headings; the earlier Ars Notoria, however, signals chapter beginnings and endings with 'incipit' and 'explicit capitula' (markers likely to be quite helpful when I get around to looking at them more closely). Finally, as already noted, the early modern text (in both Latin and English versions) is missing the *notae*, or figures. More medieval texts will have to be examined before we can begin to put together a picture of the lines of transmission of these versions of the Ars Notoria.

10 The headings in the seventeenth-century editions do nothing to clarify this distinction of parts, which I have extrapolated from the often confusing internal indications in the text.

11 After an introductory prayer beginning 'Alpha and Omega', the first heading of the discursive text runs, 'Here beginneth the first Treatise of This Art, The Golden Flowers', which describes what follows as 'a general introduction to all Natural sciences' [Turner, *Ars Notoria*, p. 4]. Then follows a statement in the first person: 'I, Appolonius, Master of Arts . . . am intended to treat of the Knowledge of Liberal Arts . . .', which suggests that Appolonius is meant to be seen as the author of at least some of the discursive text which follows. In other discursive sections of the text, however, Master Appolonius is referred to in the third person, which suggests either that the writer momentarily forgot he was supposed to be impersonating Appolonius, or that someone else's hand may have intervened. Throughout this section, prayers are interspersed with commentary by Appolonius (or his proxy). Appolonius does not claim to have composed any of the prayer texts, which he indicates were transmitted by God directly to Solomon; rather Appolonius seems to appear

as a kind of intermediary between Solomon and his medieval successors, translating and interpreting the prayers, and explaining how they ought to be used.

12 Curiously enough, the figures vary considerably from manuscript to manuscript; though the known Ars Notoria figures preserve some similar elements, the designs are by no means identical.

13 It may be noted, however, that in his introductory treatise Master Appolonius tells us that the text is in two parts (not three) and that the part concerning the 'generals' comes before the part concerning the 'specials'.

14 The Graz text contains a quantity of ritual material at the end which is not present in Munich. Like McMaster, the Graz text includes instruction for the consecration of a ring; however, there appears to be additional material not present in McMaster either, some of which may belong properly to the *Liber visionum*, some of which may have been separately circulated. All of this requires closer examination.

15 This structure is signalled in various loci, e.g., f. 48r. col. 2: '. . . opus liber confitendi incepi ut inferius apparet et ad finem produxi eiusdem Virginis auxilio suffragante' ('I began the work of confessing this book in order that she might appear below, and I brought it to a conclusion with the help and support of the Virgin herself'.)

16 Though an 'opus figurarum' is mentioned in the McMaster text, it seems to relate to the visualizations of Part I. The Munich text mentions a 'liber figurarum' in such a way as to imply that it was a separately circulated work. A 'liber figurarum' (unfortunately without figures) is included in the additional ritual materials at the end of the Graz text, but more analysis is necessary to determine how these references relate to each other. There is still hope that some other manuscript of the *Book of Visions* will actually contain the figures.

17 A partial list of condemnations of the Ars Notoria is found in Klaassen, p. 30, n. 44.

18 *Speculum Morale*, Libri III, Dist xviii, Pars III.

19 For an overview of Thomas' ideas about knowledge in the context of thirteenth-century attitudes to curiosity, see Hans Blumenberg, 'The Trial of Theoretical Curiosity', Part III of *The Legitimacy of the Modern Age*, trans. Robert M. Wallace (Cambridge, Massachusetts and London: MIT Press, 1983), pp. 325–42.

20 Quotations drawn from Watson's translation in this volume, p. 164.

21 The Prologue to the Graz text is much more extensive, and gives a comprehensive account of John's early life including a detailed narrative of his visions, both those induced by the Ars Notoria rituals, and the subsequent visions by which he was delivered from the magic arts.

22 The term 'exceptive arts' is an unusual currency which requires some explanation. John clearly uses it as though it were equivalent to 'magic arts', and indeed the McMaster text includes helpful tables listing the liberal arts, mechanical arts and exceptive arts, where, 'exceptive arts' does indeed head a list of the magic arts (pyromancy, aeromancy, hydromancy, nigromancy, gyromancy, geomancy and geonegia) and the mechanical arts also are appropriately listed (woolworking, building, medicine, theatre, hunting, agriculture and navigation). However, the Solomonic texts I have seen (including the fifteenth-century version in Clm 276), refer to the 'exceptive arts' only to say that they are included in the liberal arts, and proceed to describe the *mechanical* arts as including 'hydromancy, pyromancy, nigromancy, chiromancy, geomancy, geonegia and neogia' – in other words, the magic arts. Whether this frequently reproduced coupling of the mechanical arts with the magic arts is an error or a

deliberate blind must remain unknown at least until some earlier texts have been examined. However, it is noteworthy that the term 'exceptive arts' does not seem to occur at all outside of contexts pertaining to the Notory Art: the word 'exceptive' is listed in the OED with usages going back to medieval Latin, but the 'exceptive arts' do not occur, nor have I found the *artes exceptive* listed in any Latin dictionary. It seems sufficiently clear, at least, that John understood the term 'exceptive arts' to cover the magic arts and not the mechanical ones. The Graz text makes it clear that John was involved not only with angelic magic but also, at a later stage, with necromancy; in his usage the term 'exceptive arts' seems to be used in reference to magic of both types.

23 This may be an oblique reference to the knowledge which 'puffs up' mentioned in I Corinthians 8:1, 'Scientia inflat, charitas vero aedificat'.

24 'Ego, frater Iohannes, monachus de Mariginato . . . in preteritis temporibus artium et scientiarum exceptivarum sectando fui sepius involutus, et ab hijs tenebris ignorantie per sacras revelationes et inmutationes spirituales ex parte beate et intemerate gloriose virginis Marie et sanctorum angelorum Dei, [n]olentes me per ignorantiam condempnare quasi per quedam temporis spatium ad suam misericordiam revocare; set postea quadam sufflatione demorata temptatus, et temptatione illa prevalente cetatus, quasi hesitans, non credendo sacras revelationes et inmutationes in futuras esse ex bono spiritu, aritibus quibus ignoranter vocaveram iterum in detrimentum anime mee sicut canis qui [Proverbs 26:11] recurrit ad vomitum quasi scienter cucurri et prohdolor adhesi in contumeliam creatoris. Set non wlt mortem peccatoris set patius ut convertatur et vivat; michi tamquam musce in extremo fluvie Egipti [Isaiah 7:18] posite sibile sue gratie misericorditer sibilavit: primo per vocem spiritus minando me multas subire passiones propter quod talia que contra ipsum erant facere presumebam; secundo verberationes spirituales in presentia ipsius in sompnis michi crudeliter illatas; et ad hoc non credidi omnibus set potius hesitam. Et cum timor Dei a malo non revocaret, saltem cohercet persecutionum seu passionum promissarum disciplinis. Tertio et idem Deus persecutiones temporales et corporales etiam me a predictis erroribus nephariis non meis meritis set sui gratia misericorditer revocavit. Cognoscens per adventum persecutionum in sompnis omnia quecumque prius spiritualiter videram vel audieram indubitabiliter esse vera.' I reproduce the manuscript text as closely as possible, standardizing u/v and c/t according to principles also in use by Watson. I have kept emendation to a minumum, not emending in some cases where the manuscript reading is clearly wrong; 'cetatus', e.g., as shown, is probably for 'citatus'; 'aritibus' for 'artibus'. The scribe's most common error is to confuse 'a' with 'o' – hence 'Mariginato' ('Morigny'; elsewhere in the text written 'Moriginato') and 'patius' for 'potius'. References to this text throughout will be to folio and column numbers in Clm 276 as well as to section headings in the synopsis provided with Nicholas Watson's essay.

25 The reference to 'spiritual transformations' probably does not refer to any transformations taking place in John, but rather to the transformation of Mary's statue into a living, speaking body which occurs in the first vision truly to come from God, after John has sworn off the exceptive arts, as detailed in the Graz text.

26 A supposition confirmed by Graz. John describes the Ars Notoria as a book which was very beautiful and had the appearance of being most holy. Also, the doctor who first told him about the practice expressly maintained that it required nothing illicit.

27 'Verum quia principalis causa seductionis mee in predictis fuit quod per illas scientias et artes

exceptivas errore seductus credebam me posse ad culmen omnium scientiarum protingere, quod esse non potuit bono modo, idcirco impetravi apud beatamVirginem gloriosam Mariam ut unum librum, nomine suo, si sibi placeret, conponerem, per quem de spiritis antiquis erroribus ad culmen scientiarum et artium ego et quicumque ipsum haberet et operaretur attingere posset.'

28 'Et cum hec multotiens quesivissem, tandem illa beata virgo Maria . . . apparens in sompnis, predictum librum et conponendi modum tantummodo de 30 orationibus finibus ut iam in visionibus superius ostensum et michi lic[entiam] [MS reads 'licitiam'] contulit et concessit. Qui opus liber confitendi incepi ut inferius apparet et ad finem produxi eiusdem Virginis auxilio suffragante.'

29 A common proverb found in Isidore's *Sentencie* and elsewhere.

30 Or perhaps 'studies of living well'. The sentiments are roughly equivalent in either phrasing since 'bene vivere' would be assumed to be the ultimate goal of study. Writing about eighty years later in England, the poet John Gower gives condensed expression to the idea that studies are superior to other forms of labor and more directly related to celestial reward in Latin verse IV.vii of the *Confessio Amantis*: 'Expedit in manibus labor, vt de cotidianis/Actibus ac vita viuere possit homo./Set qui doctrine causa fert mente labores,/ Preualet et merita perpetuata parat.' [Manual labor's useful, so a man/Can live in daily life by daily deeds;/But he who toils in mind for wisdom's sake/ Prevails, for lays up perpetual meed.'] Translation from Echard and Fanger, *The Latin Verses in the Confessio Amantis* (East Lansing: Colleagues Press, 1991), p. 53.

31 '. . . scio quod ista prenominata que peto secundum auctoritates quorundam non proprie pertinere ad salutis beatitudinem consequendam, quia 'non est bonum multa scire sed potius beatum bene vivere'; tamen primi motus et principaliter sunt studii bene vivendi, et sic per consequens causa felicitatis eterne et celestium premiorum; et idcirco ad ipsam impetrandam a domino nostro Ihesu Christo filio tuo sis in adiutorium meum et quod ab ipso merear exaudiri ad laudem et gloriam sancte Trinitatis et tuam tociusque curie celestis et sancte ecclesie katholica utilitatem et ad gloriam perpetue beatitudinis anime mee et aliarum multarum animarum, per gloriam et operationem virtutem omnipotentem(?), et amirabilem dispensationem sancta et individue Trinitatis, et per tua gratissima et potentissima suffragia; amen.'

32 A movement traced by Hans Blumenberg through the writings chiefly of Peter Damian, Albertus Magnus and Thomas Aquinas in *The Legitimacy of the Modern Age*, 325–42 cited above, n. 20.

33 Concerns to some extent shared by the Solomonic Ars Notoria.

34 'Incipit liber . . . per quem si devote dixeris in intimo cordis effectum namque in ipso secuntur, non temptando, non mirando, et sine peccato criminalium'; and farther down 'Cavendum est ne temptando vel presumendo ipsas orationes dicas quia in temptatione et presumtione peccatum est' (f. 49r. col. 2; Watson synopsis Second Incipit and Prologue).

35 'Item nota quod tam in compositione orationum quam institutionum huius scientie nos spoliasse vasis aureis et argentis (id est verbis divinis et bonis) Egiptum (id est Artem Notoriam) et ditasse Ebreos (id est fideles et sanctos operationes huius scientie). Quia componendo ipsas plura extorsimus ab Arte Notoria – nec immeritis nos sic fecisse, cum ipse meus dominus precepit Ebreis exeundo de terra prima spoliare Egyptios, sicut et nobis fuit permissum exeundo de Arte Notoria et transcendo ad istam scientiam spoliare et ditare istam – Dyabolus enim nobis revelavit maliciam Artis Notorie et ipsa per precepta recessimus spoliando ipsam – unde Dyabolus, videns se deceptum et delusum, multum nos molestabat in visionibus et multas iniurias faciebat. Set ultra hoc Deo non

permittente aliquid facere non valebat sed confusus semper recedere cogebatur. Hoc ideo scripsimus ut si contingerit successionibus nostris ipsum apperere dormiendo, vel aliquo modo ipsum sentire, non timeat, cum quia semper recedat confusus, nec potest aliquid mali facere nisi permissus a Deo. Nec Deus permittitur ipsum tibi inferre aliquid nisi quantum te scit posse sustinere; et ideo non est timendum et inde non recedas ei.'

36 'Queret aliquis quare compilatio figurarum facta et edita in principio a nobis non valuerit vel non potuerit confirmari sicut antiqua formis quod antiqua erat confirmata, et ista erat revelanda' [f. 65r. col. 2]; ('If anyone wants to know why the compilation of figures made and published by us in the beginning would not or could not be confirmed in its designs like the old [one] that was confirmed of old, this also was bound to be revealed'); however it does not subsequently become clear precisely what was revealed.

37 In the miscellany of additional ritual materials included in the Graz text (after the main text of the *Liber visionum*, but before the conclusion) there is a 'Liber figurarum', from which unfortunately the figures have been omitted.

38 Translation in Watson essay, p. 164.

39 As Watson notes, they are apparently heavily retouched, and it is possible that some 'prayers and characters' have been covered up by a more recent layer of paint, but about this at present we can only speculate.

40 It is clear that this is the case from the Graz text, where he also admits to writing (secretly, during the period of his 'relapse'), a book of necromancy.

41 'Item nota quod ista nova compilatio fuit presignata, quod futura erant a principio antique compilationis argumenta cuiusdam visionis; set non intelleximus donec ipsa nova compilatio fuerit conpleta. In qua visione petebamus si librum ad finem componeremus, et respondit ridendo beata virgo Maria quod 'non' – et verum dixit, etiam hystorice – quamvis aliomodo interpretati sumus dictam visionum in antiqua compilatione, et tamen bene, quia patet quod nos non finivimus istum librum set ipse Deus et beata virgo Maria.'

42 'cum polita voluntatis', Graz.

43 *Sic* Graz.

44 'Lac nobis in principio istius scientie beata Virgo in potum dedit, ut satis significatur per mammillam suam sanctam quam posuit in ore meo lacte gratie spiritualis – me lactando ostendens me ad huc iuvenem esse. Et ideo permisit me tingere in ista scientia et ambulare per ipsam quocumque vellem ludendo cum puero, domino meo Ihesu Christo, curpilota (?) voluntatis, constituendo et inveniendo figuras qualescumque valebam et institutiones ipsarum dicendarum. Et omnia mihi tamquam puero in flerem fletu dimissionis uel renunctiationis huius scientie sancte. Ab ipso domino Ihesu Christo et ab ipsa beata Virgine fuerit confirmata, unde hec omnia ex antiqua compilatione colligimus. Sed quia crevi iam et senui in scientia iam amplius non lac sed escam dedit mihi ipsa Virgo in cibum. Ita quod amplius non possunt me tingere sed or (?) brachia virtutis extendere et alius tinget me, scilicet ipsa Virgo dicendo me "quo non volo cum placet"; tradendo mihi et revelando istas figuras et earum operationes quomodo non voluntatem meam sed Dei et ipsius Virginis oportuit fieri et etiam confirmari. Ex hiis ergo omnibus patet hanc scientiam fuisse propheticis visionibus designatam quasi miraculis pronunctiatam et figuris et enigmatibus presignatam.'

45 F. 66v. col. 1, top: 'set in pluribus videatur dum hoc opus vel has orationes dixerit quia magis se wult esse in publico quam in oculto.' ['but in many things let it be seen when (the operator) recites this work or these prayers that he is willing to be in public rather than in hiding'.]

46 Donald Tyson, in the bibliographic note on the Ars Notoria contained in his edition of Agrippa's *Three Books of Occult Philosophy* (St Paul: Llewellyn Publications, 1993), p. 852.

APPENDIX

Synopsis of the Prologue to the Liber Visionum *in* Graz, University Library MS 680

The Prologue, which runs about ten folios, starts at the top of f. 94r and continues through 104r, halfway down the first column, where we pick up the beginning of the Munich text. Unfortunately the rubrics grow increasingly illegible in my copy (although they should pose no problem when I am able to see the manuscript *in situ*). Here I present a summary account in which I represent at least the locations of rubricated text (in italics), what the rubric contains (where I am able to read it), and a brief synopsis, in English, of the following text.

The narrative is remarkable for its level of detail (much of which I have omitted in this synopsis) concerning such things as the clothing, actions, and physical positioning of John and his various interlocutors, human, diabolic and angelic. There is also a quantity of dialogue which I report only where it is crucial. It may be noted that the dialogue does not in the main reduce but rather increases the essential ambiguity of many of the visions, especially those induced by the Ars Notoria.

[f. 94r. 1] Incipit liber apparicionum et visionum beate et intemerate et sacratissime virginis Marie dei gentricis alma Maria procurante et eciam revelante et supremo deo concedente . . .

[f. 94r. 1] *Incipit primo prologus in nomine domini nostri ihesu christi amen.*
Nemo cum laternam accendit sub abscondito ponit eam neque sub modio ymmo pocius super candelabrum ut ingredientibus lumen appareat claritatis . . .
[Here follows a defense and advertisement of the work, continuing the metaphor of not hiding one's light under a bushel; it would be wrong to boast of learning, but it is good to manifest divine revelation and helpful knowledge (like Solomon); how the book drives away evil spirits and procures good; etc.]

f. 94v. 2 (large cap) Supposicioni omnia quecumque in hoc libro scripta sunt penitencie sacramentis scilicet ut septem sacramentis spiritualibus principalibus

mistice supponantur. Mistice propter plures rationes diximus et specialiter ex eo quod in omni visione semper figura vel misterium reperitur.
[How the first vision of Mary is as a theme for all the rest, though he did not realize it at the time.]

Finit prologus. Incipit [f. 95r. 1] *Liber visionum Et primo de prima visione que est quasi thema omnium sequencium visionum quam habui existens quasi xii annorum*
Ego enim iohannes dum essem circa estate xiiii [sic] annorum et moraer [sic] apud anitatem carnocensium in claustro beate Marie satis prope ecclesiam quasi per iactum unius lapidis mihi tamquam abortiuo talis visio est ostensa.
[The vision was at night; he knew not whether he was in his body or out of it; he was chased by a horrible figure whom he sensed was inimical to the human race; he dashed into the church toward the image of the blessed Virgin Mary, who makes a sign to him; she gives him refuge and solace; he wakes up.]

[f. 95r. 2] *Finit thema et quomodo a dyaboli deceptus. Incipit pars prima ipsius libri et quid accidit mihi post huius visionem primam*
[Tells what happened after the visions which follow (that is, after the narrative of the Prologue closes, and after the first prayers are written) in the year 1308, in September. He is at this point at Morigny in a cloister with other brothers, and one day he asked the blessed Virgin three questions by means of the prayers of this book. 1. Should he remain a scholar as he has been? 2. Should he remain in the abbey? 3. Should he manifest (ie publish) his former visions from her? Her answer: 'You will be a monk, and you will move, and you will tell what I have told you'. His actions in remaining a monk, but moving around and publishing his book, all follow her advice.]

[f. 95v. 2] *De erroribus meis, scienciis meis nefariis, et pecia scilicet in Arte Notoria que est dyabolo tradita*
[This took place after the first vision and around his fourth year as a Benedictine; he describes receiving a book of necromancy from a certain cleric; being tempted by the devil to pursue this, he goes to a certain Lombard medical expert named Jacob for advice. Jacob advises him instead to seek out a book called the Ars Notoria which will give him all the knowledge he wants in a better way.]

[f. 96r. 1] *(rubric partly illegible) Ars Notoria . . . fallacissime est contexta et fabricata*
[Here follows a long digression on the evil of the Ars Notoria, which is all the more dangerous because of the holy appearance of the book. Prefaced by a description of the book itself, 'which outwardly appears . . . the most beautiful and useful and even the most holy of all books'; yet its honey conceals venom etc.]

[f. 96r. 2] *Sequitur visio secunda*
[Here follows the first vision induced by the Ars Notoria. After a fast and a prayer, he goes to bed and seems to himself to be in a yard by his mother's house and sees a frightening apparition: a shadow of five fingers deriving from a malign spirit, a figure so so great it extends from zenith to horizon. He is frightened and runs into his house. Pointing out of the window for everyone to look, he sees only a figure very simply dressed in black attire and wearing a black diadem. He repents a little that he had called it a malign spirit, and awakes.]

[f. 96v. 1] *De 3a visione que est exposicio precedentis*
[Seeking the meaning of the first vision, he says a prayer for intelligence, and finds himself in a crowded church. In the chorus he sees one of the brothers minor reading a psalter with some students; the brother gestures to him to come and he reads the words 'Vidi impium super exaltatum et elevatum sicut cedros lybani'. But then he loses his place, and it cannot be found; when he remarks on this the brother answers 'He who was showing himself, who was he?' He wakes glorifying God and giving thanks.]

[f. 96v. 2] *Quomodo Artem Notoriam didici et quomodo per eam operata fui*
[How as a student he endured poverty in books and many other necessities but above all desired knowledge of all the sciences; he puts aside other studies to pursue the Ars Notoria.]

[f. 96v.2] *Quarta visio . . . (rubric partly illegible)*
[Here follows a vision in which he is lying in bed and sees the room filled with great light. He sees two men whom he believes from their conversation to be the Father and the Son; another, whom he perceives but cannot see, he understands to be the Holy Spirit. At the time he believed this was a good and true vision; later he comes to understand it was the devil disguised as an angel of light.]

[f. 97r. 2] *Quinta visio*
[He sees a proud and arrogant man enter through the window as he lies in his bed; circling the chamber the man says 'If you adore me and pay me homage you will have all you seek'. He refuses; two others dressed as brothers minor enter through the same window and threaten to pour boiling lead down his throat if he does not comply with the man's request; he says no but they continue to pressure him with threats of violence. Finally, he asks how this homage is to be done; they show him and he wakes. He wonders whether this art is not evil after all and asks God: 'If there is anything in this science which is contrary to you, or yours, or the Christian faith, don't let it have any further effect on me.']

[f. 97v. 1] *(illegible rubric, but presumably seventh vision)*
[When he again took up the work he had been in the middle of, and followed it

all the way to the end, it was twice revealed to him by all the angelic spirits that into the prayers in outlandish tongues of this book were subtly and ingeniously inserted invocations of malign spirits, in such a way that this could not be perceived. He begins to have much doubt of this science.]

[f. 97v.2] *Sequitur visio octava*
[He explains he has many other visions which do not pertain to his point, through which he learned necromancy in both kinds with the help of this book. Similarly geomancy, pyromancy, hydromancy, and the rest. It would take too long to tell all this. He does not wish to leave this science, but then he has another vision, in which an angel of the cherubim comes to him, dressed in a black tunic, and orders him to come down from his chamber. And when he doesn't wish to, the angel pushes him down the stairs. On the bottom step a malign spirit ('i.e. dyabolus') takes him and leads him about, looking for an opportune place to kill him. John calls to the angel for help, but the angel recedes. Terrified, John imagines himself confessing his sins; the devil lets go of him and he hears the angels singing sweetly. This long vision has a second part in which the confession is realized and he is congratulated and embraced by John the Evangelist and the Virgin Mary. Here in truth he knows that the Ars Notoria was evil, and he begins to renounce it, but not entirely.]

[f. 98v. 1] *Nota (nona?) visio de inhibicione Artis Notorie*
[He has uttered the prayer for memory and finds himself pursued by a malign spirit with a drawn sword. He is terrified and flees, but then a figure enters his room dressed in a tunic not exactly white, but the colour of ashes, 'as though it had been burnt'. This figure takes John by the hand and leads him to a bench and induces him to confess. When this is done, John says, 'then I knew and understood without doubt that the book of the Ars Notoria was entirely malign, and it did not please the Creator that I should operate through it any more'. He dismisses the Ars Notoria completely.]

[f. 98v. 2 bottom] *(rubric partly illegible)* . . . *artes nigromancie decima visio*
[Narrative commencing on f. 99r. 1. After his dismissal of the Notory Art he lapses into to the necromantic arts; indeed he becomes so proficient he is in the process of composing a new necromantic book. He is also in the process of making the Rings of Solomon when he has the tenth vision. He has just finished off the fourth ring, when a voice comes to his ears saying 'Fool! Fool! Fool!' He is afraid and says 'Truly I am a fool!', and again the voice says 'Truly you are a fool, and if you are to know how much of one then you must suffer for the things you are doing.' The voice recedes; he is very much frightened but nevertheless continues composing the book of necromancy.]

[f. 99r. 1] *(Rubric partly illegible) undecima visio qualiter . . . coram . . . creatore*
[One night as he is sleeping John sees a figure come into his solarium dressed in a
red toga. Others in similar habits accompany him. The figure seats himself 'in
katedra tamquam magister'. John, knowing the master to be the lord Jesus,
prostrates himself and asks for mercy, but the figure of Jesus begins to beat John,
saying 'Stop what you have done and are doing, for it is contrary to your
Creator.' The pain of the beating is so severe it wakes John up, and he continues
to experience pain in his shoulders and elsewhere for an hour afterwards.
Because of this John lays aside the necromantic arts, and the book he is writing,
for good.]

[f. 99r. 2] *Explicit prima pars visionis @Incipit 2a pars de visionibus quas habui post
confessionem sanctam et revelacionem huius librum et hec visio prima a deo procedens*
[After he has forgone the magic arts, John has a vision in which is before the
great altar in the church of the blessed Virgin. Her silver statue is transmuted to
flesh and comes to him. Leading him to the altar she tells him to stand, adore
God and give thanks. He asks her a question: 'if my book of unlawful
necromancy is discovered, will it be said that it was no miracle, but by that art I
made your image change? And will I be removed and hidden from society on
account of this book?' The Virgin does not answer, but he thinks about this and
then wakes up. In memory of this vision he composes the prayer <u>Gracias ago tibi
gloriose flos celorum</u>.]

[f. 99v. 1] *Nota visio 2a Qualiter fui in societate angelorum*
[An angel comes to him, dressed in red and beautiful beyond measure, with a
multitude of other angels in train. John finds the society of angels so sweet and
beautiful he desires to enter it but does not dare. One of the angels invites him in,
but John insists that he does not dare. The angel explains that it is now the Lord's
will and pleasing to God and again invites him in. John goes with them and
experiences such joy that he wishes to remain always and wakes giving thanks to
God.]

[f. 99v. 2] *Tercia visio de confirmatione prose que incipit Ave gloriosa virgo regina . . . (rubric
partly illegible)*
[Narrative commencing f. 100r. 1. John prefaces the vision by noting that he has
a great desire to say this 'prosa oratio' but one of his companions warns him
against it, saying that anyone who said it would be excommunicated, as the
author had been condemned. John has a vision in which the canons of the
church are singing it, demonstrating that it is not displeasing to the Virgin.]

[f. 100r. 1] *(rubric completely illegible)*
[John has many glorious visions which it would take too long to narrate word for

word. He has seen a city above the clouds and heaven clear as crystal and so forth. The first prayer of this book he composed after the ninth vision. Other information about composition of certain prayers is given.]

[f. 100r. 2] *Nota visio . . . de licencia . . . (rubric mostly illegible)*
[At this point John describes asking for and receiving permission to write a new book 'ad destructionem alterius libri Artis Notorie'; he prays before the image of the Virgin for thirty simple prayers through which he might be able to obtain knowledge of all scripture and the arts and sciences. The Virgin's wooden image is tranformed and she speaks 'as though unwilling and heavily'; but she grants permission and says that when the time comes she will give him the eloquence to do it.]

[f. 100v blank]

[f. 101r. 2] *(another rubric illegible except for the first word 'finit')*
[He explains that Jesus Christ and the blessed Virgin desire him to summon two or three witnesses against the Ars Notoria. He describes how his sister Gurgeta at the age of fifteen very much desired to learn to read and write. He felt it was unlikely that she could acquire proficiency because of her age, but she insisted. He gives her the Ars Notoria and she learns to read and write proficiently in a very short space of time.]

[f. 101v 1] *(yet another illegible rubric)*
[But after his sister had started on the Ars Notoria she had many horrible visions which kept her awake at night. Malign spirits hurt her and she was frightened. He told her to sign herself with the cross and say a Pater Noster, but this had no effect. Finally he tells her that she must renounce the Ars Notoria and its pomps and works and tomorrow promise this to God and the blessed Virgin before her image in the church. As soon as she decides to do this the devils begin to recede. He testifies that this is all true and meant to show the evil of the Ars Notoria.]

[f. 102r 1] *De visionibus bonis sororis mee postquam dimisit Artem Notoriam*
[After setting aside the Ars Notoria his sister begins to have good visions. She has a vision of the Creator in a church. She herself is entirely nude and says to him 'I give myself to you untouched'; to which He responds 'do you have the power to do this?' and she says 'I have'; and he says 'then I receive you, my daughter'. And she awakens.]

[f. 102r 1] *Alia visio eiusdem*
[Here follow more of his sister's visionary experiences, all briefly told, a number involving the Virgin.]

[f. 102r 2] *Item alia visio*
[This vision is John's. Here the Virgin appears to him at his request to answer the question of how his sister can become a nun when she lacks in temporal necessities. The Virgin promises that she will provide what is required when the time comes. Many other things not written in this book were promised and performed by the Virgin for them, which shows that the Ars Notoria is evil but the present art is good.]

[f. 102v 1] *De tercio teste contra Artem Notoriam*
[Having described the second witness, the third witness follows. A certain monk of the order of Saint Bernard had asked John many times to be taught the Ars Notoria. At length John gave in and taught him, and when this monk had pursued the art for some time he asks a question by means of the art concerning the interpretation of certain words or names in the art. Thereupon he has a vision in which he enters the cloister of his abbey and sees a figure holding a psalter and reading the psalm 'Deus iudicium tuum etc.'. And when this monk tried to look on in the psalter, the reader looked at him indignantly and said 'What are you looking for? What you seek is not here'. By which he understood divine law was not in the Ars Notoria, and that the Ars Notoria was not pleasing to God. (Note that in this case, as in the case of his sister, it is quite unclear when, in the sequence of John's own spiritual autobiography, he becomes involved in teaching the Ars Notoria to others. The fact that he has to be pressured in both cases, and that he knows the cure of his sister's nightmares must lie in the renunciation of the Notory Art, suggests that this happens later in his career, perhaps even after he has renounced its use for himself.)]

[f. 102v. 2] *Finit . . . que est de reprobacione Artis Notorie et de presentis Artis revelacione . . . liber virginis marie et prima de explicatione lectori et . . .(rubric partly illegible)*
[A lyrical section beseeching the right readers to come to this work in the right spirit; it is not for the proud or rich or luxurious or malevolent etc., but for the faithful, the meek, the chaste, the poor etc.]

[f. 103r 1] *De . . . operatione que debent hic volentes . . . hanc Artem . . . (i)ndicia ipsorum (rubric partly illegible)*
[The blessed Virgin appears to him in a vision and shows him the many false monks whose outward holiness belies the abominations of their secret hearts. She pleads with him to come to her in the spirit of poverty and simplicity and informs him that she does not wish prayers or figures otherwise, and if the petitioner is not true to her none of the prayers or figures will have any effect.]

[f. 103v 1] *Qualiter et ubi consuevit apparere et ut plurimum virgo Maria*
[Describes the various forms in which Mary is known to appear and gives various

signs by which the apparition may be known as genuine and distinguished from the devil in the guise of an angel of light.]

[f. 104r 1] *Incipit liber visionum eate et intemerate virginis marie genitricis dei. Cogita hic quod tu sis in itinere paradisi*
[This is the beginning of the Munich text; see Watson synopsis for ritual text proper.]

9

THE DEVIL'S CONTEMPLATIVES: THE *LIBER IURATUS*, THE *LIBER VISIONUM* AND CHRISTIAN APPROPRIATION OF JEWISH OCCULTISM

Richard Kieckhefer

The author of *The Cloud of Unknowing* refers to certain misguided souls as 'the devil's contemplatives' – hypocrites and heretics, prone to frenzy and other inappropriate behavior.[1] Through much of his work the *Cloud* author was profoundly concerned with what he saw as perversions of the spiritual life, and he identified various types of person as led by deceptive spirits into practices harmful to their souls. Absorbed as he was in such matters, he might not have been surprised at a phenomenon likely to perplex the modern reader: the fusion of devotion, contemplation and the occult in two Continental writings from generations shortly before the *Cloud* author's own; the *Liber iuratus* ascribed to one Honorius of Thebes and the *Liber visionum* composed by a monk of Morigny named John. Both of these texts involve the use of contemplative and apparently magical means to gain visions, whether of God or of the Virgin Mary, and in both cases there is disarming combination of holy with unholy purposes.

This article will discuss these two works in their cultural setting, but will first set the stage by examining some of the more ordinary ways magic mingled with religion in European Christendom. The central contention will be that what distinguishes these texts from other forms of occultism in late medieval Christendom is that they draw upon Jewish precedent, not so much for particular techniques but rather for fundamental conceptions of spiritual process – conceptions ultimately alien to the culture of European Christendom.

MAGIC AND DEVOTION JUXTAPOSED AND FUSED

Ritual magic commonly resembles mystical practice in its asceticism, as when texts insist that the magician remain chaste three days before operating, must have his hair and beard cut, and must be dressed in white, or that one who prepares magical objects must be chaste for nine days, must be bathed, and must wear clean clothes.[2] One may read the requirement of ritual purity as merely an operative procedure, a set of external acts needed for the efficacy of the ritual but not implying any transformation of the practitioner. While admitting this as a possible reading, I incline to take more seriously the occasional suggestion that the magicians' asceticism did transform them, by giving them more intense energy – a higher spiritual voltage, as it were. The magician was transformed, not morally, yet personally and in a sense spiritually.[3]

More relevant to this study is the magicians' use of devotional practices, often of a highly elaborate nature. Devotionalism was increasingly important in late medieval Europe, and the pious exercises encouraged by prayerbooks and devotional artifacts became increasingly complex, sophisticated and imaginative in the fourteenth and fifteenth centuries.[4] Devotionalism is not the same as contemplation; indeed, contemplative works commonly urged their readers to set aside the outward devotions they had cultivated and turn instead to the pure and simple discipline of contemplative prayer.[5] Yet devotional reading and prayer was commonly a prelude to contemplation: the *Cloud* author, like others, recommended the standard triad of reading, prayer and meditation as a preparation for the higher prayer of contemplation.[6] If the *Liber iuratus* and the *Liber visionum* are exceptional in their attempt to fuse occultism with contemplation, combination of devotionalism with magic is far more common, perhaps routine.

The ways in which devotional piety could intersect with magic may be illustrated by a compendium of recipes on ff. 186r–187v of Bodleian Library MS e Mus. 219, a manuscript of the later thirteenth century or perhaps the early fourteenth. These formulas serve various ends, some practical and constructive, others frivolous, yet others antisocial: discovering a thief or recovering a lost object, silencing enemies, making a dead fish leap out of a pan, causing those who enter a house to dance, making men appear headless, causing women to leap from their bath water, arousing a woman's lust, and so forth. The techniques recommended are largely traditional. A thief may be found out by driving a nail into an eye drawn on a wall (the manuscript shows the pertinent drawing, rubricated), which will cause the culprit to cry out in pain.[7] Magical characters are given for silencing enemies and other purposes. Discord is overcome by sympathetic magic, while use of a hoopoe's heart or kite's tongue gives understanding of the language of the birds.[8] At one point the text uses a crude cipher.[9]

While the compilation as a whole is not markedly pious, four of the recipes are of particular interest for their recommendation of devout words and deeds. The first of these procedures, identified as a tried and proven exorcism taught by a demoniac, involves writing sacred words from the beginning of John's gospel on a piece of parchment, then scraping the letters into a bowl and administering the scrapings to the energumen with holy water. The ascription of this recipe (called a *carmen*, or charm) to a demoniac probably means that an exorcist conjured the demon possessing a person to reveal how he could be expelled, and thus the demon, speaking through a human being's mouth, was coerced to aid in its own exorcism. This theme could be seen as related to that of the demon preacher constrained to speak against his own interests.[10] The second procedure is meant for perceiving clearly the enchantments of a trickster (*ioculator*): one must go into a garden on the night before the feast of St John the Baptist, before daybreak, saying the Lord's Prayer, extract a leek from the ground, and place some of the leek in one's mouth whenever the enchantments are performed. The blending of magic and devotionalism in these two prescriptions is no different in principle from what we find in many other sources, including the Greek magical papyri and the Anglo-Saxon charms. Both the means and the ends are holy, or at least not obviously transgressive. The use of sacred words scraped into a drink *need* not be thought of as magic; it *could* be construed as a kind of sacramental. If ecclesiastical scrutiny took exception to either procedure it would have to be chiefly because the means were not officially regulated or were not clearly adequate to the intended ends. In either case, the recipes might be defined as superstitious, in the sense that they involve pious usage, but deployed in an improper way.[11]

The third recipe is actually a set of procedures for various purposes: if a person has lost something, he should recall the Cross of the Lord, which was found, and should give bread to four paupers; one who has been smitten should recall the blows suffered by the Lord, and he will not be hurt or afflicted; one taken captive should remember the Lord's captivity, and he will be released quickly (*not* like Christ!) Finally, the collection gives a set of pious acts to be performed before undertaking a duel: one should fast, pray, give as much in alms as possible, have three masses sung (those for the finding of the Holy Cross, the exaltation of the Holy Cross, and the Ascension, each time with a specified gospel), and wash the hands and feet of three, five, seven, or thirteen paupers. These experiments appear to involve nothing more than highly specific forms of petitionary prayer, tied to very particular expectations. The very specificity of both means and ends, and of the adaptation of means to ends, might be seen again as superstitious. But it would be difficult to define clearly how these procedures differ from many others that were widely tolerated and sometimes encouraged by ecclesiastical authorities, such as ringing church bells as protection against storms, gazing at a painting of Saint Christopher for its protective efficacy, or even saying a set of specific prayers to gain an indulgence.

Perhaps the most important point about these four prescriptions, however, is the company they keep in the manuscript. Why does the compiler include these along with procedures for sympathetic magic, recommendations for the use of magical characters, and recipes for using the occult virtues of hoopoe hearts? It is *prima facie* reasonable to suppose that a person who includes these procedures along with all the others on ff. 186r–187v of the manuscript thinks of them in similar terms – which is to say, as manifestations of occult or magical power. Even the performance of pious deeds can be recognized as magical if seen as releasing some occult force other than a strictly divine or moral virtue. The relevant question for the historian is not whether this or that practice was magical in some neutral sense, but whether it would or could have been so perceived by contemporaries, and a critical medieval reader would *understandably* have seen even the more pious formulas as tainted, in large part by guilt through association. Terms such as 'heretical' and 'magical' were often used broadly; indeed, it is a common characteristic of pejorative terms that they lend themselves to loose employment. (One might go further and say that pejorative *thinking* as well tends to paint with a very broad brush; it comes as no surprise to find the Jacobus who compiled the canonical collection *Omne bonum* speaking of constellations and astrology but moving quickly to other forms of divination and superstition, including charms said over herbs.)[12] More importantly, in medieval usage to refer to an act as magical was to identify the power by which it was thought to operate, and even an ostensibly pious deed or prayer could be conceived as activating an occult power. When such deeds and formulas occurred mingled together in a manuscript along with magical (and thus, for many, by definition evil) prescriptions, it would be reasonable to suppose they were in fact so conceived.

We can only speculate about how a critical medieval reader might have read the materials in this Bodleian manuscript – an exercise useful insofar as it helps to see some of the problems such a reader would face in categorizing and reacting to such materials. Yet we have other texts for which speculation is less necessary: texts that contemporaries did in fact find problematic, and ones identified even by their authors as magical. The remainder of this article will focus on the two texts mentioned above as extreme examples of magic fused with piety.

THE *LIBER IURATUS* ASCRIBED TO HONORIUS OF THEBES

The *Liber iuratus (Sworn Book)* or *Liber sacer (Sacred Book)* is attributed to one Honorius, son of Euclid, of Thebes. The earliest manuscripts are of the fourteenth century. The work's pretense is that a convention of magicians met at Naples after their art had been condemned by the pope and his cardinals, and the 811 masters there assembled commissioned Honorius to distill the essence of magic and set it forth in this consummately secret manual. All of this I take to be fiction. We know that Pope John XXII was obsessed with the workings of magicians and that cardinals such as William of Santa Sabina labored with him in the suppression of magic; as early as 1317 cardinals, along with Pope John, were the targets of supposed and perhaps real magical assaults.[13] This seems to me (as it did to Norman Cohn) the most likely setting for the composition of the

Liber iuratus in its present form, or at least for the account of its composition in the prologue. Robert Mathiesen (along with Lynn Thorndike and Edward Peters) dates the work to the first half of the thirteenth century, largely because William of Auvergne refers to an 'accursed and execrable' work known as the *Liber sacratus (Consecrated Book)*. Mathiesen takes this to have been the same as the *Liber iuratus*, and tentatively identifies the pope in question as Gregory IX.[14] This earlier dating is possible, but I find the later one more plausible on three grounds: first, there are many books of magic that might have been characterized as sacred, sworn or consecrated, and the use of a similar title for a thirteenth-century work is at best very weak evidence for its identification with a work first found in fourteenth-century manuscripts; second, while Gregory IX was chiefly concerned with the eradication of heresies, and appointed inquisitors to try them, these inquisitors were not authorized until later to proceed also against magicians, and it is only with John XXII and his successors that we find pope and cardinals joined in sustained action against magicians;[15] third, as I will suggest later, there are elements in the work that probably derive from Jewish sources accessible only in the later thirteenth century.

The *Liber iuratus* contains a variety of material, but of greatest interest to the author and of greatest relevance to this article is its set of detailed instructions for gaining a vision of God. One begins with several days of purification, including a fast on bread and water, with prayers and masses. If the visionary detects any sin in himself he must purge it, presumably in confession, then receive communion, and recite a prayer beseeching Christ to purge his body, 'so that being cleansed I may see thee with thy nine order of angels while yet I live'. This concluding petition is repeated in a versicle to be recited, along with other prayers, as the preparation continues in a secret place. The visionary eventually makes a couch or mattress of blessed or 'exorcized' hay, places this mattress in the middle of a clean chamber, surrounds it with ashes, and in the ashes writes a hundred specified names of God. He then washes himself in clear spring water, while reciting a prayer for purification of all his sins. He dons a hair tunic or hairshirt, and over it wears black garments.

When evening comes, he sits on the mattress and recites vespers, followed by a long prayer. This begins with a series of unaccustomed words or names. It then addresses God almighty, 'whose angels and archangels do fear, worship, and praise'; Orha, also known as Gabriel; Christ; Hospek, who made Joseph's rod burst into flower; Gofgar, who sent testimony to Israel through John the Baptist; Occynnomos, who sent a star to guide the three kings; Elyorem, who was presented in the Temple and revealed himself to Simeon as God; Theloy, who turned water into wine at Cana; Archima, who preached the Catholic faith for thirty-two years; Rabuch, who fasted in the desert and was tempted. The prayer leads to its climax, asking the Lord to deliver the visionary's soul from the darkness of his body, 'that I may see thee with thy nine orders of angels while yet

I live, and that my soul may look upon thee and praise thee and glorify thee'. The prayer concludes with a series of arcane names and a recollection of Christ's words *Consummatum est*. The visionary then goes to sleep, and will behold the celestial palace, the majesty and glory of God, the nine orders of angels, and all the company of the blessed.

The purpose is now completed, but the text adds a series of warnings: one who works in this 'magical art' must not be in any mortal sin, which will impede the vision of God; one must be pure, for God cannot be constrained, but must be prayed to and entreated; even given this state of purity, the vision of God is difficult to attain, for it is beyond natural reason. Thus ends Book One of Honorius' compilation. Books Two and Three proceed to list and describe a vast array of spirits, planetary, aerial, and terrestrial, which may be summoned through appropriate use of magic circles, conjurations, and suffumigations that may require mandrake root mixed with the brain of a black cat and the blood of a bat (along with much else), all for the sake of gaining secret knowledge, avenging injuries, securing favor, inciting love and lust, and accomplishing myriad further goals, none of them so noble as the vision of God.

The basic inspiration for this book seems ultimately derivative from medieval Jewish mysticism in the Merkabah tradition rather than from Christian traditions of either mysticism or magic.[16] Christian theology promised the *visio Dei* as a reward for the blessed after death, and the Christian contemplative tradition of the early Middle Ages did speculate on how it was possible to see God during life here below,[17] but when Christian writers spoke of beholding God in visions they typically had ineffable perception in mind rather than visual representation, and before the mid-fourteenth century it was rare for artists to depict God the Father except in the form of Christ, who as God incarnate served as the sole icon of divinity.[18] And while magical invocation or even conjuration of angels was certainly known in Christian culture, it was less common than either ecclesiastically approved prayer to the specifically Biblical angels or conjuration of demons and neutral spirits.[19] The invocation of non-Biblical angels was vigorously repudiated in the early medieval West.[20] Jewish mystical tradition was far more daring. Early Merkabah mysticism led to visions in which the mystic ascended to the divine throne or Chariot and came back to describe the majesty of God and his celestial court, with its ranks of angels. This kind of vision, rather than any Christian antecedent, seems implied in the *Liber iuratus*. The use of the divine name, not simply as one of many sources of magical power, but in its embellished form and as a primary means for magic, is clearly derived from Kabbalah; at least in one version the *Liber iuratus* straightforwardly identifies the elaborated name of God as the Shemhamphoras, which is to say *Shem ham-M'forash*, a Hebraicized Aramaic term usually rendered as the 'Ineffable Name'. In Book One of Honorius' book, *before* the instructions for a vision of God, the magician is told to construct the 'seal of God' on a sheet of virgin parchment or vellum. This seal consists of an intricate design with a pentagram at its core, and with arcane names inscribed, and with the 'Sehemhamphoras', the great divine name in seventy-two letters, in a surrounding circle. It is not clear whether or how this seal is to be used in attaining the dream-vision; Honorius does say that if the magician wishes to use it for invoking spirits he should use ink made with equal parts of mole, turtle, hoopoe and bat blood. Not all these details need to have come from Judaism, but the conception of the divine name as integral to a great 'seal' does seem to imply Jewish influence. Furthermore, the expectation that the vision of God should come in a dream is plausibly derived from Jewish sources. The long-standing Jewish interest in dream revelations is only indirectly relevant and not specific to Judaism. More to the point, in medieval adaptations of Kabbalah not only spontaneous but cultivated dream-visions were known; the mystic would ask a 'dream question', a *she'elat halom*, anticipating a revelation in his sleep that might be a theophany or might address some practical problem.[21] Jewish texts are also the most likely source for the insistence on moral (and not merely ritual) purity; this requirement may not be exclusively Jewish but it is most characteristic of the magic used within Judaism, in which ritual and moral purity are to an exceptional degree associated and even fused. Thus, in the Greek magical papyri it is an exorcism constructed of allusions to the Hebrew Bible that concludes with the injunction, 'Keep yourself pure, for this charm is Hebraic and is preserved among pure men'.[22] The text's use of 'prayers', with intricate variation of closely similar words, is probably a reflection of the Kabbalistic practice of Abraham Abulafia.[23] The author's insistence that the book should be buried if the owner cannot find a suitable successor may reflect the Jewish custom of burying worn out books containing the name of God.[24]

Clearly aware of his own indebtedness, Honorius nonetheless explicitly distances himself from his Jewish sources by telling us that they cannot effectively use the very techniques he has borrowed from them: because of their infidelity Jewish magicians cannot attain the true vision of God, and even if they conjure demons by the power of the divine names, the spirits will not answer their questions truthfully because they do not sign themselves with the sign of the Cross; only Christians can attain the vision of God and succeed in other magical works. Confident as he is of his superiority, however, Honorius seems to have plundered the gold (or perhaps the dross) of the Hebrews. The *Liber iuratus* is thus an interesting and important witness to the kind of use Christian magicians might make of Jewish materials in the era before the rise of fully fledged Christian Kabbalah. Frances Yates traces the history of Christian Kabbalah to Ramon Lull, who claimed a vision on Mount Randa in 1274, roughly the time the *Zohar* was written, also in Spain; as Yates points out, Lull shares with this Kabbalist classic a reliance on combinations of letters and speculations about the divine Names or Dignities. But the next stage in Yates' itinerary is the work of Pico della Mirandola in the late fifteenth century.[25] The work of Honorius helps fill the gap, and testifies to a different kind of borrowing from Jewish occultism, relying on elements from it different from those of concern to Lull, but sharing with him (and not with Pico) a refusal to acknowledge the dignity or superiority of Jewish magic.

THE *LIBER VISIONUM* BY JOHN, MONK OF MORIGNY

The next text I wish to examine is the *Liber visionum*, which in 1323 a monk of Morigny named John was found to have written; the chronicle of St Denis described it as a book of devotions inspired by curiosity and pride, although the monk claimed to have been inspired rather by visions of the Virgin Mary. The monk's book contained many pictures of the Virgin, and prescribed 'invocations' (presumably of the Virgin); it was to be copied specifically for the user, and the user's name was to be inscribed in it twice. Beyond this the chronicler gives very little information about what this monk's book actually contained, and it is not clear that he knew at first hand exactly what its contents were. Instead, the chronicler tells us that with his devotions John was attempting to revive the 'heresy and sorcery' known as the Ars Notoria. The chronicler gives a capsule description of this Ars Notoria, which he characterizes more fully and clearly than he does the monk's volume: the art, he says, involves the use of special figures, contemplation of these figures amid prayer and fasting, and invocation of mysterious and presumably demonic names, all for the sake of knowledge, wealth, honor or pleasure.

This was by no means an isolated case of Marian visions linked with elaborate cycles of devotional practice. James of Porta, a Franciscan friar from the province of Strasbourg, presents an interestingly comparable but little known case. According to the biographer, his mother offered him 'to God and to Saint Francis' in the year 1301, went before an image of the Virgin during his first year in the order and, weeping, asked for the grace of perseverence in his new life.[26] When he lay down in bed, he had what seems to have been a dream vision of the Virgin coming to him and placing a finger in his mouth; he clenched it firmly with his teeth, and she pulled him up to a sitting position, filling him with great sweetness. Afterward he was inspired to devise a system of Ave Marias, Salve Reginas, and other prayers, to be said in fixed numbers, typically in the thousands, along with the special prayer, 'Obtain for me and all true penitents who beseech you that you may stand before the Son and show him your breasts [*pectus et ubera*], and the Son may show the Father his side and his wounds, and may there be no refusal where there are so many signs of love. Obtain for us (or for me) indulgence of all sins.' This plea for intercession was to obtain an indulgence analogous to that granted for pilgrimage to the Porziuncula for those who could not make the journey. James prayed that this favor be confirmed by a series of miracles. The first miracle was his own ability to go seventy-two hours without eating or drinking, while nonetheless continuing to perform all his normal actions with full strength. The second and third were healings, one of a girl expected to die of an illness, the other of a Franciscan nun who had been blind and dumb. Lest the miraculous nature of these happenings be doubted, James also experienced the healing of a finger that he injured while carving a plaque showing the scene of the Virgin before her Son and the Son before the Father. On another occasion James commissioned a painter to depict this scene; the painter set out to ignore James's specifications, but found himself nonetheless following them exactly. James's biography is not a conventional *vita* but is devoted to a cluster of themes related to his Marian devotion, in particular his motif of the double intercession by Virgin and Christ, a theme which later was to attain some significance in Western art;[27] his visions; his hairshirt and other mortifications, his use of penitential crosses, analogous to those of Henry Suso.[28]

Beyond the association of Marian visions with Marian devotions, how does the piety of James of Porta compare with that of John of Morigny? In both cases we find not simply fervent devotion to the Virgin but a systematic and perhaps even obsessive manifestation of that fervor. In each case the petitions were to be accompanied by specifically relevant artwork which the devotee produced or commissioned. And both of these religious had highly specific ideas of what they expected from the Virgin in return for their devotion; indeed, the level of specificity both in their exercises and in their expectations makes it clear that the devotees were seeking not an intense mystical relationship or the free bestowal of favor but a *quid pro quo*. Yet James attained an honorable position in the annals of his order, while John's work was condemned and burned as one of heresy and sorcery.

We are in a better position to discuss the *Liber visionum* since Nicholas Watson and Claire Fanger have discovered more than one version of it: Watson analyzes at some length a version now in Munich (Clm 276), which he takes to be close to John's original composition, although it was copied in the late fifteenth century, and a version of 1461, now at McMaster University (McMaster University Library, Unnumbered MS), which he characterizes as a later reworking of the text for the use of a person named Bernard. Among the further manuscript copies now known, one at Graz, dated 1414, contains a prologue that is of special interest for its account of how John came to write his work.

Let us look carefully at certain key passages from the McMaster text, which may be a reworking, but is nonetheless of special value because it makes clear and explicit the principles for use that are less fully spelled out in the Munich manuscript: it is, in essence, a practical adaptation of the work. The opening sections proceed auspiciously enough, with elaborate prayers to the Virgin and to God, with readings from the Psalms and other books of the Bible, hymns, and other elements taken from a less unusual office. In the opening folios as elsewhere the devotee adopts a posture of insistently humble supplication:

Hear me, Bernard, a sinner, thy slave and servant, crying unceasingly to thee, and praying with thy most holy and glorious names here uttered by me, a wretched sinner, with my unworthy mouth.

In part I, section 5, the devotee prays for command of each of nine arts. He enlists the aid of the angels for knowledge of grammar, the archangels for logic, the thrones for rhetoric, the powers for arithmetic, the virtues for music, the dominations for geometry, the principalities for astronomy or astrology, the cherubim for metaphysics, and the seraphim for theology. The prayers for a grasp of music (ff. 52v–53r) read in part:

O holy and glorious spirits, O Virtues [*virtutum*], by whom all miracles occur before God and humans, whose names are these: Virtues of salvation, Virtues of medicine, Virtues of health, Virtues of grace, Virtues of virtues, Virtues of signs, Virtues of miracles, Virtues of manifestation [*ostentationis*], Virtues of testing [*probationis*], Virtues of subtlety, Virtues of disposition, Virtues of dispensation, Virtues of life, Virtues of curing, Virtues of clemency, Virtues of goodness [*pietatis*], you who stand in the sight of God in the empirean heaven, I, Bernard, ask and beseech you that you may entrust the power naturally bestowed on you to the angels and archangels, that they may teach me every art, and may you impart [*precipiatis*] the science of music and its divisions. Amen.

The McMaster manuscript, unlike the Munich version, inserts rubrics instructing Bernard to stand at the beginning of this prayer, and to beat his chest at the mention of his own name. Following this passage are prayers (f. 53v) for command of geometry, addressed in part to God himself, again interspersed in the McMaster manuscript with rubrics guiding the user's gestures:

I pray and beseech that I may progress straightway in the art of geometry, and may a ray of thy Holy Spirit [of fear, *timoris*] descend into my heart and into my soul from thy most glorious heavenly habitation, that he may bestow, minister, provide, and concede, now and forever, ease, fluency, [and] eloquence, for the knowing and understanding and measuring of all geometry – altimetry, palmimetry, confinitactry, and all other divisions – so that I may be able to grasp, learn, and teach it, and to construct its figures, and to know [its] divisions, and to measure all things proportionately. And grant to me, thy servant Bernard, that I may be quick in learning, discriminating in the use of reason, [and] firm in remembering, so that whatever I hear, see, or read I may commend permanently to memory, by that ineffable miracle which you accomplished when on the sixth day you formed every creeping thing on Earth and all animals according to their kind, and created humans according to your likeness.

When this cycle and certain related prayers are complete, the book proceeds to further exercises involving visions. The devotee prays to the Virgin Mary for a vision, and following this revelation, presumably in accordance with its instructions, he consecrates a ring and a book, presumably this very book. The ring, carved with an image and with the names of Jesus and Mary, is used not only for gaining visions but for acquiring skill in argument and exposition, and perhaps for other purposes as well. At one point the practitioner stands in a chapel or oratory with burning incense in a thurible; he must stand before an image of the Madonna, and should place the ring and book on the altar. As the incense arises he prays, 'May my prayer rise to the Lord like incense in thy sight'. Among the prayers that come next is the following, in which are inserted instructions for bowing and breast-beating:

> O Lord Jesus Christ, creator of all creatures, visible and invisible, I thy servant, Bernard, [thy] humble servant, pray, implore, and beseech and invoke you today and now, that as on Mount Sinai you wrote the law on stone tablets with your own hand and finger, and sanctified it, and having done so gave it to Moses for the salvation of the Israelite people, so too you may deign to ✠ cleanse, ✠ bless, ✠ sanctify, ✠ and confirm this book unto the salvation of all those who enjoy it, and all things that are written in it, especially for the salvation of me, Bernard, thy unworthy servant and humble servant, by thy goodness, sweetness, graciousness, [and] mercy [*misericordie*?], by thine own hand, and that of the blessed Virgin Mary thy mother, and of thy holy angels, and of the entire heavenly court, so that all things written in it may obtain the force and power that we desire, that is, for the knowing and learning of all letters and arts and sciences and virtues.

Even more interesting for our purposes is the section that follows immediately:

> May it disclose [*pandat*], banish, and release all enchantments [*incantamenta*] of whatsoever kind, art, and virtue. . . . And may the malign forces withdraw at once, nor may they remain any further. . . . May it [this book] remove the magical and illusory arts. And may it release those whom malign spirits ✠ have conquered [and] ensnared by [their] magical arts. And may it put all evils to flight. . . .

Four conclusions emerge even from this glimpse at a few passages from a long and complex text. First, substantial portions of the manuscript, including the invocation of angels and the plea for the Virgin's aid, are essentially orthodox in *content*. The angels addressed are squarely planted in the nine orthodox choirs. There is no suggestion of intent to conjure demons in any way. When the devotee prays that the consecrated book may banish incantations and related works of the

Devil, there is no contradiction. But second, and perhaps more importantly, crucial passages in the book are absolutely and unmistakably magical in their *form*: when John prescribes the use of a ring, the consecration of the ring and the book, and the linkage of the book with the ring, both to be kept secret, he is using the ritual and symbolic language of magic rather than that of orthodox devotion. The very idea of consecrating the book is more likely to have been derived from precedent in the traditions of magic than from consecration of liturgical manuals. The *Liber sacratus* referred to by William of Auvergne was not the only consecrated book of magic, and indeed a text called the *Liber consecrationum* was expressly intended to render the experiments in a magical book efficacious.[29] And third, the *purposes* his devotions served were those more often pursued by magic than by prayer.

The idea of conjuring spirits to gain knowledge of the various arts is articulated here in a Christian framework, but what might be the source for the notion itself? There is at least one close parallel in the explicitly demonic magic of the late Middle Ages: a necromantic manual from fifteenth-century Germany had prescribed an experiment designed to summon a demonic tutor who could bestow knowledge of the liberal arts.[30] The Solomonic Ars Notoria which the *Liber visionum* purports to replace, uses prayers and invocation of angels to gain mastery of the liberal and mechanical arts.[31] The legends of Christian necromancers also assume that their traffic with demons is the best explanation for their scholarship: a tradition dating to the late eleventh century claims that Gerbert of Aurillac, who became Pope Sylvester II, gained his prodigious learning and influence dishonestly, through magical means. Dietrich of Niem, reflecting on this report in the late fourteenth century, saw it as a product of the Romans' animosity toward the overly learned outsider elevated to the papal throne.[32] But the ultimate source for all these Christianized versions of magic to gain knowledge is almost certainly Jewish magic used for the same purpose. Early Kabbalistic texts suggest that angels attempted to thwart the transmission of Torah to the human race, and that it was because of angels' opposition that students had difficulty committing it to memory. Adjuration of spirits, especially the 'Prince of the Torah' (*sar ha-torah*), was thus required to master the Torah.[33] Although the *ars notoria* did not call upon demonic aid, and the *Liber visionum* revolved around the recitation of devotions to the Virgin and to unfallen angels, their techniques were untraditional and superstitious, and an unsympathetic observer might pardonably have categorized these texts alongside the first experiment in the necromantic manual mentioned above.

CONCLUSION

We find, then, that both of the texts under examination are indebted to Jewish precedent – but it is different precedent in the two cases, and they are differently indebted. The *Liber iuratus* more directly and more uncontestably echoes the central themes of Kabbalah, and its author feels obliged to grapple with this indebtedness and argue the superiority of Christian over Jewish occultism. The *Liber visionum* draws more indirectly and in all likelihood unwittingly on Jewish precedent, but is nonetheless heir to a tradition more at home in Jewish than in Christian circles.

The close connection between mysticism and magic is a well-known feature of Kabbalah. Gershom Scholem speaks recurrently of the magical dimension of Jewish mysticism. The intense concentration or 'intention' (*Kawwanah*) cultivated in Lurianic mystical prayer, he says, lends itself to magical employment, even if few Kabbalists have succumbed to this temptation.[34] Sholom Ansky's play *The Dybbuk* brings the relationship between the mysticism of 'theoretical Kabbalah' and the magic of 'practical Kabbalah' into clear focus, with its portrayal of a wizened rebbe who recognizes the danger of falling from spiritual heights to spiritual depths, and a young student who rushes in where rebbes fear to tread.[35] The play is a modern text, but the tension central to it has deep roots in Jewish tradition. In the magic of Christendom, however, at least before the rise of explicit Christian Kabbalah in the fifteenth century, one finds little intermingling of this sort. Meister Eckhart and his critics, the author of *The Cloud of Unknowing*, Teresa of Ávila – all these figures recognized mystical contemplation as having potential for self-deception or false doctrine, and some feared that visions and locutions could be demonic, but the idea of a fundamental continuity between mysticism and magic, integral as it is to Kabbalah, appears foreign to Christian culture. Far more common within Christianity is a semi-Quietist insistence that contemplation and mystical withdrawal will remove a person from mundane concerns and lead to *apatheia* regarding worldly affairs. The radical extreme to which Christian mystics inclined was not that of using mystical powers for magical or otherwise practical ends, but the opposite one of encouraging the annihilation of personal will, and thus a state of will-lessness regarding all ends.[36] Furthermore, mainstream Christianity made rich provision for orthodox use of intermediaries – more than mainstream, normative Judaism – and it made ample provision also for contemplative prayer within monasteries. The religious functions performed by the Kabbalah were thus not relegated to the periphery quite so much in Christianity as in Judaism, which may have been one reason they combined less often with magical elements.

One way in which the *Liber iuratus* and the *Liber visionum* hold special interest, then, is that they combine the mystical and the magical in ways more typical of Judaism than of Christianity, under direct or indirect Kabbalistic influence. They provide some of the missing links in the early history of Christian appropriation of Jewish magic. The history of early Christian Kabbalah still needs to be written; these writings will occupy a significant place in that story. Honorius of Thebes and John of Morigny in their rather different ways imbibed a mentality that would more readily be perceived as coherent within Jewish culture. This is not to say that the book of either writer was condemned specifically on these grounds; neither book was criticized, so far as we know, because it was Jewish or Judaizing. Rather, the *Liber visionum* was presumably repudiated for reasons that Claire Fanger has articulated in her analysis.[37] The affinities with Kabbalah help us to see why, approved or disapproved, the *Liber iuratus* and the *Liber visionum* were so anomalous, taken as specimens either of Christian mysticism or of Christian magic.

Notes

1 *The Cloud of Unknowing*, chs 18 (þe deuels seruauntes & his contemplatyues) and 45 (þe deuil haþ his contemplatyues, as God haþ his), in *The Cloud of Unknowing and Related Treatises*, ed. Phyllis Hodgson (Salzburg: Institut für Anglistik und Amerikanistik, 1982), pp. 27, 48. I am indebted to Barbara Newman, Claire Fanger and Jeffrey Hamburger for the help they provided for this article.

2 See, for example, Richard Kieckhefer, *Forbidden Rites: A Necromancer's Manual of the Fifteenth Century* (Stroud: Sutton Publishing, 1997), p. 59, 105f. For a fascinating study in religiomagical asceticism see A.G. van Hamel, 'Oðinn hanging on the tree', *Acta Philologica Scandinavica*, 7 (1932–3), pp. 260–88.

3 See my article, 'The holy and the unholy: sainthood, witchcraft, and magic in late medieval Europe', *Journal of Medieval and Renaissance Studies*, 24 (1994), pp. 355–85, reprinted in Scott L. Waugh and Peter D. Diehl, eds, *Christendom and Its Discontents: Exclusion, Persecution, and Rebellion, 1000–1500* (Cambridge: Cambridge University Press, 1996), pp. 310–37.

4 On this theme see my article, 'Major currents in late medieval devotion' in Jill Raitt, ed., *Christian Spirituality*, 2 (New York: Crossroad, 1987), pp. 75–108, and, more recently, Henk van Os, with Eugène Honée, Hans Nieuwdorp and Bernhard Ridderbos, *The Art of Devotion in the Late Middle Ages in Europe, 1300–1500*, trans. Michael Hoyle (Princeton, NJ: Princeton University Press, 1994).

5 *The Cloud of Unknowing*, chs 6–8 (Hodgson, ed., pp. 14–18); Meister Eckhart, German sermon 5b and *Die rede der underscheidunge*, ch. 3, in Meister Eckhart, *Werke*, ed. Niklaus Largier (Frankfurt am Main: Deutscher Klassiker Verlag, 1993), vol. 1, pp. 66–75, and vol. 2, pp. 338–41.

6 *Cloud of Unknowing*, ch. 35 (ed. Hodgson, pp. 39f., with commentary p. 166).

7 See *Papyrus graecus magicus* V.70–90, in Hans Dieter Betz, ed., *The Greek Magical Papyri in Translation, Including the Demotic Spells*, 1 (Chicago: University of Chicago Press, 1986), p. 102.

8 A friend of the quarreling parties cooks two lizards in a pot, pulverizing them, and sews the powder into the clothes of the enemies, causing them to become friends. Knowledge of the language of birds is gained by marinating the heart of a hoopoe or the tongue of a kite in honey, then placing it under one's own tongue.

9 Ff. 186r–186v: *ad graciam cznc&orum [cunctorum] h&m&um [hominum]*. . .

10 On this theme see Barbara Newman, 'Possessed by the spirit: devout women, demoniacs, and the apostolic life in the thirteenth century', forthcoming in *Speculum*, July 1998. An alternative possibility is that the formula was given by a *former* demoniac, testifying to the means that had proven effective for his cure; I take this as a less likely reading.

11 On the concept of superstition see Dieter Harmening, *Superstitio: Überlieferungs-und theoriegeschichtliche Untersuchungen zur kirchlich-theologischen Aberglaubensliteratur des Mittelalters* (Berlin: E. Schmidt, 1979).

12 British Library MS Royal 6.E.VI, ff. 396v–97v; see Richard Kieckhefer, *Magic in the Middle Ages* (Cambridge: Cambridge University Press, 1989), p. 181.

13 Joseph Hansen, ed., *Quellen und Untersuchungen zur Geschichte des Hexenwahns und der Hexenverfolgung im Mittelalter* (Bonn: Georgi, 1901; repr. Hildesheim: Olms, 1963), gives the key documents for John XXII (pp. 2–8) and Benedict XII (pp. 8–15); Benedict's involvement in these matters was scarcely less than John's, although it is perhaps less well known.

14 Mathiesen gives the appropriate citations to Cohn, Thorndike and Peters.

15 See the articles in Peter Segl, ed., *Die Anfänge der Inquisition im Mittelalter, mit einem Ausblick auf das 20. Jahrhundert und einem Beitrag über religiöse Intoleranz im nichtchristlichen Bereich* (Cologne: Böhlau, 1993), for inquisitorial activities in the thirteenth century. The most relevant papal document is that of Alexander IV, who in 1258 specifically directed inquisitors *not* to act in matters of divination and sorcery, which he saw as diversions from their proper role as heresy-hunters; see Hansen, *Quellen und Untersuchungen*, 1.

16 The classic work on Kabbalah is Gershom G. Scholem, *Major Trends in Jewish Mysticism* (New York: Schocken, 1946), but see more recently Moshe Idel, *Kabbalah: New Prespectives* (New Haven: Yale University Press, 1988).

17 See Cuthbert Butler, *Western Mysticism: The Teaching of SS Augustine, Gregory, and Bernard on Contemplation and the Contemplative Life: Neglected Chapters in the History of Religion* (London: Constable, 1922), pp. 77–88 ('The vision of God').

18 W. Braunfels, 'Gott, Gottvater' in Engelbert Kirschbaum, ed., *Lexikon der christlichen Ikonographie*, 2 (Freiburg: Herder, 1970), cols 165–70.

19 For one example of conjuring angels see *The Commonplace Book of Robert Reynes of Acle: An Edition of Tanner MS 407*, ed. Cameron Louis (New York: Garland, 1980), p. 169f.

20 See especially Jeffrey B. Russell, 'Saint Boniface and the eccentrics', *Church History*, 33 (1964), pp. 235–47.

21 'Visions' in *Encyclopedia Judaica*, 16 (Jerusalem: Keter; New York: Macmillan, 1971), cols 166–70; Gershom Scholem, *Jewish Gnosticism, Merkabah Mysticism and Talmudic Tradition* (1960); E. Gottlieb, in *Fourth World Congress of Jewish Studies: Papers*, 2 (1968), pp. 327–34.

22 See Betz, *The Greek Magical Papyri*, p. 97. The insistence on moral purity is a leitmotif also in works such as the *Sepher-ha-Razim: The Book of Mysteries*, trans. Michael A. Morgan (Atlanta: Scholars Press, 1983), and 'The Sword of Moses', ed. Moses Gaster in *Journal of the Royal Asiatic Society*, 1896, 3–52, reprinted in Moses Gaster, *Studies and Texts in Folklore, Magic, Medieval Romance, Hebrew Apocrypha and Samaritan Archaeology*, 1 (1928; repr. New York: Ktav, 1971), 288–337.

23 On Abulafia see the works of Moshe Idel, *Studies in Ecstatic Kabbalah* (Albany: SUNY Press, 1988); *Language, Torah, and Hermeneutics in Abraham Abulafia*, trans. Menahem Kallus (Albany: SUNY Press, 1989); and *The Mystical Experience in Abraham Abulafia*, trans. Jonathan Chipman (Albany: SUNY Press, 1988).

24 See 'Genizah' in *Encyclopedia Judaica*, vol. 7, cols 404–7. The term 'genizah' refers to a room connected to a synagog where such materials are concealed or buried.

25 Frances A. Yates, *The Occult Philosophy in the Elizabethan Age* (London: Routledge, 1979), chs 1 ('Medieval Christian Cabala: the art of Ramon Lull') and 2 ('The occult philosophy in the Italian Renaissance: Pico della Mirandola').

26 ed. Collegium S. Bonaventurae, *Analecta Franciscana* 3 (1897), 617–39.

27 For the theme of the double intercession see D. Koepplin, 'Interzession Mariä und Christi vor Gottvater' in Engelbert Kirschbaum, ed., *Lexikon der christlichen Ikonographie*, 2 (Freiburg: Herder, 1970), cols 346–52, but without reference to James of Porta. See further figures 6.6 (Metropolitan Museum, New York, Cloisters, a painting of *c.* 1402) and 3.13 (Öffentliche Kunstsammlung in Basel, painting in the style of Konrad Witz, *c.* 1450), in Caroline Walker Bynum, *Fragmentation and Redemption: Essays on Gender and the Human Body in Medieval Religion* (New York: Zone, 1991). I have not been able to consult François Boespflug, 'La Double Intercession en procès: de quelques effets iconographique de la théologie de Luther' in Frank Muller, ed., *Art, religion, société dans l'espace germanique au XVIe siècle* (Strasbourg: Presses Universitaires de Strasbourg, 1997), pp. 31–53.

28 Henry Suso, *The Life of the Servant*, i.16, in *The Exemplar, with Two German Sermons*, trans. and ed. Frank Tobin (New York: Paulist, 1989), pp. 88–91.

29 See Richard Kieckhefer, *Forbidden Rites*, pp. 8–10.

30 Kieckhefer, *Forbidden Rites*, pp. 116–20.

31 Lynn Thorndike, *A History of Magic and Experimental Science*, vol. 2 (New York: Macmillan and Columbia University Press, 1929), pp. 281–3.

32 Johann J. Ign. von Döllinger, *Fables Respecting the Popes in the Middle Ages: A Contribution to Ecclesiastical History*, trans. Alfred Plummer (London: Rivingtons, 1871), pp. 265–70.

33 Michael D. Swartz, *Scholastic Magic: Ritual and Revelation in Early Jewish Mysticism* (Princeton, NJ: Princeton University Press, 1996). See also Kieckhefer, *Forbidden Rites*, p. 120, and the sources there cited.

34 Gershom G. Scholem, *Major Trends in Jewish Mysticism*, pp. 277f.; cf. 33, 77, 102f.

35 S. Ansky, *The Dybbuk: A Play in Four Acts*, trans. Henry G. Alsberg and Winifred Katzin (New York: Boni & Liveright, 1926).

36 Bernard McGinn has emphasized the centrality of this theme for the vernacular theology of the later Middle Ages in various of his writings; see the forthcoming third volume of his history of mysticism, *The Presence of God*.

37 Fanger, pp. 216–49.

SELECT BIBLIOGRAPHY

(Printed matter list includes works cited pertaining to the history of magic, codicology and manuscripts. Manuscript list includes extant manuscripts cited which contain magic texts.)

PRINTED MATTER

Agrippa, Heinrich Cornelius von Nettesheim. *Opera*, Lyons, Beringos Fratres, conjectural date 1620; micro-facsimile Landmarks of science, New York, Readex Microprint, 1974

——. *De occulta philosophia*, ed. V. Perrone Compagni, Studies in the History of Christian Thought, Leiden, Brill, 1992

——. *Three Books of Occult Philosophy* trans. James Freake, ed. Donald Tyson, St Paul, Llewellyn Publications, 1993

al-Kindi. *De Radiis*, ed. M.T. d'Alverny and F. Hudry, *Archives d'Histoire Doctrinale et Litéraire du Moyen Age* 41 (1974), 139–260

d'Alverny, Marie Thérèse. 'Récréations monastiques: les couteaux à manche d'ivoire' in *Recueil des travaux offert à M. Clovis Brunel*, vol. 1, Paris, Société de l'école de Chartres, 1955

——. 'Survivance de la magie Antique' in Paul Wilpert and W.P. Eckert (eds), *Antike und Orient im Mittelalter*, Berlin, De Gruyter, 1962, pp. 154–78

——. 'Translations and Translators' in Robert Benson and Giles Constable (eds), *Renaissance and Renewal in the Twelfth Century*, Medieval Academy Reprints for Teaching 26, Toronto/Buffalo/London, University of Toronto Press, 1991

Armstrong, C.A.J. 'An Italian Astrologer at the Court of Henry VII' in E.F. Jacob (ed.), *Italian Renaissance Studies, A Tribute to the Late Celia M. Ady*, London, Faber and Faber, 1960

Ars Notoria; The Notory Art of Solomon, Shewing the Cabalistical Key of Magical Operations, The Liberal Sciences, Divine Revelation, and the Art of Memory, written originally in Latin and now English'd by Robert Turner, London, Cottrel, 1657; rpt Seattle, Trident, 1987

Ayscough, Samuel. *A Catalogue of Manuscripts Preserved in the British Museum*, 2 vols, London, Rivington, 1782

Bandini, A.M. *Catalogus codicum latinorum Bibliothecae Mediceae Laurentianae*, 4 vols, Florence, s.n., 1774–8

Barb, A.A. 'Birds and Medieval Magic', *Journal of the Warburg and Courtauld Institutes* 13 (1950), 316–22

Bateson, Mary (ed.). *Catalogue of the Library of Syon Monastery*, Cambridge, Cambridge University Press, 1898

Bell, David N. *The Libraries of the Cistercians, Gilbertines and Premonstratensians*, London, British Library, 1992

Bernard, Edward. *Catalogi librorum manuscriptorum Angliæ et Hiberniæ*, Oxford, Sheldonian Theatre, 1697

Betz, Hans Dieter (ed.). *The Greek Magical Papyri in Translation, Including the Demotic Spells*, Chicago, University of Chicago Press, 1986

Bloom, William. *The Sacred Magician: A Ceremonial Diary*, Glastonbury, Gothic Image, 1992

Boehm, Fritz. 'Losbücher' in E. Hoffmann-Krayer and Hanns Bächtold-Stäubli (eds), *Handwörterbuch des deutschen Aberglaubens*, vol. 5, Berlin/Leipzig, Walter de Gruyter, 1932–3

Bolte, Johannes. 'Geschichte der Losbücher' in Johannes Bolte (ed.), *Georg Wickrams Werke*, vol. 4, Tübingen, Litterarischer Verein Stuttgart, 1903

The Book of the Sacred Magic of Abramelin the Mage, trans. S.L. MacGregor Mathers, London, Watkins, 1900

Boyle, Leonard E. *Medieval Latin Palaeography: A Bibliographical Introduction*, Toronto, University of Toronto Press, 1984

Braekman, W.L. 'Fortune Telling by the Casting of Dice. A Middle English Poem and Its Background', *Studia Neuphilologica* 52 (1980), 3–29

Britton, Derek. 'Manuscripts Associated with Kirby Bellars Priory', *Transactions of the Cambridge Bibliographical Society* 6 (1975), 267–81

de Bujand, J.M. *Index de Venise 1549, Venise et Milan 1554*, Index des Livres Interdits, vol. 3, Sherbrooke: Centre d'Études de la Renaissance, 1987

Burnett, Charles. 'Adelard, Egraphalau and the Science of the Stars' in C. Burnett (ed.), *Adelard of Bath: An English Scientist and Arabist of the Early Twelfth Century*, Warburg Institute Surveys and Texts 14, London, Warburg Institute, 1987, pp. 133–45

——. 'Arabic, Greek and Latin Works on Astrological Magic Attributed to Aristotle' in J. Kraye, W.F. Ryan and C.B. Schmitt (eds), *Pseudo-Aristotle in the Middle Ages* Warburg Institute Surveys and Texts 11, London, Warburg Institute, 1987, pp. 84–96

——. 'Talismans: magic as science? Necromancy among the Seven Liberal Arts' in *Magic and Divination in the Middle Ages*, Aldershott, Variorum, 1996, pp. 1–15

——. 'The Translating Activity in Medieval Spain' in S. K. Jayyusi (ed.), *The Legacy of Muslim Spain*, Leiden, E.J. Brill, 1992

Butler, E.M. *Ritual Magic*, Cambridge, Cambridge University Press, 1949

Carmody, Francis J. *Arabic Astronomical and Astrological Sciences in Latin Translation: A Critical Bibliography*, Berkeley, University of California Press, 1955

——. *The Astronomical Works of Thabit B. Qurra*, Berkeley, University of California Press, 1960

Chronique Latine de Guillaume de Nangis de 1113 à 1300 avec les Continuations de cette Chronique de 1300 à 1368, ed. H. Géraud, 2 vols, Paris, Jules Renouard, 1843

La Chronique de Morigny (1095–1152), ed. Léon Mirot, 2nd edn, Collection de textes pour servir à l'étude et à l'enseignement de l'histoire, Paris, Librairie Alphone Picard et fils, 1912

Cohn, Norman. *Europe's Inner Demons: An Enquiry Inspired by the Great Witch-Hunt*, New York, Basic Books, 1975

The Commonplace Book of Robert Reynes of Acle: An Edition of Tanner MS 407, ed. Cameron Louis, New York, Garland, 1980

Crossgrove, William C. 'The forms of Medieval Technical Literature: Some suggestions for Future Work', *Jarbuch für Internationale Germanistik* 3 (1971), 13–21

Davidson, Gustav. *A Dictionary of Angels, Including the Fallen Angels*, New York, Free Press, 1967

Delisle, Léopold. *Le cabinet des manuscrits de la Bibliothèque Impériale*, Paris, Imprimerie Impériale, 1868–81

Delmas, Bruno. 'Médailles Astrologiques et Talismaniques dans le Midi de la France, XIIIe–XVIe siècle' in Congrès national des sociétés savants, *Archeologie Occitane: Actes du 96e Congres National des Société des Savantes*, Paris, Ministère de l'éducation nationale, 1976, pp. 437–54

Deonna, W. 'Abra, Abraca, la croix talisman de Lausanne', *Genava* 22 (1944), 116–37

Dold, A. and R. Meister. 'Die Orakelsprüche im St. Galler Palimsestkodex 908 (die sogenannten 'Sortes Sangallenses')', *Österreichische Akademie der Wissenschaften Philosophisch-historische Klasse Sitzungsbericht* 225, Vienna, Verlag der Akademie der Wissenschaften, 1948, 1–115

Duffy, Eamon. *The Stripping of the Altars: Traditional Religion in England* c. *1400*–c. *1580*, New Haven, Yale University Press, 1992

Duling, D.C. 'Testament of Solomon', in James H. Charlesworth, *The Pseudepigrapha and Modern Research*, Missoula Montana, Scholars Press for the Society of Biblical Literature, 1976, 935–87

Eamon, William. *Science and the Secrets of Nature: Books of Secrets in Medieval and Early Modern Culture*, Princeton, Princeton University Press, 1994

——. *Studies in Medieval Fachliteratur*, Scripta, Medieval and Renaissance Studies 6, Brussels, Omirel, 1982

Eis, Gerhard (ed.). *Wahrsagetexte des Spätmittelalters aus Handschriften und Inkunabeln*, Texte des späten Mittelalters 1, Berlin, Erich Schmidt Verlag, 1956

——. *Gottfried's Pelzbuch*. Südosteuropäische Arbeiten 38, Brünn, Rudolph M. Roherer, 1944

Elworthy, Frederick T. *The Evil Eye: An account of this Ancient and Widespread Superstition*, London, Murray, 1895

Evans, Joan. *Magical Jewels of the Middle Ages and the Renaissance, Particularly in England*, Oxford, Clarendon Press, 1922

Flacciere, Robert. *Greek Oracles*, trans. Douglas Garman, London, Elek Books, 1965

Flint, Valerie I.J. *The Rise of Magic in Early Medieval Europe*, Princeton, Princeton University Press, 1992

French, Roger. 'Astrology in Medical Practice' in Luis Garcia-Ballester et al. (eds), *Practical Medicine from Salerno to the Black Death*, Cambridge, Cambridge University Press, 1994, pp. 30–59

Friedman, John B. 'The Cipher Alphabet of John de Foxton's *Liber Cosmographiae*', *Scriptorium* 36 (1982), 219–35

——. '"Dies boni et mali, obitus, et contra hec remedium": Remedies for Fortune in Some Late Medieval English Manuscripts', *Journal of English and Germanic Philology* 90 (1991), 311–26

——. 'Les images mnémotechniques dans les manuscrits de l'époque gothique' in Bruno Roy and Paul Zumthor (eds), *Jeux de mémoire: Aspects de la mnémotechnie médiévale* (Montréal-Paris: Presses de l'université de Montréal, 1985), pp. 169–84

——. 'The Prioress's Beads "of Smal Coral"', *Medium Aevum* 39 (1970), 301–5

Fürbeth, Frank. *Johannes Hartlieb. Untersuchungen zu Leben und Werk*, Tübingen, Niemeyer, 1995

Gaster, Moses. *Studies and Texts in Folklore, Magic, Medieval Romance, Hebrew Apocrypha and Samaritan Archaeology*, vol. 1, 1928; repr. New York, Ktav, 1971

Gaster, Theodore H. 'Amulets and Talismans', in L.E. Sullivan (ed.), *Hidden Truths: Magic, Alchemy, and the Occult*, New York, Macmillan, 1987

Gauthier, Marie-Madeline. 'Iris, le peinture et l'alchemiste: di savoir-faire au style', in Centre national de la récherche scientifique, *Colloque International du CNRS: Pigments et Colorants de l'Antiquité et du Moyen Âge: Teinture, peinture, enlumineure études historiques et physiochimiques*, Paris, Diffusions, Presses de CNRS, 1990, pp. 59–70

Gilson, Julius P. and George F. Warner. *Catalogue of Western Manuscripts in the Old Royal and King's Collections*, 4 vols, London, British Museum, 1921

Giordano Bruno, *Cabala del cavallo Pegaseo*, 'Paris, A. Baio' [= London, J. Charlewood], 1585

Les Grandes Chroniques de France, ed. Jules Viard, vol. 9, Paris, Librairie ancienne Honoré Champion, 1937

Grattan, J.H.G. and Charles Singer. *Anglo-Saxon Magic and Medicine*, London, Oxford University Press, 1952

Great Britain, Historical Manuscripts Commission. *The Manuscripts of the Corporations of Southampton and King's Lynn*, Appendix, Part III of *Eleventh Report of the Royal Commission on Historical Manuscripts*, London, Eyre and Spottiswoode, 1887

Greenfield, Richard P.F. *Traditions of Belief in Late Byzantine Demonology*, Amsterdam, Hakkert, 1988

Habiger-Tuczay, Christa. *Magie und Magier im Mittelalter*, Munich, Diederichs, 1992

Hansen, Joseph (ed.). *Quellen und Untersuchungen zur Geschichte des Hexenwahns und der Hexenverfolgung im Mittelalter*, Bonn, Georgi, 1901; repr. Hildesheim, Olms, 1963

Hansmann, Liselotte and Lenz Kriss-Rettenbach, *Amulet und Talisman: Erscheinungsform und Geschichte*, Munich, Callwey, 1966

Harmening, Dieter. *Superstitio: Überlieferungs-und theoriegeschichtliche Untersuchungen zur kirchlich-theologischen Aberglaubensliteratur des Mittelalters*, Berlin, E. Schmidt, 1979

Hartlieb, Johann. *Die Kunst Chiromantia des Dr. Hartlieb. Ein Blockbuch aus den Siebziger Jahren des 15. Jahrhunderts*, ed. Ernst Weil, München, Verlag Münchner Drucke, 1923

——. *Johann Hartliebs Buch aller verbotenen Kunst*, ed. Dora Ulm, Halle, Erhardt Karras, 1914

Hils, Hans-Peter. 'Von dem herten: Reflexionen zu einem mittelalterlichen Eisenhärtungsrezept', *Sudhoffs Archiv* 69 (1985), 62–75

Hübl, Albertus. *Catalogus codicorum manu scriptorum qui in biblioteca monasterii B.M.V. ad Scotos Vindobonae servantur*, Vienna, Braumüller, 1899

Humphreys, K.W. (ed.). *The Friars' Libraries*, London, British Library and British Academy, 1990

Hurley, J. Finley. *Sorcery*, London, Routledge & Kegan Paul, 1985

Idel, Moshe. *Kabbalah: New Prespectives*, New Haven, Yale University Press, 1988

——. *Language, Torah, and Hermeneutics in Abraham Abulafia*, trans. Menahem Kallus, Albany, SUNY Press, 1989

——. *The Mystical Experience in Abraham Abulafia*, trans. Jonathan Chipman, Albany, SUNY Press, 1988

——. 'Ramon Lull and the Ecstatic Kabbalah. A Preliminary Observation', *Journal of the Warburg and Courtauld Institutes* 51 (1988), 170–4

——. *Studies in Ecstatic Kabbalah*, Albany, SUNY Press, 1988

Institut Filozofii i Socjologii, *Magia, Astrologia e Religione nel Rinascimento*, Warsaw, Zaklad Narodowy im Ossonlinskich, 1974

James, Montague Rhodes. *A Descriptive Catalogue of the Manuscripts in the Library of Gonville and Caius College*, 2 vols, Cambridge, Cambridge University Press, 1907–14

——. *The Western Manuscripts in the Library of Trinity College, Cambridge*, 4 vols, Cambridge, Cambridge University Press, 1901

——. *The Ancient Libraries of Canterbury and Dover*, Cambridge, Cambridge University Press, 1903

John de Foxton's Liber Cosmographiae (1408): An Edition and Codicological Study, ed. John B. Friedman, Leiden, E.J. Brill, 1988

Johnston, Mark D. *The Spiritual Logic of Ramon Llull*, Oxford, Clarendon Press, 1987

The Key of Solomon the King (Clavicula Salomonis), ed. S.L. MacGregor Mathers, York Beach, ME, Weiser, 1989

Kieckhefer, Richard. *Forbidden Rites: A Necromancer's Manual of the Fifteenth Century*, Stroud, Sutton Publishing, 1997

———. 'The holy and the unholy: sainthood, witchcraft, and magic in late medieval Europe', *Journal of Medieval and Renaissance Studies*, 24 (1994), pp. 355–85, repr. in Scott L. Waugh and Peter D. Diehl (eds), *Christendom and Its Discontents: Exclusion, Persecution, and Rebellion, 1000–1500*, Cambridge, Cambridge University Press, 1996, pp. 310–37

———. *Magic in the Middle Ages*, Cambridge, Cambridge University Press, 1989

Kren, Claudia (ed.). *Medieval Science and Technology: A Selected Annotated Bibliography*, New York, Garland, 1985

Lea, Henry Charles. *A History of the Inquisition of the Middle Ages*, 3 vols, New York, 1887, repr. New York, Russell and Russell, 1955

Lehmann, Paul (ed.). *Mittelalterliche Bibliothekskataloge Deutschlands und der Schweiz . . . Zweiter Band, Bistum, Mainz, Erfurt*, Munich, C.H. Beck'sche Verlagsbuchhandlung, 1928

Lerner, Robert. 'Ecstatic Dissent', *Speculum* 67 (1993), 33–57

Lex, Barbara. 'The Neurobiology of Ritual Trance', in Eugene G. d'Aquili et al. (eds), *The Spectrum of Ritual: A Biogenetic Structural Analysis*, New York, Columbia University Press, 1979, pp. 117–51

'Liber hermetis de quindecim stellis quindecim lapidibus quindecim herbis et quindecim imaginibus' in Louis Delatte (ed.), *Textes latins et vieux Français relatifs aux Cyranides*, Liège, Université de Liège, 1942

Ein Losbuch Konrad Bollstatters aus CGM 312 der Bayerischen Staatsbibliothek München, ed. Karin Schneider, Wiesbaden, Dr Ludwig Reichert Verlag, 1973

Ein Losbuch Konrad Bollstatters aus CGM 312 der Bayerischen Staatsbibliothek München. Transkription, ed. Karin Schneider, Wiesbaden, Dr Ludwig Reichert Verlag, 1976

Llull, Ramon. *'Doctor Illuminatus.' A Ramon Llull Reader*, ed. and trans. Anthony Bonner, Princeton, Princeton University Press, 1985

Luaces, Joaquin Yarz. 'Fascinum: Reflets de la Croyance au Mauvais Oeil dans l'art médiévale Hispanique', *Razo* 8 (1988), 113–27

Luhrmann, T.M. *Persuasions of the Witch's Craft: Ritual Magic in Contemporary England*, Cambridge, MA, Harvard, 1989

McAllister, Joseph Bernard. *The Letter of Saint Thomas Aquinas De Occultis Operibus Naturae Ad Quemdam Militem Ultramontanum*, Washington, Catholic University of America Press, 1939

Maloney, Clarence (ed.). *The Evil Eye*, New York, Columbia University Press, 1976

Mowat, J.L.G. *Alphita: A Medico-Botanical Glossary from the Bodleian Manuscript, Selden B. 35*, Oxford, Clarendon Press, 1887

Newman, Barbara, 'Possessed by the spirit: devout women, demoniacs, and the apostolic life in the thirteenth century', forthcoming in *Speculum*, July 1998

Obrist, Barbara. *Les Débuts de L'Imagerie Alchemique (XIVe–XVe siècles)*, Paris, Le Sycamore, 1982

Pereira, Michela. *The Alchemical Corpus Attributed to Raymond Lull*, Warburg Institute Surveys and Texts XVIII, London, Warburg Institute, 1989

Peters, Edward. *The Magician, the Witch and the Law*, Philadelphia, University of Pennsylvania Press, 1978

Petrus Peregrinus de Maricourt Opera Epistula de magnete, ed. Loris Sturlese and Ron B. Thomson, Pisa, Scuola Normale Superiore Ufficio pubblicazioni classe di lettere, 1995

Picatrix, The Latin Version of the Ghayat Al-Hakim, ed. David Pingree, Studies of the Warburg Institute, no. 39, London, Warburg Institute, 1986

Pingree, David. 'The Diffusion of Arabic Magical Texts in Western Europe', *La Diffusione delle Scienze Islamiche nel Medio Evo Europeo*, Rome, Accademia nazionale dei Lincei, 1987, pp. 57–102

Ploss, Emil et al. (eds), *Alchimia: Ideologie und Technologie*, Munich, Moos, 1970

Powicke, F.M. *The Medieval Books of Merton College*, Oxford, Clarendon Press, 1931

Rhodes, D.E. '"Provost Argentine of Kings' and his Books"' in *Transactions of the Cambridge Bibliographical Society*, London, Bowes and Bowes, 1958, vol. 2, pp. 205–11

Roberts, Julian and Andrew G. Watson, *John Dee's Library Catalogue*, London, The Bibliographical Society, 1990

Roger Bacon. *Opus Majus*, trans. Robert Belle Burke, 2 vols, New York, Russell and Russell, 1962

——. *Part of the Opus Tertium of Roger Bacon*, ed. A.G. Little, Aberdeen, University Press, 1912

Roy, Bruno. 'L'illusion comme art libéral. Interprétation du Secretum Philosophorum (XIIIᵉ S)' in Marie Louise Ollier (ed.), *Masques et déguisements dans la littérature médiévale*, Montreal and Paris, Vrin, 1988, pp. 75–81

Russell, Jeffrey Burton. *Witchcraft in the Middle Ages*, Ithaca, Cornell University Press, 1972

Salter, H.E. *Mediaeval Archives of the University of Oxford*, 2 vols, Oxford Historical Society nos. 70 & 73, Oxford, Oxford Historical Society, 1920–1

Schneider, Karin. *Die deutschen Handschriften der Bayerischen Staatsbibliothek München. CGM 201–350. Catalogus Codicum Manu Scriptorum Bibliotecae Regiae Monacensis*, vol. 5, pt 2, Wiesbaden, Otto Harrassowitz, 1970

Scholem, Gershom. *Jewish Gnosticism, Merkavah Mysticism and Talmudic Tradition*, 2nd ed., New York: Jewish Theological Society of America, 1965

——. *Kabbalah*, The New York Times Library of Jewish Knowledge, New York, Quadrangle/The New York Times and Jerusalem, Keter, 1974

——. *Major Trends in Jewish Mysticism*, New York, Schocken, 1946

——. *Origins of the Kabbalah*, ed. R.J. Zwi Werblowsky, trans. Allan Arkush, The Jewish Publication Society, Princeton, Princeton University Press, 1987

Schwab, Moïse. *Vocabulaire de l'angélologie*. Milan, Archè, 1989

Schwartz, Dov. 'La magie astrale dans la pensée juive rationaliste en Provence au XIVᵉ siècle', *Archives d'Histoire Doctrinale et Littéraire du Moyen Age* 61 (1994), 31–55

Scott, Edward J.L. *Index to the Sloane Manuscripts in the British Museum*, London, British Museum, 1904

Segl, Peter (ed.). *Die Anfänge der Inquisition im Mittelalter, mit einem Ausblick auf das 20. Jahrhundert und einem Beitrag über religiöse Intoleranz im nichtchristlichen Bereich*, Cologne, Böhlau, 1993

Sepher-ha-Razim: The Book of Mysteries, trans. Michael Morgan, Atlantis, Scholars Press, 1983

Singer, Dorothea Waley. *Catalogue of Latin and Vernacular Alchemical Manuscripts in Great Britain and Ireland*, 3 vols, Brussels, M. Lamertin, 1928–31

Sotzmann, 'Die Loosbücher des Mittelalters', *Serapeum* 20 (1851), 305–16

Struik, Dirk J. 'The Prohibition of the Use of Arabic Numerals in Florence', *Archives Internationales des Histoires des Sciences* 21 (1968), 290–7

Swartz, Michael D. *Scholastic Magic: Ritual and Revelation in Early Jewish Mysticism*, Princeton, Princeton University Press, 1996

The Sworn Book of Honourius the Magician, As Composed by Honourius through Counsel with the Angel Hocroell, ed. Daniel J. Driscoll, Gillette, NJ, Heptangle Press, 1977; repr., 1983

Talbot, C.H., and E.A. Hammond. *The Medical Practitioners in Medieval England: A Biographical Register*, London, Wellcome Historical Medical Library, 1965

Taylor, F. Sherwood. *The Alchemists: Founders of Modern Chemistry*, New York, Henry Shuman, 1949

Tepl, Johannes von. *Der Ackermann aus Böhmen*, trans. Felix Genzmer, Stuttgart, Philipp Reclam, 1984

———. *Der Ackermann aus Böhmen*, ed. Günther Jungbluth, Heidelberg, Carl Winter Universitätsverlag, 1969

Thetel. 'Cethel aut veterum Judaeorum Physiologorum de Lapidibus Sententiae' in Jean Baptiste Pitra (ed.), *Spicilegium Solesmense* III, Paris, Instituti Franciae, 1852, pp. 335–7

Thomas of Cantimpre. *Liber de natura rerum*, Berlin and New York, Walter de Gruyter, 1973

Thomas, Keith. *Religion and the Decline of Magic*, New York, Charles Scribner's Sons, 1971

Thomas Norton's Ordinal of Alchemy, ed. John Reidy, Early English Texts Society, OS 272, London, Oxford University Press, 1975

Thomson, R.M. *Catalogue of the Manuscripts of Lincoln Cathedral Chapter Library*, Woodbridge, Suffolk and Wolfeboro, NH, D.S. Brewer, 1989

Thorndike, Lynn. *A History of Magic and Experimental Science*, 8 vols, New York, Macmillan and Columbia University Press, 1923–58

———. 'Traditional Medieval Tracts Concerning Engraved Astrological Images', *Mélanges Auguste Pelzer . . . à l'occasion de son soixante-dixième anniversaire*, Louvain, Bibliothéque de l'Université, 1947, pp. 217–74

———. 'Unde Versus', *Traditio* 11 (1955), 163–93

Thorndike, Lynn, and Pearl Kibre. *A Catalogue of Incipits of Mediaeval Scientific Writings in Latin*, rev. edn, Cambridge, Medieval Academy of America, 1963

Trithemius, Johannes, *Antipalus malificiorum*, in Johannes Busaeus (ed.), *Paralipomena opusculorum Petri Blesensis et Joannis Trithemii aliorumque*, Mainz, Balthassar Lippius, 1605, pp. 291–311

———. *Polygraphiae libri VI*, Basel, Johannes Haselberg, 1518

———. *De scriptoribus ecclesiasticis*, Basel, Johannes Amerbach, 1495

van Hamel, A.G. 'Oðinn hanging on the tree', *Acta Philologica Scandinavica*, 7 (1932–3), 260–88

van Lennep, Jacques. *Alchimie: Contribution à l'histoire de l'art alchimique*, (Bruxelles, Crédit Communal de Belgique, 1982

Voigts, Linda Ehrsam. 'The Character of the *Carecter*: Ambiguous Sigils in Scientific and Medical Texts' in A.J. Minnis (ed.), *Latin and Vernacular: Studies in Late-Medieval Texts and Manuscripts*, Cambridge, Brewer, 1989, pp. 91–109

———. 'The "Sloane Group": Manuscripts from the Fifteenth Century in the Sloane Collection', *British Library Journal* 16.1 (1990), 26–57

von Döllinger, Johann J. Ign., *Fables Respecting the Popes in the Middle Ages: A Contribution to Ecclesiastical History*, trans. Alfred Plummer, London, Rivingtons, 1871

Waite, Arthur Edward. *The Book of Black Magic and Pacts*, London, Redway, 1898; repr. as *The Book of Ceremonial Magic*, London, Rider, 1911

William of Auvergne, *Opera Omnia*, Paris, Pralard, 1674; facsimile reprint, 2 vols, Frankfurt a/M: Minerva, 1963

Yates, Frances A. *The Art of Memory*, Chicago, University of Chicago Press, 1966

——. *Lull & Bruno, Collected Essays Vol. 1*, London, Routledge & Kegan Paul, 1982

——. *The Occult Philosophy in the Elizabethan Age*, London, Routledge, 1979

Zambelli, Paola. *The Speculum Astronomiae and its Enigma; Astrology, Theology, and Science in Albertus Magnus and his Contemporaries*, London, Kluwer Academic Publishers, 1992

MANUSCRIPTS

Ars Notoria

Kues, Hospitals zu Cues, MS 216

London, British Library, Harley 181

London, British Library, Sloane 513

London, British Library, Sloane 1712

Munich, Bayerische Staatsbibliothek, Clm 276

Oxford, Bodleian, Ashmole 1515

Oxford, Bodleian, Bodley 951

Paris, Bibliothéque Nationale, MS 7170A

Paris, Bibliothéque Nationale, MS lat. 9336

Turin, Biblioteca Nazionale MS E.V. 13

Divination Device and Alphabetic Keys

Munich, Bayerische Staatsbibliothek, CGM 312

Vienna, Österreichische National Bibliothek, Cod. 145 (A. Hübl 209)

Wolfenbüttel, Herzog August Bibliothek, Cod. Guelf. 75.10 Aug. 2°

Image Magic

Cambridge University Library, MS Ff.vi.53

London, British Library, Sloane 312

London, British Library, Sloane 1784

London, Institution of Electrical Engineers, Thompson Collection S.C. MSS 3/5

London, Society of Antiquaries, MS 39

London, Wellcome History of Medicine Library, MS 116

Oxford, Bodleian, Ashmole 346

Oxford, Bodleian, Ashmole 1416

Oxford, Bodleian, Ashmole 1471

Oxford, Bodleian, Bodley 463

Oxford, Bodleian, Cannon. Misc. 285

Oxford, Bodleian, Digby 228
Oxford, Bodleian, Selden Supra 76
Oxford, Corpus Christi 125
Oxford, Corpus Christi 221

Liber de angelis
Cambridge University Library, MS Dd.xi.45

Liber sacer sive iuratus
London, British Library, Royal 17 A. XLII
London, British Library, Sloane 313
London, British Library, Sloane 3826
London, British Library, Sloane 3854
London, British Library, Sloane 3883
London, British Library, Sloane 3885

Liber visionum
Graz, University Library, MS 680
Hamilton, Canada, McMaster University Library, Unnumbered MS
London, British Library, Additional 18027
Munich, Bayerische Staatsbibliothek, Clm 276
Vienna, Schottenkloster, MS Scotensis-Vindobonensis 61(140)

Magical Recipes
Oxford, Bodleian Library, MS e Mus. 219

Necromancy
Cambridge University Library, MS Dd. xi. 45
London, British Library, Sloane 314
London, British Library, Sloane 3849
London, British Library, Sloane 3853
London, Society of Antiquaries, MS 39
Oxford, Bodleian, Rawlinson D. 252

Secretum Philosophorum
Cambridge, Caius and Gonville College, MS 413/630
Cambridge, St John's College, MS 109
Cambridge, Trinity College, MS O.1.58
Cambridge, Trinity College, MS O.2.40
Lincoln Cathedral Chapter Library, MS 226
Oxford, Bodleian, Rawlinson D. 1066

INDEX

Bold numbers = main or substantial entries. *Italic* numbers = illustration captions. Continuous page references ignore intervening illustration pages. Space does not permit detailed indexing of notes, but attention has been drawn to some explanatory notes by 'n' after the page number.

AN = Ars Notoria
GD = German divination device
HT = Honorius of Thebes: *Liber iuratus*
JM = John the Monk: *Liber visionum*
OB = Osbern Bokenham: *Book of Angels . . .*
RL = Ramon Lull
SP = *Secretum Philosophorum*

Abelard, Peter (attrib.): *Liber sacratus petri abelardi* 9, 10
Abulafia, Abraham 94, 256
Adelard of Bath 6
Agrippa von Nettesheim, Cornelius: *De occulta philosophia* 20, 36, 145, 219
Albertus Magnus: *Speculum astronomiae* 5, 6, 11, 12–13, 17, 18, 112
Albertus de Judenberga 165
alchemy 8, 9, 13, 77, 95, 111
  Alkmonute 80, 81
al-Ghazzali 94
al-Kindi 17
  De radiis stellarum 5, 9, 10, 11, 12
alphabets
  ephesia grammatica 112, 113
  exotic 76–7
  HT author of 158
  see also German divination device
Alverny, Marie Thérèse d' 111–12
Amalricus, King 93
Amandel/Mandal 146
amulets 35, 112
angels
  angelic magic xi
  angelic/demonic magic compared vii–ix
  in diagrams 124, 126
  in HT 149–51, 255
  in JM (*notably*) 173, 174–5, 176, 228–9, 259

in OB 34, 38, 46/47–52/53
  Tractatus de nominibus angelorum 9
Anglo-Saxon charms vii
animal sacrifice (OB) 34, 46/47, 48/49
Ansky, Sholom: *The Dybbuk* 262
Arabic
  general influence 92
  letters and language 133–5, 221–2
  magic 7, 12–13, 24, 25, 34, 112
  numerals 119–21
  and RL 87–8, 94, 97
Aramaic 153
architecture, personification of *134*, 135
Argentine, John 6–7
Aristotle/pseudo-: *de Secretis Secretorum* 76, 79, 82, 83, 112
arithmetic (liberal art) 77, 119–21, *120*, *121*, 124
Ars Notoria
  condemnations 14–15, 110–11, 112, 217, **222–5**
  JM's adaptation *see* John the Monk
  similar 'Artes Notorie' 16, 22
  texts and context xii, **14–19**, 25
  title xvii–n
  visual art in xiii–xiv, **110–35**
    figurae 115, **124–6**, *127*, *128*, *129*, *130*, *131*, 220
    notae 111, **113–24**, *114*, *116*, *120*, *122*, 220